IN PLACE OF AUSTERITY

In Place
Of Austerity

Reconstructing the economy,
state and public services

Dexter Whitfield

SPOKESMAN

First published in 2012 by Spokesman
Russell House, Bulwell Lane,
Nottingham NG6 OBT, England
Phone: 0115 9708381 Fax: 01159420433
e-mail: elfeuro@compuserve.com
www.spokesmanbooks.com

ISBN 978 0 85124 793 9

A CIP Catalogue is available from the British Library

Printed by the Russell Press Ltd. (www.russellpress.com)
Cover and Layout by Kavita Graphics (dennis@kavitagraphics.co.uk)

Contents

Part 1: DESTRUCTING DEMOCRACY

Part 2: THE ALTERNATIVE: RECONSTRUCTION

New public service management
Public infrastructure investment strategy

Part 3: THE CASE FOR THE ALTERNATIVE STRATEGY

iv

Figures

Tables

Abbreviations

AAA	Anti-Academies Alliance
AES	Alternative Economic Strategy
AIG	American International Group
ALMO	Arms Length Management Organisation
APPG	All Party Parliamentary Group
ATTAC	Association for the Taxation of financial Transactions and Aid to Citizens
BRIC	Brazil, Russia, India and China
BSF	Building Schools for the Future
BT	British Telecom
CBI	Confederation of British Industry
CCA	Corrections Corporation of America
CM@R	Construction Management At-Risk
CPS	Centre for Public Services
CSR	Corporate Social Responsibility
CTF	Child Trust Fund
DBFO	Design, Build, Finance and Operate
DCH	Defend Council Housing
DCLG	Department for Communities & Local Government
DfE	Department for Education
DfT	Department for Transport
DH	Department of Health
DoE	Department of the Environment
DWP	Department for Work and Pensions
ECT	Ealing Community Transport
EFSF	European Financial Stability Facility
EIB	European Investment Bank
EPSU	European Public Service Unions
ERSA	Employment Related Services Association
ESOP	Employee Share Ownership Plan
ESSU	European Services Strategy Unit
ETUC	European Trade Union Confederation
EU	European Union
FE	Further Education
FTA	Free Trade Agreement
FTE	Full Time Equivalent
FOI	Freedom of Information
GAO	Government Accountability Office

GATS	General Agreement for Trade in Services
GATT	General Agreement on Tariffs and Tade
GDP	Gross Domestic Product
GLL	Greenwich Leisure Ltd
G20	Group of 20 Industrial and Emerging-Market Countries
GP	General Practitioner
GVA	Gross Value Added
HEFCE	Higher Education Funding Council for England
HM	Her Majesty
HMO	Health Maintenance Organisation
IBM	International Business Machines
ICB	Independent Commission on Banking
ICT	Information and Communications Technology
ILO	International Labour Organisation
IMF	International Monetary Fund
IPPR	Institute for Public Policy Research
ISTC	Independent Sector Treatment Centre
JVC	Joint Venture Company
LABV	Local Asset Backed Vehicle
LATC	Local Authority Trading Company
LEP	Local Education Partnership and Local Enterprise Partnership
LSVT	Large Scale Voluntary Transfer
MBS	Mortgage-Backed Security
MRSA	Methicillin-resistant Staphylococcus aureus
MSA	Medical Savings Account
NAMA	National Asset Management Agency
NAO	National Audit Office
NASUWT	National Association of Schoolmasters Union of Women Teachers
NESTA	National Endowment for Science, Technology and the Arts
NGO	Non Governmental Organisation
NLGN	New Local Government Network
NHS	National Health Service
NOMS	National Offender Management Service
NPPF	National Planning Policy Framework
NUT	National Union of Teachers
OCS	Office for Civil Society

OECD	Organisation for Economic Co-operation and Development
OFSTED	Office for Standards in Education
OFT	Office of Fair Trading
OGC	Office of Government Commerce
OJEU	Official Journal of the European Union
PbR	Payment by Results
PCS	Public and Commercial Services Union
PCT	Primary Care Trust
PEAT	Patient Environment Action Team
PFI	Private Finance Initiative
PfS	Partnerships for Schools
PPP	Public Private Partnership
PSA	Public Services Alliance
PwC	PricewaterhouseCoopers
QE	Quantitative Easing
RAB	Regulated Asset Base
RBS	Royal Bank of Scotland
RDA	Regional Development Agency
REIT	Real Estate Investment Trusts
RIA	Regulatory Impact Assessment
SAP	Systems Applications and Products
SCAT	Services to Community Actions and Tenants
SIB	Social Impact Bond
SIF	Social Investment Fund
SME	Small and Medium-sized Enterprise
SOCITM	Society of Information Technology Management
SPV	Special Purpose Vehicle
SSP	Strategic Service-delivery Partnership
TARP	Troubled Asset Relief Program
TRIPs	Trade-Related Aspects of Intellectual Property Rights
TUC	Trade Union Congress
TUPE	Transfer of Undertakings (Protection of Employment) Regulations 1981
UCU	University and College Union
UK	United Kingdom
US	United States
UN	United Nations

URC	Urban Renewal Company
UNESCO	United Nations Educational, Scientific and Cultural Organisation
VAT	Value Added Tax
VFM	Value For Money
WTO	World Trade Organisation

Preface

I have written *In Place of Austerity: Reconstructing the Economy, State and Pubic Services* with four key objectives in mind.

Firstly, to develop a theoretical framework to better understand neoliberal transformation of public services and the welfare state. Cuts in public spending are just one manifestation of the financial crisis.

Secondly, to expose the myths of commissioning, localism, big society and empowerment. Neoliberal public sector transformation commodifies children and the elderly, fragments public provision and deconstructs democracy. We need to better understand the scale of failure in public service markets and expose how corporate welfare has reached a new zenith.

Thirdly, to promote action strategies that can stop, slow down and/or mitigate the negative consequences of these policies.

Fourthly, to advance a framework of policies for the reconstruction of the economy, state and public services. There is an alternative to neoliberal economic strategies, and 'another world is possible'.

This book develops the theory and strategies set out in *Public Services or Corporate Welfare* (2001), *New Labour's Attack on Public Services* (2006) and *Global Auction of Public Assets* (2010). The book concentrates on the UK, which is in the vanguard of marketisation and privatisation of public services and the welfare state, although it draws on European and US evidence and responses to the global financial crisis.

Sincere thanks to Andy Mott (USA), John Spoehr (Australia), Richard Whyte, John Burgess, Nick Grant, Keith Hayman, Nigel Behan and Dave Orr for their assistance.

To Kenny Bell, who died in August 2011, who had a rare ability to combine organising, education, developing strategies, building alliances and advancing public service alternatives.

Tony Simpson and staff at Spokesman Books demonstrated their commitment throughout this project. The Australian Institute for Social Research, University of Adelaide, provided valuable support.

I sincerely thank Dorothy Calvert for her love, solidarity, political input and editorial support.

CHAPTER 1

Deepening crisis

Across Europe, trade unions and community organisations are opposing cuts in public spending, closure of community facilities, home foreclosures, increased charges for services, outsourcing, wage cuts and job losses. Organised resistance is crucial and is empowered by understanding the root causes of the crisis and having alternative policies and strategies.

More equitable taxation and reduction of the tax gap could reduce deficits and debt levels and the need for public spending cuts. But increased revenue is not going to fundamentally change the implementation of core neoliberal policies for health, education and other public services. Furthermore, there has been a high degree of continuity in the policies pursued by Tory, New Labour and Coalition Governments and the differences between governments has narrowed as neoliberalism is embedded into public policy. These policies have four objectives.

Firstly, marketisation and privatisation provide *new opportunities for accumulation*. This is much more than just about money and investment, the marketisation of services and the public infrastructure. These policies are designed to create markets that lead to the transfer of government functions and service provision to the private sector. Private investment in public services increases opportunities for profit and to design and organise services in the interests of capital, thus ensuring business has an ever-larger role in public policy making.

Public Private Partnerships (PPP) are a *wealth machine* and public assets sold cheap when privatised have soared in value after the sale. Business and the political right's longer-term strategy is to control key parts of the public infrastructure – transport, energy, communications and the welfare state infrastructure. This is a key route into the provision of core public services (Whitfield, 2010a). The emerging social investment market is another phase in this process, with new opportunities for private investment, brokers and service providers.

Secondly, marketisation and privatisation are a mechanism to *gain more power and control in the economy,* to reduce the role of the state and to *change public values* and expectations of public services and the welfare state. They are designed to transfer more power from the state to capital, from employees to employers and from service users to private contractors.

Community budgets, participative budgeting, big society, voluntary sector contracting, mutuals and social enterprises will be 'celebrated' but will only be mainstreamed if they benefit a minority. They are 'tolerated' because, in parallel, capital is gaining control of a far larger share of public and welfare state provision. *Deregulation* is used to weaken trade unions and community organisations, and to marginalise other civil society organisations.

Thirdly, financialisation and personalisation (personal budgets, vouchers, social investment market) are *a means of transferring risk, cost and responsibility to individuals* as a means of reducing the scope of the welfare state. Programmes designed to benefit those most in need of public services, such as 24-hour care, are being adapted and mainstreamed to marketise and privatise virtually all public services. Fewer and fewer services are provided by public employees. Instead, they are delivered by private contractors working to contract as agents of the state.

Fourthly, these policies are a means by which capital can radically reduce the role of the state, yet *safeguard corporate welfare*, which consists of tax breaks, subsidies, contracts and regulatory concessions. They are a means of deepening business involvement in the public policy-making process and increasing secrecy.

Who delivers public services and who owns the public infrastructure are vitally important, but are only part of the agenda. These policies are designed to *dispossess, disinvest, destabilise, depoliticise* and *disempower*.

This amounts to the *de-construction of democracy* at local, national and international levels.

Neoliberalism is pervasive

Neoliberal ideology has dictated economic policy and public sector transformation over the last three decades. It promotes free trade, competition and markets to determine resources allocation and who delivers services. The capitalisation of income streams and the securitisation of assets through financialisation have played a crucial role in commodifying services and assets, and in extending markets.

Deregulation of trade, financial and labour markets has created light-touch, self-monitored regimes that permit the free flow of capital, goods and services globally to provide new opportunities for accumulation. 'Flexible' labour markets with strict regulation of trade union activities are designed to maintain management's 'right to manage'. The state is reconfigured so it commodifies and outsources services, develops markets, privatises public assets, and creates a pro-business climate (Whitfield, 2006a).

The reconfiguration of the state was intended to reduce intervention in the economy, to open up new markets in public services and to deepen business involvement in the public policy-making process (Whitfield, 2001 and 2006a). A narrow performance management regime was devised to focus on outcomes and basically ignore the quality of inputs, processes and outputs which are a fundamental part of public provision. The privatisation of nationalised industries reduced the role of the state in the economy, and new forms of marketisation and ownership were created to privatise public services and the welfare state. This was not just about ownership of bricks and mortar, but also who, and how, services are delivered and funded.

The restructuring of labour is taking place differentially because many public services must be delivered locally, for example, waste collection, primary education, child care, health and social care, and cannot be relocated or offshored. Certain related functions such as medical records and back office support services are more mobile and can be relocated. Public services are under intense pressure to increase efficiency and productivity. Deskilling and de-professionalisation of work continues so that services can be delivered by assistants and generic workers.

The UK became a neoliberal model for the way it privatised state assets, developed PPPs and an infrastructure market, and marketised public services. Personal budgets and whole-service outsourcing, a combination of strategic partnership and PPP models, could be the next exports.

The remainder of this chapter outlines the causes, scale and consequences of the 2008 financial crisis, the subsequent recession and emergence of a corporate welfare state.

Causes and consequences of the financial crisis

Market and regulatory failure originated in the US mortgage market then spiralled across financial markets and institutions. The *"...search for increased growth and profit led to the origination and securitization of hundreds of billions of dollars in high risk, poor quality mortgages that ultimately plummeted in value, hurting investors, the bank, and the U.S. financial system"* (US Senate Permanent Subcommittee on Investigations, 2011).

The US national inquiry concluded the financial crisis was caused by widespread failures in financial regulation and supervision, corporate governance and risk management, and a systemic breakdown in accountability and ethics in key financial institutions. Excessive borrowing, risky investments, and lack of transparency combined with *"...collapsing mortgage-lending standards and the mortgage securitization pipeline lit and spread the flame of contagion and crisis.... Over-the-counter derivatives contributed significantly to this crisis and the failures of credit rating agencies were essential cogs in the wheel of financial destruction"* (Financial Crisis Inquiry Commission, 2011). Equally important, they concluded failures were systemic, but avoidable. The Inquiry Commission's and US Senate's reports are 650 pages of chilling reading.

Spiralling UK house prices, low interest rates, the buy-to-let and second home boom, and large-scale equity withdrawal increased consumption, but primarily of imported cars and electronic goods.

The ultimate cause of the financial crisis was a failure of neoliberalism that prioritised deregulation, marketisation, competition, debt-driven consumerism, privatisation, and the erosion of democratic accountability and transparency. It generated greed, profiteering, illegal and corrupt practices.

Bailouts

The 2008 financial crisis led to the bankruptcy of investment bank Lehman Brothers followed quickly by the collapse and sale of investment banks Bear Stearns and Merrill Lynch; the rescue and sale of mortgage lenders Ameriquest, Countrywide Financial and Wachovia by Citigroup, Bank of America and Wells Fargo banks respectively and Washington Mutual to JP Morgan; and the government had to rescue Fannie Mae and Freddie Mac, both government-sponsored enterprises, to provide liquidity, stability and affordability to the U.S. housing and mortgage markets.

The largest US banks required cash injections under the government's US$700bn Troubled Asset Relief Program (TARP) launched in October 2008. Some banks, such as Citigroup, *"...needed multiple infusions of federal cash"* (McLean and Nocera, 2010). Insurance giant, American International Group (AIG) required over US$100bn support and had $32.4bn outstanding at 30 June 2011, with the government owning

1.45bn AIG shares (American International Group, 2011). TARP was also used to bail out the US motor industry, General Motors and Chrysler receiving $79bn. The final public cost of TARP is estimated to be between US$19bn-$64bn after loans are repaid and assets sold (Congressional Budget Office, 2011a). But the scale of government financial support was much greater than revealed at the time.

Over US$16 trillion (a thousand billion) of public money was loaned to banks and financial institutions between 2007-2010 to prevent financial collapse (Government Accountability Office, 2011). The ten biggest US banks and brokerage firms made US$104bn profits in 2006, but a year later these same companies negotiated trillions of loans under four Federal Reserve Bank emergency programmes. European banks, such as Royal Bank of Scotland, Barclays, UBS, Deutsche Bank and Credit Suisse, accounted for half the top twenty banks. The four large UK banks borrowed US$1.6 trillion. The unprecedented scale of support indicates the scale and depth of the crisis in banks and financial markets, and the dependency on the state to bail out financial institutions regarded as 'too big to fail'. Meanwhile bankers continue to receive annual multi-million performance bonuses. Taking the billions spent on fiscal stimulus programmes around the world and the billions spent on banks rescues in Europe and elsewhere, the total financial support runs into many more trillions.

The public cost of bank bailouts, fiscal stimulus programmes and falling tax revenues/increased welfare state benefits caused by the recession, led to the sovereign debt crisis with Ireland, Portugal and Greece being bailed out by the EU/IMF. But their debt, as a percentage of Gross Domestic Product (GDP), is expected to be higher at the end of 2012 than it was at the start of the crisis. One banker concluded *"... this situation resembles a pyramid or a Ponzi scheme. Some of the original bondholders are being paid with the official loans that also finance the remaining primary deficits"* (Blejer, 2011). But as McNally has reminded us *"...always follow the money ...The difference is that the new loans are coming from public funds, which is another way of saying that private banks are being rescued once more by the people. Just as in the global bank crisis of 2008-09, bank profits are private, but their losses are public. Not exactly the free market. But it's a nice deal for profligate bankers"* (McNally, 2011).

UK Treasury support to financial institutions included the recapitalisation of the Royal Bank of Scotland (RBS) and Lloyds Banking Group (Lloyds) when the government acquired 83% of RBS (but 68% of the voting rights) and 41% of Lloyds, and nationalised Northern Rock and Bradford & Bingley. A number of schemes were set up to provide guarantees and indemnities and loans to insolvent banks so they could repay customer deposits of over £50,000. The original scale of the support was £955bn in guarantees, shares and loans by December 2009, but the maximum liability for taxpayers declined to £512bn by December 2010 (National Audit Office, 2011a). The Treasury estimate the eventual total cost of support could be between £20bn-£50bn, but *"...further shocks could still lead to significant losses for the taxpayer"* (ibid).

The collapse of banks and the property market in Ireland required a €70bn-€90bn bailout with the government establishing a 'bad bank', the National Asset Management Agency (NAMA), to take over property loans from banks that would otherwise be bankrupt. Anglo Irish Bank was nationalised in January 2009 with the Bank of Ireland and Allied Irish Bank recapitalised. Three other financial institutions, EBS Building Society, Irish Nationwide and Irish Life and Permanent, were part of the Government Guarantee Scheme and received bailout funds. The crisis exposed a network of illegal practices, corruption and incompetence on an unprecedented scale (O'Toole, 2010). Irish bank funding from the European Central Bank and the Central Bank of Ireland had reached €154.6bn by the end of July 2011 (RTE News, 2011).

Most G20 countries implemented fiscal stimulus measures to try to maintain/increase economic output and create or sustain employment. Infrastructure investment commonly accounted for between a quarter and a half of measures, alongside tax cuts and other fiscal policies.

Recession impacts

The financial crisis led to the worst recession in OECD countries since the 1930s. Unemployment soared to 14% in Spain, 13% in Ireland and 9% in the US, with even higher rates for young people. The share of people unemployed for more than 12 months had risen by over 30% in in the UK, US, Spain, France and Japan and by 50% in Ireland, Portugal, Hungary and Italy between 2007-2010 (OECD, 2011a).

The property market collapse and falling house prices were particularly severe in Ireland, Spain and the US. A record 2.9m US properties received notices of default, auction or repossession in 2010 (www.realtytrac.com). Nine per cent of Nevada households were in foreclosure in 2010, the highest US foreclosure rate, followed by Arizona and California. House prices had fallen an average 33% between 2006-

2010 (based on the Standard & Poor's/Case-Shiller Index of 20 cities). Over 800,000 UK homeowners were in negative equity in 2011 and up to 300,000 in Ireland.

The bulk of the economic and social costs have been borne by millions of families and individuals. They have suffered job losses, pay cuts, home foreclosure, negative equity and increased personal debt. Increased insecurity and personal risks have health and social consequences in addition to personal and public costs. The ability to avoid or mitigate these consequences and costs is directly related to income and class.

In the UK, on average, lower-income households had higher inflation rates over the last decade than higher-income households. The second-to-lowest income group of the population experienced the highest average inflation rate of the period from 2000 to 2010, with a rate of 3.5% in contrast with the highest income group, who experienced the lowest inflation, with a rate of 2.9% (Institute for Fiscal Studies, 2011).

Rising deficits and debt

In addition to the cost of bank bailouts, government finances were under pressure from the cost of fiscal stimulus (increased public spending and/or lower taxes) measures, the higher cost of unemployment and social welfare benefits, and declining tax revenue caused by the fall in economic activity and the property market crash. Consumer and government debt levels soared. In advanced G-20 economies, the increase in debt was driven mostly by the collapse of output and the related loss in revenue. *"Of the almost 39 percentage points of GDP increase in the debt ratio, about two-thirds is explained by revenue weakness and the fall in GDP during 2008-09"* (IMF, 2010a). The costs of fiscal stimulus support to the financial sector and lending (student loans, car loans and support to small and medium enterprises) also accounted for the increase in debt (ibid).

Public spending increased in all G-7 countries (US, Canada, UK, Germany, France, Italy and Japan) in recent decades (measured by the ratio of spending to potential GDP). Healthcare and pensions accounted for over 80% of increased spending, with the provision of a wider range of services having a relatively small impact (IMF, 2010b).

Government gross debt is forecast to increase in all major advanced economies by 2016 (Table 1). The UK and US have the largest increase. In contrast, emerging and low-income economies have had relatively stable gross debt levels since 2008 and are forecast to be 34.3% and 41.3% of GDP respectively in 2012 (OECD, 2011a). Some countries, such as Japan, Belgium and Italy, had significantly higher levels of debt for many years before the current financial crisis.

By 2016, net debt (defined as gross debt minus financial assets of the general government, which include assets held by the social security insurance system) is forecast to be 68.6% in the Eurozone. Net debt in France and the UK is forecast to be between 7% and 10% respectively below the level of gross debt. In contrast, Canada has had a significantly smaller net debt in recent years, which is forecast to be 33.3% of GDP in 2016. However, the scale of fiscal retrenchment, primarily from cuts in public spending, is forecast to exceed the OECD average (Jackson, 2011).

Table 1: Government gross debt (as a percentage of GDP)

Major advanced economies	2008	2009	2010	2011	2012	2016
		Actual			Projections	
United States	71.6	85.2	94.4	100.0	105.0	115.4
Euro Area	70.1	79.7	85.8	88.6	90.0	86.6
France	68.2	79.0	82.3	86.8	89.4	87.7
Germany	66.4	74.1	84.0	82.6	81.9	75.0
Italy	106.3	116.1	119.0	121.1	121.4	114.1
Japan	195.0	216.3	220.0	233.1	238.4	253.4
United Kingdom	52.0	68.3	75.5	80.8	84.8	80.4
Canada	71.1	83.3	84.0	84.1	84.2	73.0

Source: IMF, World Economic Outlook, September, 2011

The Maastricht Treaty and the Stability and Growth Pact fiscal rules were suspended as the crisis intensified and countries failed to keep government deficits below 3% of GDP and government debt below 60% of GDP (in case of a higher debt ratio, on a decreasing trend). However, they remain as fiscal targets.

There has been wide misuse of deficit and debt data, for example, the Coalition's use of the 'general deficit' (total expenditure minus total revenue) instead of the 'primary deficit' (total expenditure excluding interest payments on public debt, minus total revenue). The first was -10.7% of GDP in 2010 and the second -7.7% (Burke et al, 2011). Net deficit was only -2.7% if public investment in assets is taken into account (ibid). Another misuse refers to the ramping up of 'unfunded liabilities', in particular pensions, claiming pay-as-you-go public sector pension schemes funded by current revenue are 'liabilities' when 'funded' schemes, primarily relying on share and property prices, are not!

The 'right' make constant claims about the 'insolvency' of the US Social Security system, when in fact amendments, improvements and increasing its universality would maintain sustainability (Rivlin, 2011).

Government response - spending cuts and tax increases

Austerity programmes have followed a common pattern in Europe and North America, with deep cuts in public services and large job losses for public employees. The UK adopted a rapid four-year deficit reduction strategy with a 70%/30% expenditure/revenue ratio. This ratio was more balanced elsewhere, for example, in France, Spain and Portugal (OECD, 2011a).

The focus of public expenditure cuts in OECD countries is clearly illustrated in Figure 1 which shows welfare spending was the most targeted programme followed closely by health, pensions and infrastructure. Germany and Ireland are reducing welfare spending more than other countries, with a 10% cut in unemployment benefits in Ireland in 2009-10. Cuts in health expenditure are not a significant proportion of cuts, although in Greece and Ireland they contribute 0.9% and 0.7% of GDP respectively. Ireland imposed a 13.5% public sector

Figure 1: Targeting of spending cuts in OECD countries

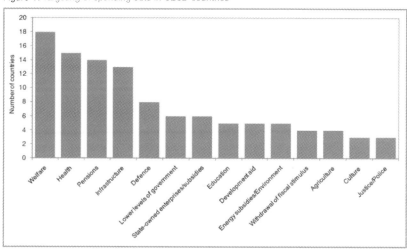

Note: Out of a total of thirty countries. Source: OECD Fical Consolidation Survey, 2010

wage cut in 2009-10 with 5% cuts in Spain and Portugal and wage freezes in the UK and France. Several countries have public sector staff reduction targets with 400,000 in the UK, 100,000 in France, 25,000 in Ireland. Taxes have been increased, particularly VAT (UK, Ireland, Greece, Portugal), and changes in income tax thresholds and the elimination of tax breaks have been common (OECD, 2011a).

Income inequality has increased as wage cuts, increases in the retirement age, reduced pensions and the termination of private sector-defined benefit pensions have been accompanied by the abolition or watering down of employment rights. More than 20 US states have introduced anti-trade union legislation. Meanwhile, increased casualisation and offshoring bring new insecurities. Productivity increases have not been reflected in wages. Austerity increases health, social and environmental inequalities.

Neoliberal governments and business interests have sought to exploit the financial crisis to demand further restructuring of the state, bigger and deeper cuts in welfare states, whilst protecting corporate welfare subsidies.

Fiscal crises of cities and states
States and cities in many countries have had to confront increased demand for services caused by the recession and infrastructure investment at a time of falling tax revenue and the collapse of property markets. Most US states and cities are facing severe financial crises. In early 2011 it was feared attempts were being made to engineer a collapse in the municipal bond market (Bloomberg News, 2011). At the same time it was argued that states should be allowed to go bankrupt, so they could tear up public sector terms and conditions and pension agreements (Bush and Gingrich, 2011). Detroit has a 20% unemployment rate (May 2011), a 25% population decline in last the decade, 59 school closures in last two years in a school district with a US$327m deficit. It has an estimated 47% of adults (more than 200,000 individuals) who *"...are functionally illiterate, referring to the inability of an individual to use reading, speaking, writing, and computational skills in everyday life situations"* (Detroit Regional Workforce Fund, 2011, Wall Street Journal, 2011a, Cohen, 2011). The graphic photos of an abandoned library, school, central station, police station and other buildings in Detroit demonstrate the dramatic decline of a major city (Marchand and Meffre, 2011).

Sovereign fiscal crisis
Ireland (€85bn in 2010), Portugal (€78bn in 2011) and Greece (€110bn in 2010 and €109bn in 2011) required EU/IMF bailouts. In each case the

respective government had to approve further austerity measures, including €50bn privatisation proceeds by 2014 in Greece. The EU established the €440bn European Financial Stability Facility (EFSF) in 2010 and was forced to extend its powers at the time of the second Greece bailout. The ESFS buys up bonds of debtor countries as a 'precautionary' measure to try to prevent a crisis, and could supply loans to any struggling Eurozone country to help them recapitalise banks.

The Eurozone crisis was exacerbated because European governments took a conservative step-by-step approach to dealing with the sovereign fiscal crisis. No sooner than one bailout was agreed, market speculators turned their attention to the 'next' country in crisis. A significantly larger initial EU bailout fund would have at least more rapidly quelled speculation and achieved a degree of stability.

Sovereign bailouts have involved multi-billion loans and financial support by other states, the EU and IMF. Whether bondholders should be required to take a 20%-50% 'haircut' (loss) has been hotly debated. Bondholders are primarily insurance companies, pension funds, mutual funds and wealthy individuals who lend to governments and large companies by purchasing short to long-term bonds (gilts). Bonds are more stable than equities and enable these financial organisations to better align their assets and liabilities than other forms of investment.

The situation is more complex because of the scale of government bonds held by financial institutions in other countries. For example, the percentage of government debt held abroad in 2011 (as a percentage of GDP) in Greece, Ireland and Portugal was 91.3%, 60.8% and 53.3% respectively. Thus, governments have been reluctant to press for bondholders to suffer losses, fearing financial markets would 'retaliate' by making investment in their economy more difficult and pushing up the cost of borrowing. Bank shares fell sharply in late 2011 because of their exposure to the sovereign debt crisis.

The creation of new Eurobonds has been advocated as a means of financial rescue and to investment. A share of national debt would convert into EU bonds, modelled on the 50-year experience of bond issues by the European Investment Bank. *"Many EU member states are deeply indebted after salvaging banks. But the Union itself has next to no debt. Even with the buy-outs of bank and national debt since May last year, its own is scarcely 1 per cent of EU gross domestic product. This is less than a 10th of the level from which the US issued the bonds that financed the New Deal"* (Amato and Verhofstadt, 2011). Bonds need not be traded. *"This would ring fence the converted bonds from rating agencies and enable governments to govern rather than the agencies rule"* (Holland, 2011). Financial initiatives should be part of a wider plan for the socialisation of investment and state intervention in the economy because *"...this crisis is not just a financial crisis, but a capitalist crisis: it is part of an attack on labour"* (Bellofiore, 2011).

The 2011 crisis over raising the US debt ceiling, resulting in the lowering of the long-term credit rating (Standard & Poor's, 2011a), was engineered by the 'right' to try to achieve a substantive longer-term reduction in public spending and the role of the Federal government. *"The political brinkmanship of recent months highlights what we see as America's governance and policymaking becoming less stable, less effective, and less predictable than we previously believed"* (ibid).

Economic growth in the G-7 economies has slowed (Figure 2) and *"...appears to have come to a halt in the major industrialised economies, with falling household and business confidence affecting both world trade and employment"* (OECD, 2011a). Continued growth in the emerging economies, in particular Brazil, Russia, India and China (BRIC) has had a key role in sustaining the global economy, offsetting recession in much of the developed countries, despite soaring commodity prices.

The IMF forecast growth in advanced economies of 1.5% in 2011 and 2% in 2012, but *"...this assumes that European policymakers contain the crisis in the euro area periphery, that U.S. policymakers strike a judicious balance between support for the economy and medium-term fiscal consolidation, and that volatility in global financial markets does not escalate"* (IMF, 2011).

Figure 2: Deceleration of growth in G-7 countries (excluding Japan)

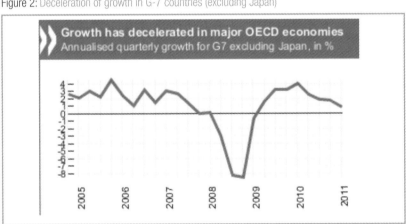

Source: OECD Economic Outlook, 2011

Global bodies, regional development agencies and nation states are confronted by other fundamental changes and crises within and between nation states. Continued urbanisation has led to the rapid growth of megacities that impose heavy demands on infrastructure and public services; adapting infrastructure to the effects of climate change will require significant investment and a new international energy order has developed in the search to procure energy supplies; extremes of water shortages and flooding whilst competition intensifies for resources and access to clean water and basic sanitation; ageing populations create new demands on health, social care, housing, pensions systems and fiscal regimes. A global shift in political power is evident as emerging economies continue to grow.

The emerging corporate welfare state

A *corporate welfare state* is emerging as neoliberal policies continue unabated. It is a state that is primarily dealing and negotiating with private capital through contracts, markets, and regulatory frameworks. A corporate welfare state will continue to have political and democratic responsibilities but these will constitute a minor part of its focus. This puts a different perspective on localism and empowerment (Chapter 3).

The transfer of physical resources and assets, such as staff and premises to the private sector, is partially replaced by new responsibilities to manage markets, undertake procurement, contract management, and coordinate local economic development in increasingly difficult conditions. The loss of in-house intellectual capability is only partially compensated by the increased, and costly, use of management consultants and lawyers who reinforce business values. A corporate welfare state will have fewer assets to manage, as they will be increasingly leased or sold to the private sector.

Managing markets, designing and monitoring regulatory frameworks and undertaking market research, is much more labour intensive and costly, particularly in monitoring abuse and corruption. It may lead to a decrease in costs for some public bodies but this will be offset by increased costs in others. It will spawn a raft of impact consultants and advisers. Capital has rarely valued 'social' impacts but now contracts are to be awarded on the basis of social outcomes! Contracts will have many more vested interests – investors, contractors, financial institutions, consultants and lawyers, before service users and staff are even considered!

The state has been claimed to be hollowing out (fragmentation of the centre and loss of central control), but there is little UK evidence to support this thesis (Holliday, 2000). The latest model is the 'post-bureaucratic state', which would eliminate hierarchies and build networks of people and contacts and 'knowledge sharing'; it would liberate public spending information; and 'permanent audit' of service providers would create pressure to deliver 'what users want', high quality services at low cost and innovation (Network for the Post-Bureaucratic Age, 2010). Commissioning will shrink the state by limiting it to a client role that plans and funds services. Delivery will increasingly be outsourced and assets leased to private and voluntary sector contractors. Market forces will be unleashed across public services and the welfare state.

The belief that local authorities could be run like companies took root in the 1970s when Nicholas Ridley, then Secretary of State for the Environment, promoted the 'contract city' model adopted by some small US towns. These towns outsourced most services with elected members meeting only occasionally to award contracts. This underpinned the concept of the 'enabling' council, which extended the client/contractor split under competitive tendering of manual services in the 1980s to the whole council. The London Borough of Barnet's recent claim to become an 'easyCouncil' (Chapter 8) is based on an extension of this model (although it is impossible for local government to be run on the same basis as a cheap airline); *"...economics and business are not the same subject, and mastery of one does not ensure comprehension, let alone mastery, of the other"* (Krugman, 2009).

The private sector has always sought to provide public services, particularly where this work had previously been privately delivered; for example, railways, gas and electricity had been nationalised because of private sector failures (Whitfield, 1992). The Tories sought to sell the first council houses built under the Wheatley Act of 1924 and again in the 1950s, sales that preceded the 1980s right-to-buy for council tenants.

The UK is politically obsessed with localism, community budgets, social enterprises, and community asset ownership of libraries, leisure centres, and post offices. They are a diversion, because the bidders for larger contracts are inevitably national and transnational companies. David Harvey was concise in concluding, *"...we are witnessing a consolidation and centralisation of class power into the hands of a few institutions that escape public control"* (Harvey, 2010).

Neoliberal governments, supported by transnational ICT companies, are using 'innovation' to extend marketisation and privatisation. Advances in information and communications technology have created millions of users with individual mobile phone, social and professional networking accounts. Because we have personal phone accounts does not mean that we should automatically have personal health, education, training or social care accounts. It is increasingly possible to electronically charge for road usage and other services with payment directly from bank accounts or credit cards. Technological viability does not automatically make policies politically, economically and socially desirable or feasible. The notion that 'we can', therefore 'we will', is not an acceptable guide.

Innovation is crucial, but when it is used to extend and embed marketisation, it must be challenged and opposed before large parts of the public sector and welfare state are subjugated to the interests of transnational communications companies.

CHAPTER 2

Neoliberal transformation of public services and the welfare state

Neoliberal transformation of the public sector and welfare state consists of four processes – financialisation, personalisation, marketisation and privatisation (see Figure 3). Transformation of public services was intensified in an attempt to retain and strengthen the neoliberal model, to extend wealth creation in the public sector, to reconfigure the state and reformulate social relations. In some respects the financial crisis was a setback for neoliberalism, because of the failure of securitisation, deregulation and the property market collapse. However, it created opportunities to accelerate marketisation and privatisation. It brought the role of the state back centre-stage in the bailout of banks and financial institutions as corporate welfare (the well-being of corporations at public expense) reached a new zenith.

Individualisation and personalisation could potentially improve user involvement in the planning and design of services and align with people's needs. Services should be more flexible, so individuals can learn, develop and receive the services appropriate to their circumstances. Equity of access, respect and engagement in ideas, observations and complaints is essential. But these aspects have marginal status in the neoliberal agenda. The overriding priority is to change the individual's relationship from a service user to a customer-market relationship. Individuals must access, or buy, the service from competing providers, and if they don't like it, either challenge or change the provider. The objective is to atomise, or fragment the user relationship and to have it prescribed by market relations. Neoliberalism focuses on individual needs and prioritises them over collective responsibility and the public interest. The intention is clearly to minimise opportunities for collective action. It allows the state *"...to relinquish moral obligations"* (Judt, 2010).

Social enterprises and mutuals are often presented as the nirvana of a 'new economy', but this is fraudulent. The Coalition's objective is to provide a diversion from the big business colonisation of public sector contracts and assets and to create a secondary market so private contractors can later acquire social enterprises. In addition, they hope to reduce the cost of public services by hiving off responsibility to community organisations, increasing the use of free labour by volunteers, and engaging voluntary organisations in contracting, which inevitably compromises their capacity to advocate and campaign (see Chapter 9). The idea that public service innovation can only be developed and nurtured by the 'social sector' is simplistic and untrue.

Figure 3: Neoliberal public sector transformation

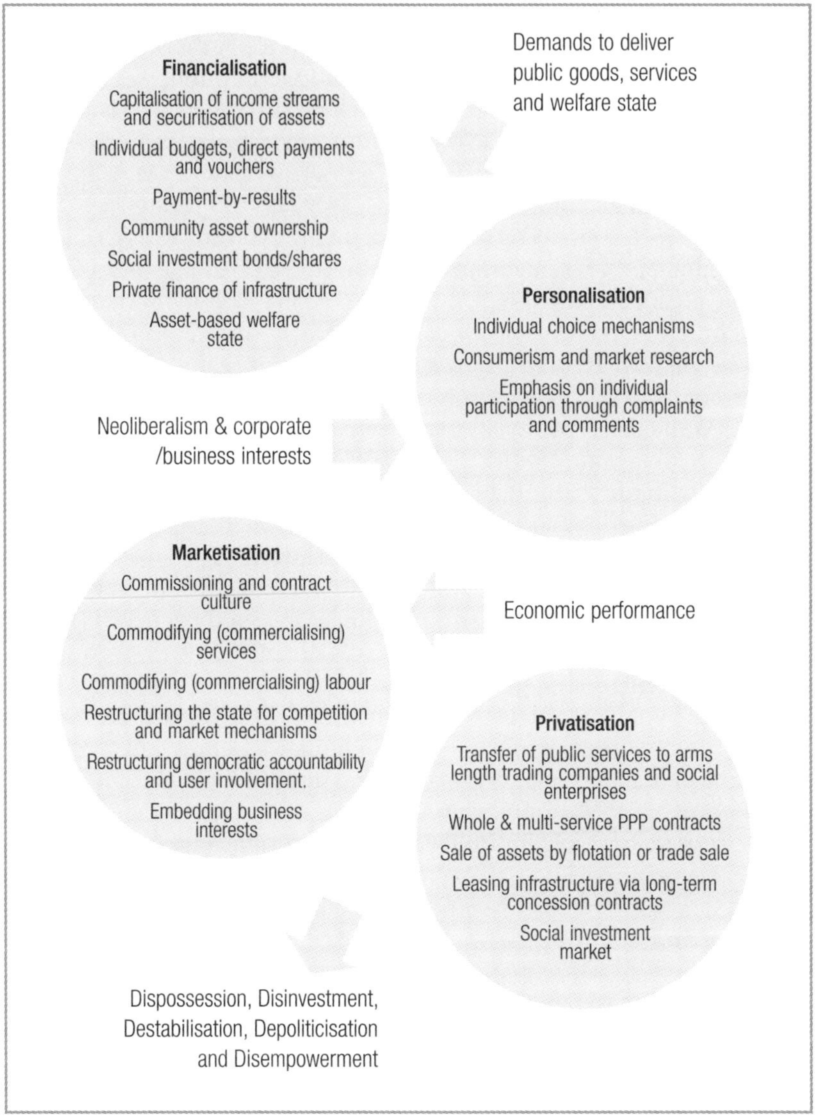

Financialisation

Capitalisation of income streams and securitisation of assets

Individual budgets, direct payments and vouchers

Payment-by-results

Community asset ownership

Social investment bonds/shares

Private finance of infrastructure

Asset-based welfare state

Demands to deliver public goods, services and welfare state

Neoliberalism & corporate /business interests

Personalisation

Individual choice mechanisms

Consumerism and market research

Emphasis on individual participation through complaints and comments

Marketisation

Commissioning and contract culture

Commodifying (commercialising) services

Commodifying (commercialising) labour

Restructuring the state for competition and market mechanisms

Restructuring democratic accountability and user involvement.

Embedding business interests

Economic performance

Privatisation

Transfer of public services to arms length trading companies and social enterprises

Whole & multi-service PPP contracts

Sale of assets by flotation or trade sale

Leasing infrastructure via long-term concession contracts

Social investment market

Dispossession, Disinvestment, Destabilisation, Depoliticisation and Disempowerment

Financialisation

Financialisation has affected the public sector in seven important ways.

Capitalisation of income streams and securitisation of assets

The capitalisation of income streams (the process of converting an income stream, such as rents, to a lump sum capital value), and the securitisation of assets (mortgages, credit cards, student loans, car loans, in fact, any loan or debt can be bundled together and sold to other investors), have enabled banks and financial institutions to transfer a degree of risk, make profits from these transactions, and create new markets. This drive to create further tiers of financial ownership, new financial products and to financialise services, is evidence of the increasing penetration of formal finance into the transaction of ordinary life: housing, pensions, insurance and consumption (Lapavitsas, 2008).

Public health and secondary education remain free of charge, but this applies only to a narrowing concept of the core service. Budget cuts in the US, UK and Ireland are resulting in the growing imposition of charges for 'extras', for example, enrolment fees, materials, field trips and sports such as $660 per student for cross country running and track (Wall Street Journal, 2011b). 'Voluntary contributions' are commonly sought to help fund running costs in Ireland's public schools.

However, big differences remain in charging policies between England and the devolved administrations. Prescriptions are free in Wales, Scotland and Northern Ireland; Scottish students do not pay tuition fees, whilst Wales and Northern Ireland have frozen them at 2011 levels.

The introduction of charges and tolls enables services and assets (roads, airports, parking garages and meters) to be converted into long-term concessions operated by the private sector in return for a lump sum. Asset monetisation is expanding in the US as states and cities bear the brunt of the financial crisis and recession (Whitfield, 2010a). The sale of equity in PPP companies (Whitfield, 2011a) led to the growth of a secondary market, which could emerge in the social investment market too (JP Morgan, 2010).

Individual budgets, direct payments and vouchers

The switch to individual budgets and direct payments, in which service users receive a cash payment, or a voucher instead of delivery of a service, has a number of consequences. Currently, a personal budget can be taken as a direct (cash) payment with each person purchasing services; as an account held and managed by the local authority with decisions taken by the user; as an account held by a third party provider and called off by users; or as a mixture of these approaches. There is wide support for people receiving ongoing care to have more control over the design and delivery of long-term, high intensity services. However, mainstreaming individual budgets and direct payments to other services will have drastic consequences for the NHS, education and other services. Receiving payments for health and education in the same way as older people receive their pensions will increase market forces, competition and accelerate privatisation of the NHS.

The 2010 Spending Review announced that personal budgets would be extended to special needs education, support for children with disabilities, long-term health conditions, adult social care and other services. The Vision for Adult Social Care concluded *"The time is now right to make personal budgets the norm for everyone who receives on-going care and support – ideally as a direct cash payment, to give maximum flexibility and choice"* by April 2013 (Department of Health, 2010a). The mainstreaming of individual health budgets is likely to accelerate the growth of a healthcare market faster than the Coalition's other NHS 'reform' policies.

Why would they stop at these social needs and services? Surely the danger is that there is no cut-off point and individual budgets, direct payments or vouchers could eventually become the norm for most public services. And why are legal constraints put in the way of direct payments being used to access publicly provided services? Users who transfer to private and voluntary sector providers only help to expand the care and health markets. This in turn creates secondary or niche markets for brokers and advisers.

Finance and service delivery are no longer confined within local authority boundaries. Information and communications technology enables the government or local authorities to change the value of individual budgets with the flick of a switch. It is an easy mechanism to force service users to top-up budgets with their own money to maintain the quality and level of service or purchase additional services in the private sector.

Private companies will try to attract budget holders, agglomerate competing firms and accumulate profits. The switch from defined to contributory pensions, the continued push for home ownership, more insurance products and the compensation culture are other aspects of financialisation. Increasing personal debt, behavioural or attitudinal changes, and certain social norms, are reinforced by individualised budgets, for example, self-interest and loss of collective identity. Financialisation and individualisation have affected important parts of daily life – tolls for roads, tunnels and bridges; tuition fees for college students; charges for television in hospitals; fees for homecare; charges for music and other 'non-core' activities in schools. This system of multi-tax collection is inefficient and masks the extraction of profit by an array of contractors and consultants delivering public services. It inevitably leads to the monetisation of social relationships between state and citizen, between client and contractor, between service user and worker, and between users.

These developments occur at the same time as UK household debt (mortgage, credit card and other debt) is set to soar by a further £303bn by 2015 to £2,126bn, an average £77,309 per household and a 17% increase on previous projections (Office for Budget Responsibility, 2011). *"This is the downside of the chancellor's deficit reduction plan. As tax increases and public spending cuts squeeze household's disposable incomes, they will be forced to take on more and more debt in an attempt to maintain their living standards"* (Dolphin, 2011).

Student loan debt in the US now exceeds total credit card debt. The latter was $792.5bn in July 2011, down from a peak of $975.7bn in September 2008 (www.federalreserve.gov/releases/g19), whilst student loan debt had continued its inexorable rise to $946.2bn by October 2011 (www.finaid.org).

Different types of personal budgets such as Health Spending Accounts or Medical Savings Accounts (MSA) exist in the US, Singapore, South Africa, China and have been considered in Canada.

"Close scrutiny of existing MSA plans around the world reveals the benefits to be concentrated among the healthier members of those populations; indeed, most of the sickest are not members of such plans. ….A plan that strips specialty services, escalates costs, adds bureaucracy, undermines privacy, and erodes health care has little to recommend it" (Deber et al, 2004).

"Our results reinforce and expand our understanding of the distributional impacts of MSAs. Compared with the existing method of public funding, MSAs generate a number of undesirable distributional impacts across those of differing health statuses, incomes, utilization levels, and ages, both with respect to the distribution of public funds and the distribution of out-of-pocket payments" (Hurley et al, 2008).

Other evidence suggests that the cost of care had increased through the loss of bargaining power over providers. They represent an explicit rejection of risk pooling across populations, and co-payments from patients were common (Deber, 2011).

Payment-by-results

The obsession with the performance management regime's wide range of indicators and targets has finally become less dominant, but 'payment-by-results' has become the new performance management mantra. There are two models – phased incentive payments and the social impact bond mechanism with payment at the end of the contract (see social investment below).

The Work Programme, the Coalition's five-year welfare-to-work project, has a phased payment system with a small start fee for each new participant, which is reduced each year and eliminated after three years. Contractors will receive a job outcome payment after a participant has been in a job for three or six months, depending how *"...far they are from the labour market"*, in plain English how long they have been unemployed. Contractors can also claim 'sustainment payments' every four weeks when a participant stays in work for up to one year, 18 months or two years, again depending on how long they are unemployed (Department for Work and Pensions, 2011).

Payment-by-results in the NHS was designed to improve efficiency and value for money, facilitate choice and plurality of providers to increase contestability, and to get the price right for services which reflects true costs and incentivises patient care. But it is not a results-based system because it does not take account of the quality of treatment (Leys and Player, 2011). Hospitals are paid only for operations and procedures performed, a national tariff of over 1,000 procedures each with a Health Resource Group code. It forces hospitals to operate like businesses. If they perform an operation at less than the national tariff they retain the difference, but if their costs are higher than the tariff the hospital will be forced to cut costs, do more operations to generate additional income, or terminate the service. The system is designed to make money follow patients and to spur competition between hospitals. A Market Forces Factor, consisting of staff, buildings and land indices, is used to adjust the national tariff to give the local price for each Trust.

Community asset ownership

There are a number of plans to extend and embed financialisation in the public sector and welfare state. 'Capitalise the poor and civil society' policies are intended to encourage and incentivise individuals and groups to acquire community assets such as libraries, swimming pools, community centres, council offices, police stations, courts, prisons, and the road network. ResPublica (a public policy think-tank), the Development Trusts Association and the National Endowment for Science, Technology and the Arts (NESTA) propose *"...a truly popular and meaningful Big Society to simultaneously capitalising civil society and spreading ownership....to achieve a bottom-up prosperity that builds resilient and independent communities capable of providing individuals with sustainable exits from poverty and entrances into wealth and well-being"* (Wyler and Blond, 2010). A community right to buy, to build, to try, to bid, to work and to know with community shares and community vouchers would *"...help to liberate people from social inequality, economic dependency and entrenched poverty"* (ibid). This is another manifestation of Thatcher's 'real public ownership'. The plan to allocate 10% of Royal Mail shares to staff will be the largest employee share scheme in privatisation. However, this is individual, not collective, share ownership.

Social investment state
Social investment and 'impact investments' are a *"...new alternative for channelling large-scale private capital for social benefit"* (JP Morgan, 2010). They are a new form of financialisation. A social investment market will enable social projects to obtain private investment with a financial return, for example, via Social Impact Bonds (SIBs) or equity investments, and hence create a new asset class. Local projects, which deliver services, provide activities, operate buildings and/or provide transport that generate social value and are self-sustaining, will ensure that investors get a return on their investment (JP Morgan, 2010 and Cabinet Office, 2011a). A number of Wall Street investment banks and large foundations such as Ford and Rockefeller are developing this model.

Following UK and US initiatives in the last decade, (such as the Social Investment Task Force, the Global Impact Investing Network, the Impact Reporting and Investment Standards and the Coalition government's Social Investment Market strategy, together with various trusts and foundations), plans for a 'new asset class' have emerged. *"As this movement gathers steam, we recognize the potential for impact investments to attract a larger portion of mainstream private capital and anticipate that more investors will seek to generate positive social and/or environmental impact when making investment decisions. In fact, we believe that impact investing will reveal itself to be one of the most powerful changes within the asset management industry in the years to come"* (JP Morgan, 2010).

The social bond payment mechanism is dependent on the successful performance of the contract. A Social Investment Fund will raise funds for a project and select a contractor to deliver the project. The contractor will be paid in the normal way but the investors funding the project via the Social Investment Fund will only be paid if the project is successful. For example, payments for the Peterborough Prison contract, the first UK project, have three consecutive two-year periods, with payments made to the Social Investment organisation in the fourth, sixth and eighth years. Payment to the investors is contingent on the contractor reducing reoffending by 7.5% compared to the recidivism rate in a selected group of similar prisons. The greater the reduction in reoffending rates, the higher the return to investors up to a maximum of a 13% return. The return to investors is financed by reducing the cost of police work, court, community sentence, and prison costs (Social Finance, 2010 and Center for American Progress, 2011). Four social impact bond pilots have been launched in Birmingham, Leicestershire, Westminster and Hammersmith and Fulham to raise up to £40m *"...to help families blighted by anti-social behaviour, crime, addiction and poor education"* (Cabinet Office, 2011b).

In this model the Social Investment Fund (SIF), not the state, selects the contractor. Because it is initially financed by private investment, it gives the impression that projects are privately financed when, in fact, they are the same as PPPs, entirely publicly financed. Government claims, that voluntary and private service providers will have access to capital markets, are not relevant if they are ultimately financed by the public sector. Advocates make comparisons with the Private Finance Initiative (Young Foundation, 2011 and Hems, 2011), which should be a warning.

The focus on paying only for demonstrated results shifts the focus to those who bear the risk and away from the needs of service users to investors and the contractor. If the project performs poorly or fails, then the support and sympathy needs to be directed to the children, unemployed and prisoners who have a poor service, rather than affluent or wealthy investors. Furthermore, political risk cannot be transferred and government will take the brunt of criticism where projects fail.

Social impact bond projects require *"...sufficiently high net benefits to allow investors to earn their required rates of return"*, the outcomes must be measurable, the treatment population must be well-defined, impact assessments must be credible, and unsuccessful performance must not result in early closure if it becomes evident to investors that performance targets will not be met and they will not be paid (Center for American Progress, 2011). There is the potential for high transaction costs with independent impact assessment and potential for disputes arising over the measurement of impact and cause/effect of outcomes; gaming with contractors concentrating on the 'easier' users to maximise 'success' (Office for Fair Trading, 2011a); the sustainability of outcomes after the contract; and the longer term consequences of creating a social investment market. The wider impact on marketisation and privatisation is completely ignored by the social market advocates.

The Coalition government believes *"...individual investors will be receptive to simple retail products from credible suppliers that give them a chance to 'invest for good', as long as they believe there is a reasonable chance of getting their money back, possibly with a positive financial return. Our vision calls for the creation of a new 'asset class' of social investment to connect social ventures with mainstream capital"* (Cabinet Office, 2011a). This strategy is dependent on mainstreaming commissioning and outsourcing to open up the provision of public services to new providers, reducing the 'bureaucratic burden' on small civil society organisations and increasing social ventures' access to capital.

The UK government plans to accelerate the growth of the social investment market by dedicating resources to promote a new class and range of investment products, increase share ownership in local pubs and post offices, and develop a secondary market for the sale and purchase of shares in social ventures. Voluntary organisations will inevitably be pressured into considering social investment for projects.

The government will use a proportion of the savings that result from improved social outcomes to reward private investors who fund projects. This 'payment-by-results' model depends on developing an agreed performance regime. Safeguards to prevent cherry-picking the most likely successes and leaving the difficult complex cases to the prison service should remain a concern. Social Impact Bonds (SIB) are said to be a paradigm shift to *"...catalyse positive cycles of government spending, improving social outcomes and reducing costs"* (Social Finance, 2009).

Basically, private investors finance early intervention projects, such as preventing reoffending, and receive a share of the savings in public spending as a return on their investment. It is just another way of monetising efficiencies.

The rise of a 'new social economy' is claimed to have *"...profound implications for the future of public services as well as the daily life of citizens"* (Murray, 2009). It is anticipated to involve *"... changing the way in which whole systems of production and service are conceived and delivered or the need for them avoided"* (ibid). This includes *"...all areas of the economy which are not geared to private profitability"*, the state, the third sector, *"...social enterprises and cooperatives operating in the market"*, households, social networks and social movements. But the role of the market, democratic governance, the quality of jobs and the reform of the core functions of the welfare state are just some of the issues missing from, or obscured by, the rhetoric.

Similar Community Bonds have been developed to acquire buildings for community use in Toronto, Canada, where a minimum C$10,000 investment with 4% return attracted investors to fund improvement work. The US government has launched a pilot programme with seven projects and the State of New South Wales is planning the first Australian project.

This social bond model leads to additional risks, over and above the normal procurement and outsourcing risks (see Chapter 3). The new risks include the identification of savings, the difficulty of assessment, and investment, complexity and scaling up risks. The potential for market gaming (see Chapter 10), in which contractors cherry pick 'easy' clients and park 'difficult' ones, is much greater. Transaction costs could be relatively higher because of the need for independent assessment. This 'market' is a major threat to universal public provision and could ultimately lead to entirely private services, reliant on state subsidies.

Private finance of infrastructure
PPPs have facilitated the financialisation of public infrastructure (Whitfield, 2010a). Construction companies and banks finance the design, construction and operation of public buildings and transport systems, effectively owning and managing them under long-term contracts. The sale of equity in PPP project companies is highly profitable, averaging 50.6% (see Chapter 8). Total profits were estimated to be £2.2bn, based on a sample of 154 projects, although this excluded the undisclosed profits obtained in the sale of secondary market infrastructure funds. The number of UK infrastructure funds operating from tax havens has increased (Whitfield, 2011a).

Asset-based welfare state
The growth of an asset-based welfare state, to increase the value of property and financial assets of the poor, has been uneven in the UK. It has ranged from widening home ownership via the sale and shared-

ownership of social housing and child-care vouchers, to the 'personalisation of pensions', encouraging people to start individual third-tier defined contribution pensions. The recently abolished Child Trust Fund (CTF) enabled parents of children born after September 2002 to receive vouchers worth £250 (£500 to those receiving child tax credit and earning less than £13,230), to be deposited in special accounts, topped up by families and friends and a government top-up at the age of 7, 11 and 18 when children could access the tax-free funds. The Coalition abandoned the Savings Gateway, similar to Individual Development Accounts in the US, due to start in July 2010. The government would have added 50 pence to every pound saved by people receiving benefits and tax credits, to a maximum of £300 over two years.

Instead of addressing inequality of opportunity, redistribution of wealth and social solidarity, the CTF *"...became a tool for changing the behaviour of the poor rather than a challenge to prevailing patterns of ownership"* (Finlayson, 2008). The policy *"...in form and presentation, was dominated by commercial concerns and by an individualised approach to welfare, concerned to create new kinds of attitude in people"* (ibid). New Labour's attempt to 'build the assets ladder' could be interpreted as little more than saving for tuition fees, other service charges and tolls.

The asset-based model sought to direct welfare state benefits to the elderly and those seeking work and to minimise middle class benefits. This meant widening the introduction of fees and charges for services. For example, the Scottish 'independent' budget review concluded *"... there is scope to look again at eligibility, as well as the selective introduction of means testing and user charging for all universal services. This will help to ensure that public services are focused on those with greatest need as well as helping to control future costs"* (Scotland's Independent Budget Review Panel, 2010). This review advocated the concept of a residual welfare role for public services, the same model used for council housing, even though it started out as good quality general housing.

Education, health and social care could eventually be individually purchased via vouchers, individual budgets and direct payments. The more affluent are likely to continue to opt out of publicly financed, into entirely private financed and provided services. A two-tier system would lead to a fractured and residual role for public provision. The loss of social solidarity, and collective provision, would erode social rights and concern for inter-generational needs reinforcing 'self/today' societal values. New forms of insurance would develop as the private sector sought to group individual purchasers to obtain economies of scale and organise the market. Tolls and charges for virtually everything electronically collected, as you inhabit the city or suburb. The erosion of universal provision could speed-up new and/or increased charges.

A new market is growing in equity release for elderly homeowners, to supplement low pensions and the cost of care, thus, potentially, reducing public welfare spending and family inheritance except for the wealthy. Real Estate Investment Trusts (REITs) are intended to expand access to a wider range of savings products and to provide investment mechanisms, which are an alternative to the falling value of pensions. These policies help to expand and create new financial services markets in savings, insurance and pensions.

Personalisation

Individual budgets, direct payments and vouchers/credits transfer the risk and responsibility to individual users, by forcing them to select their own service provider. It atomises collective provision because individuals are encouraged to make decisions based solely on their own circumstances. Trading restrictions placed on public sector providers, combined with other destabilising tactics, help to expand private provision, whilst creating the conditions for public provision to wither on the vine and to avoid direct privatisation.

The transfer of risk and responsibility has four dimensions. Firstly, individual budgets and direct payments make the selection of a service provider a personal responsibility, although this is dressed up in the language of choice, but these are in practice contrived and fake choices. The state is effectively transferring risk to the user and their advisers or agents.

Secondly, the withdrawal of the Code of Practice on Workforce Matters in 2011, and the planned restriction of transferred staff having access to public sector pensions, ensure that the consequences of a two-tier workforce are transferred to staff. An analysis of the risk of changes to terms and conditions of service, pensions, staff consultation and representation and problems with a secondment agreement, revealed that 84% of risks are in the high to medium risk category with the TUPE transfer model, compared to none to 8% with the secondment and TUPE Plus models respectively (ESSU, 2010a).

Thirdly, payment-by-results is intended to incentivise contractors, with payment conditional on the completion of agreed outputs or outcomes. This can include achievement of savings targets, with the benefits shared between client and contractor. This attempt to increase the transfer of risks to contractors is not without its risks, such as gaming, concentrating on easy wins or 'cream skimming' (see Chapter 10) and disputes could arise over the cause and effect of change.

Fourthly, there is evidence that some authorities adopt risk denial, particularly the risk of contract failure, to minimise opposition to outsourcing policies. For example, options appraisals and business cases in the London Borough of Barnet have systematically failed to address operational risks (ESSU, 2010b and 2011a).

Marketisation of public services

Marketisation creates the conditions whereby full privatisation becomes inevitable. Competition and contestability impose commercial values and operational systems on in-house services, often resulting in the sale of direct service organisations. It encourages public sector arms length companies and trusts to expand and diversify, become more independent, which in turn is used to legitimise 'greater freedom' and full privatisation. Marketisation sets the culture where the public sector assign prices to functions and services that have not traditionally been priced and have economic and social value, not simply a financial value.

Market forces are imposed in different ways at different speeds in different services. Markets do not evolve naturally, nor do they emerge through self-regulation. States create the conditions, regulations and financing, and provide the legitimacy to create and sustain markets in public services. This is a political decision as much as a technical or organisational process and has five key elements, detailed in *New Labour's Attack on Public Services* (Whitfield, 2006a).

Commodifying (commercialising) services – users are treated as consumers and purchasers; services are quantified and organised so they can be readily specified and packaged in a contract; operational values are remoulded to meet commercial criteria; risks are commodified so they can be priced; public agencies replace grants with contracts; and market research and soft market testing enable the private sector to influence the scope and packaging of services.

Commodifying (commercialising) labour – tasks, working practices and jobs are standardised, routinised and reorganised to increase productivity, reduce the cost of labour and assist transfer to another employer. New working methods are accompanied by changes to job descriptions and restructuring of the workforce to increase deskilling and casualisation. Management will seek to renegotiate agreements or impose changes.

Restructuring the state for competition and market mechanisms – client and contractor roles are separated with public bodies becoming 'commissioning' agents rather than providers; market mechanisms are introduced, such as money follows patients and pupils, pricing of tasks and activities and payment-by-results; schools, hospitals and other facilities are compelled to compete against each other; options appraisals, soft market testing, business cases and the formal procurement process increasingly dominate management of public bodies.

Restructuring democratic accountability and user involvement – services and functions are transferred to quangos, arms length companies and trusts with separate governance structures that undermine traditional structures of democratic control; participation and disclosure is limited to consultation because of 'commercial confidentiality'.

Embedding business interests – business is more deeply involved in the public policy making process; trade bodies promote free market in services, wider use of PPPs and the infrastructure market, and promote liberalisation of public services.

Commissioning, competition and contract culture

The separation of purchaser/provider, or client/contractor functions, is a key pre-condition for mainstreaming marketisation in the public sector. Commissioning is based on the belief that it does not matter who provides services and that public, private and voluntary organisations should compete to deliver services. It is a re-hash of the earlier 'enabling model' of local government and requires the separation of client and contractor roles. The procurement process (service reviews, options appraisals, business cases and tendering procedure) is mainstreamed across all services and embedded in public management (see Chapter 10).

The economics of competition and outsourcing assumes that a combination of:

- reducing the cost of labour (increased productivity, fewer staff and changes to terms and conditions);
- the introduction of new technology and working methods; a competitive drive and business values;
- the relocation of work to areas with lower wage levels; and the reduction in overheads;

will produce savings and better services. Reality is different (see Chapter 10).

The state is required to manage demand for services (such as pupil numbers and population needs for heath and social care), procure and manage contracts, and monitor the implementation of regulations. Public bodies retain statutory duties and must have strategic plans to ensure broadly equitable provision. The state must research market trends, prevent monopoly control and corruption, and take action in the event of contract and/or market failure. It must also mediate between conflicting interests of community needs, political and business interests.

Commissioning requires the state to provide financial and regulatory support for markets and contestability between providers. The notion of a 'level playing field' ignores structural and operational differences between public and private sectors. It requires the commercialisation of in-house services and the establishment of arms length trading companies to compete with private firms and voluntary organisations. Staff are transferred between employers with a modicum of protection. Advocates claim it promotes 'partnerships' between the public and private/voluntary contractors. But this is disingenuous, because the partnerships in question are contracts and *"...suggest a more closely balanced relationship than is really present"* (Grout, 2009).

Public service principles and values are replaced by commercial values and business practices. The loss of public sector capacity and the extension of 'commercial confidentiality' impacts negatively on democratic accountability and transparency. A reduction in the implementation of corporate policies is another consequence. Only corporate policies specifically applicable to the service being contracted are legally enforceable. The development of new or improved corporate policies is likely to be stymied because the interface between service provision and corporate policy will be fractured. Employment and equalities policies require constant assessment and review, but weak public sector monitoring means that contractors can make commitments in the procurement process, in the knowledge that most monitoring regimes are under-resourced and scrutiny is less than rigorous.

The deregulation of service, labour and other markets is a consistent feature of neoliberalism (see Chapters 1 and 10). Business interests want four things – a reduction in the regulatory framework in which they have to operate to reduce costs, for example, health and safety laws; a large measure of self-assessment of performance so that they can ensure assessment is not rigorous; contract conditions that are not too onerous and incur small financial penalties for poor or non-performance; and the re-regulation of labour and trade union regulations to impose more restrictions on trade unions organising and taking industrial action.

The mutation of privatisation

Privatisation was never simply about the sale of nationalised industries and utilities but included restructuring the economy to increase capital accumulation. It is *"...a comprehensive strategy for permanently restructuring the welfare state and public services in the interests of capital"* (Whitfield, 1983).

Changes in genes, caused by viruses, radiation or chemicals or error in replication, may result in changes in DNA sequences that prevent a gene from functioning properly, alter the product of a gene or have no effect. Privatisation has mutated into a variety of forms. The transfer of ownership and control of public assets was initially concentrated in state owned corporations and real estate, for example, the sale of oil, gas, electricity, telecoms and water. Once the scale of privatisation reached a threshold where further sales were complex or politically untenable, the emphasis moved to different forms of ownership and control. New forms of privatisation emerged as the focus moved to the marketisation of services by outsourcing, joint ventures, public private partnerships, combined with a new 'gene' of personalisation which gave service users individual budgets and direct payments/vouchers. This widened and deepened the role of the private sector in the design and delivery of public services.

Although the sale of assets took centre stage, privatisation was never intended to be solely about selling assets to increase government revenue in order to minimise taxation, or to improve economic efficiency. Private ownership was a means of marginalising democratic accountability, and reducing the cost of labour and the power of trade unions. Commodified services and markets with minimal regulatory oversight ensured profits and transferred risk. New forms of privatisation were needed to outsource public goods and encourage a 'privatisation of life' perspective to address 'cradle to grave' needs and the privatisation of land, sea, air and space.

Thatcherism triggered a new, more intensive sale of public assets in the early 1980s, beginning with the privatisation of nationalised industries and utilities, plus the sale of council housing. Privatisation developed, by political and economic necessity, into a multi-dimensional process. Because of political, staff, trade union and community opposition most of the core functions and services of the state could not be privatised by a stock market flotation or trade sale. The market mechanisms were not in place and required more complex arrangements with a longer timescale. Political values and social attitudes had to be changed, not least the belief in 'public service' had to be eroded and embedded trade union and professional interests challenged.

Three key areas remained in the public sector – the welfare state infrastructure (such as health and education), the criminal justice system, and defence. Labour commenced with a two-year commitment to the Tories' spending plans and a rapid speed-up and broadening of the role for the private finance initiative. The 'modernisation' agenda consisted of a centralised performance management framework of targets and inspection, Best Value, mainstreaming procurement, strategic partnerships, outsourcing, the transfer of services to quangos and arms length companies, and a new 'efficiency' drive.

New Labour, subsequently, increased public spending, but public sector transformation was rooted in a neoliberal ideology of competition and market forces. They attempted to redefine privatisation, claimed that PFI projects, strategic service-delivery partnerships (SSPs) and outsourcing were 'partnerships' and not privatisation, and that marketisation was little more than the application of the principles of a mixed economy. However, these policies involved the transfer of resources (staff, land, buildings, equipment, and intellectual capital) to private companies, private investment in the public infrastructure, and private management of a wide range of public services. This was, and is, privatisation.

New pathways to privatisation have been created to diversify the routes to and speed up the mutation of privatisation process. The transfer of services to an arms length or trading company is one route. A few Local Authority Trading Companies (LATC) have been established for social care services. The London Borough of Barnet is planning to combine its care service and the arms length housing management service, Barnet Homes, into a new LATC. Capita Group has recruited Barnet Homes to be a subcontractor in its bid for a £300m planning and regulatory services contract. This creates the opportunity for full privatisation at a later stage when the decision-making process might be carried on less transparently than under direct democratic control.

Unless social enterprises have a *"...water-tight trust-based model, closed to carpet-baggers"* with an asset lock-in legal mechanism to prevent members of the mutual selling the asset, they will be prey to private companies seeking to build market share (Davies, 2010). The expansion of leisure trusts in Scotland to become Community Trusts to include libraries, museums, parks and community education services is another pathway. Bilateral Free Trade Agreements provide international pathways by supporting opportunities for new projects and funding mechanisms.

New forms of marketisation and privatisation are constantly emerging. Networks of publicly owned schools and hospitals are fractured and fragmented, so that each becomes a stand-alone business which must compete for survival against its neighbours, such as academy and 'free' schools. This usually leads to increased commercialisation and detachment from democratic control (see Chapter 8).

A 'whole' service approach combines the design, build, finance and operation of a PPP, with the provision of services in a strategic partnership. The £2.9bn Birmingham 25-year highway contract (and similar contracts in procurement in Sheffield, Hounslow and the Isle of Wight) is almost certain to be followed by several more 'whole' service contracts.

Independent Sector Treatment Centres (ISTCs) that provide routine clinical services on behalf of the NHS, are an example of private sector provision of core services. The outsourcing of the management of the NHS Hitchingbrooke Hospital to a private company set another precedent. Chief executives of Innisfree and John Laing, who gave evidence to the House of Lords respectively, said it would be a *"... natural extension"* to provide nursing services and *"...there is no reason why the private sector could not embrace the provision of the service rather than just provide the hardware from which the service is delivered"*. *The Select Committee on Economic Affairs agreed "...there is scope to transfer more demand or output-related risks"* (House of Lords, 2010).

Privatisation has enabled the state to absolve responsibility for staffing policies in outsourced contracts. Fremantle Trust operates care homes privatised by the London Borough of Barnet in 2000. It subsequently imposed draconian cuts in terms and conditions, despite a concerted UNISON campaign. The Council claimed: *"This is a matter between Fremantle and its employees....The Council is not involved as it transferred the staff over 5 years ago and does not engage in third party employer/employee industrial relations. The Council's sole concern is to ensure the welfare of residents in the Homes."* (London Borough of Barnet, 2006).

Strategic infrastructure assets and public services cannot be allowed to fail, such as rail services, airports, water and energy supply. Private companies know this and can terminate a loss-making contract in the knowledge that the government would take over provision or rapidly organise another operator. National Express walked away from the East Coast rail franchise in 2009 in the full knowledge that another operator would take it over, in this case, the government. In a similar way, the big banks believe they are 'too big to fail' and thus demonstrate moral hazard. They do not take full responsibility for high-risk investments, knowing that they will either make a high return, or be bailed out by taxpayers if they do not succeed.

Deconstructing democracy

Financialisation, personalisation, marketisation and privatisation are designed to dispossess, disinvest, destabilise, depoliticise and disempower, in effect the de-construction of democracy at local, national and international levels. I now examine each of these in turn.

Dispossession

Home foreclosures, the loss of jobs, reduced employment protection in staff transfers, the erosion of public sector pensions and the closure of local facilities due to spending cuts are forms of dispossession. The community-right-to-challenge, and right-to-buy local facilities are a blatant attempt to divert attention from the impact of spending cuts and to hand community organisations a poisoned chalice, whereby they have to redirect their effort and resources to managing facilities. It will turn many community activists into community centre and volunteer managers! Most community organisations don't have the level of active membership and resources to divide up responsibilities between management, organising and campaigning (see Chapter 9).

The offshoring and relocation of public service jobs is another form of dispossession. The loss of locally provided services results in job losses and reduced spending in the local economy. The claim that increased economic efficiency (taking advantage of lower wage rates elsewhere) will enable the local authority to increase expenditure in other services is fallacious because the benefits are outweighed by the loss of local economic activity. Most of the gains are captured by the private contractor organising offshoring or relocation.

US conservatives are planning the ultimate dispossession by abolishing the welfare state. *"It will require extraordinary sacrifices from today's young Americans, who will need to continue paying the taxes necessary to support the retirements of their parents and grandparents while denying themselves the same level of benefits so their children and grandchildren can thrive"* (Levin, 2011). It would be replaced by free market health insurance, minimal education and social services provision, means testing of benefits, and contracting out of the remaining government functions. Two thirds of the \$4.3 trillion cuts in the House of Representatives Budget Committee's 10-year budget plan would come from low-income housing, food stamps and other programmes for low and moderate income individuals and families. People retiring after 2021 would no longer have direct access to Medicare but would have to select a private insurance plan, subsidised by the government at a level below health care cost inflation to either drive down demand or increase personal costs. Further analysis of the proposals revealed that most of federal government, except for social security, health care and defence, would cease to exist. Medicare beneficiaries' expenditure on premiums and out-of-pocket expenses would more than double to 68% of health care costs (Congressional Budget Office, 2011b).

Disinvestment

"The process of retrenchment begins with spending cuts and targeting, extends to changing universal to selective systems, focusing on core services at the expense of support and other activities, and switching public resources to alternative providers" (Whitfield, 2001). Disinvestment includes the reduction or withdrawal of investment in existing and new infrastructure, failing to ensure staff are fully trained to deliver the required service and/or using high levels of agency staff, and failing to prepare service improvement plans, so any innovation and improvement reduces to a snail's pace.

Disinvestment often includes promoting private finance as the solution, exaggerating the need for spending cuts, and making the case for the rundown and withdrawal of public services (ignoring the fact that it is ultimately entirely financed by the public sector and/or user charges). It is not limited to financial matters, and includes the decline in capability and expertise, and fails to recognise a need for capacity building. Central government capability reviews have been narrow in scope and focus on identifying the skill shortages to implement neoliberal transformation.

The use of management consultants for basic functions, such as service reviews, options appraisals and business cases, further undermines public sector capability and reinforces the ideological drive of neoliberal public management. The lack of controls on the transfer of knowledge, training and capacity building, allows consultants to obtain, and then re-sell, public information.

The degree of embeddedness of these processes varies between local authorities and public sector bodies. There is sometimes an element of ebb and flow in their implementation, due to fluctuating political control and priorities.

Destabilisation

The destabilisation strategy is designed to challenge the affordability, capability and viability of continued state provision of public services and the welfare state. It takes several forms – creating doubt, fear and insecurity about the quality of public services; deliberate simplification of the complexity of delivering public services; promoting and state-funded capacity building of alternative providers; and exaggerating private sector ability, efficiency and performance in delivering public services.

There is a strong element of self-destruction, or 'creative destruction', in the process of imposing the neoliberal model of the state and delivery of 'public services'. This has only a limited connection to innovation, the driving force being to marketise and privatise as widely and rapidly as possible. The notion that this is a seamless or orderly process, with minimal negative consequences, is nonsense and perpetrated by those who stand to gain most. There have been repeated attempts to privatise state provision and mainstream market forces in the 20th/21st centuries, for example in health and social care, council housing, schools, higher education, and bus services. The process pays scant regard to people's lives and incomes, social needs, careers, democratic accountability and transparency (Whitfield 1992 and 2010a).

Welfare programmes, often with different levels of entitlement and applicable conditions, have a level of complexity that is not evident in other public services. Control mechanisms to prevent fraud and abuse and protect the public interest often add another layer of complexity. These programmes are vulnerable to not being fully understood either by recipients or by the public. Contractors brazenly claim they could deliver services more efficiently. They are, therefore, vulnerable to being exploited for political ends.

Personalisation creates new constituencies and interest groups of service users with individual budgets who will usually want to retain those budgets, irrespective of their cost or public policy issues. This creates further uncertainty and conflicting interests, ostensibly pitting vested groups of service users against each other whilst ultimately being pawns in a wider struggle of political and economic interests. A good example is Medicare Advantage, a US programme outsourced to private firms such as UnitedHealth and Humana, provided extra benefits for senior citizens. The Obama health care bill radically cut back on this programme reducing subsidies in line with traditional Medicare benefits. However, many elderly recipients did not understand the rationale for the changes and believed, wrongly, that the government was reducing the main Medicare programme. The right exploited this situation in the 2010 mid-term elections where the Democrats' senior citizen vote declined significantly in many states.

The introduction of market systems causes distortions, which lead to further destabilisation, for example in the NHS, with a structural imbalance of power between purchasers (Primary Care Trusts) and providers (acute trusts) and perverse incentives caused by payment-by-results such as *"...if we prevent an admission by good quality care we lose money"* (Civitas, 2010). These distortions usually lead to the private sector demanding speedier implementation of market systems and regulatory changes and further criticism of the public sector.

Making the case to 'rebalance the economy', (in particular reducing the role of the public sector in the north of England, Scotland and Northern Ireland), is another aspect of destabilisation. A radical rebalance on the basis of power, equity and regional disparities should be addressed. The 'rebalance' advocates do not have this agenda (Erturk et al, 2011).

Depoliticisation

The privatisation of public services attempts to depoliticise the design, finance, delivery and employment in service provision by transferring decision making to the private sector and establishing an individual commercial relationship between provider and user.

Depoliticisation has been defined as a governing strategy as *"...the process of placing at one remove the political character of decision-making"* (Burnham, 2001). He cites three forms of depoliticisation. Firstly, a *"... reassignment of tasks away from the party in office to a number of ostensibly 'non-political' bodies as a way of underwriting the government's commitment to achieving objectives"* (ibid). The granting of operational independence for monetary policy to the Bank of England in 1997, the establishment of 'regulators' for privatised utilities and in services to be marketised, and the formation of arms length companies in local government are examples. Secondly, the adoption of *"...measures ostensibly to increase the accountability, transparency and external validation of policy"* such as the adoption of rules or codes of practice (ibid). New Labour tied fiscal policy over the economic cycle to borrow to invest and ensure public debt, as a proportion of national income, would be held stable. Thirdly, the *"...adoption of binding credible rules"* that constrain government, such as World Trade Organisation agreements on trade, services and procurement that *"...remove or significantly diminish the discretion of politicians"* (Flinders and Buller, 2005).

There is a further dimension to depoliticisation. Financialisation and personalisation, in effect, transfer decisions about service delivery from the state to the individual. This changes the nature of those decisions from 'collective' to consumer selection in a market of alternative providers. It changes the emphasis from public service principles and values into 'indisputable' business and commercial values, and thus reduces the scope for debate and challenge. In doing so, it nurtures passivity and apathy, or at most a complaints culture.

This is not simply another aspect of arms length depoliticisation, because the objective is not only to transfer decision-making to another arena, but also to depoliticise the decisions and reduce the ability of service users to take collective action. Individual decisions are privatised and atomised, irrespective of the claims for increased accountability and participation, through social enterprises and voluntary organisations, which affect only a small part of economic and social life. The simplification or 'dumbing-down' of complex issues into sound bites reinforces depoliticisation, in part dictated by media and social network communications.

Disempowerment

Despite the empowerment rhetoric, personalisation will disempower many community organisations, as volunteers replace paid labour, contracting reduces advocacy, and community initiative is directed into financing and managing facilities (see chapter 8). Depoliticisation is not simply a consequence of financialisation and personalisation, but part of the neoliberal strategy. Individual choice, customer care, market research, and individual participation reinforce personal decision making, whilst further undermining collective or public interest. The financial crisis and recession have dispossessed many of their jobs, livelihoods and status.

Phases of marketisation and privatisation

There have been three distinct phases of marketisation and privatisation since the early 1980s.

The first phase of neoliberal transformation of public services in the UK begun in the 1980s, focused on 'rolling back' state interference in the economy and promoting the free market ideology, deregulating labour markets and fracturing trade union power. The government carried out significant restructuring before privatisation, including organisation and financial rationalisation, and debt write-offs.

The second phase began in the early 1990s with increased emphasis on competition, commercialisation and quasi-markets in public services. Competitive tendering in central and local government was extended to white-collar services, with market mechanisms imposed in core services such as health and education, which could not be privatised in the same way as nationalised industries had been for political and economic reasons. The establishment of agencies led to the growth of performance management, later expanded by Labour's Best Value regime, which removed compulsory competition in local government but extended competition to all services via service reviews. Commissioning was mainstreamed in social care and later housing, with varying degrees of 'success'. This phase saw the emergence of public service consumerism and consultation. Most significantly, the Private Finance Initiative provided long-term design, build, finance and operate infrastructure contracts for the private sector. By the end of the 1990s transport, energy, utilities, telecommunications and industrial state-owned corporations had been privatised leaving most of the social infrastructure of the welfare state (education, health, council housing, leisure), defence, security, and the criminal justice system still in public ownership.

The third phase of neoliberal transformation began in the early 2000s with a new emphasis on creating markets in public services. Commissioning and contestability became paramount, with New Labour sanctioning the use of public sector assets and intellectual capital to fulfil these objectives. Again, the state was not 'rolled back' or 'hollowed out', but reconfigured to extend the introduction of market mechanisms and to support and sustain markets. There was a rapid increase in arms length public/private organisations, such as foundation hospitals and foundation schools, arms length management organisations in council housing and urban regeneration companies. Strategic partnerships, essentially large multi-service contracts for ICT and corporate services, and long-term 'whole service' contracts for highway services also emerged in this phase.

Privatisation mutated in this phase into different forms; it expanded from state-to-business transactions, to transferring responsibility and risks to individuals and families via direct payments, individual budgets and wider use of fees and charges.

Typology of marketisation and privatisation

The marketisation and privatisation typology provides a framework to explain and understand the method, scale, scope and impact of neoliberal transformation of public services and the welfare state. It has been adapted, as new pathways to marketisation and privatisation have developed (Whitfield, 1992, 2001 and 2006a). The different forms of marketisation do not take place in isolation. They are part of a broader restructuring of the state in the interests of capital.

The typology has four parts: the marketisation and privatisation of assets and services; the privatisation of governance and democracy; the privatisation of the public domain; and the marketisation of global public goods (see Table 2). The vertical columns identify the different forms of marketisation and privatisation, the methods used to implement these policies, the political, social and economic objectives and the impact on the state and public services.

The public domain, or commons, consists of public access to the countryside, forests, oceans, lakes and rivers, air and space; social spaces in towns and cities; inheriting, sharing and creating music, art and literature; and public access to the internet, information, and collaborative development of open source software. Public domain has a degree of regulated access to prevent expropriation, exploitation and over-use, together with collective and social responsibility and trust, to ensure continuity of the public domain for future generations.

Global public goods are those with benefits, which extend across borders, population groups and generations (Kaul et al, 2003). Ten global public goods are fundamental to the implementation of the UN Millennium Declaration. They include basic human dignity for all people, including access to basic education and health care; respect for national sovereignty and global public health, particularly communicable disease control. Global security, a global public domain free from crime and violence, and global peace are, of course, important.

Public goods are being redefined to the extent that they can be privately delivered. Public goods have two key characteristics. They are non-excludable (users cannot be excluded from consuming the goods) and non-rival (consumption by one user does not reduce the supply available to others). Nor is it possible to charge for their use, for example street lighting, where the use by one person does not affect the use by others. Local or national public goods include law and order, public health, macro-economic management, roads, parks and open spaces. Public goods are usually under-provided and are primarily specified and financed by government.

Central and local government are increasingly outsourcing the delivery and maintenance of public goods. For example, several local authorities have PPP projects for the renewal and maintenance of street lighting. Private security companies are employed to carry out law and order functions, for example, the London Borough of Barnet engaged MetPro Rapid Response Ltd for housing, child protection, the youth offending service, evictions and security at Cabinet meetings, until the company went bankrupt (London Borough of Barnet, 2011a).

Some public goods could, in theory, be privately provided, but not without social costs, public subsidies, increased inequality, stringent regulations, and the likelihood of increased contract collusion and corruption.

Table 2: Typology of marketisation and privatisation

Marketisation and privatisation of publicly-owned assets and services			
Type of Marketisation and Privatisation	Method	Political, social and economic objectives	Impact on the state & public services
Sale of assets to private sector via flotations, trade sales and sale of shares	Sale of assets such as state owned companies, utilities, housing, land and property. Re-nationalisation of stakes in banks and financial institutions.	Extend property and company ownership. Increase government revenue for tax cuts or maintain services that would otherwise be cut.	Asset stripping as sales undervalue public assets. Public sector responsible only for increasingly residualised services.
Concessions (asset monetization)	Long-term leasing to private sector of new or existing toll roads, airports, parking garages/meters or any facility with user fees and charges.	Attraction of upfront lump sum payment to offset budget crises. Private sector gets regular increases in tolls and charges.	Fragmentation of infrastructure being sold to different companies. Danger of being used as 'cash machines'.

Table 2: Typology of marketisation and privatisation (continued)

Marketisation and privatisation of publicly-owned assets and services			
Type of Marketisation and Privatisation	Method	Political, social and economic objectives	Impact on the state & public services
Sale and leaseback of government buildings	Public buildings and offices are sold with a long lease to a private investment company, which leases them back to the government or public body.	Commercialise public asset management. Also short-term financial benefits for public bodies.	Public sector loses direct control of the offices and buildings from which it operates. Accessibility undermined.
Commissioning of public services – separation of client & contractor functions with outsourcing or franchising to private and voluntary sectors.	Marketisation process - commodifying services and labour, restructuring the state for competition and market mechanisms, restructuring democratic accountability and user involvement, embedding business interests and promoting liberalisation internationally.	Mainstream contestability and competitive forces across the public sector. Restructure the role of the state from direct provision to making and sustaining markets. Creation/expansion of global and European markets in services.	Decline in public provision and reduced state capacity. Two tier workforce with equalities marginalised. Withdrawal or reduction of public services to spur private sector. State support for market with subsidies, tax concessions.
Private finance of infrastructure and services	Private Finance Initiative (PFI) and Public Private Partnerships (PPP) to design, build, finance & operate infrastructure & services. Private sponsorship of Academy schools. Ramping up user charges and replacing student grants with loans. Secondary market in sale of PPP equity and refinancing.	Access to private capital and expertise. Legalised off-balance sheet financing of public investment. RAB - equity risk transferred to users and/or taxpayers.	Long-term financial commitment with private sector. Design, build, finance and operation by private contractors. Support staff transfer to private sector, longer-term threat to core services. RAB - Method of guaranteeing investment returns to private sector via user charges.

Table 2: Typology of marketisation and privatisation (continued)

Marketisation and privatisation of publicly-owned assets and services			
Type of Marketisation and Privatisation	**Method**	**Political, social and economic objectives**	**Impact on the state & public services**
Choice mechanisms via financialisation and personalisation	Individual budgets, direct payments and vouchers for services – social care, child care and training. Individual purchases of services from private and voluntary sector companies.	Choice through competition and contestable markets.	Fragmentation of public provision. Public facilities run as stand-alone businesses to compete against each other. Ultimately limits choice for many users.
Deregulation, liberalisation and re-regulation	World Trade Organisation (WTO) and European Union liberalisation and marketisation of services. Regulators appointed to deregulate and increase role of markets. Increased regulation of trade unions. Regulatory impact assessments to reduce obligations on business.	Increase competitive pressure on 'failing' services. Promotes middle class opting out. Create global markets in publicly funded services. Regulators operate 'independently' of government to open up and manage markets. Laws to limit industrial action by trade unions.	Reduced power and capacity of state to intervene in markets. Market forces increasingly determine service provision. Increased competition and outsourcing.
Commercialisation of the public sector	Public sector bodies run as business units with business values. Sponsorship of events. Public sector bodies urged to take on 'corporate citizen' and corporate social responsibility model.	Market forces applied more widely across the public sector. Create conditions for further privatisation, marketisation.	Increasingly fragmented provision and internal trading. Business values gradually replace public service ethos.

Table 2: Typology of marketisation and privatisation (continued)

Marketisation and privatisation of publicly-owned assets and services			
Type of Marketisation and Privatisation	**Method**	**Political, social and economic objectives**	**Impact on the state & public services**
Asset Based Welfare State	Child Trust Fund – vouchers issued to start savings schemes. Savings Gateway & Individual Learning Accounts to access training.	Promotion of individual rather than collective responsibility for future social needs.	Encourage private suppliers and new markets to marginalise public provision.
Increased domestic & family responsibility	Reduce scope of services and assume family (women) take over responsibility for care of elderly & children. Separation of health and personal care.	Financial savings, promote family and social networks.	Service reductions and targeting. Means tested welfare state.
Privatisation of governance and democracy			
Type of Marketisation and Privatisation	**Method**	**Political, social and economic objectives**	**Impact on the state & public services**
Contract governance – separation of client and contractor roles	Mainstreaming national procurement policy across the public sector with larger and longer-term contracts. Partnership Boards and Joint Venture Companies operate managed services contracts. Wider use of management consultants for reviews and procurement.	Separation of strategic policy making from service delivery. Establish organisational structures to extend contracting to wider range of services. Extend private markets by increasing outsourcing.	Loss of political control by elected members and erosion of democratic accountability and transparency. Growth of corporate welfare complex.

Table 2: Typology of marketisation and privatisation (continued)

Privatisation of governance and democracy			
Type of Marketisation and Privatisation	Method	Political, social and economic objectives	Impact on the state & public services
Transfer of services to arms length companies or social enterprises	Hospitals and schools operate as stand alone businesses. Formation of arms length companies for council housing, economic development and regeneration activities.	Create pathway to privatisation and delegate employment responsibility to company board. Increase business role in policy making process and delivery of services.	Reduce range of directly provided services. Reinforces 'enabling' model of the state. Loss of democratic accountability and transparency. Loss of provision of central and support services as transferred & corporatised bodies procure services from private sector.
Private companies established within public services	Transfer of assets and services to third sector organisations such as housing associations and leisure trusts. Gated communities with 'self governance'.	Extend the role of the private sector in state education and marketise educational services.	Marginalisation and run-down of in-house services. Loss of democratic accountability.
Privatisation of development and regeneration responsibilities	Privately-run Academy and free schools. Establishment of Urban Development Corporations, Urban Regeneration Companies and Business Improvement Districts in city/town centres.	Increase business involvement and influence in public policy making in growth and regeneration areas. Draw on business expertise and experience to speed up development.	Erosion of democratic accountability, reduction in capacity of local government and public bodies. Business interests have greater role in setting policy agenda.

Table 2: Typology of marketisation and privatisation (continued)

Privatisation of governance and democracy

Type of Marketisation and Privatisation	Method	Political, social and economic objectives	Impact on the state & public services
Privatisation of citizenship and political power	Focus on citizens panels, polls & market surveys and 'armchair' voting. Community organising constrained by lack of resources.	Increase voter turnout to sustain legitimacy. Promote consumerism. Capacity building limited to aiding government policy implementation.	Users, community organisations and trade unions less involved in policy-making process.
Privatisation of public interest information	Widening scope of contracting and PPP's results in parallel use of 'commercial confidentiality' – much contract information exempt from Freedom of Information Act.	Protect commercial interests of the state and private capital.	Separation of policy and performance information/data. Reduced accountability, transparency and disclosure.

Privatisation of the public domain

Type of Marketisation and Privatisation	Method	Political, social and economic objectives	Impact on the state & public services
Public service values and principles replaced by market ideology and commercial values	Extol virtues and abilities of the private sector whilst failures are ignored. Create 'no alternative' to private finance as economic orthodoxy.	Embed market forces and state support for market mechanisms. Create conditions for capital accumulation and profits from provision of public services.	Loss of legitimacy for in-house provision and increasing reliance on outsourcing and privatisation.

Table 2: Typology of marketisation and privatisation (continued)

Privatisation of the public domain			
Type of Marketisation and Privatisation	Method	Political, social and economic objectives	Impact on the state & public services
Privatisation of public knowledge and skills	Extended use of consultants by public bodies. WTO Trade-Related Aspects of Intellectual Property Rights (TRIPS) – patents on products and processes for 20 years, protects monopoly rights. Nearly a fifth of known human genes have been patented – 63% owned by private biotechnology companies.	Enable work to be carried out by either public or private sectors. TRIPS obliges governments not to disclose information of commercial value. Patents, knowledge, research, industrial designs and processes in private control and ownership.	Loss of knowledge of needs, the history and understanding of local systems. TRIPS hinders knowledge and technology transfer. Misallocation of public funds to corporate marketing. Research & Development focused on market and profit potential, not public social needs.
Privatisation of public space and the commons	Pressure to de-communalise public land by privatizing forests and open spaces. Secured private villages (gated communities). Public spaces in city centre shopping streets and retail centres privatised and controlled by private security.	Increase safety for middle classes. Respond to business interests in cities.	More private control of 'public' spaces and activities in cities restricting protest, limiting activities and accessibility.

Table 2: Typology of marketisation and privatisation (continued)

Marketisation and privatisation of global public goods (Examples)			
Type of Marketisation and Privatisation	Method	Political, social and economic objectives	Impact on the state & public services
Carbon market in response to climate change	Emissions trading system for greenhouse gases established under Kyoto Protocol. Corporate-led self-monitoring and verifications schemes run by big business.	Retain business control with minimum commitments at minimum cost.	Large sums of public money required to establish trading system. Largely privatised system which is difficult to scrutinise.
Deregulation of protection of natural resources and the global commons	Privatisation of water and sanitation systems. Deregulation of environmental protection.	Attract inward investment and create new markets. Permit exploitation of minerals and natural resources with minimum controls.	Business claims ownership of natural resources and related property rights. Environmental degradation with knock-on effect on climate change.
Public health	Privatisation and commercialisation of health care systems including demands for trade and services liberalisation. Global Public Private Partnerships for specific diseases, drugs and vaccines.	Creation of global markets. Harnessing public and private finance in Global Public Private Partnerships but remain under multilateral agency and commercial control.	Demise of health for all, segmentation and fragmentation of health care systems. Business interests more able to dictate responses to diseases and epidemics.
Privatisation of global governance	Promotion of corporate citizen and corporate social responsibility (United Nations Global Partnership with business). Democratic accountability given low priority in development agenda.	Increase power of business and ensure business-friendly operating environment.	Lack of accountability of international agencies. Democratic accountability marginalised at national, regional and local levels.

Table 2: Typology of marketisation and privatisation (continued)

Marketisation and privatisation of global public goods (Examples)			
Type of Marketisation and Privatisation	Method	Political, social and economic objectives	Impact on the state & public services
Rise of privatised military industry	Outsourcing services and PPP projects for equipment for armed forces. Growth of private armies and security firms hired for civil wars.	Extend the military industrial complex beyond equipment and supplies to a wide range of services and functions.	Privately financed civil wars/defence.

Source: Whitfield, (2001 and 2006)

CHAPTER 3

Corporate welfare reaches a new zenith

Corporate welfare reached new heights with the bailout of banks and financial institutions in 2007/08. The injection of billions of public money in asset protection, credit guarantee and special liquidity schemes, loans, share acquisitions and other multi-billion government guarantees was unprecedented in the US and many European countries, particularly the UK, Ireland, Greece and Portugal. The UK government had committed £955bn by December 2009, although the scale of support had halved a year later because of loan repayments and lower than anticipated take-up of support schemes (NAO, 2009a and 2011a). Corporate welfare ensured the socialisation of losses, financed by public money, government guarantees, and the privatisation of profits.

The US *"...corporate safety net was extended from commercial banks to investment banks and then to an insurance company – to firms that not only had paid no insurance premium for the risks against which the taxpayer was protecting them, but also had gone to great lengths to avoid taxation"* (Stiglitz, 2010).

In *Public Services or Corporate Welfare* I described how a three-part 'corporate welfare complex' was emerging, comparable to the military-industrial complex of the 1960/70s. This comprised a network of companies, politicians, government agencies, civil servants, trade organisations, lawyers and lobbyists who built political support for continued or increased spending and policies that prioritised business opportunities and profits over economic and social policy (Whitfield, 2001). Corporate welfare is even more evident today.

A US 'prison-industrial complex' has been developed with the rapid expansion of private prisons (Schlosser, 1998), often promoted as economic development initiatives in depressed rural areas (Whitfield, 2008a). Private companies have a vested interest in demand and supply, and hence in continuing public policies that embed their role. Continued marketisation and privatisation could lead to the emergence of sub-sections of a corporate welfare complex in criminal justice, health and social care, and education – the basic elements are already in place.

"Contractors develop a dependency on government contracts which leads them to search for, and gain access to, insider information and intelligence in order to pursue corporate objectives, influence the procurement process and to participate in government policy making. It also leads to contract

collusion and corruption. Contractors become major employers in localities and this, in turn, is used to lever further concessions, financial contributions are made to candidates as political payoffs, and a system of common values and interests makes the triangle increasingly difficult to penetrate.

Corporate welfare is a hidden subsidy to capital, inflating profits and enabling transnationals to minimise their own investment in new factories and offices. …But corporate welfare is not solely about money, it also consists of shared values and ideology, revolving doors as officials move from public to private sector jobs and vice versa" (Whitfield, 2001).

Corporate welfare has three parts. Firstly, a system of tax reliefs, subsidies, guarantees and regulatory concessions to business. Secondly, an outsourcing system with a shared client/contractor ideology, value system and vested interests in which the state outsources an increasing range of services and functions. Thirdly, a growing infrastructure market in which construction companies and banks design, build, finance and/or operate public buildings, transport systems, social facilities and the welfare state infrastructure.

Protectionism

The global financial crisis has exposed protectionism in the belief that large banks and financial institutions are 'too big to fail', because they are so large, and their activities extend to all sectors of the economy, that failure would be inconceivable. Since Bear Stearns became the first federal bailout of a bank in 2008, banks and trade associations have *"…hired over 240 former government insiders as lobbyists and spent hundreds of millions of dollars on an influence game designed to thwart reform, shape bailout programs and maintain their status as 'too-big-to-fail' institutions"* (Institute for America's Future, 2010).

The big US banks – Goldman Sachs, Bank of America, JPMorgan Chase, Citigroup, Morgan Stanley, and Wells Fargo – *"…lobbying spree is taxpayer-funded – it follows $160 billion in bailouts from Congress and trillions in cheap loans from the Federal Reserve. And as their influence has come to be viewed as increasingly toxic in Washington, the banks have shifted segments of their political activity to a 'shadow lobby' that includes such front groups as the U.S. Chamber of Commerce"* (ibid).

This level of protectionism effectively means that large banks can continue to take hidden high risks in their lending policies and financial products but *"…insuring private sector mistakes with public money merely transfers the problems from one party to another"* (Joye, 2011).

Tax breaks and subsidies

Financial concessions to business are a standard part of corporate welfare, such as tax relief, reduced corporation tax rates, public subsidies, local and regional business grants, training and labour market concessions, research and development grants and investment guarantees. Creative accounting practices and tax regimes permit transnational companies enormous leeway in transfer pricing and minimising tax responsibility. The US Treasury Department has forecast that corporate tax breaks will cost the federal government over $1.2 trillion between 2008 and 2017 (Labor Notes, 2010). The effective tax rate for large UK and US corporations is significantly below the statutory rate. Furthermore, large UK companies pay a lower rate of tax than other companies (Devereux and Loretz, 2011).

Barclays Bank is at the centre of a multi-billion foreign tax credit dispute. Stars – 'structured trust advantaged repackaged securities' – were deals between Barclays and US banks that *"…worked asymmetries in tax systems…. Barclays realized at least $800 million in tax savings from the UK government – benefits it shared with other parties in the deals"* (ProPublica and Financial Times, 2011). Other tax loopholes have enabled corporations to move profits from subsidiaries in high tax countries to locations with low or no taxes.

Twenty-five of the 100 highest-paid US corporate chief executives took home more in pay than their company paid in 2010 federal income taxes – big rewards for tax dodging. And twenty of the twenty-five companies spent more on lobbying than they paid in corporate taxes (Institute for Policy Studies, 2011). The US corporate sector solution to the jobs crisis included a 'repatriation holiday' by reducing the tax rate on profits earned and accumulated overseas, *"…U.S. multinationals could be encouraged to bring as much as $1.2 trillion back to the American economy"* (US Chamber of Commerce, 2011). The letter to Congress and President Obama called for a temporary cut in the corporate capital gains tax on the sale of assets.

There are various types of tax incentives for business in economic development. Companies often claim that they are planning to relocate headquarters or plants to another city, state or country to try to obtain tax breaks. They may use the threat of relocation to obtain concessions and a greater role in regeneration or development areas. Exploiting wage and labour market differences are also a factor.

For example, Wal-Mart's rapid expansion in the United States has been financed by public money including over $1.2bn in tax breaks, free land, infrastructure assistance, low-cost financing and outright grants from state and local governments. In addition, taxpayers indirectly subsidise the company by paying the healthcare costs of thousands of Wal-Mart employees who don't receive coverage on the job and have to rely on public programmes, such as Medicaid. A recent US Commission identified 75 different tax breaks and 30 different tax credits offered to business, citing the system *"...a patchwork of overly complex and inefficient provisions that creates perverse incentives for investment"* (National Commission on Fiscal Responsibility and Reform, 2010).

The design of regulatory frameworks has become an increasingly important part of the corporate welfare complex. Business lobbying has resulted in extensive deregulation in the last three decades. The social relations of regulation, the way in which companies are treated in corporate welfare, are in stark contrast to the way benefit claimants are treated in the means tested welfare state. Business lobbying has focused on establishing self-regulatory regimes and deregulation of labour markets, weakening health and safety and environmental requirements and restricting trade union organising. For example, EU Commission investment powers, under the Lisbon Treaty, allow multinational companies to claim compensation when national environmental or public health laws damage their profits (Corporate Europe Observatory, 2010).

The UK's Regulated Asset Base (RAB) model for privatised infrastructure incorporates an element of corporate welfare, because it guarantees profits via an investment and price regime. The regulator has a duty to ensure that the private sector is properly remunerated. *"The RAB is a number which represents the past investments, comprising what investors paid when the assets were originally privatised, plus the completed efficient capital expenditure since then, adjusted for depreciation. Once assets are in the RAB, there is nothing that management can do to change their value. The RAB is an accounting number, protected by the duty that is placed upon regulators to finance the functions of the business, including the RAB. Understood in this way, the equity risk in the RAB for the company is zero – it has been transferred to the customers who are compelled to pay for the RAB (or, in the case of government guarantees and subsidies, to the taxpayers)"* (Policy Exchange, 2009).

Another concern is 'regulatory capture', when regulators are aligned to business interests as a result of lobbying, political pressure and ideological sympathy, and consequently prioritise and protect business interests first and foremost.

The 'protection' of business interests is another aspect of corporate welfare, for example, failing to identify the source of poor performance or complaints. An Audit Commission investigation of the performance of 14 strategic partnerships refused to name the contractors and local authorities, even when contracts had been terminated (Audit Commission, 2008). This ludicrous situation was heavily criticised (Whitfield, 2008b) but local government and trade unions failed to address the Commission's research shortcomings and the misuse of commercial confidentiality to protect contractors.

Contract culture

Contractors develop a dependency on government contracts, which leads them to search for, and gain access to, insider information and intelligence in order to pursue corporate objectives, influence the procurement process, and government policy-making. They poach key public sector staff, finance trade groups and right-wing causes. Regulatory capture is another feature of corporate welfare. Private firms lobby government to ensure that regulation benefits them, rather than the public. A system of common values and interests makes the state-politician-contractor triangle increasingly difficult to penetrate. Contract collusion and corruption become inevitable.

Public procurement increasingly dominates the public management agenda as commissioning, outsourcing and market mechanisms are embedded in local government and the NHS. This leads to a shared client/contractor ideology and a contract culture with commercial values and business interests, aided by the 'revolving door', where public managers move to private contractors or management consultants and private sector managers become 'commercial directors' in the public sector. The private sector increasingly shapes the scope of contracts through the Competitive Dialogue process and contractual terms, including the right to compensation in the event of termination in contract clauses. Larger, longer-term multi-service contracts ensure a feast for global management consultancies and law firms.

The engagement of business interests in the public policy making process isn't confined to procurement (Whitfield, 2001 and 2002, Farnsworth, 2004). The corporatisation of public bodies with business representation on boards, task forces and policy reviews further embeds commercial interests in the public sector. Most contractors are members of business organisations and trade associations, which are part of national and global networks that campaign to minimise regulation and create the best possible climate and conditions to 'do business'. This includes intensive lobbying of the European Union and World Trade Organisation by business organisations, such as the European Services Forum (representing over 30 transnational companies and 30 business federations), promoting the liberalisation of public services. They fund right-wing think tanks, political parties and candidates.

The increasing power of transnational corporations lies not just in the production and sale of goods and services, but in branding and defining values through the media and information channels. The concentration of land ownership and resources and the funding of research and political organisations have increased their influence in the global, regional, national and local policy making process.

This collusive process helps to ensure that capital is able to exploit new forms of accumulation with minimal intervention by government, for example rights to intellectual property (TRIPS) and minimal state rights to nationalisation in investment and bilateral/multi-lateral trade agreements. Marketisation feeds the growth and power of the corporate welfare complex.

The terms 'Corporate Social Responsibility' and 'Corporate Citizen' are used interchangeably to describe the role of business in society. However, citizenship comprises a set of individual rights: civil rights (freedom from abuse and interference from the state, companies and other third parties; freedom of speech, the freedom to own property and intellectual property rights); social rights (the right to education, health care, welfare and the freedom to participate in society); and political rights (the right to vote, to hold office, to organise, to join a trade union, and to participate in collective and public activity). Clearly a company or corporation cannot have social and political rights under the concept of citizenship. Acting responsibly and claiming to be a citizen are two entirely different concepts. Business must fully respect all human rights, labour, environmental mandates and regulations, and should not be 'rewarded' for doing so.

In this context, it is salutary to note the US Supreme Court ruled in 2010 that it is unconstitutional to limit how much money corporations can spend to influence elections, as this would violate the First Amendment of free speech. In effect, they ruled that corporations have the same rights as individuals! The case arose from a right-wing lobby group after lower courts had prevented the screening of a film critical of Hillary Clinton during the presidential election campaign in 2008.

Infrastructure
PPPs are a classic example of corporate welfare. Specific legislation protects corporate interests and establishes regulation frameworks acceptable to the construction and financial services industries. The creation of national agencies and special project units in government departments creates a system that virtually guarantees high profits with minimal disclosure. Equally important, a contract system and financial mechanism are created, that gives the private sector freedom to accumulate publicly funded assets, develop new secondary markets, locate assets in tax havens, and capture efficiencies and financial innovation for further accumulation. The infrastructure market has grown rapidly in the past decade, slowed only by the global financial crisis.

Growth of contract and services markets

Government competition policy has been influenced by a series of reports on public service markets by the Office of Fair Trading (OFT), case studies by PricewaterhouseCoopers, KPMG's Payment for Success, and the Julius review of the public services industry (OFT, 2011a and 2011b; PricewaterhouseCoopers, 2011; KPMG, 2010; Julius, 2008). They are pro-market, pro-private sector and uncritically accept neoliberalism. They use selective evidence, ignore private sector failures and disregard the quality of employment (staff transfer rights are important only because they give new providers ready access to skilled workers). Not surprisingly, there is little or no acknowledgement of equity, equalities or social justice. The OFT studies appear to be written by economists with little or no interest in, or understanding of, the political economy of the welfare state and public services.

A contract market has grown as governments have outsourced service delivery to private or voluntary sector contractors and extended the role of PPPs (Table 3). In addition, a services market is growing in which users purchase services directly from companies (voluntary organisations have a minor role), paid for out of their income, individual budgets and/or direct payments.

Myth of a 'public services industry'

The concept of a 'public services industry' is ill-conceived and it is politically short-sighted to give it credibility. It was defined by the Julius Review as *"...all private and third sector enterprises that provide services to the public on behalf of government or to the government itself,"* a shameless New Labour plan to demonstrate its commitment to business

(Julius, 2008). The public sector spent about £220bn or 15% of GDP on the purchase of goods and services from the private and third sectors in 2008/09 (OFT, 2011b). About £79bn per annum was spent on outsourcing public services in 2007-08 (Julius, 2008).

The 'public services industry' is not an economic definition, as it is solely related to whether the provider is in the private and voluntary sectors. It does not constitute an industry because it excludes in-house providers simply because they are in the public sector. The definition excludes water, transport, telecoms and energy services, presumably because they have largely been privatised in the UK and are, therefore, considered private services. It is thus a very English & Welsh definition with limited use at European level. It excludes the financial institutions funding PPP projects. The definition considers public services to be those that have yet to be privatised! It would be more accurately named the 'privatisation industry'.

Table 3: Public service markets

Public sector provision (non-market)	Contract market	Service Market
In-house organisation and management. May include joint or shared service provision between public sector bodies.	Public delivery plus outsourcing to private and voluntary sector contractors, joint ventures, Public Private Partnerships. Private delivery of some public goods.	Ultimately leads to full private market with insurance schemes combined with state and self-funding. User choice and payment systems, individual budgets, vouchers and government initiatives help to create markets.
Role of the state		
Direct delivery with client and contractor roles combined. State finances and delivers services.	Commissioning separates client and contractor roles. State responsible for planning, contracting, monitoring, securing improvements, governance and fulfilling specific duties such as equalities. State finances services, but directly delivers fewer services.	State regulates the market seeking to 'balance' business and user interests. State provides only residual (unprofitable) services.

Furthermore, there is not a separate 'public services industry'; it is part of the services sector of the national, European, and, in many cases, global economy. There are few firms that rely wholly on public sector contracts, and the companies and consultancies that dominate services markets also operate in the private sector. It represents the vested interests of service providers. Ironic given that the same people regularly criticise trade unions for representing producer interests! More accurately, we should simply refer to this industry as the 'big business lobby'.

The expansion of this 'industry' cannot constitute economic growth, because services merely transfer between sectors (see Chapter 9). For example, 'secondary healthcare (ISTCs)' was forecast to have the largest relative growth in annual expenditure. ISTCs were publicly financed and took over non-urgent operations from the NHS. A switch in provider of a service does not generate economic growth and, in fact, the overall consequences for jobs and the local economy would be negative if the contractor reduces jobs, terms and conditions.

The Review's evidence was highly selective and mainly from academics who have regularly peddled the competition model and savings claims. It excluded government research evidence of significantly smaller savings (DoE, 1993 and 1997) and Equal Opportunities Commission evidence identifying discrimination and public costs, not savings (Escott and Whitfield, 1995).

The European and British Chambers of Commerce, the Confederation of British Industry (CBI) and Institute of Directors, the Coalition of Service Industries, Transatlantic Business Dialogue and the World Economic Forum are just a few of the business interests that have well-resourced campaigns demanding liberalisation and free trade. They are represented at all levels in the European Union, the Organisation for Economic Cooperation and Development and World Trade Organisation negotiations.

Free Trade Agreements (FTAs) have proliferated as the World Trade Organisation (WTO) negotiations have stalled. FTAs cover trade in goods, services and investment and include chapters on labour and the environment and will be recognised by the WTO if they are consistent with specific articles in the General Agreement on Tariffs and Trade (GATT) and the General Agreement on Trade in Services (GATS).

European law exempts 'non-economic services of general interest' (police, judiciary, prisons, social security, air traffic control, border security carried out in the exercise of government authority) from the single market and competition law provisions. This is reinforced by the

Lisbon Treaty (Protocol 26), which clarifies that European law *"...does not affect in any way the competence of Member States to provide, commission and organise non-economic services of general interest"* (European Union, 2007). Services of General Interest consist of network industries (telecoms, transport, energy and postal services) and a group of non-network services (such as health and social care, education, environmental services, employment and training services, certain cultural services). The European Commission is using the negotiation of bilateral FTAs to seek a backdoor change to create a third sub-category of network industries that will include water supply and disposal, waste disposal and environmental services (European Commission, 2011). It introduces a new negotiating model for opening up service markets that may limit the scope to organise, finance and provide public services. Unlike in the GATS and other free trade agreements ratified by the EU, liberalisation obligations themselves are not listed explicitly in the 'Schedule of Commitments'. Without the inclusion of appropriate exemptions, liberalisation obligations apply automatically (Krajewski, 2011).

Outsourcing company strategies

National and transnational corporate strategies are aided and abetted by legislation and the government's public spending and reform policies, together with local authorities' and public bodies' decisions on a service-by-service basis. Business and trade organisations, together with outsourcing and PPP agencies, provide a stream of propaganda.

The scope of outsourcing has widened over the last thirty years. Initially, a few authorities outsourced building maintenance, cleaning, catering, refuse collection, street cleansing, grounds maintenance and leisure management, later extending to social care, ICT and other corporate or back-office services. Many of these services were outsourced as part of 25/30-year facilities management, as PFI became 'the only show in town'. The first strategic partnerships, long term multi-service contracts, began in the late 1990s. Management consultants have been commissioned to undertake a wider range of tasks such as the design and management of transformation projects, the production of options appraisals and business cases, and to advise and manage the procurement process. This results in the loss of public sector skills and the erosion of public sector principles and values.

A few local authorities are outsourcing statutory functions such as planning, environmental health and trading standards, in effect widening the scope of outsourcing to most professional and technical roles. Attempts to outsource the client or commissioning function have been considered and are likely to increase – the ultimate position of private sector managing and monitoring the private sector – a new extension of corporate welfare.

Some companies have acquired offshore (primarily in India) and/or near-shore companies in Eastern Europe, to enable them to transfer work from the UK, for example, Capita's 'blended delivery model' includes four near-shore centres in Poland, Ireland and two in the Channel Islands and three offshore centres in India at Mumbai, Pune and Bangalore.

Building market share by takeovers and mergers has enabled companies to have a dominant position in the provision of supply teachers, pensions administration and in private education. Most managed services companies initially focused on information technology services, however, the increasing dependency of services on ICT has enabled them to broaden provision to most white collar or professional services.

Other companies have developed partnerships that provide additional facilities, for example, university-based foreign language centres that 'facilitate' university entry and provide a base to extend to other university functions (see Chapter 8). Companies often form consortia with others to bid for PPP or joint venture projects.

Diversification has been another strategy. For example, the growth of PFI projects led construction companies to diversify into facilities management and more lately some, (Carillion, for example), have extended into managed services. Management consultants have widened their capabilities. Large highway 'whole service' contracts, which combine elements of PFI and strategic partnership projects, are likely to develop in other services (see Chapter 8).

Outsourcing theory but not reality

Outsourcing is primarily cost driven, with budget savings achieved by increased efficiency, improved productivity and reductions in jobs, terms and conditions. However, the savings claimed at the award of a contract are rarely achieved (Chapter 10). Claims about innovation are undermined by the fact that this is most effectively obtained by specific short-term contracts that target best-in-class providers rather than long-term contracts with one contractor.

The lessons of outsourcing are clear, and have been learnt the hard way, but there is little evidence that they are put into effect because the scale, scope, value and length of contracts keeps on rising (see Chapter 4 for radical changes to the procurement process).

Many complex UK public sector ICT projects have failed (Whitfield, 2007b and Chapter 10). For example, the £11.4bn National Programme for IT in the NHS has been beset with delays, contract failures and the plan for a standardised electronic care records system for every patient has been abandoned (House of Commons Public Accounts Committee, 2011b). The government later announced *"...an acceleration of the dismantling of the National Programme for IT"* having spent £6.4bn (Department of Health, 2011a). Another analysis concluded contracts *"...tended to be too big, leading to greater risk, complexity and limiting the range of suppliers who could compete....the infrastructure was insufficiently integrated, leading to inefficiency and separation"* (Public Administration Select Committee, 2011). The recommendation that ICT contracts should not exceed £100m lifetime value seems to have had minimum effect.

The problems encountered by Boeing are legion, when it outsourced a large part of production of the 787 Dreamliner. This proved disastrous. The plane is over three years late and billions over-budget. Problems across the supply chain included part defects, failure to meet deadlines, design flaws, lack of qualified staff, non-alignment of components and Boeing had to take over some suppliers (Hart-Smith, 2001, Economist, 2011, Hiltzik, 2011, Airbus, 2008).

Offshoring of call centres has been reversed in many cases following customer complaints about the quality of service and breaches in data security.

The commodification and transfer of risk

The identification, allocation of responsibility, elimination and mitigation, and pricing of risk have been key tools to justify PPPs and outsourcing. The level and cost of risk transfer is frequently exaggerated to 'prove' value for money, but may also mask hidden profits for contractors and banks. However, commissioning and public spending cuts are leading to risks being significantly understated at each stage of the planning and procurement process. This takes several forms.

Risk denial, for example, understating transaction costs; inflated forecasts of savings and private sector performance, are common in options appraisals and business cases (see www.european-services-strategy.org.uk). This approach understates the increased risks that are transferred to staff and service users, particularly when the government is deregulating staff transfers. Personal budgets and direct payments transfer the risk that the funding will be sufficient to purchase the required level and quality of service to users. Otherwise service users will have to top up with personal contributions. Direct payments transfer employment risk to the service user.

Risk uncertainty is relevant to the promotion of personal budgets, social investment bonds and whole service PPPs, because these are untested initiatives undertaken, in the case of new social enterprises, by organisations with no track record and limited assets. New market mechanisms bring risks and uncertainty, because they are often untested on the scale planned. Exogenous risks have increased, for example, the effects of the government's fiscal strategy, disinvestment and continued recession.

There have been only limited moves to transfer *demand* risk to the private sector but this would increase if outsourcing and PPPs extend to core services.

Risk profiteering has increased, for example, in the sale of equity in PPPs once they are operational and construction risk has been virtually eliminated (Whitfield, 2011a).

Local authorities with several outsourced services and/or PFI projects, are at risk of cumulative failure, with one contract impacting on related contracts. New risks could arise where a handful of private firms, that effectively have monopoly control in a local authority, exercise collective power to leverage changes in contracts and service provision. Government policy is creating new risks in restructuring services, fracturing and replacing organisational structures and the commercialisation of public services.

Large multi-service contracts introduce new risks, particularly in services and/or public bodies, where there is little experience of outsourcing. Risks are inherent in new providers, for example, social enterprises and voluntary sector contractors, which are either recently formed organisations that have a limited track record, or may be obtaining a contract for a service they have little experience in delivering.

The risk of delays and cost overruns in public sector infrastructure contracts has been continuously exaggerated. The UK Treasury 'evidence' claims that cost overruns occur in 73% of conventional construction projects with delays in 70% of projects. Only one of the five studies cited by the Treasury is comparative and even this is fundamentally flawed (Pollock et al, 2007). A rigorous evaluation of the evidence concluded, *"...the Treasury's claims about the superiority of the PFI is based on time and cost overrun arguments for which there is no evidence"* (ibid). Furthermore, the PPP track record had deteriorated by 2008 with cost overruns and delays increasing to 35% and 31% of projects respectively (NAO, 2009b).

CHAPTER 4

Reconstructing the economy

The proposals outlined in this and the next two chapters are a starting point in creating an urgently needed framework for strategic policies for reconstruction of the economy, state and community. They are intended to encourage political debate in order to develop strategies that are positive and not merely defensive. We need to demonstrate that there is an alternative to neoliberal economic strategies. We need to promote the belief that 'another world is possible' is more than rhetorical and to recognise the limits of the 'stop privatisation' or 'stop the cuts' approaches. It is important to demonstrate the connections between the policies for financial reform, climate change, industry, infrastructure, public services and the welfare state, with taxation and public spending. The aim is to generate debate about policies and strategies, and to help to join up the separate campaigns and initiatives with common goals. Alternative visions and policies have a vital role in giving confidence, and have a key role in organising and exposing the consequences of neoliberalism and deconstructing their vision for the economy and society.

Reconstruction has three inter-connected parts – new economic policies, alternative policies for public services and the welfare state, and a new public service management. The three chapters need to be considered as a whole. Some elements of the economic strategy are discussed in detail in other sections to avoid duplication, for example, taxation in Chapter 5, and infrastructure and public services are consolidated in Chapter 6 (see Figure 4).

The reconstruction strategies are intended to strengthen the organisation, capacity and resources of community, civil society and trade union organisations in opposing neoliberalism. The objective is to establish a fundamental return to values of collective solidarity, public interest and social justice from speculation, greed, exploitation and self-interest. The strategies should cover a range of demands ranging from those that could potentially be implemented in the short term together with transitional demands that are longer-term but equally important in achieving socialism.

Resources, such as government revenue, skills and organisational capacity, are vitally important, so too is the design and scope of policies,

Figure 4: Reconstruction vision and strategy

Reconstructing the Economy
Economic and industrial policies
Financial and regulatory reform plan
Reconstructing the State
Inter-generational responsibilities
Core functions of the state
Changing public spending priorities
Reconstructing Public Services
Public service and welfare state policy changes
The case for in-house provision
New public service management
Public infrastructure investment strategy

projects and programmes together with the method of implementation. Resources, policies and process are inseparable and interconnected and all three must be an integral part of alternative strategies.

Reconstruction proposals must avoid being trapped in the ideology of recession and austerity, often used to divert attention and avoid debate about the Coalition's marketisation and privatisation programme. Longer-term goals and objectives, such as 10-year plans, should be rooted in principles, including the provision of core services, not simply the latest trend or fad. The political blame game – 'the crisis was caused by the previous government' – is myopic and puerile.

Reconstruction should focus on how the economy, public services and the welfare state can be radically changed and improved. It should, therefore, be much more than just an alternative budget. Even if the Coalition Government or local authorities accepted a revised budget and changed various economic and financial policies in the process, this would not alter their privatisation plans for health, education, the sale of assets and the promotion of large-scale outsourcing of local government services. An alternative budget may have short-term tactical benefits and focus on social needs and progressive taxation, but wider strategic policies are usually not within their remit.

Alternative visions, blueprints and badging of policies with 'progressive' prefixes must be critically assessed. Much of the language of these proposals is framed in rhetoric about a new epoch, new era, reclaim, rebirth and the proclaimed 'death' of neoliberalism or New Labour. All too often policies are persuasively wrapped and marketed, but are disappointingly familiar on closer inspection. Rhetoric has its place. But fine words often turn into weasel words.

New measures of well-being and quality of life are being developed to supplement measuring economic production through Gross Domestic Product (GDP). They include France's Stiglitz Commission, the European Commission's GDP and Beyond, the EU-funded Well-being 2030 project and the OECD's Better Life Index. Most include income, employment/unemployment, health, education and environmental criteria and some even venture into subjective indicators such as 'happiness'. However, indicators remain crude, based on averages that mask the realities of economic and social inequalities, class, gender and age differences, and have limited effectiveness in policy-making.

Social science would be better served if well-being and quality of life criteria were developed for equality-based impact assessment and the evaluation of local policies and projects. Local judgements about social needs for different groups and ages, arising from their participation in the policy making process, aspirations and quality of life, would identify how income, employment/unemployment, health, education and environmental policies interconnect to improve or worsen people's life satisfaction, expectations and quality of life. Such attempts, in their current format, change nothing, but feed costly banks of statistics and market research.

The Alternative Economic Strategy (AES) in the 1970/80s included job creation plans and an industrial strategy, the case for planned trade, control of inflation and workers' control (Conference of Socialist Economists, 1980). There was much debate about the cause of the then economic crisis, the potential consequences of the AES, the role of the state and economic strategies. An alternative strategy must reflect the reality that services now account for over 70% of GDP and infrastructure about 12% in industrialised economies.

Fundamental principles

A reconstruction strategy should be underpinned by seven core principles:

1. democratic accountability, participation and transparency with a commitment to user, civil society and employee/trade union involvement in the design, planning and policy making processes;
2. social justice to eliminate victimisation and discrimination, and to eliminate or mitigate adverse impacts and inequalities;
3. public investment to ensure democratic control and public interest in the management of assets and to minimise risks;
4. quality integrated services of a good standard, responsive and flexible that meet social and community needs through in-house provision;
5. sustainable development to take account of global, national and local economic impact, production and supply chains, and to conserve natural resources;
6. universal provision available for all unless specifically targeted;
7. quality employment with good terms and conditions, pensions, equalities and diversity, training and workforce development.

The ethical standards required in public management are discussed in Chapter 6.

Economic and social strategy

The strategy should have the following objectives. Firstly, to significantly increase government revenue by tax increases on higher earners and the wealthy, improved tax collection rates and reduced avoidance. Secondly, a fiscal stimulus to increase aggregate demand and create jobs by a combination of public infrastructure investment and targeted tax breaks in key manufacturing and service sectors. Thirdly, the creation of good quality jobs with training, workforce development and pensions. Fourthly, to create a clean energy economy with investment in renewable energy and the adaptability of homes and buildings to climate change. Fifthly, to increase the sustainability of local/regional economies with investment, training and social provision. Finally, to ensure rapid agreement and implementation of national and international regulatory reforms.

Economic policies

An alternative economic strategy must address current economic and political realities, and consist of strategy, policy, implementation and sustainability.

Clean-energy economy: One million new climate change jobs could be created by a programme targeted to reduce emissions by 80% in electricity, buildings and transport over twenty years (Campaign Against Climate Change, 2010). The new climate change jobs, not so-called green jobs, would be producing renewable electricity (425,000 jobs), refitting buildings to make them adaptable to climate change (150,000), changing transport (325,000), industry and landfill (50,000) and education (50,000). In addition a further half million jobs will be created in the supply and service industries plus the new jobs will generate additional employment through increased household spending on goods and services in the local economy. The net effect will be a gain of 1.33m jobs in the economy after 20 years of the programme.

A National Climate Service should be established by the government to employ teams of construction workers to refit homes and buildings, engineers to design and build wind farms and to plan, build and operate public transport systems. Previous government policies of subsidies, tax breaks and outsourcing have failed to achieve the required step change in investment in renewable energy. The total cost of the programme is estimated to be £52bn per annum, with the net cost of about £18bn per annum, after taking account of higher tax and National Insurance revenue from the new jobs, lower unemployment benefit costs, energy payments and public transport fares (ibid). In terms of affordability, the UK government spent £200bn on 'quantitative easing' in 2009 and financed the bank bailouts. A phased approach with lower initial investment but increasing over an 8-10 year period would be feasible and ensure investment was targeted and evaluated. The national infrastructure plan is discussed in Chapter 6.

Industrial investment and innovation strategy: An Industry and Innovation Investment Bank should be established to finance and to actively promote research, technology and key manufacturing sectors. Germany's KfW Bankengruppe (government owned) and France's Fonds Strategique D'Investissiment (FSI) provide different models (TUC, 2011a). They could support investment in specific manufacturing industries, in particular biotechnology, nanotechnology and low carbon manufacturing. Whether industrial investment should be combined with a national infrastructure bank requires further analysis. There are advantages in having two separate organisations with specific skills and objectives. The Coalition Government's plan for a Green Bank is too little, too late.

Research and development accounted for only 11% of UK investment in innovation between 2000-07 with *"...product and service design, training staff in new skills, software development, and even branding and marketing"* being vitally important (Westlake, 2011). The priority *"... should be on how to make the innovation system work better. Critical to this are strong university-business links; the right support for clusters and other ways for businesses to access platforms for innovation; harnessing the power of public procurement; expanding markets; removing barriers to finance, especially for risk capital; and investing in the quantity and quality of education"* (ibid).

Long-term deficit reduction plan: Deficit reduction should be extended over a longer period, a minimum six years. This would be possible using a combination of narrowing the annual £120bn tax gap, increased tax income from a financial transaction tax, rate increases for higher earners, cuts in corporate welfare subsidies and changes in public spending priorities.

Job creation: The immediate focus should be on initiatives that will generate significant new good quality jobs and policies that will prevent further job losses and the erosion of pay, pensions and other terms and conditions. Growth policies that accelerate marketisation and privatisation must be avoided. For example, one recent 'going for growth' strategy recommended public investment only in marketised services to generate revenue to service the debt instead of taxes. *"The investment must be in assets whose output would be sold, rather than being provided free at the point of delivery. Railways quality but not schools; toll roads but not free roads.....Instead of getting the private sector to raise expensive finance to build assets and lease them to the public sector, a public sector entity would raise cheap finance to procure assets and lease or sell them to the private sector for operation, thereby servicing its debt"* (Holtham, 2011). This would be US asset monetisation on a national scale, accelerating the growth of the global infrastructure market and privatisation (Whitfield, 2010a). It is an example of narrow financial objectives being diametrically opposed to wider economic policy, public service and welfare state objectives.

Monetary policy: The government has two key fiscal policies to stimulate spending in the economy. The application of these policies depends entirely on prevailing economic conditions.

Quantitative Easing (QE) increases the amount of money in the economy and aims to keep interest rates low, provide banks with money to maintain lending and prevent deflation. The Bank of England does not print more money but the Bank's Monetary Policy Committee buys UK government bonds (gilts) or high-quality debt from private sector institutions such as insurance companies, pension funds and banks. They, in turn, have more money in their bank accounts, which boosts the supply of money in the economy. But there is a lack of agreement over the effectiveness of QE. Green QE would target direct investment in new infrastructure, investment in the economy through a new national investment bank, with funds fed directly into the economy instead of through the banks. The £200bn injected into the UK economy in 2009 was thought to have helped to restore bank profitability but little else (Hines and Murphy, 2010).

Fiscal Stimulus consists of increased public spending and/or lower taxation to generate economic activity. The timing, scale and targeting of fiscal stimulus, to boost growth and prevent deflation, will depend on prevailing economic circumstances. It should include a public infrastructure investment programme to finance investment and jobs in public transport, housing and other public facilities. It would achieve economic and social objectives, generate economic activity and jobs in a range of supply industries, and increase government revenue.

Unlock cash hoardings of corporations: The corporate sector is globally hoarding cash on an unprecedented scale. UK-based non-financial companies had cash and bank deposits of £652.4bn by the end of 2009 (Weldon, 2010). The holdings of cash and liquid assets of US non-financial corporations reached $1.93 trillion by the end of the third quarter 2010, an increase of 14.4%. The cash mountain represented 7.4% of total company assets, the largest for 50 years. *"Nationally, cash and checking deposits held by corporate businesses rose by just over 200%, or almost $300bn, from the beginning of the recession in December 2007 to September 2010"* (Sadowski, 2011).

The top 50 publicly traded non-financial companies had $1.08 trillion cash and short-term investment holdings by late 2010 (Standard & Poor's, 2011b). Seventeen were US-based companies, 17 in Europe and 13 in Asia and Australia. A later analysis identified 22 non-financial companies where cash balances exceeded the market value of the companies (Standard & Poor's, 2011c). Meanwhile, UK public sector financial balances have fallen as a percentage of GDP.

Whilst profits have recovered, business investment has not, for example, investment in new equipment and machinery in Canada was just 5.5% of GDP in early 2011 compared to 7.7% in 2000. In the US it was 15% lower in late 2010 compared to pre-recession levels (McNally, 2011b). But cash hoarding was increasing before the financial crisis as capital expenditure decreased and corporations shored-up balance sheets in response to the recession (Hunt, 2011).

The policies for manufacturing outlined above would help to unlock these assets and increase investment, which would, in turn, increase demand, employment, tax revenue and reduce the cost of unemployment. Alternative productive investment must be a priority, otherwise the cash hoardings could be diverted into dividend pay-outs, share buy-backs, merger and acquisitions, benefiting only the few.

Retain public ownership of banks rescued in state bailouts: The four banks which the state has full or partial ownership should be moved into full public ownership and control with immediate cessation of the current Treasury arrangements, which are limited to shareholding.

Procurement policy: The abolition of commissioning will significantly reduce procurement, with priority given to in-house provision and improvement strategies negating the need for procurement. Similarly, the replacement of PFI/PPP with a new public sector contract will reduce the scope and complexity of contracts by eliminating the design, build, finance and operate model (Chapter 6).

Where procurement of services is required, the following radical changes should be prioritised:

- well-resourced in-house bids should be standard (social enterprises or mutuals do not constitute in-house options);
- award criteria should be widened to include economic, social, equalities, environmental, health and sustainability matters (this will require more imaginative interpretation of existing EU regulations plus new evaluation criteria);
- full impact assessment to identify the advantages and disadvantages of proposals, including economic impact on production and supply chains, and the local/regional economy;
- a whole public cost analysis including transaction costs and government revenue and expenditure based on the Centre for Public Services model (Centre for Public Services, 1995);
- democratisation of the procurement process to enable service

user/community organisations and staff/trade union involvement and full public scrutiny;
- wider disclosure and transparency of proposals (whilst respecting the public interest);
- strict terms and conditions imposed on role of consultants and advisers including training and building public sector capacity requirements;
- comprehensive continued monitoring and scrutiny built into contract management;
- comprehensive employment policy including terms and conditions, pensions, training and education, and equalities for the contract period.

The Coalition Government's response to the European Commission Green Paper on the 'modernisation' of EU procurement policy (European Commission, 2011) is predictably centred on further deregulation and a three-year avoidance of procurement for employee-led organisations/mutual (Cabinet Office, 2011c).

An important example is the award of the £1.5bn Thameslink train contract to a Siemens plant in Germany instead of Bombardier (and the resultant 1,400 redundancies at the Derby plant). This was rooted in the privatisation of the railways, private under-investment, the use of the PPP model, and declining public investment. The narrow 'best buy' procurement decision was flawed but inevitable (Centre for Research on Socio-Cultural Change, 2011).

Improving workforce skills: The reinvention of apprenticeships, a revival of broadly based technical education for 16-18 year olds combined with continuing training plus a significant expansion of training within firms are required in manufacturing (Froud et al, 2011). The TUC have proposed a review of the £5bn tax relief granted for work-related training because there is little information on how it is being used by employers and could be more effectively targeted (TUC, 2011). Mid-career education and training at Further Education Colleges and Universities should be linked to training in new public service management skills (Chapter 6).

Investment in education: There is a compelling case for increasing investment in higher education. The UK has slipped below the average OECD's proportion of the population participating in higher education (equivalent to a UK university, non-vocational degree). Debate has centred on the financial benefits of higher education to the individual, which has been used to justify escalating tuition fees. The returns to the public sector in the form of taxes, social contributions and lower unemployment benefits have been largely ignored. However, for the UK the *"...net present value of investment in higher education for men is $95,318 and for women is $82,289. Put another way every £1bn invested in higher education yields £3.36bn in a return to government finances, so providing a net present return of £2.34bn."* A rate of return on investment is 220% for males and 252% for females (Burke, 2010). *"Even these may be severe underestimates, as they only take account of income-related taxes and disregard the taxes derived from the consumption or savings of those higher incomes, which, depending on the tax regime, may be nearly as high again"* (ibid).

Employment and labour market policies: The objective is to increase the bargaining power of labour, to be achieved by a number of measures. New legislation would give mandatory protection to terms and conditions for staff transferred between employers and for new staff engaged on contracts. This would be part of new UK and EU labour laws to strengthen job security; the protection of jobs, terms and conditions, and pensions; rights to organise, represent members and take industrial action; and rights/procedures for staff/trade union and user/community organisation participation in the design, planning and delivery of services and access to information. Monitoring and reporting obligations would be imposed on client and contractors.

A Trade Union Freedom Bill should abolish restrictions on balloting, confirm the right to strike, freedom to take solidarity action for workers who are in dispute, and strengthen protection against the exploitation and discrimination of migrant, agency and temporary workers, and ethnic minorities.

Local and regional economic development: Widen the scope and borrowing powers of local authorities so they can take a more direct and influential role in economic development. Build on current local sustainability initiatives that promote production and supply chains, particularly in food and agriculture, to reduce emissions, value fresh quality produce and support local economies. Business development and incubator centres can provide physical space, support and creative environments in the formation of new ventures.

Enterprise Zones: The planned 21 zones will provide a business rate discount of up to £275,000 per business over a five-year period, costing £80m by 2015-16 (Department for Communities and Local Government, 2011). These should be abolished.

Terminate privatisation programme: The planned privatisation of Royal Mail should be stopped and a new strategy devised to continue improvement and investment. Closure of Post Offices should be reversed and a new strategy devised to address postal service, banking and community needs in urban and rural areas. The planned privatisation of other assets in the Coalition's programme must be terminated and replaced by new strategies and investment plans.

Anti-poverty strategy: A national anti-poverty strategy should provide resources and strategies for national, regional and local implementation, focusing on health, housing, education, income and unemployment with specific targets to reduce inequalities. There is an urgent need for decisive anti-poverty strategies at both European and national levels which should *"...propose appropriate measures that address the key causes of poverty of the group concerned. For example, to overcome in-work-poverty in the EU, a macroeconomic strategy for full employment through public investment, working time reduction and an extension of public employment should counter the trend towards more precarious working conditions and low-paid jobs"* (EuroMemo Group, 2011).

Rapid roll-out of National Superfast Broadband: Ensure all homes, public bodies, organisations and businesses have access to superfast broadband by 2015 at the very latest.

Rapid development of Cloud Computing: Cloud computing provides on-demand internet access to a shared pool of computing resources such as applications, data storage, networks and servers. Individual computers need very little software. *"Cost savings will be founded on driving down the number of unique public sector services through rationalising, sharing and re-using software and infrastructure across organisational boundaries.... by introducing standard, automated processes across the entire ICT lifecycle"* (Cabinet Office, 2011d). Data security and guarantees that personal data will not be offshored are essential.

Sustainable food and agriculture: Produce more food by sustainable means with priority given to horticulture, including local and regional food production to generate employment and minimise transport impact and costs; support diversification, marketing advice and support for new products, local brands and formation of agricultural/ horticultural and producer cooperatives; sub-regional sustainability plans should combine production, marketing, exporting, environmental protection, waste minimisation, food hygiene and more comprehensive rural impact assessment methodology (Sustainable Development Commission, 2011).

Transparency: new disclosure requirements in both public and private sectors to include contracts, agreements and other documents of contracts and projects involving public and private sector organisations falling within a generic description of public private partnerships. New rights of access to documents and policy reports are required to facilitate participation in the options appraisal, business case, procurement and contract management processes.

Re-nationalisation and re-municipalisation: The renationalisation of water, energy and the railways (Network Rail and the East Coast line are already in public ownership) should be prioritised. Re-municipalisation, such as the transfer back to local authorities of housing arms length management organisations, community and leisure trusts, can be implemented at relatively low cost. Outsourced contracts should be returned to in-house provision, either on the grounds of poor performance or at the completion of the contract.

Multilateral and bilateral trade agreements: Negotiations with the World Trade Organisation (WTO) General Agreement for Trade in Services (GATS) and the EU Services Directives proposals to extend marketisation and privatisation should be abandoned immediately. Trade agreements should be based on equal treatment of foreign and host state investors under the municipal laws and courts of the host country and avoid investor state dispute resolution mechanisms. Technical and financial support are required to develop local and national public services and welfare state and advice on methods to replace business support for marketisation and privatisation policies.

Financial and regulatory reform plan

Taxation must be reformed to increase revenue for public services and investment, and to eliminate or minimise tax avoidance and evasion. A revenue and taxation strategy based on redistributive taxation and tax justice must be designed to eliminate avoidance, evasion and non-collection of unpaid taxes and to maximise resources and achieve equity objectives.

A Financial Transaction Tax: A financial transaction tax *"...set at a rate of just 0.01 per cent (but retaining stamp duty at 0.5 per cent for equity purchases) would raise gross revenues of £36 billion, even if there is a large effect on transaction volumes. After allowing for the effect on other tax revenues, the net increase in revenues would be around £25 billion"* in Britain alone (Dolphin, 2010). Previously called the Tobin Tax, now the Robin Hood Tax, it could *"...slow down the most speculative elements of international capital flows and raise the significant sums needed to provide the newly required global collective goods – especially green technologies and development aid"* (Ha-Joon Chang and Green, 2011).

Reducing the Tax Gap: The gap is estimated to be £123bn per annum, consisting of £70bn tax evasion, £28bn unpaid tax and £25bn tax avoidance. At least £20bn could be collected annually by reducing these three components by £7bn, £5bn and £8bn respectively if HM Revenue and Customs employed additional staff. Currently each tax officer collects more than 30 times their cost in tax (Tax Research UK, 2010).

Higher tax rates for high earners: Additional annual revenue of £8.4bn could be obtained by reducing or eliminating tax relief for those on gross incomes over £100,000 per annum (TUC, 2008).

Corporate welfare tax breaks and subsidies should be rigorously examined and those that are not specifically geared to contributing to implementation of the reconstruction strategy should be terminated.

A multi-lateral blockade of tax havens: Annual UK tax revenue lost to tax haven activities is estimated at £18.5bn comprising £8.5bn from UK resident high net worth individuals, £3bn by large UK companies and £7bn as a result of tax evasion and related activities – equivalent to 4.5p off basic UK income tax (Tax Research, 2009). *"Jersey, Guernsey and the Isle of Man should simply be absorbed lock, stock and barrel into the UK, with English laws, rules and regulations applying across the board. The special status of these strange entities is not cute; it's an enabler and facilitator of unethical and illegal behaviour"* (Buiter, 2008). The European Union has made commitments and resolutions on 'tax governance' but *"...there is* *still a long way to go and many proposals have yet to be implemented. Furthermore, important rules, such as mandatory disclosure of the beneficial ownership of all economic entities, including trusts and funds, still need to be included"* (World Economy, Ecology and Development, 2011).

The US Senate recently recommended tax haven banks that impede US tax enforcement should be barred from doing business with US financial institutions, together with extensive widening of powers of the Inland Revenue Service (US Senate Permanent Subcommittee on Investigations, 2008).

Country by country reporting would require transnational corporations to be taxed on the unitary basis to permit tax authorities to effectively reverse the false shifting of profits to low-tax jurisdictions. The residency principle should be universally applied for corporate taxation (Murphy, 2009).

Rating agencies should be brought under public control: The outsourcing of regulatory judgements to three entrenched ratings agencies, Standard & Poor's, Moody's and Fitch who control about 90% of the global market, enabled the securitisation of subprime mortgages that led to the financial crisis. The high credit rating of mortgage-related securities enabled them to be marketed and sold to financial institutions and banks. Ratings agencies are US private companies with an 'issuer pays' business model, with financial institutions and banks paying the charges for ratings, not investors.

"… [I]n calculating appropriate ratings on the tranches of securities backed by subprime mortgages, the credit rating agencies were operating in a situation where they had essentially no prior experience, where they were intimately involved in the design of the securities, and where they were under considerable financial pressure to give the answers that issuers wanted to hear. Furthermore, it is not surprising that the members of a tight, protected oligopoly might become complacent and less worried about the problems of protecting their long-run reputations" (White, 2010).

New EU regulations on transparency and due diligence came into effect in September 2010 but have been overtaken by demands for an independent, transparent, accountable and responsible European rating agency (Public Service Europe, 2011).

Off-balance sheet financing should be prohibited in both public and private sectors: New International Financial Reporting Standards, amendments to the EU Capital Requirements Directive (EU 2006/48) and the Basel 3 global accord which raises the quality and quantity of core capital requirements and liquidity of banks are designed to significantly reduce off-balance sheet financing. However, the effectiveness of these regulations will depend heavily on financial regulators and political scrutiny. They leave other financial institutions, such as hedge funds, untouched. *"A radical form of increasing regulatory coverage should be considered by including all financial intermediaries in the same core capital requirements regime in order to avoid such asset-shifting"* (Thiemann, 2011).

Demerger of financial conglomerates into separate banking, investment banking and securities trading activities has been widely demanded (Elliot and Atkinson, 2008 and Stichele, 2008). However, the Independent Commission on Banking (ICB) recommended only *"...retail ring-fencing of UK banks, not total separation"* by use of separate subsidiaries (ICB, 2011). Neil Lawson, chair of Compass, concluded: *"[t]hree years on from a crash that they created and the banks are given 8 years to find their way through a ring fencing system that is bound to leak information and capital flows. Instead of recommending the simple and effective step of complete bank separation the British establishment has bottled it and the City has won again. Nothing changes; the state will have to under-write the banks, people's savings will remain in jeopardy, businesses will be starved of investment funds and the bankers will still be rewarded with £millions in bonuses for taking reckless risks"* (http://goodbanking.org.uk/).

New controls on private equity and hedge funds on short-selling: Short-selling bans were introduced on about sixty European bank stocks in early August 2011 following a spike in the trading of banks shares. Short-sellers aim to profit from the fall in share prices, but could threaten the viability of banks. The ban reduced trading in the banned shares by 62% (Financial Times, 25 August 2011).

Potential resources: Changes in public policy could produce significant resources: the cancellation of Trident nuclear weapons submarines – construction costs are estimated to be £25bn with total lifetime costs of at least £76bn; the annual cost of government measures to establish public service markets (excludes one-off costs) were estimated to be £30bn over ten years (Whitfield, 2006a); the consolidation and elimination of quangos, such as arms length agencies, companies and trusts, could save £2bn over 10 years; and more effective public sector asset management could reduce spending by £40bn over ten years (HM Treasury, 2009).

A Land Value Tax has many benefits and could potentially replace council tax. It is *"...an annual tax on the market rental value of land, not the development that is built upon it. It is levied at a fixed rate and is charged whether or not the land has been sold. It is simple and cheap to administer, it can replace other taxes like council tax, and it can be collected locally with receipts mostly retained locally. It can also be tapered by area so that those in areas with high land values would pay more"* (Centre for Research on Socio-Cultural Change, 2011).

"Unlike most other taxes, LVT is transparent and cannot be avoided by any individual or business. Land is highly visible and cannot be hived off into an offshore tax haven in order to avoid tax. Therefore, taxes collected for public expenditure will be shared more fairly by all individuals and businesses, including foreigners and non-domiciles, and businesses with headquarters abroad" (Labour Land Tax Campaign, 2011). An independent review of taxation also recommended replacement of business rates by land value taxation (Mirrlees, 2010).

Private Finance Initiative profit sharing: Profits from the sale of equity in PFI project companies averaged 50.6% between 1998-2010 based on a sample of 154 projects (Whitfield, 2011a). Total equity sale profit could have been as high as £4.2bn for this period if the sale of secondary market funds are included. Most equity sales occur shortly after the project is operational and represent only one source of PFI profits, which are built into the financing, construction and facilities management contracts. The main dividends to PFI companies are structured to come towards the end of the contract period. An equal profit sharing scheme, similar to that for refinancing gains, could produce about £250m per annum. A House of Commons Select Committee recommended gain sharing in new and existing PFI projects (Public Accounts Committee, 2011).

Regulation offices: Legislative requirements for Regulator Offices to expand services markets must be repealed. They should focus on monitoring and controlling existing markets and price controls. European Union Single Market regulations for Services of General Interest must be amended to remove the requirements for competition and markets.

European Union policies: A new Treaty should replace the Treaty of Lisbon and the Europe 2020 plan and should include proposals to reduce the role of the internal market and competition; re-draw Europe's role in trade agreements with other countries to exclude reference to privatisation, PPP and marketisation elements; strengthen workers rights, particularly in transfers between employers; new public procurement regulations to recognise the need for sustainable local employment policies; and immediate termination of further WTO negotiations on the liberalisation of public services.

Policy reform of multinational and global bodies: The World Bank, International Monetary Fund (IMF), World Trade Organisation, United Nations and Development Banks need to adopt macroeconomic and financial policies with effective regulatory frameworks, strengthen domestic capability, improve public sector provision and employment, and cease the prescription/conditionality of neoliberal policies. Multilateral development banks should not have the right to pressurise borrowing countries to pass legislation to facilitate wider use of 'alternative financial instruments' (Fried, 2008) and should eliminate privatisation and PPP requirements from bilateral and multilateral agreements.

An effective monitoring system should be established for state and international implementation of the United Nations Convention Against Corruption together with more decisive rules and binding procedures put in place to minimise fraud, corruption and bribery (Transparency International, 2008).

The next chapter examines reconstruction of the state.

CHAPTER 5

Reconstructing the state

Basic rights and responsibilities

Nation states and international bodies have a central role in fulfilling duties and responsibilities established by the United Nations (UN) and other international agencies.

The UN Declaration of Universal Human Rights sets out the fundamental principles of dignity and self-determination, rights, living standards, access and opportunities and fair distribution of wealth and resources. The UN Global Compact's ten principles draw on this declaration plus the International Labour Organisation's (ILO) Declaration of Fundamental Principles and Rights at Work, the Rio Declaration on Environment and Development and the UN Convention Against Corruption. They include the fundamental principles of dignity and self-determination for individuals, families, communities; maintenance of a standard of living with guarantees to food, clothing, housing and medical care to provide the ability to live and to participate in the economy and civil society; understanding and respect for cultural diversity; opportunities for all, irrespective of race, gender, age or religion, to education, training, and employment; and fair distribution of wealth and resources. The promotion of cultural diversity is enshrined in the UNESCO Universal Declaration on Cultural Diversity (2001) and the Convention on the Protection and Promotion of the Diversity of Cultural Expressions (2005). Duties (ethical and moral obligations) and responsibilities are legally binding obligations under international law.

The United Nations Millennium Declaration in 2000 set eight goals with specific targets for 2015 – to eradicate extreme poverty and hunger; achieve universal primary education; promote gender equality and empower women; reduce child mortality; improve maternal health; combat HIV/AIDS, malaria and other diseases, and ensure environmental sustainability (including access to safe drinking water and basic sanitation and improvement in lives of the urban poor). The final goal is to develop a global partnership for development (develop further an open, rule-based, predictable, non-discriminatory trading and financial system, good governance, deal comprehensively with the debt problems, and implement strategies for decent and productive work for youth). The private sector were especially required to cooperate to provide access to affordable essential drugs in developing countries and to make available the benefits of new technologies, especially information and communications.

Inter-generational responsibilities

The assets, debts and economic, social and environmental conditions that are passed on to future generations impact on their living standards and ability to address poverty and social needs. A balance has to be attained between meeting the demands of today's population and ensuring that adequate resources are available for future generations. This can be distinguished between intra-generational equity (fairness among the current population) and inter-generational (fairness between members of succeeding generations) with respect to family responsibilities, debt and pensions, environment, infrastructure and democratic governance.

Wide differences exist in Europe in the way that responsibility for the old and the young is shared between family and the state. This is reflected in legal duties on parents, attitudes and public opinion surveys. However, "*...alternative or complementary services in the more generous welfare states in western Europe have made the family less duty-driven, and other values have become more important*" such as autonomy and independence. "*When public services to both the young and the old are available, it is easier for adult children, parents and grandparents to help out as their help does not substitute for, but complements services*" (Herlofson et al, 2011).

Intergenerational debt

Responsibility for fiscal stewardship and economic management requires dealing with deficits and debts in a way that does not sanction the deterioration of living standards for the poor, unemployed and working families today, whilst not burdening future generations with excessive debt, which prevents them from addressing future economic and social needs.

Minimising intergenerational debt is both a collective and individual responsibility. Individual citizens and families have a responsibility to ensure that rampant debt-fuelled consumerism does not burden future generations with debt and/or financial obligations (but must avoid the sterile debate about 'funded' and 'unfunded' pension schemes that are legitimately funded from current resources).

Intergenerational environmental justice

"*Sustainable development requires the promotion of values that encourage consumption standards that are within the bounds of the ecologically possible and to which all can reasonably aspire ... At a minimum, sustainable development must not endanger the natural systems that support life on Earth: the atmosphere, the waters, the soils, and the living beings"* (World Commission on Environment and Development, 1987).

However, the continued depletion of natural resources, deforestation, environmental degradation and threatened extinction of plants and animals, continued privatisation of the commons or public domain, are having significant impacts now, as well as storing up serious long-term consequences. The Stern Review of the economics of climate change concluded that the producers of *"...greenhouse-gas emissions are bringing about climate change, thereby imposing costs on the world and on future generations, but they do not face directly, neither via markets nor in other ways, the full consequences of the costs of their actions"* (Stern Review, 2006).

Present resource consumption and production patterns by nation states and companies are threatening environmental quality and economic development today but drastically reducing the resources that will be available to future generations. *"To achieve sustainable development and a higher quality of life for all people, States should reduce and eliminate unsustainable patterns of production and consumption"* (Principle 8 of the Rio Declaration).

Major infrastructure projects such as transport networks, large hospitals, energy and other facilities should be designed and financed to be intergenerational. Hence, the design, quality, building flexibility and funding have an important effect on future generations. For example, implementation of EU transport objectives of ensuring sustainable and accessible urban mobility, encouraging and increasing co-modality and decongesting transport corridors, the greening of surface transport, improving safety and security and innovative and cost-effective production systems, would have significant benefits now and for future generations.

The shift from funding projects from general revenue to PPPs, particularly transport projects that are reliant on achieving forecasted levels of fares and tolls, could lead to local or central government having to step in to rescue projects, thus imposing additional burdens on future generations of taxpayers. The more that public infrastructure is based on hypothecated private finance, the greater the risk that public intervention will be needed. *"Future generations therefore may be forced to assume a larger share of the costs of financing a facility than is fair, given their use of the facility"* (Rosenbloom, 2009).

Intergenerational governance

The power, scope and effectiveness of national and international democratic institutions and participation in public affairs are another matter of intergenerational justice. The extent to which commitments and declarations to eradicate crime and corruption, collective security and disarmament to reduce military expenditure, can be implemented now, will shape the international order for future generations.

Nation states and international institutions have a much longer-term mandate than the private sector, which is governed primarily by market forces, short-term financial returns and private, rather than public, interest.

The global economy is currently confronted with demographic change, urbanisation and the growth of mega-cities and regions, natural disasters, climate change and ecosystem degradation, mass unemployment and rising poverty and inequality, in addition to surges in technological change and geo-political power shifts, and accompanied by market failures and economic crises.

Core functions of the state

The nation state has three broad duties and responsibilities. Firstly, it must recognise the UN and international fundamental principles and rights and ensure they are fulfilled individually and collectively. Secondly, it must ensure that future generations are not burdened with unsustainable levels of debt; political, economic, social and environmental conditions or democratic governance that is not fit for purpose. Thirdly, among many functions it has duties and responsibilities to manage the economy, fulfil international obligations, and maintain law and order.

These roles and responsibilities are organised under five core functions: democratic and civil society; national and international responsibilities; human needs and development; economic and fiscal management; and the regulation of markets, firms and organisations. Each core function has a range of other functions, activities and services (see Table 4).

The ability to fulfil these functions requires legislative powers, political and moral authority, governance and accountability and adequate resources to plan and implement decisions. This in turn requires skills and capacities such as leadership and political strategy; fiscal and economic management; the ability to design, plan and manage projects; powers of regulation, intervention and enforcement; to raise revenue to finance and invest; and ensure equity and redistribution.

The state must both provide and directly deliver the vast majority of

Table 4: Core functions of the state

Democratic governance and civil society

- Governance, representation and public accountability
- Participation in public policy-making process
- Civil rights and freedom of information
- Law and order
- Justice and penal system
- Enhanced engagement and capacity of civil society
- Transparency of policies, performance & public procurement

National and international responsibilities

- Global, European and national policy-making
- Macro-economic, infrastructure and transport planning
- International aid and development, and multi/bilateral trade agreements
- Reduce carbon emissions, promote renewables and infrastructure adaption.
- Foreign relations policy
- Defence and security
- Protect and sustain the environment & joint action on climate change

Human needs and development

- Education and learning
- Public health, health and social care
- Shelter and housing
- Income support
- Poverty reduction and social inclusion
- Equalities and social justice
- Identify and quantify social and economic needs
- Promote social economy
- Promote the arts, culture and heritage
- Protect the public domain/commons

Economic and fiscal management

- Manage inflation through interest rates and money supply
- Progressive taxation
- Manage public expenditure
- Invest in infrastructure
- Redistribution
- Plan regions, cities, urban and rural areas
- Economic development and regeneration
- Job creation and training

Table 4: Core functions of the state (continued)

Economic and fiscal management (continued)
■ Manage public assets effectively ■ Research, development and innovation
Regulation of markets, firms and organisations
■ Regulation of and intervention in financial, trade, utility and services markets (standards, rights, prices, performance) ■ Property, land and intellectual property rights ■ Regulation of the labour market and compliance with labour rights ■ Regulation of corporate sector ■ Regulation of public sector, social and voluntary sectors ■ Regulation of development

Source: Developed from Whitfield, 2001.

these functions and services (see Chapter 6). Voluntary and private organisations, and social enterprises have an important but limited role.

Role of the state

The precise role of government in financing, planning, providing and regulating each of these functions and activities draws sharp political differences. Nevertheless, the vast majority of these responsibilities and functions cannot be provided and delivered by the market (see Chapter 10). The state must have the resources and ability to fund, plan, provide and regulate for the medium and long term, taking account of generational interests, innovation and transformation of the economy, redistribution, and the need to legislate and enforce regulations, protect rights, advance a social justice agenda and protect the environment.

The state plays a crucial role in minimising negative externalities and promoting positive externalities through taxation, regulation, monitoring and inspection, planning and the provision of activities and services. They regulate monopolies and afford consumer protection in the provision of public goods and services (see Chapter 2). Public goods suffer from under-provision.

Quality, social justice and public interest are inherent in both the provision and delivery of the core functions of the state. In addition, the push to separate the provision and delivery is driven by claims of efficiency benefits. The IMF reported that there is extensive literature on the relative efficiency of the private sector, but concluded, *"...the theory is ambiguous and the empirical evidence is mixed"* (IMF, 2004). The full transaction costs are rarely identified, let alone taken into account. There are additional economic and social costs, such as changes to wages, terms and conditions that affect workers' earnings, government tax revenue, and a knock on effect on consumer expenditure on food, household goods and entertainment in the local economy. This in turn affects employment in retail and other sectors. The only detailed UK study of these impacts revealed that outsourcing had a negative impact (Escott and Whitfield, 1995).

There are, of course, other important dimensions, and the case does not rest on efficiency alone. Employment conditions have a direct effect on the quality of service and the commitment of the workforce to operate to and implement public service principles and values. The relationship between staff and service users is a key part of service delivery. Management skills and employment conditions affect the ability and commitment of the workforce to seek out service improvement and innovation.

Operational principles
The principles of universal provision, public ownership and others crucial in determining the role of the public sector in the economy were set out in Chapter 4. Universality is vitally important, eloquently summed up by Standing *"It is the only principle that can reverse growing inequalities and economic insecurity. It is the only principle that can arrest the spread of means testing, conditionality and paternalistic nudging"* (Standing, 2011).

Ethical standards in public bodies, such as honesty, integrity, objectivity, leadership, equality, inclusivity, competence and selflessness, must shape the decision-making and service delivery processes.

A new model of local democracy
Local authorities should be responsible for education, primary care and public health, social care, housing, transport, cultural and leisure services, welfare and employment services, environmental services, with a direct role in police and criminal justice. The creation of one democratically accountable and transparent governance system would revitalise involvement in these services. It would present an opportunity to create genuinely integrated and joined up services, combined with responsibility for the economic and social well-being of the area. It would reinvigorate local government by making it more democratic,

accountable, and participative with wider powers to provide and deliver services combined with the financial power to raise resources and borrow for capital investment. Increased capacity, skills and capability of local government should be a pre-condition for its much wider role and new responsibilities.

The new model should include new governance and accountability arrangements for trading, arms length and joint venture companies. A moratorium should be imposed on the transfer of services or functions to new or existing trusts or companies; there should be plans to transfer services back to in-house provision and where closure of companies is not immediately feasible, renegotiate agreements and contracts to limit their scope (see new public service management in Chapter 6).

Sub-regional (city regions) and regional economic strategies are increasingly important to counter centralisation in London and the south-east and to redistribute resources. However, the mistake of creating non-accountable regional agencies must not be repeated. Sub-regional and regional bodies must be representative, democratically accountable with wide participation.

Funding public services through taxation
International, national and local taxation should be the prime revenue source to fund public services and the welfare state. It provides funding to revenue budgets to pay for the wide range of state functions summarised in Table 4, including the welfare state, social security system of benefits and pensions. It includes the costs of governance and representation, elections, democratic services, select committees and other public bodies. Capital budgets finance borrowing for public infrastructure projects such as public transport, roads, hospitals, schools and other public buildings.

Taxation helps government manage the economy, for example, tax relief is used to encourage research and development or it can be used to prioritise some manufacturing or service industries over others.

The tax system is a means to redistribute income and wealth to reduce poverty and inequality. Progressive taxation, in which the percentage tax rate increases as income rises, has an important role in promoting social justice. The breadth of the tax base is equally important. The system can be designed to encourage personal saving.

Governments can use the tax system to reallocate resources by changing the price of goods and services to reflect public health, social and environmental costs and the public interest. For example, the pricing of cigarettes and tobacco is set to discourage smoking on personal and public health grounds and environmental taxes to increase sustainability and protect natural resources.

The tax system should minimise the negative effects on welfare and economic efficiency; minimise administration and compliance costs; be fair in its distribution, procedures, avoidance of discrimination, and with respect to legitimate expectations; and be transparent so that people can understand it (Mirrlees, 2010).

The reverse is equally true. Unpaid taxes and tax evasion/avoidance schemes reduce the level of resources available to fund services, infrastructure and may increase inequalities. Likewise, corporate welfare will distort the tax system by giving private companies tax breaks, subsidies and guarantees. The fairness, sustainability and credibility of the tax system should be undermined and challenged.

The design of the tax system should incorporate two features. Firstly, it should focus on the collection of taxes on personal income, corporate profits, resources, property and consumption. There is a role for charges, tolls and fares on some services, for example car parking and public transport. But the drive to impose new and higher charges on a widening range of public services must be opposed, together with the increasing use of individual budgets, direct payments, vouchers, and insurance schemes. A user-pays taxation model will prove much more expensive than public provision through general taxation. It is inequitable, regressive and significantly reduces collective provision and hastens the demise of public services and the welfare state. There has been a shift away from trade taxes, reduced corporate and personal income tax rates and a shift towards goods and services taxes, particularly Value Added Tax.

Secondly, it should avoid hypothecated taxes, in other words, the allocation of a particular tax to fund a specific service or capital project. For example, the roads lobby has long argued that vehicle and fuel taxes should be spent only on improving and building new roads! This would set a dangerous precedent.

Changing pattern of public expenditure

Public spending has a vital role in economic development and social life (Hall, 2010). However, an increasing proportion of public expenditure goes directly to transnational companies via outsourced public sector contracts, PPPs, management consultants and corporate welfare subsidies. The finance of individual budgets, direct payments and vouchers, most of which goes to private and voluntary sector contractors, is public money. Just as it is vitally important to systematically challenge the figures in the accounts of transnational companies, the same applies to public expenditure. Total expenditure obscures how public money is spent. A government or public body can have a relatively high level of public spending, but a large proportion may go directly to private contractors. It makes the benchmarking of expenditure and costs more complex with scope for even wider abuse in comparisons.

The following observations illustrate why demands to increase public expenditure must be specifically targeted – what, how, when and to whom it is allocated.

Under-valuing public expenditure

The cost of democracy (Council meetings, accountability procedures, town halls, Parliament, European Union and public spending on foreign relations) is too often perceived as a 'burden', but the administrative cost of central and local government alone runs into several billion pounds annually, and is priceless. It is an essential cost and could increase if public services are democratised. Expenses claims have been a key issue, but account for only a small proportion of the cost of democratic governance.

Under-estimating costs

The cost of privatisation is frequently limited to the sale costs and ignores the restructuring, preparation, debt write-offs and other costs. For example, a privatisation audit 1979-91 identified the cost of sales, debt write-offs, cash injections, discounts and other costs amounted to £47.3bn or 39% of gross privatisation proceeds (Whitfield 1992). Many of these costs never appeared in government audit reports.

Outsourcing expenditure data does not include the cost of contract management, consultants and other advisers, 2% of the contract value (Office of Government Commerce, 2009), 3% for PFI contracts and up to 7% for ICT contracts (Audit Commission, 2008). On average, 5% - 12% of the contract value is company profit and is not spent on the provision of frontline services. The cost of outsourced public services was estimated to be £79bn in 2007/08 (13.5% of total managed public expenditure) but included some internal public sector transactions estimated because of complexity and limitation of the data sources (Oxford Economics, 2008).

The public cost of market mechanisms is often substantial, for example, New Labour's market initiatives incurred one-off costs of £8.4bn by 2006 with annual costs of £3.1bn (Whitfield, 2006a). Independent Sector Treatment Centres (ISTC) alone cost £200m for operations that did not happen because of contracts with a guaranteed flow of patients, £186m 'buying back' treatment centres at the end of contracts and £60m compensation to companies when planned ISTC's were axed (Bureau of Investigative Journalism, 2011a and 2011b).

Concealing costs, risks and liabilities

Annual PPP unitary payments from public sector revenue budgets are £8.9bn in 20011/12 rising to £10bn by 2017/18 (Office for Budget Responsibility, 2010), plus £800m annual payments for strategic service-delivery projects (Whitfield, 2010b). Future commitments in PPPs and strategic partnership contracts contribute to an increasing proportion of ring-fenced revenue payments, thus reducing the scope to meet changes in needs and circumstances. Total UK PPP debt was £240bn at March 2011 (HM Treasury, 2011a) and a further £9.2bn for strategic partnerships in corporate, highways and waste services (Whitfield, 2010b).

Transfers payments

The transfer of pensions, unemployment and other social benefits from the state to individuals, accounts for a significant part of public expenditure.

Another form of transfer occurs when public services are outsourced. Supply chain spending and back-office services previously delivered locally will flow out of the local economy, together with profits, to corporate headquarters and ultimately in dividends to shareholders.

Concealing the cost of corporate welfare

The maximum public cost of guarantees and indemnities, loans and shares to UK banks was £512bn in December 2010, down from £955bn a year earlier (NAO, 2010a). Northern Rock and Bradford & Bingley banks were nationalised and the recapitalisation led to the state owning 83% of RBS and 41% of Lloyds. A further £5bn is paid in interest charges, 11% of the total £44bn interest paid on public sector debt in 2010/11 (ibid).

The percentage of public expenditure absorbed by central government gross debt interest reflects the level of debt and interest rates and thus reduces expenditure available for productive spending on services and benefits. Central government gross debt interest was £30.9bn in 2009/10, or 5.1% of total public sector current expenditure. It is forecast to rise to £66.8bn by 2015/16 or 9.4% of current expenditure (HM Treasury, 2011c). Although public sector net debt averaged 33.1% of GDP from 2000/01 to 2007/08, it is forecast to rise to 69.1% of GDP by 2015/16. Debt interest payments averaged 2.1% of GDP in the same period but will rise to 3.5% of GDP by 2015/16 (House of Commons Library, 2011).

The cost of the corporate welfare complex is often difficult to quantify, particularly regulatory and financial concessions to business, such as tax relief, reduced corporation tax rates, public subsidies, local and regional business grants, training and labour market concessions, and investment guarantees. Most of this public spending directly benefits business interests and should, therefore, not be counted as direct investment because it falsely implies a similar economic impact of other forms of public spending.

Inequalities
The local or regional impact of public expenditure is highly correlated to wage levels (both directly employed and outsourced) and the sourcing of the production supply chain. Low wages and conditions will have a dramatic impact on employment multipliers by significantly reducing standard input/output multipliers. In addition, the switch from local to global or national sourcing of goods and services will result in further negative impact on the local economy. Input/output multipliers should only be used as a guide and adjusted downwards to take account of cuts to terms and conditions and changes in supply chains. Analysis of the regional distribution of public expenditure should take account of national redistribution policies and those within sectors, such as housing and health, in response to differential needs (HM Treasury, 2011, Institute for Fiscal Studies, 2011).

Public spending includes income from user fees and charges
Public spending is based on forecasts of income raised from user charges, rents, tolls, penalties and fees – gross income from the sale of goods and services was £52.6bn in 2009/10 (National Statistics, 2010b). The level of rents, fares and user charges is a material concern in assessing the impact of public expenditure.

The wider use of individual budgets, direct payments, vouchers and personal top-ups will result in a widening gap between expenditure in government programmes and total public and private expenditure on a service, because it will be difficult to track the level of personal top-up payments. Individual budgets/direct payments were £900m in 2010 (6% of adult social care) to 170,000 budget holders (Audit Commission, 2010a).

The growth of a social investment market and the substitution of public services could make classification and tracking public spending more difficult, even assuming improved networking and wider use of ICT. Changing boundaries between public, private, social investment and voluntary sectors will lead to further obfuscation.

CHAPTER 6

Reconstructing public services

The third part of the reconstruction strategy makes proposals for public service and welfare state policy changes, the case for in-house provision, a new public service management strategy, and public infrastructure investment. The proposals are an integral part of the strategies in Chapters 4 and 5.

Alternative economic strategies rarely tackle the means of implementation. Yet public management of the NHS, education and other local government services determines the degree of shift between policy design and implementation and determines whether four million staff are directly employed or outsourced. This effects their terms and conditions, pensions, equalities and diversity and level of trade union organisation. If staff and trade unions are not engaged in service delivery, then it is highly probable that service users and community organisations will not be involved to any significant extent. Public management has suffered from a series of neoliberal 'fads' over the last three decades – compulsory tendering, performance management, best value, champions and leadership and partnerships, with efficiency savings again having priority. More widely, local government has an important role in democratic governance. Local and sub-regional economic strategies have renewed importance given the abolition of Regional Development Agencies.

The strategy for the welfare state must build on the principles of social solidarity, access to a basic income, elimination of inequalities, redistribution of resources, and universal provision. Long-term visions are limited because policy making and implementation can radically change objectives and their impact. Rigorous critical analysis must be undertaken of innovation proposals, stripped of rhetoric and vested interests – how is collective provision improved, what are the socio-economic costs and benefits, who designs and delivers, how is mid- and long-term provision of public services affected?

The demand for a 'level playing field' (competitive neutrality in commissioning language) has been described as 'arrant nonsense', because the structural differences between the public and private sectors are not taken into account (Whitfield, 1992). The public sector has statutory, democratic, economic, social and environmental responsibilities to deliver and regulate public goods and services. This limits the extent to which government can benefit from economies of scale, diversification and withdrawal from service provision. The public sector has public service principles and values in contrast to commercial values in the private sector.

The private sector has none of these responsibilities, and has the freedom to start and stop activities, expand and diversify, take over or merge with other companies. It can abandon contracts at short notice to reduce losses. The private sector's claim to corporate social responsibility is tokenistic and minimalist. Accounting differences between the sectors are significant, particularly the treatment of trading surpluses in the public sector whereas the private sector has no such restrictions and can spoon and ladle between subsidiaries, submit loss leader bids, cross-subsidise contracts, and take advantage of tax regimes through transfer pricing.

The public sector must adhere to statutory democratic procedures and standards of accountability and ensure a degree of transparency and disclosure that, except for meeting company law, are absent in the private sector. The structural differences mean that the public sector has duties, responsibilities, costs and operational constraints that are not borne by the private sector. Furthermore, the private sector benefits from economies of scale by spreading costs between contracts and companies and can raise capital more freely. It can source the cheapest goods and services globally, whereas the public sector is committed to supporting local economic development, SMEs and sustainable development.

Public service and welfare state policy

Decommodification

The process of financialisation, personalisation and commodification must be reversed. This will not happen overnight, but a number of initiatives are essential to stop further application, beginning the process of reversal and replacement with methods of new service delivery. Charging for 'additional' services in health, social care and education should be stopped immediately, together with payment and monitoring systems. Service specifications should also be changed. New funding systems should be designed to replace payment-by-results and payment-follows-patients or pupils. Proposals should be developed to replace fee-based provision, such as tuition fees. Service users and community organisations that organise non-payment campaigns should be supported by trade union non-collection action.

The abolition of commissioning and termination of options appraisals, business cases and procurement to outsource services, will provide an opportunity to redesign service delivery. Individual budgets should be closed for all but the high-dependency users for whom the scheme was originally designed. This is likely to be a difficult process, because some service users are likely to resort to legal action.

Policy changes
The following is only a sample of the policy changes necessary in each service or sector.

Health: Primary Care Trusts should be transferred to local government and combined with public health functions to form a new health division under democratic control (accountable to elected members, subject to scrutiny and other forms of accountability). Monitor's regulatory function should be abolished with statutory requirements amended so that Foundation Trusts are accountable to local government and Parliament (as proposed by Keep our NHS Public and NHS Unlimited). Independent Sector Treatment Centre contracts should be terminated, and where not immediately feasible, renegotiated to ensure patients and the NHS obtains the maximum benefit for the remainder of the contract.

Public health: The relocation of health and public health to local government would afford an opportunity to get genuine joined up housing, transport, leisure and sport, planning, environmental health and other services.

Education: Academies and 'free' schools should transfer back to local authority and community control. New local authority or sub-regional education plans would set out proposals to enhance pre-school, primary, secondary and 14-19 education and adult education. They should focus on skills and training. Schools and colleges should be required to develop principles and values of collective provision and innovation to address social needs. This would be an alternative to the 'every child a capitalist entrepreneur' programme for schools to set up their own businesses. Citizenship courses would be redesigned to include modules on pupil/student investigation of public policy, plus organising and strategy skills. Tuition fees in England would be abolished and a living grant reinstated for further and higher education students. Adult education would be expanded with increased funding for a more extensive programme (Workers' Educational Association). Local authorities have a key role in the development of an effective education system (Campaign for State Education, 2011).

Childcare: A national programme of full and part-time good quality public sector childcare and early childhood education is needed with a national network of children's centres and nurseries. Individual and direct payments should be limited to those requiring high levels of social care, with legal certainty established, so that service users can use local authority services. Other individual and direct payments for health and other services and voucher schemes should be abolished.

Social work: Rethinking social work must have *"..prevention at its heart and recognise the value of collective approaches."* User movements have brought innovation and insight to ways of seeing social and individual problems and *"...emphasises that social work needs to engage with, and learn from, these movements in ways that will allow partnerships to form and new knowledge bases and curricula to develop ... no return to a past of professional arrogance and that progressive change must involve users and all front line workers"* (Social Work Action Network, 2010).

Housing: A three–part housing programme should begin with the termination of the 'right-to-buy' and 'right-to-acquire' council and housing association homes. The drastic consequences were forecast by ESSU, tenants federations and trade unions (National Union of Public Employees/SCAT, 1978 and SCAT Publications, 1980); stock transfers of council housing should be terminated together with PPPs for building maintenance departments; the sixty council Arms Length Management Organisations (ALMOs) should become directly accountable council services.

The second part would be a programme of new council housing for all who want and need it, making first class council housing a tenure of choice, with funding at level of need, so every council can deliver and maintain decent affordable homes. Improved standards and a retro-fitting programme should be introduced to increase the energy efficiency of council housing. These initiatives would be undertaken by directly employed building workers and apprentices in new building maintenance units.

The third part will protect existing secure tenancies and low rents, abolish fixed-term tenancies and plans for up to 80% of market rents, and no eviction of tenants in arrears due to housing benefit cuts. Subsidies to attract first time buyers into homeownership via schemes, such as Firstbuy, should be scrapped – they can lock buyers into negative equity and are exploited by developers.

New democratic governance arrangements should ensure a minimum 40% tenant representation on housing association boards and council housing tenants' representation on local government committees. Council housing and housing association rents should include a small weekly levy to finance tenants' federations.

Public transport: Significant progress towards a fully integrated public transport system linking rail, bus, tube and urban light rail networks. There is a strong case for renationalisation of the rolling stock companies and termination of the rail franchises, and with Network Rail already public owned, this would provide the opportunity for a new railway system integrating routes and timetables, the planned electrification of key routes and a new High Speed line to Scotland. Congestion charging should be based on the ability to pay and investment in public transport.

Community Reinvestment Programme: A six-part programme would, firstly, require local authorities to re-invest in community organising and development strategies and re-instate funding of local projects that tackle the effects of rising unemployment, local employment initiatives, social and youth projects, and provide other key services.

Secondly, resources currently allocated to the transfer of public services to social enterprises should be re-allocated solely to developing enterprises in private industry and commercial services (see Chapter 9). Mutual and social enterprises should only be considered an option in the delivery of public services if they commit to the key criteria such as: economic and social additionality for the local economy; proposals to extend democratic governance, accountability and participation of users and staff; good quality employment conditions including pensions, training, learning and trade union facilities; a non-competitive agreement with other public bodies; organisational regulations to ensure continuing local base and lock-in arrangements, to secure public ownership of assets in the event of takeover/merger or wind-up.

Thirdly, training a new generation of organisers and leaders to have the broad knowledge, wisdom, skills and effective strategies through Community and Social Change Studies as a recognised field of studies in academic institutions. This will require *"...creative, paradigm-shifting new partnerships between people in higher education and practitioners in social movements and non-profits so that the educational programs can skillfully combine theory and practice, classroom and experiential education, applying a 'clinical' approach to learning as medicine and other professions do so successfully. Unlike most university-community 'partnerships', these must be truly equal, showing equal respect for what grassroots leaders, other practitioners, and academics can bring to robust educational programs for community change agents"* (Mott, 2010). Community Learning Partnerships has pilot programmes in New York, Los Angeles, Minneapolis, Detroit and several other cities.

Fourthly, insistence on new arrangements for community organisation and service user/staff and trade union participation in the design, planning and delivery of public services.

Fifthly, a review should take place of the operation and performance of leisure and community trusts operating libraries, museums, and art galleries to draw up a programme for their return to public provision.

Finally, genuinely independent technical and strategic support should be available for trade union branches and community organisations to prepare alternative proposals and to critically assess local, national and EU policies. The European Services Strategy Unit (previously the Centre for Public Services and Services to Community Action and Tenants, originating in 1973), provides technical and strategic advice, training and high quality research based on key operating principles. The combination of experience of frontline staff, branch leadership, action research and community organising, drawing on national/global analysis from independent strategic advisers, can be a powerful tool. It would be jointly funded by the trade unions, government and foundations.

The case for in-house public provision

It matters who delivers services and there is a powerful economic, financial and democratic case for in-house provision.

Economic case: The economic case for in-house options and bids takes account of future needs, innovation and improvements such as long-term value for money, better coordination and integration of services, avoiding unnecessary transaction costs, cost transparency, supporting the local economy and jobs and more effective citizen engagement. A full cost comparison that takes account of client costs, contract management, the cost of variation orders over the length of the contract (for additional work or changes to the contract), transaction costs (procurement, consultants, and contract management costs) and other costs borne by the public sector, plus comparable employment costs, will usually demonstrate that in-house services can provide services at lower or equal cost (ESSU, 2010e). This is reinforced when the cost of contract disputes, reviews and/or terminations and the wider economic, social and environmental impacts are taken into account. A higher degree of cost transparency would be another advantage.

Democratic accountability: In-house services are directly accountable to elected representatives with more effective scrutiny of performance. Outsourcing imposes a contract culture, thus reducing direct democratic control and community influence. Users can be more effectively engaged in the planning, design and delivery of services thus avoiding the vested interests of contractors. The public interest can be better safeguarded and enables a public body to retain and enhance public service principles and values.

Improved quality of service: Properly resourced in-house services provide a higher standard of service, are more responsive and flexible to changing needs and circumstances, and provide continuity and security of provision. In-house services focus on meeting local needs, have the flexibility to respond to changing needs and conditions. The integration of commissioning and provider roles, and avoidance of the procurement process, minimises the role of market forces in shaping the design and delivery of services.

Quality employment: The skills and aptitude of staff, delivery processes and working methods are key determinants of the quality and effectiveness of services. Good quality jobs, terms and conditions, avoidance of a two-tier workforce, better compliance with health and safety regulations, workforce development, family friendly policies, training and learning opportunities are vitally important. The public sector has a much better record for continuing and sustainable involvement of frontline staff and trade unions in the planning, design and delivery of services. Public sector workplaces have, on average, three times the level of trade union membership compared to private sector workplaces, with higher wages and better terms and conditions compared to non-organised workplaces.

Social justice: The public sector is committed to tackling inequalities and social exclusion, improving access and to taking action to eliminate or mitigate adverse impact. It has a much better track record in addressing equalities and diversity in the workforce.

Sustainable development: In-house providers are committed to creating and maintaining local and regional supply chains that support the local economy. They have a better track record in preventing environmental damage, taking initiatives to safeguard and enhance natural resources and a commitment to improve public health to minimise pollution, improve standards of hygiene and cleanliness, disease control, and enhancing community well-being. Public bodies must retain the capacity to critically examine the potential impact of government, EU and business policies from a public service and local economy perspective.

Improved service integration: Public policies and service delivery increasingly require a multidisciplinary, coordinated approach. This requires integrated teams, the pooling of skills, experience and resources between directorates. It requires joined-up government, not quasi joined-up contracts. Identifying, assessing and prioritising social needs, as well as planning, allocating resources and operational management are integral to the quality of service. It is essential that public bodies retain ownership and control of the public sector's intellectual capital (the knowledge and information about the infrastructure, geography, and rationale of services and how they work).

Public interest: The prime purpose of in-house provision is to meet local economic and social needs and achieve the council's objectives and priorities. The prime priority of private firms is to ensure profitability for shareholders and to meet the demands of the marketplace. Procurement and commissioning can lead to 'collusion' between client officers, politicians and private firms who place the needs of the procurement system over social and community needs. Graft and corruption appear to have few boundaries. The greater the involvement of private firms in the delivery of public services, the more likely there will be corruption and collusion, particularly as contracts get larger and longer-term.

New public service management

The way that policies and projects are developed and implemented critically depends on the principles, skills and capabilities of public sector

101

staff in local and central government, the NHS and other public bodies. A radical approach is needed to erase the neoliberal ideology, which has infested public management education and the allegiance to competition, choice and marketisation. This will not be easy or rapidly achieved. A change in public management practice is a medium/longer term project and will inevitably encounter resistance, so it is essential that a retraining programme be vigorously pursued. New management teams will be needed to replace neoliberal management practices in key services.

The new public service management should recognise differences in administrative law, the distinction between public and private management and role of the state across Europe. It has five components – democratic governance, public planning and investment, management practice, new operational systems and flexible and accountable organisational structures (Table 5).

Public service management deliberately places emphasis on management and operational practices rather than organisational issues. Public sector modernisation in Britain has repeatedly focused on organisational change (Whitfield, 2001). The recent infatuation with performance management addressed only one element of public management and did so in an over-indulgent manner that was eventually discredited.

Public service management and training must be extended deep into public sector bodies and not just targeted at a handful of would-be mandarins or high-flying civil servants. Leadership, collaboration and innovation are important but they are not the only attributes or skills required. The consistent applications of public service principles and rigorous application of holistic impact assessment of policies and projects would make a big difference. A comprehensive public management education and training programme must be located outside of business schools in order to change the ideological framework.

Criticism of large hierarchical public sector organisations usually goes hand in hand with comparisons with 'new era' organisations such as Google, Apple and IBM and the 'explosion of social innovation' in the 'civil economy' discussed in chapter 2. Lessons can be learnt but a comparison of local and central government with transnational companies is misguided. Innovation that addresses social needs is rare in the private sector. Contractors and consultants usually only address social needs from a commercial perspective, and are not democratic, participative or transparent to the extent that public bodies are required to be.

In future public management will have to manage significant growth in demand for health and social care, select and apply technology that improves service quality, address the social justice agenda to reduce poverty and increase equity, adapt infrastructure and services to climate change, and confront increasing commercial vested interests. This will require managing public bodies to be more innovative, yet fulfil their statutory responsibilities to deliver services and functions, improve democratic accountability and scrutiny to give greater priority to organisational learning and facilitate service user/staff participation in the planning and delivery of services. Some claim that public management will have to manage a more complex public-private interface, advanced commercialisation of the public sector and procurement, but this reconstruction strategy is intended to minimise these developments.

Democratic governance

The consolidation of arms length companies, trusts, off-balance sheet companies and quangos is essential to improve governance, accountability and participation. Public bodies must involve service users and community, civil society and trade union organisations in the

Table 5: A radical public service management

Democratic governance
■ Democratisation and consolidation of public sector to transform governance and accountability at city and regional level.
■ User/community organisation & staff/trade union involvement in design, planning and delivery on continuing basis.
■ New disclosure and transparency regulations to broaden availability of evidence in policymaking and evaluation.
■ Continuous monitoring, evaluation and reporting of policies and projects.
■ Rigorous scrutiny with wider powers and resources to investigate and assess evidence.

Public planning & investment
■ Develop capacity and project management skills for direct public investment for infrastructure and services.
■ Design and manage a new public sector contract for infrastructure projects.
■ Comprehensive impact assessment and evaluation framework (economic, social, equalities, health, environment and sustainability) for key policies and projects.
■ Resource planning, budgeting and auditing.
■ Whole life asset management of public assets.
■ Clean-energy economy compliance in all projects.

Table 5: A radical public service management (continued)

Quality management practice

- Public service principles, values and ethical standards embedded in policies, programmes and projects.
- Increased public sector management education and training programme to build capability and knowhow.
- Delegation of responsibility, staff briefings, workshops and involvement in projects and improvement initiatives.
- New controls on role of consultants with requirements for training and knowledge transfer built into contracts.
- Quality employment, learning, training & family friendly policies and industrial relations framework.
- Quality of inputs, processes, outputs and outcomes built into policies and monitoring.
- Sharing of good practice within and between public bodies.

New improvement strategies

- Integrate client and contractor functions, terminate or re-negotiate remaining contracts.
- Public provision re-established for services, functions, development, infrastructure, welfare state, and public health and termination of market mechanisms.
- Service design, access, delivery, administrative and organisation innovation through lean systems, ICT and other techniques.
- Bi-annual service review process for improvement plans with full and continuing user/community organisation and staff/trade union involvement.
- New regulation of markets to protect public health, labour standards and user legal rights.
- Rigorous management and monitoring of supply contracts with regular reviews to maximise public benefit.

Flexible and accountable organisational structures

- Flatter management structures having self-managed teams with organisational learning culture.
- Consolidation of trading, arms length and special purpose companies into public body.
- Internal organisational structure to ensure regular flow and effective working of democratic processes in executive, select and scrutiny committees.
- Effective working between planning and provider functions to ensure maximum integration of services.
- Organisational structures to ensure effective implementation of community and trade union participation arrangements.
- Organisational review to address problems/conflicts and respond to proposals from community, civil society and trade union organisations.

public policy making process in a substantive and meaningful way on a continuing basis. They should have access to financial resources to obtain their own technical advice.

New disclosure and transparency regulations would broaden availability of evidence in policy making. Freedom of Information (FOI) channels should supplement genuine transparency and disclosure of documents in the planning, procurement and policy-making processes. Scrutiny Committees should have wider powers and resources to investigate and assess evidence including contracts, decision making processes, governance arrangements and be able to obtain evidence and to require officers, contractors, trade union and community organisations to give evidence. Advancing democratic governance, accountability, participation and transparency must be the core of a continuing agenda. Rigorous monitoring, reporting and reviewing has a key role in improving service delivery, holding service providers to account, assessing employment policies and learning from users and staff about the effectiveness of working methods and processes.

Public planning and investment

Direct public investment in infrastructure and services will require properly resourced in-house services to be responsive and flexible to meet changing needs and circumstances. Identifying, assessing and prioritising social needs, as well as planning and allocating resources and operational management, are integral to the quality of service. Infrastructure planning and project management, including access to technical resources to design and manage projects from inception to completion, should minimise delays, cost overruns and improve quality. Public sector ownership will require whole life asset management and planned maintenance programmes.

Rigorous impact assessment of policies, spending cuts, infrastructure projects, local/city plans, regeneration projects, outsourcing and privatisation proposals, and economic development investment are essential. They should assess the economic, social, health, social justice and environmental impacts of projects so that all costs and benefits, advantages and disadvantages are transparent. They provide the basis for effective demands, give confidence to challenge proposals and provide the motivation to organise. Detailed evaluation frameworks are available for options appraisal, infrastructure and PPPs (Whitfield, 2007a and 2010a).

Impact assessment objectives should identify the additionality of projects, the national/regional economic impact on particular sectors, the effect on the local economy including job creation/job loss; equalities, social justice and sustainable development; identify unintended consequences and expose double counting and inappropriate assumptions and forecasts.

Multipliers are often used to forecast the economic and employment impact of projects. This avoids carrying out detailed analysis, which may produce only marginally different figures. Multipliers quantify further economic activity stimulated by the direct consequences of policies and projects. They take two principal forms: an income ("induced") multiplier, which is associated with additional income to those employed by the project (income multipliers) and a supply ("indirect") multiplier, with local supplier purchases (supplier multipliers). Multipliers averaged 1.45 for a mix of services and functions ranging from 1.36 for people and skills, 1.40 for regeneration and physical infrastructure and 1.51 for business development (Department for Business, Innovation & Skills, 2009).

There are two important caveats. Firstly, output or expenditure multipliers, such as the proportion of public expenditure that is spent locally, are usually too vague and do not identify the full impact and effect of policies on jobs and the local economy. It is important to identify the total number of jobs. The use of Full Time Equivalents (FTE) indicates the total stock of employment, but compresses part-time jobs, thus under-estimating the total number of people employed in the local or regional economy.

Secondly, the use of national multipliers for local analysis can result in overstating the impact. The workforce concerned may have a higher proportion of low-wage and part-time employees then the national average. Consequently, the proportion of direct expenditure and induced spending that occurs in the local economy will be reduced and will vary between cities/subregions and towns/rural areas depending on travel to work patterns. For example, if the jobs affected are primarily low paid with a higher than average proportion of part-time employment, the multiplier will be reduced to about 1.15–1.20. Local multipliers are inevitably lower than regional or national multipliers because they reflect only that part of economic activity taking place in the local economy.

Impact assessment must take account of deadweight (the proportion of total outputs/outcomes that would have been secured without the investment in question); displacement (the number or proportion of outputs/outcomes that reduce outputs/outcomes elsewhere in the target area for the intervention); leakage (the proportion of outputs/outcomes that benefit those outside the target area of the intervention); and substitution (a negative effect that arises when a firm substitutes a jobless person to replace an existing worker to take advantage of public sector assistance).

Four types of public costs should be quantified and taken into account in policy and project impacts. (a) Transaction costs include officer time in options appraisal, business case and procurement process, consultants advisers and lawyers, cost of staff transfer, cost of setting up companies or organisations, cost of reviews and legal action during contract. (b) Corporate knock-on effects include the financial effect on other directorates in the authority because outsourcing could have an impact on their economies of scale and costs. (c) It should include the long-term costs to the public body and the indirect costs borne by the government or other public bodies. Direct public costs include the additional work required by other directorates or other public bodies required to support the contract, changes in local supply chains that lead to changes in number of local jobs, and additional training provided for employment of local people. (d) Indirect public costs, such as the cost of increased unemployment and other benefits and the loss of tax revenue, should be taken into account.

Equality impact assessments must engage service users and staff and be part of a social justice assessment examining the broader socio-economic implications of policies and projects. Governance arrangements must be part of a wide-ranging assessment of the impact on democratic accountability, transparency and participation, together with the effect on civil society organisations.

A US study highlighted the difference in economic impact between public investment and tax cuts. Direct spending and infrastructure have the biggest increase in economic activity ($1.75) for a one-dollar increase in the deficit. Expenditure on unemployment insurance and food stamps, aid to States and tax cuts to low and middle income taxpayers increases economic activity by $1.45, $1.25 and $1.05 for the same increase in the deficit. In contrast, tax cuts for high-income taxpayers and corporate tax breaks only increase economic growth by $0.40 and $0.20 respectively (Economic Policy Institute, 2011).

Impact assessment should identify changes in sourcing goods and services, the effect of changes in fees and charges for services, the effect of early retirement and redundancy payments, and must systematically assess visitor or user forecasts together with the knock-on economic, social and environmental impacts.

Policies and projects must be assessed under ten headings in Table 6. The level of analysis will depend on the scope and size of the project. Evaluation must be an evidence-based analysis, not a tick-box exercise.

Table 6: Evaluation and impact assessment criteria

Evaluation Criteria	
1. Core requirements and objectives ■ Needs and objectives ■ Design, vision and scope ■ Forecasts of demand ■ Quality of service/development ■ Long-term asset management **2. Financial assessment** ■ Long-term cost analysis including client and transaction costs and corporate impact ■ Risk assessment and allocation ■ Sustainability of savings **3. Public costs** ■ Public costs borne by government ■ Cost of support & indirect subsidies **4. Economic costs and benefits** ■ Direct, indirect and induced multipliers ■ Local economy impact ■ Added value and community benefits ■ Economic development issues ■ Sustainable development ■ Effect of changes in market forces ■ Cost benefit analysis **5. Quality of employment** ■ Staffing levels and forecasts ■ Terms and conditions and pensions ■ Training, learning and family-friendly policies	**6. Quality of services** ■ Technical assessment of delivery plan ■ Quality of service and performance ■ Service transformation, innovation & integration ■ Management practice ■ Urban-rural provision and access ■ Phasing of projects **7. Democratic governance** ■ Governance structures and accountability and transparency ■ Participation and involvement ■ Social and organisational impact ■ Impact on service users and civil society ■ Monitoring & regulatory framework **8. Social justice** ■ Equality impact assessment (users and staff) ■ Socio-economic impact – redistribution and improving life chances, reducing inequalities, eliminating discrimination ■ Poverty reduction ■ Assessment of 'social transformation' proposals **9. Health and Environment** ■ Public health and community well being ■ Environmental Impact Assessment **10. Public sector capability** ■ Changes in capability & intellectual knowledge ■ Public interest

Source: Whitfield 2007 and 2010.

Public management practice

Public service principles and values should be embedded in policies, programmes and projects. It is essential that public bodies retain ownership and control of the public intellectual capital. A public sector management-training programme should build capability and expertise to enable authorities to respond to changing demands and circumstances and emergencies, and to critically examine the potential impact of government, EU and business policies from a public service and local economy perspective. Contracts must include knowledge transfer, capacity building, commitment to public service principles and rigorous monitoring. The quality of inputs, outputs, processes *and* outcomes should be valued as they are key to achieving integrated and coordinated services and an holistic approach to resource allocation and the evaluation of performance.

Operational systems

Public provision should be re-established for services, functions, development, infrastructure, welfare state, and public health, although it may not be possible to immediately terminate or re-negotiate contracts.

The abolition of market based mechanisms in education, health, social care and other services would include the removal of competition requirements. Bi-annual Service Improvement Plans, agreed and monitored by Elected Members, users and trade unions, will serve as a basis for in-house service provision. Reviews would produce two-year plans, which focus on innovation, productivity and effectiveness and would assess performance, identifying lessons learnt with remedial action. Lean systems approach would be built into the design and management of services.

A degree of increased options is possible within public services by expanding in-house services, and using spare capacity (and peaks and troughs) to widen choice without establishing markets. Choice, with collective empowerment exercised with other users, would be more powerful and meaningful than individual market-based choice.

New regulatory frameworks should monitor, review, and where necessary, intervene in markets to ensure people's needs and local economy interests are achieved. Re-regulation should address social needs, increase public control and be designed to achieve environmental, health and safety, economic and sustainable development benefits. Supply contracts would be rigorously managed and monitored to maximise public benefit. This would require adequate and skilled staff to monitor service delivery, employment conditions, and achievement of economic development and sustainability objectives.

Organisational structures
The emphasis should be on new radical approaches to internal organisation rather than the usual creation of new organisations. Self-managed teams with project management skills and an organisational learning culture would create flatter management structures to promote innovation and flexibility. Internal organisational structures should ensure regular flow and effective working of democratic processes in executive, select and scrutiny committees and integration between planning and provider functions. Organisational reviews would address problems and conflicts, and respond to proposals from community, civil society and trade union organisations.

Service Improvement Agreement
Public bodies and trade unions should negotiate a Service Improvement Agreement as an essential part of Public Service Management to include:
1. Staff/trade union and user/community organisation representation in service improvement and development on a continuing basis.
2. A commitment to direct in-house provision.
3. A commitment to equalities and diversity.
4. Changes to working practices to improve coordination and integration of services subject to consultation through existing industrial relations mechanism.
5. Redeployment and retraining with no compulsory redundancies.
6. Workplace learning.
7. Contract compliance with comprehensive monitoring and review.
8. Disclosure and access to policy and performance information.
9. Flatter organisation structures and team working.
10. Secondment and TUPE Plus basis if a transfer of staff is necessary.

Public infrastructure investment strategy

Infrastructure investment is vital for the economy and to improve quality of life. It increases growth and output (a 1% increase in public sector capital stock can boost GDP by between 0.2% - 0.5%), reduces the costs of production, increases productivity, improves access, enhances the quality of services such as health and education, creates jobs (15,000 – 60,000 jobs for every £1bn investment) which, in turn, generates further economic activity and jobs in the local and national economy (Whitfield, 2010a).

A ten-year National Economic and Social Infrastructure Plan is required for public investment and ownership of economic and social public infrastructure, to meet economic and social needs and generate economic growth and jobs. It is vital that economic and social infrastructure are combined in the one plan. Social infrastructure creates significantly more, and a wider range of, jobs per £1m investment because of the higher labour content of service provision. Such a plan should prioritise improving public transport (rail, tram and bus); primary healthcare facilities and public health; integrated multi-use facilities for education, sport and leisure, library, childcare and other community services; and the national programme for low carbon construction, renewable energy, refitting and renovating buildings, public transport electrification, industry and landfill (see Chapter 4).

This infrastructure plan must recognise the importance of production and supply chains, for example, trains and rolling stock, ICT and other equipment, furniture, goods and services, in promoting economic development and employment in local/regional industries and maximising sustainability. A public design initiative would set new standards for the design and planning of public buildings and infrastructure. Service users should be involved in the design process and develop new concepts of integrated hubs/complexes providing a range of public services. Privatisation of the public infrastructure will cease.

Local authorities should draw up plans to bring vacant and under-used buildings and homes into use to maximise their use as an integral part of assessing the need for new buildings and facilities, and preparing investment strategies. A public investment funding strategy should include new sources of funding from infrastructure bonds and a National Infrastructure Bank financed through capital spending.

The current National Infrastructure Plan is only a partial plan because it ignores social/welfare state, public safety and community infrastructure. It expands the infrastructure market, fails to address key issues (except the cost of capital) and ignores the economic linkages of infrastructure investment such as production and supply chains and employment.

The trend of adopting new ICT systems because they are feasible, rather than meeting social needs and development objectives, should be challenged. The quality and effectiveness of public services is highly dependent on the quality of inputs, processes, outputs as well as outcomes and that requires direct care, teaching, and support by people, facilitated by ICT. Hence there is a limit to online delivery and self-service systems in public services.

New public sector procurement

A new public sector infrastructure contract is required that re-organises the relationship between the client (finance and operator), architect and the construction company to strengthen coordination, deliver efficiencies, minimise delays and enhance transparency. The US concept of Construction Management At-Risk (CM@R) should be adapted to the UK context. CM@R has been successfully used for building, transport-ation and highway projects (American Institute of Architects and Associated General Contractors of America, 2004).

There are two contracts in CM@R, the first between client and architect, and then between the client and construction manager. The client selects the construction manager, based on qualifications, before the design stage is completed. The architect and construction manager work together in the final stage of the design process and the latter gives the client a guaranteed maximum price and coordinates the subcontracted work. A new contract should provide evidence of public sector performance and eliminate the evidence for risk transfer and the legitimacy of PPPs. Whole life management and maintenance strategies would be an integral part of the design and quality of construction and the client would have various options how to address this without being tied into long-term contracts.

Design and build contracts that require a combination of design, manufacture and installation, for example tram systems, would continue, but not for public buildings. Parallel reforms in the construction industry are required with a vocational education and training programme to improve skills, reduce subcontracting and casual labour, better health and safety and mainstreaming green construction (Clarke, 2010).

PPP programme terminated

The PPP programme should be terminated immediately, including planned projects and those in procurement. A comprehensive case for termination on the grounds of public cost and impacts, value for money, quality of service, employment, design quality, accountability and governance and many other factors is evidenced in *Global Auction of*

Public Assets (Whitfield, 2010a). It might be argued that it is not a 'good' time to terminate the programme when public sector capital spending is being cut. However, there is never going to be an appropriate time and the longer it continues the more embedded it becomes in financial planning, public management and the public sector.

Terminating existing PPP contracts is complex. Treasury spending data shows that the current capital cost of 670 PFI projects is £56bn with a total eventual cost of £267bn that includes the finance costs, building maintenance, utilities and facilities management services over the life of the contract. These costs have to be met irrespective of whether the building is publicly or privately owned. It has been claimed that a buy-out of PFI schemes could 'save' about £200bn, which could be used to finance green new deal initiatives as part of a plan for Green Quantitative Easing (Hines and Murphy, 2010). But this is false economics, because the 25-40 year finance, management and operational costs don't disappear. The saving is only the difference between public and private provision, unless the entire PFI programme is nationalised without compensation.

Terminating the PFI programme with regard to new capital investment will require an increase in public sector capital spending. It is not simply a matter of the cost of new PFI projects to the public sector, because of lower public sector costs. These include public sector borrowing rates being about 2% lower with significantly reduced financial arrangement fees; lower transaction costs, particularly consultant and legal fees, as a result of eliminating the complexity of PFI deals; reducing the cost of risk transfer which is regularly overstated; reducing the scope of projects to take account of decentralisation, local needs and changes in technology and service delivery; better public sector project management will reduce opportunities for profiteering in the design, construction, finance and operation of the public infrastructure. Consequently, PFI projects with a £2bn capital value could be reduced by about 20% if publicly delivered. Significantly lower revenue budget commitments would, in part, compensate for increased public sector capital spending.

Strategic partnerships are financed entirely by revenue budgets and have only a small capital expenditure component, so termination will have no impact on the level of public expenditure.

Assets should be transferred to direct public ownership and management at the earliest opportunity or when contracts are concluded or terminated. Projects that are uneconomic to terminate would have improved governance, accountability and transparency.

They should transfer support services to public provision at the earliest opportunity and employ rigorous monitoring.

UNISON's alternative budget 2010 claimed *"£3bn could be saved in user fees and interest charges every year if PFI schemes were replaced with conventional public procurement"* (UNISON, 2010), which presumably relates to future rather than existing projects.

If the government were to buy out PFI projects tomorrow there would be continuing interest charges on financing a buy-out that would eat into the savings and financial/economic costs of significantly increasing public debt. Many contracts have termination fees and legal disputes would guarantee lawyers took a large chunk of savings. These are not arguments against termination, but we should be under no illusion about the real level of savings.

Taming the secondary market

A series of changes are required to restrict, and then eliminate, secondary market trading in the equity of PPP companies. New legislation should ensure the public sector has an equal share in the increased value of assets, since this arises from market value and has little to do with the quality of the building or performance of facilities management services. New transparency and disclosure requirements should be introduced that require full public notification of proposed changes in equity ownership to participants.

The unbundling of contracts would require the transfer of facilities management services to public sector in-house delivery. Increased monitoring and scrutiny of PPP performance via a bi-annual service improvement and efficiency review, with full user/staff engagement, would help to ensure the socialisation of efficiency gains and stringent action where poor performance persisted.

The buy-out of PPP/PFI contracts should proceed where this is economically feasible and in the public interest. Ultimately, the negative effects of the PPP equity secondary market can only be solved by the termination of the PPP programme.

A new value for money methodology should be devised to take account of the profits in PPP equity transactions and the other flaws in the current evaluation methodology.

CHAPTER 7

Organising and action strategies

Disempowerment, depoliticisation, dispossession, disinvestment and destabilisation must be challenged and opposed by workplace, community and civil society organising and action. The mutation of privatisation (Chapter 2) means that strategies must address much more than cuts in public spending, outsourcing or the sale of public assets.

Protecting and advancing the interests of public sector trade union members will increasingly require a more fluid and flexible approach to organising and action, educational workshops/courses on political economy, collective decision-making and alliance-building strategies.

The launch of campaigns to stop the cuts and defend public services is an understandable first reaction, but it has limited objectives. *"Defensive demands alone, to prevent this or restore that, are insufficient and merely highlight existing inadequacies in services."* Campaigns *"...need to go beyond simple calls for additional public expenditure, irrespective of the worthiness of the case, to propose how services should be planned, organised, managed and produced."* This in turn will shape the terminology and language used because *"...there must be no blurring, fudging, or dodging"*, particularly in reference to public ownership (Whitfield, 1992). Slogans, such as 'public good, private bad' have little impact.

Promoting alternative budgets is one way to highlight the Coalition's strategy. However, it is very short sighted to believe that all that is needed is a deficit-reduction strategy stretched over a longer period to reduce the level of cuts with reform of taxation to increase government revenue. New Labour's deficit reduction strategy included spending cuts but put more emphasis on growth and a more equitable tax increase/spending cut ratio.

Opposition to marketisation and privatisation is most effective through using a combination of strategies – developing alternative policies, organising and recruitment, industrial action, coalition building and joint action with trade union, civil and community organisations (Whitfield, 1983 and 1992). The combination of action research, organising and strategic advice by the European Services Strategy Unit (previously the Centre for Public Services) supported many successful campaigns that retained and improved in-house services; stopped outsourcing, PPP projects and leisure trusts; realigned regeneration projects and improved housing and public services.

115

Lessons learnt

The lessons of the last 30 years are self-evident, but yet have not been learnt. Drawing up a strategy and constantly assessing its effectiveness, is essential. Examples of successful campaigns elsewhere are important to illustrate what can be achieved and to give confidence, but they are not a substitute for strategy. Cataloguing successful campaigns globally may provide a degree of political fulfilment, but transferring successful campaigns from one continent to another, between countries in the same continent or between sectors of the economy, is complex. The political, economic and social conditions, history, organising and cultural differences are significant and need to be understood in addition to the why, what, when, who and how of strategies adopted.

There is no template but any strategy should be based on the strength, weakness and potential of your organisation and the scope to build alliances; assessing the available resources; understanding the political context and the power, strength and weakness of the opposition (government, business, local authority) and responses to your demands and tactics; clarity and agreement about organising and action tactics in short, medium and long term; and the combination of the seven elements of the strategy outlined below that are relevant and specific to each situation.

It is vital to take action before procurement commences. Evidence and policy analysis must be supported by action – the axiom 'action is louder than words' has been proven correct time and again at local, national and international levels. Advancing an alternative policy that addresses the root causes and articulates a different option, that is viable and sustainable, strengthens campaigns. Organising and learning is the core activity of community, civil society and trade union organisations that provides the basis for taking action and mobilising support. Showcase events and demonstrations, no matter how successful, have to be followed by further action. Target the business and political interests that support policies or projects, don't focus exclusively on local or central government decision-making processes. Building links and alliances with other organisations confronting the same issues and problems strengthens campaigns and reduces the scope for opposing forces to divide and rule.

Trade unions should continue to have a central role in opposition to government policies and the promotion of alternative policies. Community and civil society organisations have a key role in organising and taking action and applying external pressure for internal change within trade unions for less bureaucratic responses and positive adoption of fully-fledged alliance building strategies. This must manifest in a political struggle within the Labour Party, which has failed to acknowledge the fundamental flaws of the 1997-2010 period.

Trade unions often adopt a twin track strategy, opposing policies nationally whilst negotiating locally on individual projects. I argued in *Global Auction of Public Assets* that this strategy is fundamentally flawed if no attempt is made to build and mobilise national and transnational alliances of trade unions, community and civil society organisations (Whitfield, 2010a).

This strategy relies on the scope and power of a national alliance of trade unions, community and civil society organisations. Local organisations need to have confidence in national strategies and to have access to organisational, technical and legal support. It requires the skills to monitor contracts and projects to glean evidence and intelligence and to launch detailed investigations, such as Bedfordshire UNISON's initiative that preceded the termination of the £265m strategic partnership (Centre for Public Services, 2005). The investigation and assessment of individual contracts, or on a sector, regional or company basis, will need to be more widely undertaken by trade unions and community organisations. The ideology and practices of the big four management consultancies and of the raft of newly formed 'transformation' consultancies to advise social enterprises and big society projects should be rigorously exposed.

Building alliances and coalitions between trade union, community and civil society organisations and taking action is essential to broaden and strengthen support. Activists may be unaware of the history of previous surges of interest in the 'social economy' (see Chapter 9) and need to understand the government's primary objective of fracturing the public sector. There are likely to be divisions and differences over tactics, for example, the demand for local authorities to require a procurement process, instead of directly transferring services to mutuals or social enterprises.

Making the case for radical changes in democratic governance, participation and disclosure should be fundamental to all campaigns. The processes of financialisation, personalisation, marketisation and privatisation rely on a more direct role of business in public policy making and the wider use of commercial confidentiality to minimise disclosure. Much greater clarity is needed about the quality and type of information that should be disclosed. There are two important tasks.

Firstly, to de-construct the vision for the economy, city or local area promoted by political and business interests. This requires unravelling the rhetoric, peeling away the claims and promotional jargon to uncover the basic purpose of the vision. Does it address people's needs? What will it mean in practice and how will it be achieved? What is the real cost and who will pay? Will local labour have access to jobs? Is it a shared vision or one person's egocentric plan? How far does it fall short of community aspirations and ideas?

Secondly, to rigorously assess the impact of specific policies and projects. *"Detailed research and investigation is needed to expose the effects and failure of policies; to uncover profiteering, exploitation and corruption (financial and moral); to counter the myths and policies of the Right; to highlight the real costs of policies, and other public spending issues; and to understand companies' corporate strategies, aims and methods"* (Whitfield, 1992). Rigorous assessment of the impact of policies on the economy, equalities and social justice, health and the environment is essential. This should include:

- an assessment of the impact of policies on local and community needs;
- analysis of the effect of reconfiguration, closures and projects, the scale and quality of replacement provision and whether this imposes additional constraints and costs on service users and the community;
- challenge the rationale – efficiency, innovation, service integration – for closure, relocation or outsourcing, and the assumptions underpinning and the calculation of cost savings;
- track the accompanying changes in democratic accountability, user/staff participation and transparency;
- quantify the effect of job losses, changes in terms and conditions and changes in production and supply of goods and services on the local economy, environment, health and social justice;
- promote the viability and sustainability of alternatives (see Chapter 4).

The same rigorous approach is required to understand why other campaigns were, or were not, successful, for example, the comparative economic and political context, trade union density and organisation, support of community organisations, strength of the political parties, business interests, capability and leadership of public managers, and the strategic resources available to the campaign.

A European and international perspective is increasingly important, because the issues and policies, management responses, the firms, and effective counter strategies are increasingly similar in many countries. Links with other campaigns, particularly those confronting the same companies, can be very productive. European-wide information networks are vital. Attempts to build European-wide social movements, such as the European Public Services Network, part of the European Social Forum, and the Association for the Taxation of Financial Transactions and Aid to Citizens (ATTAC), which has organisations in most European countries, should be supported. Likewise, the European and global trade union federations and organisations such as European Public Service Union (EPSU) and Public Services International (PSI), the European Trade Union Confederation and the European Federation of Public Service Unions provide vital networks.

Equalities and social justice must underpin all organising, coalition building, alternative policies and action strategies. All forms of racism must be rigorously opposed. The scale of dispossession, disempowerment and depoliticisation (see Chapter 2), accompanied by the imposition of market forces and the denial of different interests, makes a class analysis imperative.

Organising the unemployed, low-wage workers and users of welfare state services, should be an important part of any campaign strategy. Increasing diversification of trade union membership means that *"… recruitment and organisational boundaries are becoming more porous to topics that are also dealt with by NGOs"* (Schmidt, 2005).

New forms of political organising and action have emerged, for example, UK Uncut's action against corporate tax evasion and bankers' bonuses. These are essential organising tools in their own right, and have an important role in strengthening the traditional toolkit of marches and demonstrations.

It is important to be aware of the trend to designate 'new' concepts and developments, when in fact they have been in existence for some time, or they are repeating a cycle. Another trend credits 'new social movements' with a wide-range of 'new' organising tactics and representation, but they are, in reality, a small part of traditionally organised trade union, civil and community organisations. 'New' alternative policies and coalitions may have been employed over many years, but with varying degrees of success. For example, many tenants' and residents' organisations produced alternative improvement plans for their area in the 1970s and some local authority works departments established joint committees with tenants groups to campaign for more and better council housing.

Finally, there is an urgent need for greater resources to provide independent organising and strategic advice available and accountable to trade unions branches and community organisations (see www.euro pean-services-strategy.org.uk).

The importance of planning strategies

There are differences between the threat of marketising/privatising of public goods such as water, usually delivered on a regional basis, compared to the threat to outsourced services locally. The degree to which the issue is national or local, and public or internalised in a procurement process with decisions taken behind closed doors, heavily influences the strategies that can be adopted. This, in turn, presents different opportunities and challenges in the development of alternative policies.

Clarity about strategic political objectives is crucial to ensure that policy demands go beyond 'stop the cuts', or 'stop privatisation', because even if a campaign is successful, the policy or project is likely to be subjected to other neoliberal options. For example, a public body could reverse some cuts, but then proceed to privatise services. 'Success' is frequently short-lived, for example, proposals for leisure trusts have been defeated in some cities, only for the same proposal to surface again a few years later. In other cases, services are transferred to publicly-owned arms length companies, creating a pathway for privatisation at a later date. The financial crisis has increased the rate at which previously rejected policies, such as leisure and community trusts, reappear on the agenda. Alternative policies are essential, otherwise the question ultimately arises about what we are defending.

Strategic framework

The original anti-privatisation strategy, *Improve Public Services: Shut Out Contractors*, published by the National Union of Public Employees, was designed primarily to oppose outsourcing and privatisation (Whitfield, 1983). The strategy drew on lessons learnt from earlier opposition to privatisation. The principles remain valid today at local, national or international level and take account of financialisation, personalisation and marketisation as new pathways to privatisation:

- organise in the workplace and community;
- forge coalitions and organise public service alliances;
- intervene in the transformation and procurement processes;

- organise industrial, civil and community action;
- develop alternative policies and plans;
- build political support;
- challenge the vested interests of business organisations and political allies.

The elements of the strategy are interconnected and rely on the effective implementation of each other. It is not a menu from which to select some strategies, but how to apply all the strategies in a way that best achieves objectives. Early intervention in the planning and decision-making process is essential and must include a long-term view. Individual strategies, or a selection of them, are unlikely to achieve a sufficient shift in influence and power for a decision to be reversed or a new approach adopted. Workplace and community organising, coupled with good communications, are essential in their own right, and are important facilitators of other strategies. Similarly, detailed policy critiques and alternative policies or proposals are a vital part of the overall strategy, but their usefulness is starkly reduced if they are not underpinned by a strong organisation and alliance building.

The rest of this chapter examines organising and recruitment; coalition building; intervention in transformation and procurement; workplace, civil and community action strategies; and alternative policies.

Organising and recruitment

Disempowerment and depoliticisation can only effectively be opposed by a new organising drive to strengthen existing community and trade union organisations and by creating new organisations. Organising the unorganised would include service users, the dispossessed and disenfranchised, unemployed, young people and students.

Organising should avoid the trap of imposing rigid organisational models or those associated with a particular political party. Party political positions should be debated but the emphasis should be on building self-sustaining organisations for the long term.

Five key skills and knowledge are necessary; firstly, organising and recruitment skills and an ability to forge alliances and coalitions with other trade unions, community and civil society organisations. Secondly, an ability to think strategically and put strategies in to practice; to work with service users and staff to draw on their skills and experience to prepare alternative policies. Thirdly, the ability to analyse, or access resources, to investigate and research economic and social trends and developments, profile contractor performance and evidence of failed contracts, and assessment of the impact of proposals. Fourthly, knowledge and experience of the review, appraisal and procurement processes is key to being able to intervene effectively. Fifthly, regular meetings should take place with members to report news and developments, discuss proposed action, review progress and learn lessons from earlier activities.

Strategies should encompass recruiting and organising in the workplace and strengthening representation; widening the membership of tenants and community organisations such as pensioner groups and regeneration campaigns; strengthening civil society organisations such as local branches of national organisations like Friends of the Earth; building alliances between trade unions and trades councils and community and civil society organisations; and attracting support from people who are supportive, but unaligned, for example, those who are not members of a trade union, community or civil society organisation. Living wage campaigns can bring together non-organised workers, community and trade union members to campaign for an end to poverty wages and involvement in broader alliances.

The chain of production of public services will increasingly extend from in-house provision to home-working to voluntary organisations and the social economy, to local, national and/or international locations of private firms. More broad-based movements, for economic and social justice beyond the workplace and workers' rights, will be essential. Trade unions have a vital role in organising, representing, bargaining, educating, training, and monitoring in an era of increasing insecurity.

Recruitment and organising strategies should seek to strengthen density and representation in those services that might be selected for industrial action and those where density is low. Workplace meetings should discuss the threat to services and jobs, explain the union strategy and need to strengthen membership and representation. Community forums and public meetings can increase understanding of national and local policies and engage in debate about objectives, tactics and risks.

Campaigns should draw on the support of trade union members who work for other public bodies or organisations, but live in the town or city. Regional or national records can be used to communicate with them and seek their support. Geographical rather than employer-based organising is a largely untapped organising tactic. Recruitment strategies for voluntary organisations, social enterprises and private contractors should build both local and sub-regional/regional organisation and representation.

Participation in national service-based campaigns, such as the Social Work Action Network, helps to share analysis and develop alternatives. Campaigns should consider organiser training for members that could include membership recruitment and grass roots organising, understanding the political economy context and key local issues, developing strategies, coalition building, investigation and action research techniques, understanding power relations and learning from successful campaigns.

A communications strategy should aim to keep members and supporters regularly informed about the campaign, new issues arising, progress in negotiations, responses to demands, planned events and key dates via e-newsletters, workplace meetings and use of media. Some managers have been known to support but want to remain discrete for fear that a public stance could affect their job and/or career. Maintaining lines of communication with them can provide up-to-date intelligence about management thinking and attitudes, the progress of projects, and the role of management consultants. It can be a conduit to raise best practice examples and information on the performance of other contracts.

Organisations can be strengthened with training in organising and recruitment, member education, workshops to increase understanding of policies and issues and to understand power relations. It is vital to understand who depends on whom for whose support. Predicting the likely response (or lack of it) of public bodies, private firms and government helps to develop more effective tactics.

Political support can be built up from elected representatives and community organisations through resolutions, charters, sign-up campaigns and sending delegates to a wide range of political, trade union, civil and community organisations. This could include holding briefings, workshops and forums to explain your proposals, and how they will meet people's needs. It should explain how different groups and communities would be affected by government or private sector policies and projects. Advocate public service principles and values in the formulation of policies and implementation. Build public support for public service provision, good quality services and jobs through education, information, and use of the media.

Short, targeted briefings for the public, politicians and members that document contract failures, poor service performance, employment conditions, failure to achieve savings, lack of investment, the effect on the local economy and company finances, have a vital role in publicising key issues, raising awareness and encouraging recruitment. Hold briefing sessions for elected representatives, political parties, and community organisations to explain the analysis and alternatives.

Private and voluntary sector performance and employment practices and their claims to corporate social responsibility should be analysed. Contrast these with profits, executive pay, bonuses and pension supplements for directors. Expose corporate taxation rates, including evidence of tax evasion, use of offshore locations, active involvement in national, EU and international business and trade associations, and corporate support for right wing think tanks and causes. Examine the 'investors' section on public company web sites, which contain stock exchange announcements of major contracts, recent takeovers and legal disputes.

Campaigns must challenge the policies advocated by trade associations and business organisations, demand re-regulation and rigorous monitoring of the private sector, EU proposals to extend the services market and the inclusion of privatisation and PPPs in EU bilateral agreements with other countries. The WTO/GATS and EU Services of General Interest plans for further marketisation of public services remain a major threat.

Coalition and alliance building

Local coalitions and alliances of trade unions, community and civil society organisations aim to consolidate opposition and strengthen campaigns, by bringing together a wide range of organisations and interests. Coalitions are defined *"...as involving discrete, intermittent, or continuous joint activities in pursuit of shared or common goals between trade unions and other non-labour institutions in society, including community, faith, identity, advocacy, welfare and campaigning organisations"* (Frege at al, 2004). They may have different titles such as Anti-Cuts Alliance, Public Service Alliance or Peoples Assembly, have broadly similar objectives, and be initiated by anti-cuts campaigns, trades councils or trade unions.

Building alliances must be the first, not a last resort. Too often they are organised because of perceived shortcomings in the trade union movement, but this is rarely a successful starting point. The potential for the formation of alliances between community, environmental and other local organisations, which later seek wider support, should also be recognised. Although some alliances may begin with an 'in defence of' perspective, it is vital that they quickly adopt alternative policies in order to broaden support within alliance member organisations and with other organisations.

Coalitions between trade unions, community and civil society organisations should promote public service and democratic values and challenge business values. Public Service Alliances could be formed on a city-wide basis, initiated by one or more trade unions or trades council. Barnet Alliance for Public Services, launched by Barnet Trades Union Council, draws together trade unions, community organisations and campaign groups to oppose the privatisation of public services. It has organised a series of lobbies and demonstrations against cuts and outsourcing. The TUC Northern Region, UNISON and the Public and Commercial Services Union established the Northern Public Services Alliance (PSA) with a network of eight PSAs in Newcastle, Sunderland and other key locations in 2010. The Greater Toronto Workers Assembly in Canada is an example of an umbrella organisation for trade unions and labour activists, operating through an elected coordinating committee, and supporting other campaigns, such as the Transit City campaign for adequate bus routes in under-served areas and issues of free transit.

National coalitions such as the Anti-Academies Alliance (AAA) and Defend Council Housing (DCH) are excellent examples. The AAA brings together trade unions, parents, pupils, teachers, councillors and MPs. They combine national analysis and organising, support for local campaigns, briefings and national media coverage, Parliamentary lobbying and monitoring the activities of the private sector and business interests. Likewise the DCH. In the US, a campaign of civil action against the proposed Keystone XL pipeline to carry crude oil from the Canadian tar sands in Alberta to the Gulf of Mexico, has unified the major environmental organisations to oppose the pipeline.

Experience of building and sustaining coalitions in Australia, Canada and the US identifies five important principles: coalitions are more successful when organisational membership is restricted and there are fewer groups making decisions and sharing resources; effective leadership from individuals, particularly organisational leaders and coalition coordinators are key factors; coalitions should pursue shared interests in parallel with their own objectives and broad public interest objectives with specific demands; successful coalitions have long-term organising plans and action strategies; and the most effective coalitions frequently took action at local, regional, state, national and international levels, and were most effective when this was combined with support for city or neighbourhood coalitions because this enhanced their organizational strength and political influence (Tattersall, 2010).

The organisational interests and demands from members in a coalition will not be uniform. Trade union, civil society and community organisations have different governance structures, accountability procedures, and economic and political pressures impact on them and their members differentially. Building coalitions takes time and commitment and they should not be judged solely on short-term success or failure. They are unlikely to 'succeed', either in changing policy, or in sustaining the coalition, if trade unions or political groups seek community support for, and sign up to, narrow agendas. Instead, the objectives, demands and strategies must address public or community interest, not just specific sectors or groups of workers or service users, and address future needs, not just the here and now. This requires harnessing traditional organising skills and merging them with those with different organising experience and adopting a flexible approach to action-based education and learning.

Intervention in transformation and procurement

Public services should ideally be implementing a Service Improvement Plan, using a systems approach to improve working methods, adapting to new ICT, and improving integration with other services (ESSU, 2010c). Bi-annual service reviews are an opportunity to carry out a more rigorous appraisal of service needs and performance and to update the improvement plan. Only when this approach identifies fundamental service delivery or organisational problems, should an options appraisal (examining the costs and benefits of alternative methods of service delivery) be undertaken, although neoliberal dogma frequently corrals high-performing services into options appraisal and procurement.

Staff and trade union involvement in the transformation process should include the key aspects of service design, planning and delivery, beginning with involvement in the overall approach to transformation (see Service Improvement Agreement, Chapter 6). A protocol should set out the terms of engagement, the methodologies, design of new practices or organisational structures, the role of consultants, how changes to working methods will be implemented, plans for retraining and redeployment, and the evaluation of changes. Trade unions should have a strategy for approaching transformation, identifying the make or break issues, and working out their response to different situations (ESSU, 2008a).

It is important to politicise and democratise the service review, options appraisal, business case and procurement processes (ibid and

University and College Union, 2011a). They are not simply technical and legal processes, because key political decisions are made at every stage of each process. For example, the selection of evaluation criteria, the development of in-house options or bids, the extent to which the authority 'stimulates' or creates markets, the use and selection of consultants and the shortlisting of bidders, are a combination of technical, economic and political decisions. It is vital that each stage is publicly scrutinised.

Procurement can be politicised by making elected members, staff and the public aware of the financial and operational risks, outsourcing costs, bidders' service performance and employment track record through a series of briefings. Lobby procurement meetings with bidders and/or organise a lobby at their headquarters. Don't rely on oversight and scrutiny, supply them with the questions and seek to give evidence. Organise targeted industrial action, if possible in revenue-generating services, and explain the reasons in leaflets to service users. Try to widen rifts in the ruling party, between the political leadership and senior management, and between senior management and other staff to gain a policy reversal.

Options appraisal could include an appraisal of outsourced services, with the intention of returning them to in-house provision, but it is commonly the signal to commence procurement or transfer process (Whitfield, 2007a). Critiques of options appraisals and outline business cases should scrutinise whether they have addressed social need, fully considered public sector options, assessed the impact on the local economy, employment, equalities and sustainable development, and identified the transaction costs and the basis on which financial savings are forecast. The same criteria, together with rigorous analysis, should apply to housing stock transfer appraisals and proposals for arms length trading and investment companies.

Experience shows that once a formal procurement begins, it is extremely unlikely that it will be terminated prematurely. There are a number of reasons for this. Firstly, procurement is a legal, as well as a technical and political process. European and UK legislation and statutory regulations impose processes, procedures and timeframes that cannot simply be turned on or off. There are some examples where the procurement process has been terminated or contracts not awarded, but this has invariably been the result of poorly designed contracts or lack of private sector interest, rather than the effectiveness of trade union/community challenge. Demanding innovative and improved in-house options and bids is essential. The economic case is compelling

(ESSU, 2010d). Secondly, termination of the process exposes the client authority to significant compensation claims from bidders seeking recovery of bidding costs. Thirdly, termination affects the authority's credibility in the procurement of other goods and services. The authority could conclude the procurement process and not award a contract, or continue with the current provider, but it must have significant grounds for doing so.

The procurement process must have a comprehensive evaluation framework and impact assessment (see Chapter 6); clearly specified service standards, principles and values; minimal scope for variant bids; TUPE Plus or secondment employment models; a governance structure with accountability and transparency; adequate resources for stringent contract monitoring; and review/renegotiation with non-compensatory termination clauses.

The private sector's claims of efficiency and value for money must be challenged and their contract performance, disputes and contract terminations made public. Information on companies and consultants' performance, corporate track records, and conflicts of interest are vitally important. Produce a series of briefings for elected members, staff and community organisations during the procurement process to highlight this evidence. Make the case for the exclusion of support services from the private finance initiative/public private partnership projects – facilities management services and the ICT service were excluded from Newcastle City Council's £140m Building Schools for the Future project (Newcastle City Council, 2006). An alliance of low-wage worker centers, unions, and community organizations in Mexico and in the US has launched a Prison Industry Divestment Campaign calling on public and private institutions to divest their holdings in the two largest prison companies, Corrections Corporation of America (CCA) and the GEO Group. In May 2011, Pershing Square Capital Management sold over 7m shares in CCA (http://enlaceintl.org).

It is one thing to get the authority to permit an in-house bid, but it is equally crucial that the bid is good quality and well prepared. Past and current performance will play a key role in getting an in-house service shortlisted. However, there is no guarantee that an in-house service will be able to maintain and improve performance under contractual conditions, such as a new organisational structure and financial regime, new performance targets, operating new equipment, new working practices and/or changes to staffing levels. The in-house bid must not 'rest on its laurels' and must demonstrate that it has clearly worked out, holistic, practical and effective proposals and systems. In-house and public sector consortia options and bids must be fully developed and fairly assessed. Newcastle UNISON's two-year campaign resulted in the submission of a successful in-house bid for a £200m contract, won against BT, the only in-house bid submitted in a strategic partnership procurement (Wainwright and Little, 2009). Branches in several other UK authorities succeeded in stopping strategic partnerships (Whitfield, 2010b).

Intervention in the early stages of a procurement process could put pressure on public bodies and bidders by taking industrial action and/or holding a demonstration at head offices, and at annual general meetings of firms or conferences attended by their chief executive or directors, once the shortlist of bidders is known. If transfer or outsourcing proceeds, trade unions should immediately draw up a plan to retain membership, recruit new starters, and ensure an effective industrial relations framework is established with staff/trade union participation in governance structures. They will need to monitor performance and to make the case for transfer back to public sector provision. Trade unions should follow the example set by Bedfordshire UNISON who commissioned an investigation of Bedfordshire County Council's strategic service-delivery partnership, which ultimately led to the Conservative Council terminating the £265m contract and transferring over 500 staff in-house (Centre for Public Services, 2005). See chapter 8 of *Global Auction of Public Assets* for a comprehensive analysis of contract failures (Whitfield, 2010a).

Clarity over the role of voluntary, social enterprise and community provision is essential. The replacement of paid labour by volunteers must be opposed, as this is another form of job loss. Support for social enterprises in the service and manufacturing sectors must be separated from their role in the public sector. Proposals for social enterprises must be critically assessed, employee ballots required, business cases examined to determine viability and sustainability, whether planned growth is organic or reliant on contracting, and how efficiency will be increased whilst improving jobs, terms and conditions.

Trade unions should support community campaigns opposing the closure of local facilities and resisting attempts to impose community ownership, funding and management – a poisoned chalice at the best of times, and highly toxic for the foreseeable future. Innovation, improvement and cost effectiveness should be a continuing element of service improvement plans, combined with publicly exposing the big society empowerment fraud and building political support to oppose these public sector policies (see Chapter 6).

Workplace, civil and community action strategies

Always examine issues in the wider political economy context, long-term as well as short-term, and how they affect different groups of users, communities, workers and interest groups. What action will be most effective in building political and community support? Who are the key decision-makers and what pressure can be applied to achieve a change in policy? What combination of strategies will be most effective in the current context? Distinguish between campaigning to prevent local/national spending cuts and policy changes; privatisation by asset sale; procurement to outsource service delivery; marketisation and the transfer of services to existing or establishment of new organisations such as arms length companies or social enterprises. Each has a distinct process and although the same strategies and tactics are relevant, the mix and application will need to vary.

There are many forms of industrial and community action. Industrial action and demonstrations, occupations and picketing/lobbying, are core tactics, which should be combined with creative and imaginative tactics. Combine political criticism and satire with workplace and community organising and building wider public support. Events and activities should be designed and planned to build community and political support and awareness rather than simply score political points. Work out ways of mobilising and involving people in the planning, organising and implementation of events.

Where ruling group and senior management in councils and public bodies are ideologically committed to outsourcing and privatisation, rational argument exposing flaws in their policies and alternative proposals are likely to have limited effect. It is essential that selective industrial action be organised as early as possible – a trade dispute based on the identity of the employer. If the withdrawal of labour is not feasible, then working to rule could include working to contract by refusing to work additional unpaid hours, withdrawal of cooperation to implement projects, a work-to-rule to slow down service delivery, strict adherence to health and safety regulations and agreed procedures, the use of technical/professional opinions to delay projects and low priority given to questions and information requested by elected members on other matters.

Refusal to collect user charges and fees, or recently imposed increases, is another effective tactic. Staff could take no action or use bureaucratic methods to delay action being taken against, a user/community-wide campaign that refuses to pay charges and fees. The combination of industrial action with community action can be very powerful. Ideally this action should be taken with community support simultaneously with action by community organisations. Boycotts of social investment bonds, the 'right to challenge' and similar schemes could help to make people aware and build opposition. Similarly, a campaign opposing health budgets that included education/awareness and practical advice on boycotting and opposing their introduction, could have wide community support.

Build on your strengths and understand the organisation's strengths and weaknesses and those of other organisations in a coalition. Don't embark on action that cannot be fulfilled or sustained. Be wary of provocation because governments, public bodies and/or contractors may try to 'encourage' industrial action on the basis that they could win a war of words over the impact on users and services, and may save money during a strike. They may adopt divide and rule tactics to try to fracture alliances.

Big set-piece national demonstrations can build momentum, provide an organising focus and draw media attention and must be seen as part of the overall strategy outlined above. Regionalising or localising action or the lack of follow-up action following national demonstrations is often less than successful, because of the lack of a strategic framework.

Demonstrations, rallies, lobbies and pickets can mobilise support and increase political pressure for changes in policies and projects. They are an important opportunity for people to express their solidarity and anger. The Stuttgart 21 railway campaign in Germany intensified in summer 2010 with up to 65,000 at key demonstrations, which were combined with sit-ins, occupations and attempts to stop site clearance. The €4.5bn project planned to submerge rail tracks with a new station underground to release a large area for real estate development. The start of felling 300 trees, some 200 years old, in Stuttgart's historic palace gardens was another rallying point. The campaign reached a crucial stage in April 2011 when Deutsche Bahn halted the project and agreed not to let building contracts, after the Green Party and Social Democratic Party had swept the centre-right Christian Democratic Party from power in the state elections.

Economic targets could include boycotts of companies, services, events or products, rent strikes and refusal to pay fees and charges. For example, during the Isle of Skye Bridge PPP campaign, islanders refused to pay the bridge toll fees and the government eventually bought out the contract. The objectives should be to apply political pressure, raise awareness and expose private sector performance, employment practices, disputes with public bodies and partnerships with other companies. A combination of boycotts, pickets and publicity has proven successful in many US campaigns.

Occupations have recently been revived as a key means of protest, for example student occupations of universities and colleges. UK Uncut's campaign against tax avoidance targeting Vodafone and Arcadia Group stores (Debenhams, Top Shop) with short-term occupations. Similarly, occupations of public facilities threatened with closure, council meetings and other public and private facilities are effective.

Legal action can be a useful tactic, but never build a campaign around it, or rely on 'winning'. It can never be a single tactic, only one of many tactics. Judicial Reviews (the High Court can order or make an injunction to stop a public body from acting unlawfully if it has failed to properly consult, violated people's rights or failed to carry out management duties) are sometimes successful and will force an authority to revise its approach. However, it may not change its policy, but correct the original procedural shortcomings that led to the Judicial Review, and try to implement the policy again. Or it may target other services instead, which emphasises the importance of having alternative policies.

Too many campaigns have relied on the courts to right wrongs and, irrespective of the merits of the case, have fallen foul of legal wrangles, let-out clauses and the politics of most judges and the criminal justice system. Nor should you let the long process of legal action determine your timetable.

The reconstruction of the economy, state and community agenda, highlights the need for a new kind of trade unionism: a trade unionism that combines defensive demands with alternative policies; builds alliances with community and civil society organisations; undertakes more proactive action research; provides more substantive strategic national support to local branch campaigns; and combines national, regional and local action in support of national priorities. This will mean internal reprioritising and reorganising, but is necessary given that the restructuring of public services and the welfare state includes the marginalisation of public sector trade unionism. *"The challenge now is to build a trade unionism that is actually a class organization, one that goes beyond organizing people by the workplace alone and organizes people in relation to the many facets of their lives touched by this crisis"* (Panitch, 2011).

Alternative policies

Alternative policies are important nationally and locally, such as an improvement plan for a group of services, regeneration area plan, a strategy to expand jobs in the local economy, a public-public or joint public service project, a new service to meet the needs of a group of people, or an investment plan for public transport. The objectives might include a long-term vision for a service or area, such as an integrated, publicly-owned and operated public transport system, or a plan to address community needs.

Public service workers, users and community organisations must 'own' a vision for services, facilities, communities and the economy, otherwise government and capital will completely dictate policies and plans. Alternative policies and proposals must demonstrate how public provision can meet social needs and objectives, maximise benefits and minimise negative consequences. Service user, community organisation, public and staff/trade union ideas help to sharpen critical analysis of marketisation and privatisation proposals. This helps recruitment and organising, and builds confidence and momentum in a campaign.

When governments and public authorities are embarked on ruthless implementation of marketisation and privatisation, alternative policies may have limited immediate impact. Nevertheless, alternative policies will have a long-term function in organising and recruitment, building support, creating opportunities for challenges in political parties, and in creating an evidence base to underpin industrial, community and legal action.

The status quo is rarely tenable. Rapidly evolving technology, demographic change, public sector reform, together with the economic and financial crises, mean that a defensive, 'no change' position is not sustainable. Moreover, it places trade unions in a weak negotiating position. Nor is it an effective defence against job losses and the erosion of terms and conditions. The strategy should combine proactive and interventionist campaign tactics. *"…We need to go beyond protest, or we will be trapped forever in organising the next demo"* (Panitch, 2011).

Making the case for alternative policies and proposals must not involve 'doing management's job for them'. It does not require trade unions to submit bids or tenders, but it does require intervention to promote best practice, to advocate improved in-house options and to critically assess the flaws in the scope, methodology and conclusions of management's options appraisals and business cases. It is necessary to seize opportunities. For example, the requirement to identify the current and future health and well-being needs of a local population in a Joint

Strategic Needs Assessment and the transfer of public health to local government is an opportunity to develop a community needs assessment with a radical policy agenda, more integrated health, social care and education services, and to build effective coalitions.

Alternative policies may require implementation of new working methods and reorganisation leading to some job losses, but retraining and redeployment can provide alternative employment. The threat of incorporation is often cited, because the employer's analysis of problems could heavily influence the preparation of alternative policies at the expense of service users' needs and a trade union perspective. However, alternative polices are intended to provide a broader and longer-term context for decisions about service provision, performance and funding. Incorporation is just as likely with a defensive strategy that allows the problem to be internalised and effectively privatised within the service. Alternative policies should challenge the traditional definition of 'value for money', realign the debate about public service principles and values, and widen the scope of impact assessment to include economic, social justice, health, environmental and sustainable development.

Plans for nationalisation or re-municipalisation of services must include employment terms and conditions, democratic control and accountability, proposals for public management, and a sustainable financial and business plan.

Nationally, commissioning must be abolished. The Labour Party and trade unions must take an unequivocal stand to replace this policy with the proposals set out in Chapter 6. Failure to do so will lead to the destructive consequences of market forces, detailed in Chapter 10, becoming dominant. It could also result in the rapid decline of trade union membership.

Policies and proposals alone are of limited value, and must be part of an organising and recruitment strategy to strengthen campaigns and build political support. Alternative proposals are not a panacea, but an extension of traditional organising, not a replacement tactic. Good ideas by themselves are not adequate and can easily be distorted by opponents or the media. Therefore, an alternative policy must have other key attributes – the organising and learning process undertaken to prepare proposals; links between longer-term proposals and current demands to show that they are a means to an end, are not idealistic and part of a wider strategy; proposals to control their implementation. Policies and proposals that are prepared in a vacuum are likely to have limited use and may well be diversionary.

Divisions between professional/technical and manual workers and within or between unions must be avoided. A democratic and open process, accountable to branches and/or regional structures, will help to ensure it is not exploited for sectional, political or career interests.

Alternative governance structures and ways of increasing democratic accountability and transparency should be a core part of alternative policies. The typology in Chapter 2 referred to governance being privatised, not just services. A concerted focus on the shortcomings of scrutiny in local government, and the lack of accountability in strategic partnership structures, is essential. This could run parallel with demands for improved accountability in local authority trading and arms length companies and community trusts. Proposals should go beyond changes to the composition of boards and representation, to improved decision making processes with participation of services users, community organisations and staff/trade unions. Shortcomings in accountability and representation in trade unions and community organisations need constant vigilance.

Building national (such as the Coalition of Resistance) and European alliances of anti-PPP campaigns and trade unions should focus on collective research and information sharing, targeted action against specific companies and evaluation of the effectiveness of alternative policies and campaign strategies.

CHAPTER 8

Privatisation of core public services

Public sector transformation

The Coalition Government's public service transformation has five main objectives.

Firstly, to speed up the fragmentation of the public sector into separate units and small clusters. This is promoted as increasing user choice and diversity of service providers, but is intended to destabilise current provision, increase the scope for new organisational structures, new federations of existing organisations and to increase outsourcing opportunities. The transfer of services to trusts and arms length companies has similar objectives. The government claims 'competitive neutrality' between service providers, but this is a sham because it bears little relation to the relative power, capital assets, market share and economic interests of national and transnational companies that will dominate procurement. The Open Public Services White Paper will lead to the emergence of voluntary sector opportunists, empowerment brokers, social enterprise agents and carpet-baggers, but they will ultimately have a minor economic role.

Secondly, to ramp up the marketisation and outsourcing of public services to open up new outsourcing opportunities for private capital in the delivery of public services, consolidate their presence and influence in key markets, and reduce the role of the state. The White Paper rejects a 'top down' approach in favour of a 'bottom up' approach. The division into 'individual', 'neighbourhood' and 'commissioned' services, beggars belief, particularly since all services will be commissioned.

Thirdly, to transfer risk and responsibility to individuals via a new wave of privatisation of public assets. In addition, public private partnerships will be extended to create new opportunities for the private sector.

Fourthly, to drive down the cost of employment by abolishing the two-tier code of practice (that prevented new staff being employed on worse terms and conditions), encourage local bargaining, reduce the quality and cost of pensions, and a public sector wage freeze.

Finally, to create an austere financial climate by imposing a rapid deficit reduction strategy with public spending cuts (28% cut in local government over a four-year period, front-loaded in 2011-12) with drastic knock-on effects and consequences.

Poor public management lacking the skills and ability to work with staff and trade unions to undertake service improvement is another key cause in the growth of outsourcing. This is often presented as a lack of 'leadership'. However, the question is not leadership per se, but the ideology and values of managers that underpins their practice.

easyCouncil model of local government

The London Borough of Barnet has used Future Shape, easyCouncil and One Barnet transformation brands to try to conceal privatisation of the council. The 'future shape' was a PriceWaterhouseCoopers inspired three-level structure with a strategy hub, which would have commissioned services from a new Joint Venture Company (JVC) with services provided by several 'service delivery vehicles' (Barnet UNISON, 2008). A small strategic hub would have been a 'partnership' with the Police, NHS, Middlesex University, Barnet College and Employment Service.

This model was ditched and replaced by 'easyCouncil'. The council would not automatically provide blanket coverage of services, users would pay extra for non-core services, queue jumping and individual budgets would enable users to buy services. This model was a thoughtless public relations gimmick. Designing public services for those with the minimum needs and charging those most in need for everything else would be a fundamental reversal of public service principles and human rights; likewise draconian regulations, punitive charges and 'take it or leave it' service delivery.

'One Barnet' replaced 'easyCouncil' when the focus switched back to a public sector 'total place' approach. Although a One Barnet Board exists with other public sector representation, the contracts are limited to council services. All three 'models' were promoted to mask privatisation of the council, which has remained the core objective of the Council since Future Shape was launched in 2008.

The Conservative-controlled Council, supported by neoliberal senior management, ensured that no service reviews were carried out prior to 'high-level' options appraisals, which had narrow criteria and superficial assessment. In-house options were designed to fail. Business cases were critically flawed and failed to fully address risks, affordability, investment, transformation, equalities and employment issues. The systemic lack of evidence, extensive use of mediocre consultants and lawyers (£9.2m cost between 2009-13), the fraudulent claim of a 'new relationship with citizens' and their refusal to have Gateway Reviews (peer reviews to ensure good practice), were exposed by Barnet UNISON (see www.european-services-strategy.org.uk/publications/ public-bodies/ transformation-and-public-service-reform/).

The Council is outsourcing planning and regulatory services, corporate services, customer services, transport and parking. It has concentrated on white collar services, but environmental services will follow resulting in nearly 3,000 jobs being outsourced, leaving a few hundred 'commissioners'. Adult services are being transferred to a new local authority trading company, together with the housing ALMO, the latter being a subcontractor to Capita Group plc in bidding for the Council's back office services.

Yet the Council's procurement and contract record is appalling: the £10.3m additional cost of the Catalyst care home contract (London Borough of Barnet, 2011b); Fremantle Trust slashed terms and conditions in care homes; legionella in three care homes in 2011; the £12m Aerodrome Road Bridge replacement contract almost doubled to £23m; the Council spent £1.36m without a contract with MetPro Rapid Response, which *"... failed to comply with...Financial Regulations, exposing the Council to significant reputational and financial risks"* (London Borough of Barnet, 2011a). The report identified *"...serious deficiencies in current procurement arrangements"*. The SAP (Systems, Applications and Products) project to modernise the control of payments and purchasing was initially estimated to cost £8m in 2006, but costs spiralled to £25m and many of the promised benefits of automation have not materialised. The loss of £1.5m to the Council's pension fund because it failed to require a bond from the Connaught Partnership that went into liquidation. The Receivers, KPMG, confirmed that unsecured creditors will receive less than one penny in the pound (London Borough of Barnet, 2011c).

The council plans to terminate its Greenwich Leisure Ltd (GLL) contract because the *"...planned reductions* [£1.2m] *to the revenue budgets for 2011/12 and 2012/13 are not achievable due to the contract management fees payable to GLL"* (London Borough of Barnet, 2011d). The council hired lawyers to assess the current contractual arrangements and prepare a proposal to vary the contract. They concluded the contract must be terminated and retendered. More costs, less service. The council admits it has *"...an ageing stock of leisure facilities and no long term investment plan"* so the cost of repairs to the council could increase year on year (ibid).

The Council has known for several years that Hendon Cemetery and Crematoria required investment to meet pollution regulations to reduce mercury emissions by December 2012. It outsourced an options appraisal to Capita in 2008. The appraisal was heavily criticised by the trade unions and Cabinet agreed for staff to carry out a new appraisal with an in-house option (ESSU, 2009). It assessed eight options, together with a soft market test, and concluded an in-house option was the best option – the service has an annual net income of £0.5m. The Council did nothing, but later included the cemetery and crematoria in the specification for planning and regulatory services in the knowledge that it would be subcontracted. In late 2011, the bidders informed the Council that the procurement timetable meant that there would not be enough time to complete the works between completion of the tendering process and the 2012 deadline. The Council abandoned plans for private finance and will directly fund the £1.75m investment (London Borough of Barnet, 2011e).

One Barnet seems to be a cocktail of dogmatic adherence to neoliberal ideology and some senior management practices that are incapable of meeting the basic requirements of public management and democratic governance. Barnet claims to be a 'successful suburb', but its refusal to require outsourced council services to be located in the borough is further evidence of the cost cutting objective and cynical disregard for service users, staff and the local economy.

Education markets

The Coalition Government is creating a higher education market with more intensive competition between universities and colleges. Universities will be free to recruit students with high grades (about 65,000 students). In addition, they will compete for a further 20,000 places where universities charge an average, net, full-time of £7,500 or less. This is intended to allow FE colleges, new entrants and non-traditional providers to expand to gain a share of the market. It will open a quarter of the 350,000 new undergraduate places to competition and this proportion will increase annually from 2012.

The Higher Education Funding Council for England (HEFCE) will be turned into a regulator and 'promoter of a competition system'. Routine quality inspections will be reduced but HEFCE will have more powers to respond to students' complaints, who are being treated as consumers pursuing value for money. The teaching block grant, which HEFCE currently distributes to universities, *"...will be progressively replaced by publicly funded tuition fee loans for students, paid through the Student Loans Company"* (HEFCE, 2011).

The Coalition imposed a 40% spending cut on universities with revenue 'replaced' by a maximum student fee increase from £3,290 to £9,000 per annum in 2012-13 (Browne Review, 2010). Some universities already had financial problems, a quarter failed to meet at least one of the HEFCE financial benchmarks in 2009-10 and the number 'at risk' grew from 10 to 43 between 2007-2010 (NAO, 2011b). New funding arrangements will potentially increase the number of universities at 'high risk' of failing as they compete for income. These financial problems could create opportunities for the private sector to take over the management of universities branded as 'failing', whilst soaring tuition fees create a 'market opportunity' for private companies to undercut existing universities. BPP Holdings (Apollo Group Inc) has already indicated that it has plans to take over management of ten universities and provide ICT, procurement and corporate services (Shepherd, 2011).

BPP University College (BPP Holdings) became the UK's second private university in 2010. A third private university, New College of the Humanities in London, has £18,000 annual tuition fees.

Feeder chains or networks extending from childcare, schools, FE colleges and universities are likely to develop between higher education bodies and private companies. The first partnership, a further education college, New College, Swindon, and a private company, commenced in September 2011 with degrees awarded by BPP University College.

A number of companies, such as INTO University Partnerships, Navitas Ltd (Australia) and Kaplan International Colleges (Washington Post, US) have established partnerships with UK universities to provide foreign language courses and facilities. INTO is building a new £51m foreign student centre at the University of Newcastle on a prime city centre site to provide English language pathways into a wide range of university courses. UEA London is a PPP between the University of East Anglia and INTO, with a 1,000 student centre in the City of London. In addition to foreign language courses, the Centre offers UEA graduate and postgraduate degrees in creative entrepreneurship, international business management and strategic carbon management. It hosts the London Academy of Diplomacy, which runs postgraduate courses for the London Diplomatic Corps, government departments, multinational companies and students seeking a diplomatic career. Although the degree courses will be delivered by UEA staff, the London Centre is branded as 'INTO University of East Anglia' and claiming identity with UEA's teaching and research track record! (INTO, 2011)

Many universities have rejected these joint ventures in which companies gain control of recruitment and teaching of international students on a for-profit basis.

US experience of for-profit universities

Twelve per cent of US college students are enrolled in for-profit colleges (75% public and 13% private non-profit). 60% are enrolled in four-year courses, a high proportion being under-represented minority students. Tuition fees at for-profit colleges ($15,715) were on average more than twice those at public (in state) universities ($6,393) in 2009/10. 95% of students at for-profit colleges had student loans in 2007/08, twice the level of public colleges. Federal student aid to for-profit colleges reached US$4.3bn in 2008/09 and accounted for 66% of their revenue in 2008. The University of Phoenix (Apollo Group) broke the $1bn federal aid revenue barrier in 2009/10. Yet for-profit graduation rates (four-year courses) were only 22% in 2008 compared to 55% and 65% for public and private non-profit universities in 2008 (College Results Online, 2011).

The largest for-profit is the University of Phoenix-Online Campus with 241,832 undergraduates, annual tuition of $12,840, a first-year retention rate of 36% and six-year graduation rates of 4.2% (College Results Online, 2011). New degree enrolment at University of Phoenix declined 40.5% in the third quarter of fiscal 2011 compared to the same period the previous year (Apollo Group, 2011a). Apollo spent $953m in 2010 on selling and promotional activities (Apollo, 2011b).

Apollo violated recruitment regulations that banned paying recruiters on the number of students they sign up. A government investigation of the University of Phoenix and the Institute for Professional Development, owned by Apollo, concluded the university *"...was fully aware of the incentive compensation ban; yet, it devised an illegal compensation practice and maintained two sets of books in the event of being audited"* (Government Accountability Office, 2010). In 2008 a federal jury ordered Apollo to pay shareholders $277m compensation for fraudulently misleading investors about its student recruitment policies. Apollo successfully appealed but this was overturned by the US Court of Appeals in 2010 (Apollo, 2010). In 2009 it paid $67.5m to the government plus $11m legal fees related to a 2003 case of illegal compensation in student recruitment practices (Apollo, 2009). For-profit colleges and trade bodies spent $4.5m on lobbying activities in the first quarter 2011, more than double the previous year (Youth Today, 2011).

In August 2011 the US Department of Justice and four states

(California, Illinois, Indiana and Florida) filed an $11bn suit against Educational Management Corporation, the second largest for-profit college company, claiming it was not eligible for federal and state aid in another case of illegal recruitment practices (New York Times, 2011). The suit claims the senior management of the company systematically violated federal law. Its chief executive was previously chairperson and chief executive of Apollo Group. Education Management received $2.2bn federal financial aid in 2010, which accounted for 89.3% of its net revenue. Education Management is 41% owned by Goldman Sachs.

Marketisation of the NHS

Whether a new Health Act becomes a reality or not, the key elements of a healthcare market already exist and will continue to be put in place. Without radical new plans based on universal provision and public service principles, coupled with the abolition of commissioning, competitive markets, deregulation, private healthcare and NHS hospitals run as businesses, the growth of a health care market is inevitable. Otherwise, the debate is limited to the pace of change. The proposals apply only to England! Scotland and Wales have consistently rejected marketisation and privatisation of the NHS.

The NHS Constitution affords little protection from market forces in its rights, pledges and principles. There is nothing in the Constitution that prevents delivery by the private sector. In fact, for clarity, it states *"All NHS bodies and private and third sector providers supplying NHS services are required by law to take account of this Constitution in their decisions and actions"* (Department of Health, 2010b). The Constitution protects the NHS brand and patients' rights, but not who delivers healthcare.

Key parts of the market framework are already in place. New Labour had signed a concordat in 2000 to purchase up to 150,000 procedures per annum from private health companies; created Independent Sector Treatment Centres; provided for private sector management to run 'failing' NHS Trusts; opened privately operated walk-in health centres at rail stations; outsourced under the Alternative Provider Medical Services contracts; and originally required PCTs to become commissioning-only bodies by 2008 although this was postponed.

The Coalition's strategy has five key components – the marketisation of primary care, increased competition between hospitals with opportunities for private management, increased health consumerism, a regulator to shape and direct competition, and withdrawal of the state from duties and responsibility for the NHS.

The *marketisation of primary care* is intended to widen the role of the private sector in delivering and controlling healthcare. The switch to GP commissioning immediately opens the primary care sector (it controls over 80% of NHS expenditure) to more rapid marketisation, creates significant new opportunities for health care companies to get locked into the £100bn NHS system. Primary Care Trusts will be abolished and replaced by GP commissioning consortia, thus creating a new contract culture that will promote competition, market forces and facilitate the entry of more private firms. This strategy encourages private control and ownership of the primary care infrastructure.

Commissioning, irrespective of whether it is carried out by PCTs, GPs and/or other organisations, still requires a client/contractor split and bidding for contracts in the procurement process, with the same consequences and impacts. Entire care pathways are being prepared for outsourcing in several PCTs, lending further evidence of the growth of new pathways to privatisation (Chapter 2). *"In NHS East of England, private firms, GPs and voluntary-sector providers will be able to bid for a number of pathways, including musculoskeletal, respiratory and elderly care, collectively worth more than £300m"* (Pulse, 2011).

Increased competition between hospitals runs parallel with commissioning, with a 'failing regime' that enables the private sector to take over the management of NHS hospitals. The Department of Health is reported to have held discussions with 'international players' about running up to 20 'struggling' NHS hospitals (Health Service Journal, 2011). Over a hundred major hospitals are already effectively owned by the private sector via PPP projects, many controlled by companies registered in tax havens (Whitfield, 2011a).

NHS hospitals (Foundation Trusts) are being turned, step-by-step, into businesses having to compete with other public and private hospitals and clinics. The removal of the private patient cap will allow Foundation Trusts commercial freedom to attract private patients, open new private wings/hospitals and expand overseas under the cover of being social enterprises, although they operate as stand-alone commercial businesses. Foundation Trusts must either generate surpluses or borrow against revenue streams such as PPPs. The Secretary of State's power to give grants or subsidies to Foundation Trusts will be reduced as the government intends to stimulate a market for private sector lending to Foundation Trusts. The social enterprise status of Foundation Trusts is likely to be eroded hospital by hospital.

Extending the patient's right to 'choose and book' will be another driver of competition and market forces. Continued consumerism of healthcare, particularly via individual health and social care budgets, will lead to market forces having a greater role in determining 'need and demand' and replacing local, regional and national healthcare planning. Longer term, private health companies hope for an increase in private health insurance, but this is only likely to grow significantly if a National Insurance 'opt out' were available, similar to that which propelled the growth of private pensions.

Monitor will be turned into the Office of Health Regulation. The government claims that *"...what matters is the quality of services for patients, not the ownership model of the provider"* (Department of Health, 2011b). Monitor (and the NHS Commissioning Board) will be prevented from *"...pursuing any deliberate policy to encourage the growth of a particular sector of provider. For example, the amendments would prevent a future Secretary of State seeking to increase private provision of elective care. Equally, they would prevent him from deliberately promoting the growth of state providers over voluntary sector or private ones"* (ibid). Monitor's function is to promote the provision of health care services which is *"...economic, efficient and effective, and maintains or improves the quality of the services"* (ibid). Simply removing a duty to 'promote competition' has limited effect in a health care system that is centred around commissioning.

The government plans to remove NHS employment and national pay agreements so that health organisations/companies are employers operating on local terms and conditions.

The withdrawal of the state from duties and responsibilities to provide a national health service is the final part of the strategy. The legal opinion obtained by the campaign group 38 Degrees, concludes that the Coalition's intention is to greatly curtail the duties of the Secretary of State to provide services to be replaced with a 'hands off' approach. *"...[T]he duty to provide a **national** health service would be lost if the Bill becomes law. It would be replaced by a duty on an unknown number of commissioning consortia with only a duty to make or arrange provision for that section of the population for which it is responsible"* (Cragg, 2011). These changes in powers of the Secretary of State are intended to empower individual consortia to decide which services should be provided, will make the NHS less accountable, and will reduce national health planning. Primary Care Trusts, NHS Trusts and Strategic Health Authorities will be abolished. New organisations include the NHS Commissioning Board, Health and Wellbeing Boards, and HealthWatch (yet another 'patient organisation').

The policy changes were hardly a shock, because organisations such as The King's Fund, Nuffield Trust and healthcare companies and consultants have been advocating this option, for example 'Beyond Practice Based Commissioning - the Local Clinical Partnership and Giving GPs Budgets for Commissioning' (Nuffield Trust, 2009 and 2010). *The Plot Against the NHS* describes in vivid detail the role of the private sector, lobbyists and governments in establishing the launch pad for the new drive to marketise and privatise the NHS (Leys and Player, 2011).

Polices of destabilisation, depoliticisation and disempowerment are clearly evident in the Coalition's NHS reform proposals. Wide-ranging legislative change has the effect of increasing insecurity and fear, whilst at the same time signalling new business opportunities to the private sector. The debate focuses on the rights and wrongs of different market mechanisms and not on the needs of patients and public health. Despite claims that the NHS is 'safe in our hands' with 'ring-fenced' spending, NHS expenditure is forecast to be cut by nearly 19% by 2014/15, taking account of the Spending Review 2010, Office for Budget Responsibility forecasts and health spending inflation (Burke, 2011).

The Coalition plans to shift the balance of power towards the purchaser (commissioning consortia), because of the apparent slow growth, low profitability and market withdrawals from the primary health sector and the failure of PCT commissioning (House of Commons Health Committee, 2010). The move towards establishing a 'managed care' system, similar to US Health Maintenance Organisations (HMOs), continues privatisation by stealth. This system is likely to increase unnecessary referrals and diagnostics geared to increasing income, but subjecting patients to unwanted stress.

The outsourcing of NHS services has been fraught with failure and high costs. For example, the ISTC programme of 41 centres plus 12 cataract centres cost £2.7bn. The first phase of 26 centres was paid an 11% premium on the cost of operations carried out by the private sector to take account of their set-up and investment costs and to attract foreign firms into Britain to build private sector healthcare capacity. This was despite ISTCs having lower staffing costs and inferior pensions. Primary Care Trusts were forced to pay for activity that was not used.

Commodifying children

The childcare voucher market has expanded with about 350,000 parents using vouchers that can be used to pay for registered or approved childcare from any provider. Employers commission a childcare voucher company to provide vouchers for employees, either as a 'salary sacrifice' of up to £55 per week (free of tax and National Insurance contributions) or on top of the employee's salary. Similar schemes operate in France and Spain.

The UK children's day nursery market contracted by 4% in 2009 as unemployment rose. The £3.9bn market is very fragmented with 290 nursery groups (with three or more nurseries) that accounted for 20.5% of total UK places in 2009. Twenty companies dominate the corporate sector that accounts for 9.6% of total nursery places. However, the sector has had its own global takeover saga. Councils were encouraged to seek *"...a mixed range of suppliers to help stimulate a varied and competitive market place"* (Office of the Deputy Prime Minister, 2003).

A global trade in childcare is growing rapidly. In Britain, the Leapfrog chain, owned by private schools operator Nord Anglia, was the leading company with 102 nurseries although they accounted for only 1.6% of the market (Laing & Buisson, 2005). In late 2006, Busy Bees Group, then the fifth largest nursery provider with 33 owned and 15 managed centres and a separate corporate childcare voucher system, was sold by Gresham Private Equity to ABC Learning Centres Ltd, an acquisitive Australian company, for £71m. Within a year, ABC Learning had acquired eight large nursery chains in Australia, New Zealand, the US and the UK. Nord Anglia then sold its Leapfrog chain to ABC Learning for £31.2m and merged with Busy Bees, which then became the largest UK nursery operator.

A rapid decline in ABC Learning profits and difficulty servicing its mounting debts led to a fall in the share price, the sale of share stakes by directors, the sale of 60% of its US operations to investment bank Morgan Stanley and finally to the suspension of share trading in August 2008 and receivership a few months later.

Six months later Busy Bees was acquired by Knowledge Universe, a private Singapore-based global education company. The original Busy Bees management team acquired a share stake. Knowledge Universe is the largest for-profit education and training company in the US with stakes in many early childhood education companies, schools and colleges.

A number of Children's Centres and Healthy Living Centres have formed social enterprises as a result of public spending cuts.

The Early Intervention review (by Graham Allen, Labour MP) recommended the expansion of outcome-based contracting for Early Intervention services and programmes funded by £1bn private investment (Allen Report, 2011a). The study fully accepted the Coalition Government spending plans and concluded that, without reprioritisation of public spending, Early Intervention investment will only increase with external finance. *"While bringing in external finance will diversify income sources for Early Intervention and hopefully create a future private market for social investment"* (ibid).

The Private Finance Initiative transfers some risks to construction companies, banks and facilities management contractors. Now the plan is to transfer all the risk to the private investors! Social investment *"... enables commissioners to pay for outcomes, and therefore to transfer risk outside the public sector. But rather than placing the risk on those delivering Early Intervention, this model could potentially draw on external finance from investors to take the delivery risk"* (Allen Report, 2011b).

The study acknowledges the higher costs of private borrowing but claims *"...through use of outcome-based payments the public sector is reducing the chances of having to pay out the full amount, which may mean delivery ends up being cheaper"* (ibid). The consequences for the quality of services are ignored.

The plan is to develop the market with privately financed social intermediary funds, in effect brokers; local authorities and central government (the commissioners) will contract with a fund, which selects the providers. In other words, the private sector selects the provider, not the public sector. And consultants will not be left out – *"investors have made it clear to the review team that independent verification of outcomes delivery will be essential in encouraging them to invest"* (ibid).

This is commodification and financialisation of children. Children in need do not require a variation of the Private Finance Initiative. Early Intervention must be publicly financed and provided, not by markets, private finance and investment brokers.

Breaking up the state education system

The introduction of 'free' schools and the expansion of academies are designed to break up and fragment the state education system to create the conditions for the establishment of an education market. Academies were originally created from 'poor performing' schools but the Coalition Government immediately changed this to allow any school rated 'outstanding' by the Office for Standards in Education (OFSTED), Children's Services and Skills to become a (converter) academy. Free schools now form a third tier of academies.

Academies and free schools have the same legal requirements, freedoms and flexibilities. The main difference is that an academy school replaces a maintained, foundation, trust, voluntary aided, or voluntary controlled school, whereas a free school is an additional school. Successful academies are supposed to establish 'partnerships' with weaker schools.

The operation and building of free schools and academies are state funded via the Young People's Learning Agency, a non-departmental public body or by Building Schools for the Future PFI projects. The academies programme cost £3.2bn between 2002-2010 and the *"... expansion of the Programme will increase the scale of risks to value for money, particularly around financial sustainability, governance and management capacity"* (NAO, 2010b).

The government has consistently exaggerated the level of interest in academies and free schools to create an impression of a 'tidal wave of support' when reality is quite different. By August 2011, only 62 free school applications had been submitted and only 153 schools had applied to become academies. The first 24 free schools opened in September 2011, of which *"...11 have some religious association"* and several *"... are formerly private schools which have taken the opportunity to be funded by the taxpayer"* (Anti-Academies Alliance, 2011). Building costs for this first tranche of 24 schools are estimated to be £124m (Cook, 2011).

Nearly eleven hundred academies were opened in England by autumn 2011. Nearly three hundred are sponsored academies and the remainder are convertor academies. A further 665 have applied to convert. Sixty per cent of secondary schools, nearly two thousand schools, have not applied to become academies. Although 458 Primary schools had applied or converted to academy status by autumn 2011, 97% of Primary schools have not applied to become academies.

Academies and free schools are outside local authority control, so can set their own terms and conditions for staff. They do not have to follow the National Curriculum, can change the length of terms and school days, have greater control over their budget and access the money the local authority currently spends on the school. Free schools can set their own admissions policies and there is no automatic recognition of trade unions because there is no transfer of staff, being additional schools. Sponsors of academies originally provided 10% of the capital costs with a £2m cap or £1.5m for refurbished schools but this requirement was withdrawn.

The government's cash 'bribe' to convert schools to academies is expected to cost £600m more than expected in the 2011/12 – 2012/13 period (Downes, 2011). Schools will need to expand just to stand still to take account of increases in the birth rate, but this has been marginalised by the 'dash for cash' and the ideological offensive.

The Coalition's strategy is to significantly reduce the power and influence of local authorities in education, in particular, to generate competing demands, to create chaos and to deliberately make education planning increasingly difficult. Since most schools will not survive as stand alone organisations, education companies will offer to manage schools or to provide back-office and educational support services. It is a classic example of destabilisation to create new schools and coerce existing schools to change their status.

The free school model was copied from Sweden where *"...private providers have established themselves in the bigger cities in an increasingly market-led environment"* (Wiborg, 2010). The Swedish experiment *"... has proved expensive and not led to significant learning gains overall...* [and] *appears to have increased inequality"* (ibid).

Fragmenting ownership of the educational estate
The plethora of different types of schools has led to a fragmented and complex ownership of the educational estate. Many school buildings and land have been privatised. Local authorities now own only community schools. Foundation schools are owned by the governing body, with trust, voluntary aided and voluntary controlled schools owned by charitable foundations. In all cases, the local authority must be notified of a plan to dispose of non-playing field land. They can object to proposals and claim a share of proceeds attributable to public investment. Local authorities usually own playing fields in voluntary aided and voluntary controlled schools. Secretary of State permission is required for the disposal of all playing fields. Academies' buildings and land are usually leased by the academy trust (James Review, 2011). This means that decisions and the delivery of planned maintenance and capital investment are disjointed, convoluted and rarely take full account of the public interest.

Until its termination, new academy schools were financed through the Building Schools for the Future programme, or through a design and build Contractors' Framework. The Academies Capital Maintenance programme, an £85m fund in 2011/12, allows open academies to apply for capital funds for specific projects.

Teachers' pay and conditions
The fragmentation of the education system has aided another government objective to break up teachers' and support staff national bargaining arrangements and attempt to reduce the power and role of trade unions. Free schools provide a wedge to fracture national terms

and conditions as they are new employers and can, in effect, start from scratch. New Labour outsourcing of some Local Education Authorities, such as Bradford (now inhouse), Walsall, Waltham Forest, and Leeds, to private contractors, brokerages to replace schools' purchasing services, and outsourcing via school PPP projects have undermined bargaining arrangements by increasing the diversity of employee and employer interests and creating more exemptions. *"...[L]ocal authorities have been able to contract out some core functions of their education services. This has resulted in the outsourcing to private providers of some education functions in a few local authorities. The Connexions and School Improvement markets are two examples where legal barriers have been removed and there has been the deliberate introduction of competition"* (Department for Education and Skills, 2004).

Democratic control and governance of schools

Democratic accountability is eroded in three ways. Firstly, academies and free schools are not accountable to the local community, only to the Secretary of State. Local authorities have little control over the establishment of academies and free schools or their admissions policies. Secondly, free school governing bodies need only a minimum of two elected parents with the rest appointed by the owners. Thirdly, the local authority has no control over changes in ownership, mergers and takeovers or decisions to outsource.

Academies performance

Of the Academies that entered pupils for GCSEs in 2008 and 2009, a third improved, a third stayed the same, and a third saw their results fall. *"This is a far worse proportion than for state schools"* (Anti-Academies Alliance, 2011). The attainment gap between rich and poor students in academies and maintained schools is widening. *"On average, the gap in attainment between more disadvantaged pupils and others has grown wider in academies than in comparable maintained schools"* (NAO, 2010b).

Private education market

Although the government has stated that free schools cannot be privately managed, few believe that this commitment will last. Private education companies are waiting for the opportunity to build chains of schools. The Confederation of British Industry (CBI) is considering a shift in focus *"...towards intervention designed to improve the performance of primary school pupils"* (Financial Times, 2011). The planned introduction of personal budgets for Special Educational Needs in 2014, combined with the proposals for a social investment market in Early Intervention, are likely to further increase private provision and profiteering in education.

Charter school evidence in US

Charter schools in the US are similar to free schools and academies. The first charter school was established in 1992 and there are now over 5,250 charter schools in 40 states, educating 1.6 million children. A longitudinal student-level analysis of charter school impacts on more than 70% of the students in US charter schools revealed that although 17% *"...provide superior education opportunities for their students. Nearly half of the charter schools nationwide have results that are no different from the local public school options and over a third, 37 per cent, deliver learning results that are significantly worse than their student would have realized had they remained in traditional public schools"* (Center for Research on Educational Outcomes, 2009).

A later assessment of charter schools in Pennsylvania for the period 2007-2010 concluded *"...charter schools of all ages in Pennsylvania on average perform worse than traditional public schools, and charter school students grow at lower rates compared to their traditional public school peers in their first 3 years in charter schools, although the gap shrinks considerably in math and disappears entirely in reading by the third year of attendance"* (Center for Research on Educational Outcomes, 2011).

Charter schools have a high closure rate, high teacher turnover, poor rates of student completion and teacher dissatisfaction with inadequate facilities, insufficient instructional resources and a heavy workload (NASUWT, 2010).

Evidence from other educational markets

Marketised vocational education and training in Australia provide some important lessons. Some 230 state-run institutes operating from 1,000 locations previously delivered technical and further education. By the mid-1990s this had been replaced by a competitive market with private providers given access to government recognition and funding. A national evaluation of the marketised system *"...identified several benefits and costs of market-based competition.... On balance, the weight of available evidence suggests that, currently, negative rather than positive outcomes predominate. Outcomes appear to be positive in relation to choice and diversity, responsiveness (to medium/large enterprises and fee-paying clients), flexibility, and innovation. Outcomes appear to be generally negative in relation to efficiency (due largely to high transaction costs and complexity), responsiveness (to small enterprises, local/surrounding communities, and government-subsidised students), quality, and access and equity"* (National Centre for Vocational Education Research, 2006).

Outsourcing the elderly

The social care market was constructed by successive governments, starting with the rapid increase in the use of the residential care allowance for private homes in the 1980s, the growth in outsourcing home care in the 1990s, and the closure and/or sale of local authority care homes. Originally described as creating a 'mixed economy' of care, the public sector now has a minor role in residential and home care provision.

Many local authorities systematically reduced in-house provision of social care through 'spot contracts', in other words, 'commissioning officers' with drip-fed individual care packages to the private and voluntary sectors instead of 'block contracts'. This evaded the staff transfer regulations, because an individual care package does not legally constitute an 'economic entity'. Thus there was no obligation on private and voluntary sector providers to maintain local authority terms and conditions.

Places in local authority care homes declined dramatically from 85,000 in 1994 to only 17,975 in 2010, only 8% of the total (England) as local authorities continued to sell or close care homes. The residential and nursing care home market is estimated to total £14bn of which the private sector has £9.9bn (71%), the public sector £2.2bn (16%) and the voluntary sector £1.9bn (13%). The total number of care places declined 13% between 2000-2010.

Private equity takeovers of care companies flourished in the period prior to the financial crisis. West Private Equity acquired Southern Cross in 2002 and two years later sold the company, then operating 162 homes, to the global private equity Blackstone Group for £162m. Acquisitions continued, for example, the Ashbourne Group with 10,000 beds in 193 care homes, but Ashbourne only operated the homes as it had earlier sold its property portfolio to London and Regional property group. Blackstone acquired NHP plc in 2004 for £563m. It had a property portfolio of 355 care homes and Highfield Care, a care home operator managing 165 NHP-owned homes, which was merged with Southern Cross. Two years later Blackstone floated Southern Cross on the London Stock Exchange with a £425m valuation.

A new private equity company, Three Delta, was established in 2006, funded by the Qatar Investment Authority. It acquired The Senad Group (care homes and schools for children and young people with special educational and care needs), Health Care (care homes) was acquired from Allianz Capital for £1.4bn, and the NHP property portfolio in the same year for £1.1bn, followed by Care Principles (secure hospitals, community hospitals and care homes) for £270m from 3i Investments in 2007. Care Principles defaulted on its loan in 2009 and Barclays Capital took over the company until July 2011 when Four Seasons Health Care agreed a takeover. Barclays retained ownership of the homes and hospitals. Following the collapse of Southern Cross, Four Seasons has become the largest UK care home operator with over 500 homes. It is 40% owned by the Royal Bank of Scotland. In July 2011, NHP announced formation of new care operating company that will rent and operate from the properties NHP currently lease to Southern Cross.

The sale and leaseback model became a typical model in the care sector. Care home properties were sold to property companies on the basis that the company received a lump sum, which it then used to reduce debt incurred in the original acquisition of the homes. The care company became a manager of homes leased back to them on 30-year leases with built-in annual rent increases of between 2.5% - 4.0% and assumed high occupancy levels. The financial crisis, decline of the property market, which led to a fall in the value of portfolios, and local authority freezing or cutting care home charges caused a meltdown. It wasn't just the operational/property model that failed. Most care home companies passed through several private equity owners in the last two decades. Staff had many employers in a relatively short period.

This labyrinth of ruthless takeovers, debt leveraged deals and the sale and leaseback of property assets is not sustainable. It is a direct consequence of marketisation and privatisation of care dating back to the 1980s. The financial crisis only hastened the impending crisis. Once care, or any other service is commodified, service provision and employment conditions take a back seat to the circulation of money to pay off debt and a search for new business opportunities. It generates a steady stream of consultancy and legal fees.

Whilst some private care home chains had less than 6% of homes classified as poor or adequate by the Care Quality Commission in April 2010, Southern Cross had 18.5%, Care Tech 17%, Four Seasons 15.5% and BUPA 12.2% (Financial Times, 2011). A year later Southern Cross was served with improvement orders at 164 care homes, 28% of its homes in England (The Observer, 2011).

Staff turnover rates in residential care homes are 25.6% and 20.9% in the private and voluntary sector homes respectively, compared to 11.6% in the public sector. Median hourly pay rates are significantly lower in private and voluntary sector homes and the gap widens further when other payments, training and pensions are taken into account.

A review of Canadian and US research evidence of the link between ownership and care quality, concluded that outsourcing care to private companies is likely to result in inferior care, compared to the care delivered in public and non-profit facilities. The evidence indicated that the greater the profit, the worse the outcomes (McGregor and Ronald, 2011).

The same care model is used by private equity in the US. HCR Manor Care (Carlyle Group) arranged a $6.1bn sale and leaseback deal with HCP, a real estate investment trust, in 2011. HCP also acquired a 10% stake in Manor Care. The deal enabled Carlyle to pay off virtually all the outstanding debt incurred in the $6.3bn takeover of Manor Care in 2007 and to return some funds to investors (Financial Times, 2011).

The sale of local authority care homes, for example, Essex County Council to Excelcare (ESSU, 2007b), Tameside Council to Tameside Community Care Trust (Centre for Public Services, 1999) and Barnet Council to Catalyst/Fremantle (London Borough of Barnet, 2011b) resulted in major cuts in terms and conditions for staff.

In 2011, the Dilnot Commission on Funding of Care and Support recommended a capping of lifetime contribution of adult social care costs at £35,000 after which costs would be eligible for full support from the state. People would have to contribute between £7,000 and £10,000 for food and accommodation in residential care. The Commission had 'extensive discussions' with the financial services sector as the proposals would *"...create a new space for financial products"* linked to pensions, housing assets and insurance (ibid). Private equity and venture firms will be eager to develop new products. The 'sharing cost' model instead of fully funded state provision can only exacerbate the problems. Yet the government *"...found money very quickly to bail out the banks and bankers in one year at about 40 times the year-on-year care cost that will build up over the next 20 years"* (Jones, 2011).

Profiteering from public infrastructure

More and more evidence has revealed the high cost, excessive profits, inflexibility, poor design and flawed financial model of PPP/PFI projects.

154

It lends further support to the detailed analysis in *Global Auction of Public Assets* (Whitfield, 2010a). There are over 900 UK PFI and PPP projects, with health and education accounting for half the number of projects and a third of the total capital value (HM Treasury, 2011).

"The price of finance is significantly higher with a PFI. The financial cost of repaying the capital investment of PFI investors is therefore considerably greater than the equivalent repayment of direct government investment. We have not seen evidence to suggest that this inefficient method of financing has been offset by the perceived benefits of PFI from increased risk transfer. On the contrary there is evidence of the opposite" (House of Commons Treasury Committee, 2011).

These fundamental flaws in public infrastructure investment have been brought into sharper focus by the 2008-09 financial crisis, but have been evident for over fifteen years. The high degree of 'collusion' between the main political parties, civil servants, construction companies, banks, infrastructure funds and consultants has begun to fracture because the economic and financial flaws are increasingly evident. There are powerful vested interests in retaining PPPs as one of the UK's 'successful' exports.

Taxpayers are paying £20bn - £25bn above the government borrowing rate for the £53bn capital value of current PFI projects (Timmins, 2011). The cost of capital for a typical PPP project is currently over 8% – double the long-term government borrowing rate of approximately 4% (House of Commons Treasury Committee, 2011). According to the National Audit Office between £2.8bn - £4.0bn has been paid to financial consultants, lawyers and other advisers on PPP projects (Timmins, 2011).

Public spending cuts have further exposed the inflexibility of PPP contracts. Reductions in revenue budgets with ring-fenced PPP payments means that cuts are focused on other services. This is particularly acute in NHS hospitals where fixed PPP payments account for up to 18% of the revenue budget. The PPP financing structure *"… requires negotiation with the equity and debt holders before any substantial changes are made during the life of a contract. Debt and equity holders have little to gain from changing profitable contracts so will be unlikely to agree to changes unless they significantly enhance profitability"* (House of Commons Treasury Committee, 2011).

Each PPP project has a Special Purpose Vehicle company, which is jointly owned by the construction firm, bank and facilities management company leading the consortia. Most SPVs are financed by 80% - 90%

borrowing or debt and the remainder in equity divided between the consortia. A long-term contract, 25 – 50 years, is awarded following a procurement process that commits the private sector to design, build, finance and operate the facility. The payment mechanism requires the public body to pay a unitary charge to the SPV for the availability of facilities and the provision of support services.

High profits

Profits on the sale of equity in PPP project companies, once construction is completed, reached £2.2bn by the end of 2010, excluding the undisclosed profits obtained in the sale of secondary market infrastructure funds (Whitfield, 2011a). Average profit was 50.6% (compared to average operating profits in construction companies of 1.5% between 2003-09) with health (66.7%) and criminal justice (54.9%) having higher than average profits, and transport (47.1%) and education (34.1%) below average. More than ninety PFI projects in which UK infrastructure funds own between 50%-100% of the equity, are registered in tax havens. The sale of equity in PFI/PPP companies grew rapidly in the last decade particularly from 2003 and continued largely unaffected by the global financial crisis. Yet the Treasury and National Audit Office have failed to identify the true scale and profitability of PPP equity transactions. The House of Commons Public Accounts Committee recommended gain sharing in new and existing PPP projects, the Treasury to measure tax revenue from PFI deals and to ensure this is taken into account in project assessments. It recommended Freedom of Information be extended to private companies delivering public services (House of Commons Public Accounts Committee, 2011).

Ppps expanded primarily because most projects were off-balance sheet. In terms of Public Sector Net Debt, *"...about £5.1bn of PFI deals were recorded as on-balance sheet in the National Accounts"* (Office for Budget Responsibility, 2011). However, the capital liability of on and off-balance sheet PFI contracts, was closer to £40bn (ibid). Although PFI deals are recorded in the financial accounts of government departments, they are recorded off-balance sheet for National Accounts and statistical purposes.

Coalition policies

The Coalition Government remains committed to PPPs with 61 new projects in procurement at March 2011 with a total investment value of £7bn, in addition to the £60bn capital investment (2010 prices) under signed deals (House of Commons Treasury Committee, 2011). Limiting discussion to capital investment conceals the full cost of PPPs because it represents, on average, only 25% of the total cost. Estimated payments total £239bn under PPP projects at March 2011 (in nominal terms, undiscounted) (HM Treasury, 2011).

Several housing and waste PPP projects at the planning/procurement stage were terminated as part of public spending cuts since PPP projects are funded from revenue budgets. Building Schools for the Future (BSF), a £2.2bn PPP programme to renew the secondary school infrastructure in England, was terminated in July 2010 on the grounds that it was *"...unnecessarily complex, poor value for money and unaffordable in the economic climate"* (Department of Education, 2011). However, this decision had more to do with financing the building of 'free schools'. The new £2bn schools programme was launched in 2011.

Demands for PPP savings led to a forecast of £1.5bn savings from 495 operational projects, spread over the remaining 25-30 year contracts and was widely derided following a Treasury investigation into four pilot projects (HM Treasury, 2011a). Since construction costs are sunk, the savings focused on contract management costs such as energy and insurance, more efficient use of space by subletting or mothballing, and reviewing facilities management contracts. The Treasury report was bereft of savings figures, leading to the suspicion that the bulk of the savings will yet again come from cleaning, catering, building maintenance, window cleaning and ground maintenance services and not the construction companies, banks or infrastructure funds.

Global market

The UK's large PPP programme has played a key role in the formation of the global infrastructure market, together with construction companies, infrastructure funds and increased pension fund allocations to infrastructure assets. The UK accounted for over 67% of European PPP projects between 1990-2009 and 52.5% by value (Table 7).

The global infrastructure market has continued to grow with many more countries approving PPP legislation and establishing government PPP units (Whitfield, 2010). Although the flow of projects did slow from 2008 due to the global financial crisis, only one UK project, Manchester Waste, required additional state support from the Treasury Infrastructure Finance Unit. The flow of secondary market asset sales continued, an indicator of market confidence, albeit it at a slower rate after 2007, which rebounded in 2010 (Whitfield, 2011a).

Table 7: Top Ten Country share of European PPPs (1990-2009)

Country	% of number of projects	% of value of projects
United Kingdom	67.1	52.5
Spain	10.1	11.4
France	5.4	5.3
Germany	4.9	4.1
Portugal	3.1	7.0
Italy	2.4	3.3
Ireland	1.3	1.6
Netherlands	1.2	1.8
Greece - El	1.0	5.5
Hungary	0.7	2.3
Others	2.8	5.2
Total	100.0	100.0

Source: European Investment Bank, 2010.

National infrastructure Plan

The Coalition Government's National Infrastructure Plan 2010 is a vision for *"...unlocking private sector investment in the UK's infrastructure on an unprecedented scale"* (HM Treasury, 2010a). However, the plan has two fundamental flaws. Firstly, it is exclusively concerned with the economic infrastructure – the networks and systems in energy, transport, digital communication, flood protection, water and waste management. It has nothing to say about the social infrastructure – health, housing, education, sport and culture, public safety – and is, therefore, only half a plan. Both social and economic infrastructure investment support economic development, increase productivity, generate employment, create opportunities for production and supply chains in construction, manufacturing and services, and improve community well-being. A Green Investment Bank is planned, but financed by privatisation receipts.

Secondly, the plan contains no analysis or understanding of the infrastructure market and PPPs are barely mentioned. Although the plan does recognise the growing demand for networks, the need to mitigate climate change and the effect of globalisation on infrastructure funding, this is hardly a framework for 'unprecedented' private infrastructure investment.

Continued growth of strategic partnerships

Strategic Service-delivery Partnerships (SSPs) are 10-15 year multi-service £30m-£650m contracts between a public body and a private contractor. They are financed by local authority revenue budgets. Between 50 - 1,000 staff either transfer to a private contractor or are seconded to a Joint Venture Company (JVC) established between the local authority and contractor. Most contracts focus on corporate services such as ICT, human resources, payroll, revenues and benefits, financial and legal services, property management and other professional services. Strategic partnerships are growing in planning, highways and waste services (Table 8).

Table 8: UK Local government strategic partnerships

Sector	No. of contracts	Value £m	No. of staff
Local authority/Police ICT and corporate services	40	8,201	17,000
Local authority planning	4	445	780
Highway services	1	2,700	250
Waste services	5	1,800*	650**
Total	**50**	**13,146**	**18,680**

Notes: * Based on 3 contracts. ** Based on 1 contract. Source: ESSU PPP Database 2010.

Over forty projects provide ICT and corporate services or planning services with a total contract value of £8.6bn with over 17,800 staff transferred or seconded to private contractors or JVCs (Whitfield, 2010b). Other contracts have involved private sector takeover of local authority maintenance departments.

PPP projects for the sale and leaseback of government office buildings are likely to increase. Contracts normally include the purchase of the freehold premises, facilities management of the properties and services, letting vacant space and selling surplus property. At the end of the contract, departments/public bodies retain a right to occupy the buildings that they wish to remain in, with market leases.

Selling core universal services

Privatisation by public flotation or trade sale has continued but claims of "another wave" (Privatisation Barometer, 2011) or *"...privatisation is again sweeping the world"* (Plimmer, 2011) are inaccurate.

Privatisation revenue in 2009 and 2010 is distorted by government's selling assets acquired in the bailout of banks, financial and manufacturing companies in the financial crisis 2008-09 (Figure 5). For example, the US government sale of shares in Citigroup and General Motors and warrants in Wells Fargo Bank (securities that entitle the holder to buy the underlying stock of a company at a fixed exercise price for a specified period) accounted for 23% of global privatisation revenue in 2010. The sale of Royal Bank of Scotland assets was also included as privatisation revenue, for example, the £1.7bn sale of the RBS WorldPay credit card processing business to Advent International. The bank had to dispose of certain assets to comply with European Union state aid rules following its bailout by the UK government, which acquired an 81% stake in the bank.

Some large asset sales, such as the $22.1bn sale of a 15% stake in the Agricultural Bank of China, were only partial privatisations, as were other deals in China, India and Poland. The growth of infrastructure asset monetisation or selling long-term operational leases, between 50 – 99 years, is another development. US states and cities are examining about 35 deals worth $45bn including parking garages, airports, property and water supply (Whitfield, 2010a). These asset sales are technically privatisation, but they do not have the same economic and political impact as the privatisation of core public and welfare state assets.

Figure 5: Worldwide revenues from privatisation 1988-2010

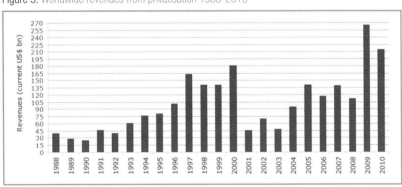

Source: Privatization Barometer

Privatisation programmes following bailouts
Three countries, Greece, Portugal and Ireland have privatisation programmes as part of the bailout conditions agreed with the IMF and European Union. Greece has agreed a five-year programme to sell €50bn of public assets by 2015. Some 31 state companies will be fully privatised and stakes sold in a further 23 companies. They include railways, telecoms, airports, ports, water utilities, electricity and natural gas companies, the state lottery, Hellenic Motorways and Hellenic Postbank and substantial land and property. Portugal's three-year €6bn programme includes the sale of energy and industrial holdings, rail freight transport, opening the postal service to private capital and re-privatising BPN bank, taken under state control in the financial crisis.

A review of the scope for the privatisation of 20 state-owned corporations and public bodies in Ireland included Dublin Bus, a 25% stake in Aer Lingus, airports, ports and six Irish banks bailed out since 2008 (McCarthy Review, 2011). However, the €5bn programme is unlikely to proceed very far given public opposition, the failures of earlier privatisations and the likely focus on the re-privatisation of the banks.

UK privatisation
The Coalition Government has endorsed New Labour's planned £16bn privatisation programme, which includes the Channel Tunnel Rail Link, National Air Traffic Services, Dartford Crossing, the Tote, the student loan portfolio, early repayment of student loans, local authority property sales, and the release of the 800MHz and 2.6GHz spectrum to support super-fast mobile services.

The Coalition immediately sold the High Speed 1 Channel Tunnel link to two Canadian pension funds. Borealis Infrastructure (Ontario Municipal Employees Retirement System) and the Ontario Teachers Pension Fund paid £2.1bn for a 30-year concession to run the 68-mile link between London and the Channel Tunnel. The government retains ownership of the tracks, stations and the freehold of the associated land.

The sale of the UK road network has again been raised. One proposal consists of voucher mutualisation (Social Market Foundation, 2010). Another, the tolling of new roads, a major programme of Motorway and A-road widening, with toll lanes financed by the private sector. The Highways Agency would be converted into 'Network Road' on a regulated utility model, partially or fully privatised and financed by diverting vehicle excise revenue for the exclusive maintenance of the road network (Confederation of British Industry, 2010).

Government debt write-offs and gap funding have played a key role in the privatisation of nationalised industries and council housing and are another cost to the public sector (Table 9). The privatisation of Royal Mail will bring the total to over £75bn since 1980. This excludes the transaction costs and the undervaluing of privatisation assets. The latter amounted to £13.4bn (at 1980-90 prices) by 1996 (Whitfield, 2001).

Table 9: Debt write-offs and discounts in privatisation

Year	Debt write-offs	Debt write-off (£bn)*
1981-1997	Privatisation of nationalized industries including telecoms, gas, electricity, water, coal, rail and other transport	28.3
2011-2012	Planned privatisation of Royal Mail – pension deficit to be transferred to state	8.0
	Sub total	**36.3**
	Value of discounts	
1988-1989 to 2009-2010	Gap funding for 295 council housing stock transfers of 1.4m homes	2.5
1980-2010	Sale of 1.9bn local authority and housing association homes @ £20,000 average discount	38.0
	Sub total	**40.5**
	Total	**76.8**

Notes: All financial data is shown in nominal prices and do not take account of inflation.
Source: Whitfield (1992 and 2001), Davis and Wigfield, (2010), Social Housing, May, 2010.

Planned Royal Mail privatisation

The Coalition Government's plan to privatise Royal Mail has been approved by Parliament, but the pension £4.5bn deficit will have to be taken over by the state (originally £8bn but reduced because of the government's plan to use the consumer price index instead of the retail price index) together with debt restructuring to significantly reduce the current £1.7bn debt.

Labour's Postal Services Act 2000 established the Postal Services Commission and a regulatory framework that *"...facilitates a competitive and innovative postal market"*, following the 1997 European Union Postal Services Directive to liberalise Europe's state-run postal services (Postal Services Commission, 2004). Royal Mail lost its 350-year monopoly over the delivery of letters in January 2006, ahead of other European countries. The regulatory agency, supposedly the guardian of the universal service, used its resources to create the conditions and regulations to increase private sector involvement in the postal service, which ultimately undermined the universal service.

Forestry Commission Estate
Coalition plans to privatise forests in England were abandoned in 2010 following intense political opposition. 15% of forestry land was to be sold to raise £100m with the remainder to be sold or managed by charitable organisations and civil society organisations, or leased to commercial companies.

Sale of council housing continues
Council housing has witnessed the largest asset sale (nearly two million homes sold to tenants in England between 1980-2009), the largest subsidised privatisation (£10.6bn in discounts since 1998 plus £20bn sale costs over 30 years (Housing Statistics, 2009) and the largest transfer of assets to third sector organisations (1.4m homes transferred to housing associations between 1988-2008) requiring nearly £5.0bn subsidies (Pawson, 2010). The sale of over 1m homes (or nearly 80% of stock transfers) took place under New Labour. It had one of the largest diversions of public investment from local government to the third sector, as public money for housing improvement was redirected to housing associations from 1974. Housing associations were deemed more efficient and innovative, although not a scrap of evidence was ever produced to support this assertion.

The Coalition Government has launched the final stage to try to decimate council housing in England. Right-to-buy is being revived with bigger discounts for two million council tenants. It claims the proceeds, once housing debt is paid off, will finance 100,000 new homes. But there are no guarantees, and the vast majority of new homes will not be council housing.

The Decent Homes programme was designed to bring council and housing association housing to a 'decent' standard but New Labour restricted the options for increased investment to large-scale voluntary transfer (LSVT), the private finance initiative (PFI), and arms length management organisation (ALMO) (Centre for Public Services, 2004). 61 ALMOs manage nearly one million homes. The Coalition government pledged that £2bn Decent Homes funding, available between 2011-14, would be allocated on the basis of need, not the organisational model (DCLG, 2010). Ealing, Hillingdon, Newham and Tower Hamlets have transferred or are considering transferring their ALMO back to the local authority.

Tote sold
The Horserace Totalisator Board (the Tote) was sold to UK bookmaker Betfred in 2011 for £265m (net £180m after debt and pension commitments, and shared equally between the government and racing industry).

Sale of nationalised banks
The bailout of UK banks in the financial crisis resulted in full state ownership of Northern Rock Bank and Bradford & Bingley plc (branches and savings accounts sold to Abbey in 2008) plus 83% of the Royal Bank of Scotland and 41% of Lloyds Bank Group.

Although Northern Rock Bank was nationalised, the government considers the reverse of this process as 'divestment', not privatisation. The Treasury created UK Financial Investments with a remit *"...to manage the shareholdings in RBS and Lloyds as if it were an institutional investor, is designed to protect taxpayer value by insulating the banks from political interference and enhancing other investors' confidence. It involves, however, the deliberate restriction of the influence that the scale of its holdings would normally provide"* (National Audit Office, 2010a). The Coalition has rejected proposals to mutualise Northern Rock.

A return to share giveaways to employees and the public is likely with the planned privatisation of Royal Mail and the sale of government bank shareholdings. Thatcher claimed share ownership was 'real public ownership' and Blair briefly promoted a 'stakeholder economy', but this was abandoned after it failed to gain traction. The proportion of shares ownership by UK individuals has plummeted from 54% in 1963 to 10.2% in 2008, despite the free shares and 'ownership' rhetoric (National Statistics, 2010c). Share ownership by the 'rest of the world' has grown from 7% to 41.5% in the same period. The remainder are owned by insurance companies, pension funds, banks and other financial institutions, with the public sector and charities owning just 1.1% and

0.8% respectively in 2008. Another share giveaway is not going to change this ownership profile.

Fragmenting public provision

Other examples of the fragmentation of public provision include planning and economic development, criminal justice and the Work Programme.

Abolition of regional bodies and growth by deregulation

Regional Development Agencies (RDAs) and regional spatial strategies are being abolished (at a cost of £1.5bn) as the Coalition seeks to localise economic development and has adopted policies to 'remove barriers to growth', encourage 'private sector led economic recovery' with a 'more even distribution of economic development' or 'rebalancing'. RDAs have been replaced by Local Enterprise Partnerships (LEPS), locally funded replacement of the centrally funded Regional Development Agencies, Enterprise Zones (tax breaks), a Regional Growth Fund (£1.4bn over three years, a fraction of RDA budgets), and deregulation of planning with a new 50-page National Planning Policy Framework (NPPF) replacing 1,000 pages of planning policy guidance and best practice.

The Coalition's growth strategy is premised on the UK's fall in international competitiveness rankings citing tax rates, regulation, access to finance and planning as problematic. Consequently the growth strategy 'ambitions' are *"...to create the most competitive tax system in the G20; to make the UK one of the best places in Europe to start, finance and grow a business; to encourage investment and exports as a route to a more balanced economy; and to create a more educated workforce that is the most flexible in Europe"* (HM Treasury and Department for Business, Innovation & Skills, 2011).

Enterprise Zones have been rehabilitated by the Coalition, with 22 designated to date in local enterprise partnerships. Zones benefit from a 100% business rate discount worth up to £275,000 over five years; business rate growth for 25 years will be retained and shared by local authorities in the LEP area to support economic development; simplified planning regulations; and superfast broadband, if necessary, publicly funded. Although nine of the eleven zones announced in the 2011 Budget are in the Midlands and North, eight of the next group of eleven zones were in the south and west of England.

Deregulation policies lead to low skill, low paid jobs that will not be available to local people because employers will prefer casualised, unorganised migrant labour, paying below minimum wage rates with few benefits that local people would not tolerate. Over 110,000 care workers in England are being paid less than the minimum wage, according to the Skills For Care database. It is frequently environmentally damaging as companies adopt a minimalist approach to compliance and public monitoring is reduced, largely as a result of spending cuts. Planned cuts in local authority regulatory services (environmental health, trading standards and licensing) average 8.8% in 2011/12 compared with an overall cut of 5.7% in local authority service delivery budgets (Local Better Regulation Office, 2011).

The NPPF proposes 'the presumption in favour of sustainable development' which is likely to be highjacked for short-term business interests. The Coalition government want the default answer to development to be 'yes', thus creating a developer's charter that conflicts with localism policies. Claims that the planning system is slow, costly, a drag on economic growth and forces house prices up have been rigorously refuted by planners. They concluded: *"The private sector has only ever been able to contribute around 150-200,000 new homes a year across Great Britain. Until the government ended mass council housing in the 1980s, the public sector helped to almost double this. If public sector housing had continued there might be at least 2 million more homes now"* (Royal Town Planning Institute, 2011). The NPPF removes local authority powers to require developers to meet affordable home targets.

Criminal justice

The Ministry of Justice Business Plan 2011-2015 *"...commits the Department to creating a functioning market in the provision of legal aid, offender management and rehabilitation"* (Ministry of Justice, 2011a). The National Offender Management Service (NOMS) had earlier been set up to commission services, undertake 'performance testing' of prisons and probation services, and estate rationalisation to increase competition and to *"...dramatically increase the level of contestability in the system"* (National Offender Management Service, 2005).

Birmingham Prison is the first publicly run prison outsourced to a private firm following a tendering process started by New Labour. Birmingham and the new Featherstone 2 prison in Wolverhampton were outsourced to G4S for 15 years and Serco retained their Doncaster prison contract. The HM Prison Service retained the smaller Buckley Hall contract. Labour originally agreed to market-test five prisons but Wellingborough was withdrawn because it *"...could not produce significant improvements without considerable financial investment"* (Ministry of Justice, 2011b). G4S now operate six prisons in the UK, Serco six (plus a Young Offenders Institution, a Secure Training Centre and two Immigration Removal Centres). Kalyx Services (Sodexo) operates four prisons.

Work Programme

A joint venture between Ingeus UK (formerly known as WorkDirections) and Deloitte, the accounting and consultancy firm, won seven of the 40 welfare-to-work seven-year contracts in 18 regions awarded in April 2011. Serco (2 contracts) and A4E (5 contracts) will have a smaller share of the programme than currently. Newcastle College was the only public sector bidder to win (2 contracts) and only two voluntary/non-profit organisations were successful, Rehab and Careers Development Group. The plan is to finance the £3bn-£5bn programme using benefit savings by getting two million people into paid employment, with contractors paid mainly on a payment-by-results basis but this is a very high risk strategy for the government, contractors and the unemployed.

Auditing public bodies

The planned abolition of the Audit Commission has led to the outsourcing of the Audit Practice, which audits 70% of public bodies. In another example of fragmentation, the work has been divided into ten contracts in four regions with a total annual value of £89.4m in 2012-13 (Audit Commission, 2011).

Restructuring employment

In 2010 the Coalition Government withdrew the civil service and local government Codes of Practice designed to prevent a two-tier workforce by requiring new staff to be employed on the same terms and conditions as transferred staff. The private sector has consistently exploited a loophole in that the transfer regulations do not specify the period to which TUPE applies. This has enabled private and voluntary sector contractors to employ new staff on lower terms and conditions, thus creating a two-tier workforce. The government is also reviewing the TUPE legislation and continued access to the local government pension scheme by staff outsourced to private or voluntary contractors. There are significant differences in the quality of public and private sector pensions with the private sector rapidly replacing final salary schemes with money purchase schemes, coupled with enrolling restrictions.

The government is proposing to extend the qualifying period against unfair dismissal from one to two years. The TUC estimates that three million workers will cease to have protection. Claimants fees and deposits may be introduced.

Outsourcing effectively means that public sector workers are being forced to bare the risks of changes to terms and conditions of service, workplace conditions and to staff consultation and representation. Staff subject to transfer have little or no choice, no involvement in the decision-making process which impacts on their lives, careers, incomes, representation and trade union organisation. An Employment Risk Matrix shows that the secondment of staff has 19% in the no-risk and 81% in the low-risk category compared to 48% and 33% respectively in the high and medium-risk category in a TUPE staff transfer (ESSU, 2010a).

The proportion of employees in trade unions in the public sector is nearly three times that of the private sector, 64% compared to 22% (2004 Workplace Employment Relations Survey). Outsourcing and transfer of services fragments trade union organisation because it increases the number of employers, negotiating machinery and consultation; disperses employees to new work locations; and factures trade union interests. Furthermore, private contractors and arms length companies frequently limit trade union representation to staff directly employed by the company. This may result in less experienced representatives and weaker trade union organisation. Many public sector trade union branches organise, represent and negotiate with an increasing variety of employers in the public, private and voluntary sectors. This can fragment resources, dilute responses and widen agendas thus forcing more selective action (Chapter 7).

The threat of near-shoring (usually in Eastern Europe) or offshoring results in a direct loss of jobs. Authorities that do not specify that service delivery must be located within the local authority area, allow contractors to relocate to regions or countries with lower wages and/or corporate tax rates. The TUC 2011 Congress resolved to oppose the use of the World Trade Organisation's Mode 4 provisions, which allow transnational companies to bring in local labour to work temporarily in the EU (TUC, 2011b). Mode 4 allows for the negation of domestic legislation that protects workers, collective agreements and trade union organising. It leads to the exploitation of migrant workers, displaces existing workers, and undercuts terms and conditions.

The commodification of services and labour (Chapter 2) requires the reorganisation of work, staffing levels, job descriptions, terms and conditions and grading structures to meet the requirements of marketised services. Service delivery is stripped of 'non-conformist' working practices to minimise operational costs. Job descriptions are adjusted to reflect working practices and responsibilities so that skill levels, job descriptions and pay rates are matched with minimum staffing levels. This optimises the way tasks are performed, simplifying jobs to minimise skills, training and wages. 'Front line' and 'back office' functions are separated to identify the minimum skills, training and professional responsibilities required for each function and the required level of management.

Eroding democratic control

Democratic accountability is being fundamentally eroded. Localism, partnerships and other participatory mechanisms simply mask this reality and offer little to mitigate the impact.

Greater use of procurement and a contract culture in the public sector leads to increased secrecy and reduced disclosure. Greater access to general public spending data is only marginally useful if the real information upon which public policy decisions are based is kept secret. The procurement process inevitably imposes certain constraints on the availability of information but this does not justify the blanket use of 'commercial confidentiality'. Increased secrecy, in effect, nullifies transparency and disclosure. For example, Sandwell Council posted a website notice for Cabinet meetings in June and August 2010 which discussed the selection of a preferred bidder 25-year £650m environmental and waste services contract. It merely stated *"[t]he report contains information which cannot be made publicly available under Access to Information legislation. Consequently the information cannot be released. The Council would like to apologise to you for an inconvenience that the unavailability of this information may cause you."* The Council could have provided significantly more information without even considering confidentiality. Serco Group plc was selected as the preferred bidder at the meeting. This firm typically claims it is committed to 'trust', 'transparency' and other corporate responsibility 'values'. This is not an isolated example.

Freedom of Information requests can sometimes lead to the provision of some information but procurement information is required during the tendering process, not after decisions have been made and contracts awarded.

Weakened accountability

Policy decisions are increasingly made by Boards of Directors with relevant decision-making taking place in closed sessions with confidential reports. The directors of leisure and community trusts, urban regeneration companies, Local Enterprise Partnerships, arms length housing management companies, irrespective of whether they are elected members, tenants/service users or independent members, have a legal duty to take decisions in the interests of the company first and foremost. The public interest or community needs come second. Furthermore, contract performance, service provision, financial matters, employment policies and other important matters are removed from directly accountable governance structures to indirect and semi-public/private bodies. Shared services or joint public-public projects raise new issues about the extension of accountability across neighbouring authorities.

New accountability issues arise when privatisation fails. For example, Railtrack was replaced by Network Rail that now owns and operates the UK's rail infrastructure. It is a not-for-dividend company so that surpluses are retained to improve the railway network. *"We are directly accountable to our members and regulated by the Office of Rail Regulation (ORR),"* but the members are 24 train operating companies, 67 members of the public and the Department for Transport! Similarly, when National Express walked away from the east coast rail franchise in November 2009, Directly Operated Railways Limited, wholly owned by the Department for Transport, established a new subsidiary company, East Coast Mainline Company Limited ('East Coast'), to operate the line until a new private sector franchisee takes over. In effect, there is a degree of creeping nationalisation without democratic accountability.

Public policy decisions are increasingly made, or are heavily influenced, by business involvement in the formation of local, national and international public policy decision-making. The transfer of services to arms length companies is swiftly followed by the formation of national associations to represent the interests of each company model. For example, the National Federation of ALMOs and the Association of Local Enterprise Partnerships are in effect trade bodies that lobby to promote these organisations irrespective of other public policy interests and to expand their role by taking over more functions. Trade bodies, such as the Employment Related Services Association (ERSA), provide a similar function for the new breed of private and voluntary sector contractors.

Management in control
New public management has resulted in increased management influence in the policy making process. Options appraisals and business

cases are rarely challenged and senior management regard the procurement process as a technical and legal process under their control. Elected members are presented with a *fait accompli* at the contract award stage. Scrutiny is a sham because it usually fails to ask the relevant questions. It leads to the rubber-stamping of proposals in many authorities. The increased complexity of contracts and wider use of consultants and lawyers, particularly in PPPs and strategic partnerships, leads to increasing managerialism with less political understanding of projects and control in decision making. New public management has ensured the near-seamless continuity between Conservative, New Labour and Coalition Governments in the UK.

Partnership politics leads to an erosion of democratic accountability. For example, strategic partnerships usually establish a two- or three-tier structure of strategic, management and operational boards that involve a handful of elected members and directors of the contracting company on the strategic board. The vast majority of elected members usually know little or nothing about the policy issues or the decision making process. The increased use of task forces and reviews under a 'partnership' umbrella engage business 'leaders' and representatives from other unaccountable public bodies in the policy making process. The growth of arms length Urban Regeneration Companies and Local Asset Backed Vehicles (a partnership between the public and private sectors, with the creation of a limited liability company) add to the erosion of accountability. Local Enterprise Partnerships (LEPs) usurp local authorities in the establishment of enterprise zones. They allow market forces to replace regional planning and promote private sector led development.

The increased use of management consultants reinforces managerial control of options appraisals, business cases and the procurement process and the establishment of commercial values.

Depoliticisation occurs as a result of the lack of rigorous evaluation of options appraisals, business cases and contract proposals combined with the failure to fully assess the impact of policies and projects through comprehensive costs benefit analysis. This is further compounded by the failure of most public bodies to rigorously monitor the performance and policy impacts of contracts.

Flawed localism

The focus on localism creates the impression that key decisions can be made at street, community and neighbourhood level. Some can, but most of the important decisions cannot be made at this level because of wider public interest objectives and priorities. Participation of service users and community organisations and staff/trade unions in design, planning and delivery of services is very limited. They are rarely involved in the procurement process, except in some regeneration projects.

The focus on localism is designed to mask the increasing centralisation of decision-making. The claims of devolution or subsidiarity are false, because they are not matched by the local power to tax, borrow or to regulate. Thus new 'leadership' models such as elected mayors and participative budgeting have little practical value. The devolution of powers to the local level will be undermined if they occur in the absence of parallel changes in local democratic governance. Community budgets represent a tiny percentage of local authority expenditure and whilst they increase flexibility into local or neighbourhood spending decisions, they are not significant and rarely represent added value.

This chapter has only summarised how key public services are being financialised, personalised, marketised and privatised. Some of these proposals may fail or be diverted or watered down so that they are less effective. Many positive initiatives are under way and will hopefully help to stem the neoliberal thrust of Coalition policies and provide the basis for alternative strategies.

To summarise the four key identifiable trends, they are:

- The continued establishment of national and local agencies to commission services that remove client and contract management from direct political control.
- The break-up of public sector provision into stand-alone organisations and businesses ready to be reconsolidated into privately managed/owned groups.
- The commitment to create markets irrespective of the costs and consequences.
- The continued reliance on public money, irrespective of increased charges, personal top-ups and social investment.

CHAPTER 9

Big society contracting

New Labour's promises of devolution, participation, empowerment and public sector delivery contracts for voluntary organisations and social enterprises have been ramped up with the Coalition's big society. The commissioning model of government is a 'wolf in sheep's clothing' because it will lead to private monopoly, commercialised services, with agendas dominated by the vested interests of private contractors (Whitfield, 2011b). Big society is dependent on outsourcing and is hypocritical in promising a new era for civil society, whilst imposing severe public spending cuts, and policies that will ensure only marginal change and further centralise power.

This chapter examines the political economy of voluntary organisations and social enterprises and their role in the delivery of public services, the impact of competition and the contract culture, the myth of empowerment, and the future of advocacy and organising.

The Coalition government has increased financial support for the creation of social enterprises, cooperatives and mutual organisations to take over the delivery of public services. The new Big Society Capital Bank, funded by £400m in dormant bank accounts and £200m commercial loans from the big four banks, will facilitate investment by bringing *"...its own resources to bear as a 'wholesaler' of capital and by attracting funding from charitable foundations, institutional investors, companies and private individuals in support of social sector intermediary organisations"* (Big Society Capital, 2011). It will not fund frontline services. A National Citizen Service will engage 16 year-olds in volunteering placement programmes. Five hundred full-time training places and 4,500 part-time/volunteer places in community organiser training will support the formation of neighbourhood groups. The government aims to devolve power from central to local government, with greater local financial autonomy.

The Localism Bill is intended to give communities the 'right to challenge' the provision of services by local authorities, and the 'right to buy' and manage local facilities, both intended to accelerate the rate of public sector 'spin-outs'. Shared equity in social housing and co-operative ownership of leisure centres, art galleries and parks will be expanded. Finally, more financial information and local crime statistics will be disclosed. The Coalition claims a commitment to equal opportunities, but is looking to water down, or to withdraw, the socio-economic impact assessment provisions in the Equality Act 2010. It has withdrawn voluntary protection for new staff in contracted services and implemented regressive public spending cuts, thus widening the gap between rich and poor.

The foundations for 'big society' were laid by New Labour. They had established a £65m Futurebuilders Fund (loans, grants and professional support to voluntary organisations, to bid for and deliver public service contracts); the Capacitybuilders Fund, for capacity building of voluntary organisations (£85m); and the Communitybuilders Fund, to build more active community organisations (£70m). The previous government prepared the Social Enterprise Action Plan to support formation of social enterprises and commissioned the Quirk Review that led to the formation of the Asset Transfer Unit to support community organisations taking over ownership and management of community facilities. The Department of Trade and Industry set up a Social Enterprise Unit in 2001 (later rebranded as the Office of the Third Sector, now the Office for Civil Society) followed by policy, procurement and legislative initiatives to remove barriers and create Community Interest Companies. NHS Commissioning, the client/contractor split in community health service and a Department of Health £100m fund to support social enterprises, led to some social enterprises in health and social care following the 'Right to Request' social enterprise proposals. With the policy and funding infrastructure already in place, the Coalition only had to widen the powers and rebrand.

In another development, the Coalition government launched 16 Community Budget pilots to *"...pool and align various national and local funding strands into a single local funding pot for tackling social problems around families with complex needs"* (Department for Communities, 2011). They hope to *"...drive down overhead costs by removing the bureaucratic financial restrictions." "...[T]he country's most chaotic families"* are claimed to cost central and local agencies up to £330,000 a year (ibid). The scheme will be extended to all areas and to 'other problems'.

European context

There were 240,000 co-operatives in the EU-25 in 2005 with 143m members and employing 3.7m people (Centre for Research and Information on the Public, Social and Co-operative Economy, 2007). Co-operatives are established in France, Italy, Portugal, Spain, Belgium,

Ireland and Sweden. For example, 7,000 co-operatives provide social care, health and employment services in Italy; childcare co-operatives account for 6.7% of pre-school day nursery provision in Sweden; and co-operative schools have increased in Spain (Bland, 2011). This 'social economy' (co-operatives, social enterprises and non-profit organisations) should not be confused with the European Social Model which nurtures fundamental social rights, social protection (universal systems, wealth redistribution and progressive taxation), social dialogue, social and employment regulation and state responsibility for full employment, public services and social cohesion (European Trade Union Confederation, 2006).

Political economy of the voluntary sector

The voluntary sector in the UK comprises many local formal and informal organisations, traditionally described as community groups and voluntary organisations, involved in local health, social care, learning and leisure, sports and cultural activities. Many of these organisations are small and fall under the radar of national and city-wide surveys of the sector (Cabinet Office, 2010). About 600,000 informal community groups operate with limited resources and volunteers. Most have little or no connection to local authorities or voluntary sector agencies. Community and voluntary organisations have a vital role in providing care, support, activities, advice, and advocacy, and are mostly self-funded and run by committed people. They would have been groups eligible to apply for small support grants.

The activities of voluntary organisations, charities and social enterprises are diverse with 13% of organisations carrying out community development and mutual aid, 24% delivery of services (social housing, healthcare, day centre, counselling, community safety) and 14% buildings and/or facilities, such as community centres, village halls, and religious buildings (Cabinet Office, 2011e). Advocacy, campaigning, representation, information or research was reported by 9% of organisations. A wide range of other activities included provision of advice to individuals (8%), accessing services or benefits (5%), making grants (12%), advancing cultural awareness (6%) and religious and/or spiritual welfare (11%). The survey excluded many small community groups, sports clubs and societies, and informal voluntary activity provided outside of a formal organisational structure.

Neoliberalism and the financial crisis have led to the re-examination of the boundaries between the state and the role of community and voluntary sectors in public service provision.

The government expanded the national survey of voluntary organisations and social enterprise organisations to include charities, community groups, clubs and societies, non-profit organisations, housing associations, trusts, co-operatives and mutuals, and faith groups. The definition includes, for example, housing associations and NHS Foundation Trusts alongside very small local community groups with few resources. The definition of civil society includes a myriad of organisations such as political bodies, think tanks, as well as national and international campaign organisations that are clearly not part of a community or voluntary sector. The claim that trade associations, professional bodies and private schools are part of civil society is bizarre (Community Sector Coalition, 2011). Trade unions are a key part of civil society, although they are rarely acknowledged.

Political motives lie behind the government's embrace of civil society. Widening the definition has led to the blurring of distinctions, causes confusion and allows the government to claim credit for changes in the sector and to 'pick and mix' promotional examples from the initiatives that it values.

A more useful approach defines civil society as having overlapping 'spheres of activity'. Firstly, local informal community/voluntary groups that provide a wide range of care, support and fund-raising activities. Secondly, many community organisations are established to represent specific interests – tenants, patients and/or to provide sport and recreational activities or to represent an area facing regeneration. Thirdly, city/regional voluntary organisations provide advice, care and other services. Fourthly, large social enterprises such as housing associations, foundation hospitals and leisure trusts operate at city or sub-regional level. Fifthly, city-wide federations and alliances of local community organisations, trade union branches, trades councils, women's organisations, and local branches of national NGOs such as Friends of the Earth, Greenpeace. The final group consists of trusts, foundations and charities, most of which are regional and national, and the Big Lottery Fund.

The structure and financing of the spheres of activity limit the degree to which community and voluntary organisations engage in political activity. Virtually all charities, trusts and foundations are prohibited from funding political activities and many community and voluntary organisations consider political activity, only in the context of being party political. The broad span of political activity by tenants' associations, community campaigns, trade unions, public sector alliances, environmental groups and the host of other organisations should be valued and not downgraded. Hypocrisy is rife since the Coalition's big society plans for civil society and the voluntary sector's enthusiasm for contracting are overtly political. Furthermore, the idea that voluntary organisations and social enterprises are the prime source of 'innovation' must be challenged. Tenants, service users and public service frontline staff have long been a rich source of ideas and proposals. The public sector's good record of innovation should be acknowledged and built on.

Voluntary organisations and social enterprises face cost pressures from the effects of public spending cuts on grants, contracts and funding from trusts, foundations and the corporate sector. The demand for greater efficiency and productivity is certain to lead to the consolidation of contracts and organisational mergers. Voluntary organisations are under pressure to take on more responsibility with fewer staff and to engage more volunteers. They are being encouraged, if not coerced, to bid for, or take over responsibility for more and more services. But the contracting process is dominated by voluntary sector entrepreneurs, seeking opportunities for aggrandisement, consultants diversifying into business advice to mutual and social enterprises, consortia and hubs, or to become agents and brokers. They and national bodies, such as the Association of Chief Executives of Voluntary Organisations, support the right to bid, to buy and the contracting agenda. But the large number of informal community and voluntary organisations, operating on a shoestring with volunteers, have virtually no connection with the business of contracting.

There are other dangers. The interests of paid staff and professionalisation could come to dominate the sector. The search for funding from the conservative charity and trust sector could result in a rightward shift in the politics of community and civil society campaigning, or community organisations face being increasingly marginalised from funding streams. And service delivery issues could come to dominate the sector agenda at the expense of identifying the cause and effect of poverty and inequalities.

Staff in voluntary organisations must be rigorously defended and represented, but this should not prevent a fundamental examination of the role of voluntary organisations. The status quo is no more acceptable in the voluntary/social enterprise sector than it is in the public sector. There are contradictions between values and expectations. For example, the idea of the London Underground or city tram services being operated by volunteers is unthinkable, but it is 'acceptable' that mental health patients and the elderly can be transported by volunteer drivers! The Coalition government claims it wants a fundamental shift in social values so that families, neighbours and communities take over more responsibility for a wider range of care, education, recreation and cultural activities. Extending social solidarity has benefits, but the current approach is exploitative and will not achieve the objectives. The neoliberal enthusiasm for 'behaviour change' assumes that supply-side reforms are 'exhausted' and substantive savings will only come about from demand-led change, such as changing service users' values and behaviour, personal budgets and co-production (New Local Government Network, 2011).

Social enterprises

There are three basic social enterprise models. A *mutual organisation* is owned by and run for the benefit of members and raises funds from its members or customers. Surpluses are reinvested in the mutual, which has a one-member-one-vote system. The governance structure must reflect the different groups of members. Employees or customers are the primary members of *worker* or *consumer co-operatives*. Surpluses have to be redistributed to members or reinvested in the co-operative. A *social enterprise* is a business with social objectives. Surpluses are reinvested in the business, or in the community. Non-profit legal models include a Community Interest Company, Industrial and Provident Society and a Company limited by guarantee or shares. The main organisation or subsidiaries may have charitable status.

The median turnover of UK social enterprises was £240,000 in 2009/10, with 8% having an annual turnover of over £8m per annum (Social Enterprise UK, 2011). A little over half reported being profitable, 19% broke even in 2009 and 23% made a loss in the last financial year. Trading with the general public accounted for 37% of income followed by 18% and 13% trading with the public and private sectors respectively with public sector grant or core funding accounting for 9% of income. Just over half (51%) of social enterprises employed between 1-9 people, 19% employed 10-49, and 12% had more than fifty staff (ibid). Training/support (18%), housing (14%), education (14%), retail/wholesale (12%), other services (11%) and youth (11%) were the main income-generating activities.

It is important to distinguish between social enterprises in manufacturing and service industries, and the delivery of public services.

Transferring privately-owned and managed manufacturing and service businesses to the non-profit sector and collective ownership can be considered a progressive move, but transferring public services from local authorities and the NHS to social enterprises is ultimately a regressive and damaging step. In this situation, social enterprises are being used to shrink the public sector, to transfer financial, employment and operational risks to new organisations and to reduce the security and flexibility of service. Furthermore, history shows they are essentially a medium/long term pathway to full privatisation by the private sector (see Chapter 10).

Recent governments have supported the growth of social enterprises, particularly ethnic minority-owned, women-owned and small and medium-sized enterprises. However, outsourcing services and functions to these organisations is no different, in principle, from outsourcing to a private contractor, although there may be some advantages to social enterprise rather than private sector provision of public services.

It is frequently assumed that mutual, co-operative or social enterprise organisations are closely controlled by the workforce and service users, who are directly involved in the design and planning of service delivery. This requires two conditions to be met concerning democratic control and workforce/user participation. They may be possible, particularly if radical new measures for accountability, participation and disclosure are introduced that are meaningful and sustainable. But this is not automatic just because they are social enterprises.

Because an organisation has a particular legal status, and uses the standard big society language on its website and publicity, does not automatically make it democratic, participatory, accountable or a good employer. For example, a leading leisure trust is registered as an Industrial and Provident Society, guided by a board of trustees with representatives of users, workforce and the Council appointed annually at the general meeting. However, it is a management-controlled organisation that has turned into a large leisure contractor, having adopted the bidding strategies and employment practices of private contractors (ESSU, 2008b).

Economic impact of transfers

Outsourcing, whether to a social enterprise or a private contractor, changes the provider, but has limited economic effect if the number of staff and employment conditions remain largely the same. There is no change in the total economic activity, because service delivery and jobs

179

transfer from one employer to another. Gross Value Added (GVA) is a measure of the total economic activity in a region and is an important indicator of the overall health of a region's economy. Local area GVA, collected by workplace rather than place of residence, is calculated as the sum of incomes earned from the production of goods and services within an area. Although a social enterprise may be a new organisation, there is no additional economic contribution if its main business is the delivery of public services previously delivered by in-house staff or a private or voluntary sector contractor. If social enterprises increase efficiency and productivity, they may make a small technical contribution to economic growth in the long term, but this is unlikely to be noticeable locally and may be accompanied by reduced employment.

Post-transfer changes in staffing levels and terms and conditions, virtually always downward, will have a negative economic effect. Furthermore, once outside the public sector, terms and conditions are subject to stronger market pressures. An increase in the local sourcing of goods and services would improve sustainability, but have marginal economic impact because, unlike labour costs, they account for a small proportion of annual expenditure. Furthermore, the abolition of the Code of Practice to prevent the two-tier workforce and further deregulation of TUPE, pensions and equalities, together with the drive to increase volunteering, will drive down terms and conditions and reduce the economic impact of civil society.

Marketisation and privatisation of services generates very little, if any, growth. Central and local government, NHS and other public services transfer from one sector to another, with relatively small changes in the cost of services, when transaction costs are taken into account. Long-term cost reductions in labour intensive service inevitably come at the expense of jobs and/or cuts in terms and conditions. So the client's economic gain is at the expense of the economic loss of the contractor's staff and spending in the local economy. It is a zero-sum game.

The growth of social enterprises could be exploited by future governments, just as housing associations and leisure trusts have been used to create pathways to further transfers and privatisation. The transfer of responsibility for housing improvement work from local authorities to housing associations in the 1970s created the vehicle for the subsequent privatisation of local authority housing stock. Similarly, in Falkirk, Highland and other Scottish local authorities, leisure trusts have provided the vehicle for the transfer of libraries, community education and other functions to community trusts. It is, therefore, conceivable that social enterprises could become a surrogate in-house bid when services are re-tendered. This will be hastened by claims of the lack of resources and borrowing restrictions for public investment, leading to claims there is no option but to rely on private finance or social investment.

Trusts, social enterprises and trading companies usually lease assets from the public sector. Lease-holders are required to maintain facilities, but responsibility for improvement and replacement is retained by the public sector. The continued transfer of services, combined with the wider sale of public sector property, could ultimately lead to the disposal of leases or freehold sale of key public assets. This would mirror the US model of asset monetisation where assets are leased on very long-term contracts to the private sector and are effectively privatised (Whitfield, 2010a). The state could, in effect, become a real estate holding organisation as a prelude to privatisation of social infrastructure.

The write-off of public debt is another cost. The Byker Community Housing Trust in Newcastle, a Grade ll listed building, required at £44m housing debt write-off as part of the financial package (Newcastle City Council, 2011).

Growth through tax avoidance

The growth of leisure trusts arose, not from entrepreneurship, but from tax avoidance, primarily the reduction or non-payment of VAT and business rates, as local authorities sought budget savings. However, a different picture would emerge about efficiency and public costs if the costs of financial support for voluntary organisations and social enterprises, the Office for Civil Society, debt write-offs and subsidies required in transfers, are taken into account.

The financial crisis has made access to borrowing extremely difficult, even for social enterprises with assets. The social enterprise sector will requires continued government assistance and public subsidy, but runs the risk of falling foul of EU state aid policies. Private contractors are almost certain to lodge complaints if they lose out to subsidised social enterprises in the tendering process.

Competition and contracting

The conservative leadership of most trusts and foundations, guided by their 'social' objectives, reinforce policies and projects that promote market-based solutions. It has traditionally been very difficult to obtain funding for projects with trade union involvement, radical community action or for small community organisations competing against established groups. The marketisation and privatisation of public services is certain to lead to a growing demand from community and trade union organisations for in-house, non-market, public service solutions, although changes in foundation or trust funding attitudes are unlikely in the short/medium term.

Voluntary organisations and social enterprises currently believe they are going to be the beneficiaries of the outsourcing of public services. However, a raft of changes are taking place that are expanding and consolidating the dominant role of national and transnational companies in the delivery of public services and infrastructure. The scope for social enterprises is relatively limited and will likely remain so. The opportunities for social enterprises to expand to become the public sector equivalent of the retail sector's John Lewis Partnership are negligible. It was no accident that only two out of 40 Department for Work and Pensions contracts in the £3bn - £5bn work programme were awarded to voluntary organisation contractors in 2011.

The vast majority of social enterprises do not have the resources and capability to tender and deliver large multi-service, long-term contracts valued between £30m and £600m. Many contracts require the formation of consortia with banks and other financial institutions, plus specialist providers. Even if a social enterprise became a consortia member, the commercial interests of other companies will dominate. Contracts may require frontloading of financial investment and, therefore, the ability to raise capital, which is refunded by the public sector later in the contract. But most social enterprises do not have the financial resources and performance record to raise capital at competitive rates. The pressure to provide integrated services leads to larger rather than smaller contracts. The outsourcing of some shared services projects will drive contract values even higher.

National and transnational companies already have a dominant position in many sectors such as information and communications technology and corporate services, environmental and waste services, construction and public private partnerships (see Chapter 8). Retaining a place at the outsourcing and grant-awarding trough could lead to appeasement and compromise in advocacy and campaigning, which could damage the sector and the people that voluntary organisations are established to support. The enthusiasm, by which most voluntary organisations embrace social entrepreneurs and the market model, spells a dilution of advocacy, with organised campaigning replaced by consumerism and individual casework. The longer-term concern is that some voluntary organisations and social enterprises sanction their conversion to private ownership, finance and management to 'recycle resources' to finance a new breed of social enterprise.

The voluntary sector has been used by successive governments as a foil to cloud the marketisation of public services. Financial aid, support and promotion of social enterprises is a strategy for reducing the role of the public sector and 'rolling back the state' (see Chapter 1). Establishing social enterprises and voluntary sector contracting may have some short-term benefits for the staff and organisations involved, but the government's medium and long-term strategy does not stop at outsourcing. It is only one stage in the financialisation, personalisation and marketisation of services process that will ultimately develop into full privatisation. The notion that social enterprises might form a new frontier of defence for the welfare state is fanciful.

Much of the capacity building programmes and support for voluntary organisations and social enterprises is designed to make them 'better contractors', to meet the demands set by commissioning bodies. The client/contractor split requires contractors to focus on service delivery performance. They have little opportunity to influence the design, planning and specification of services. Broader issues of social justice, democratic governance and sustainability are marginalised in the contracting agenda. Local authorities and public bodies often claim they have consulted 'stakeholders' in the procurement process, but this is often limited to 'internal' or 'external professional' consultees. For example, consulting school head teachers.

The procurement process raises particular problems for voluntary organisations and social enterprises because options are selected and assessed using narrow economic criteria to determine 'value for money'. Comprehensive and rigorous evaluation of the economic, social, environmental and health costs and benefits and identification of the cause and effect of outcomes and social value are complex. Good practice participatory evaluation is rare, costly and there are few off-the-shelf frameworks. Most existing models such as the social return on investment are, at best, works in progress (Arvidson et al, 2010). Whilst some trade unions have campaigned for radical changes to the evaluation of options and bids, there is little evidence of support from voluntary organisations or social enterprises. There are powerful vested interests in maintaining what are often biased, selective and superficial evaluation frameworks (Whitfield, 2010a).

Few voluntary organisations and social enterprises can compete in a system of individual budgets, direct payments and vouchers. Greater fluctuations in demand will require larger financial reserves and/or access to credit than under current contract conditions.

Some large private contractors have formed 'partnerships' with voluntary organisations or social enterprises to tender for public sector contracts, for example Balfour Beatty and Remploy. A marriage of interests, providing market and community access, is likely to be commercially beneficial to the former, but erode the values, accountability and credibility of the latter.

The emergence of consortium hubs is another development. For example, 30 voluntary organisations in Bedfordshire, Luton, Hertfordshire and Buckinghamshire have established ConsortiCo Ltd. It is a 'super contractor' that *"...identifies public service contract opportunities and then develops tender proposals in consortia with its member organisations. Once a contract is secured, Consortico will be the lead contractor and deliver financial and contract compliance services on behalf of the whole consortia. Its member organisations will deliver the services under sub contract arrangements that mirror the main contract"* (www.consortico.com). This may increase contract opportunities for some voluntary organisations, but it further embeds them in the often prohibitive procurement and contracting process.

The growth of larger agencies and hubs could have a damaging impact on voluntary organisations. Centralising funding streams, joint bidding and subcontracting, establishing bureaucratic regulations and standards, in which voluntary organisations are rewarded for implementing programmes and contracts designed by agencies and hubs, will actually reduce competition and innovation. New voluntary organisations and social enterprises could have difficulty gaining access to this system.

Most community organisations do not want, nor do they have the resources, to manage and own local facilities and services, such as libraries and leisure centres. Managing some local facilities may provide some opportunities to widen participation, but it is likely to have minimal effect. Most community organisations will be hard pressed to maintain facilities in their current condition, given the pressure on maintenance budgets. They will lose a high degree of independence through co-optation and weaken their ability to advocate for adequate funding and other local issues. Keeping buildings operational will require constant management of volunteers in addition to dealing with insurance, legal and other matters. And more organisations will be chasing the same limited public sector or charitable funding sources.

Contracting imposes new financial and sustainability risks for voluntary organisations and social enterprises (see Chapter 2). Once they are locked into the contracting system they become dependent on renewing contracts, winning new contracts to increase efficiency and are further embedded in the contract culture. Withdrawal could affect the viability of the organisation.

Social enterprises combating market forces?

Social enterprises have to operate in markets and reinforce the commissioning model and contract culture. They have cynically become one of the tools of privatisation, to enable the politically unacceptable privatisation of libraries, health and social care services to be more publicly palatable. In public service terms, social enterprises are contractors and businesses, and subject to the same commercial pressures as the private sector. The notion that social enterprises can prefigure socialist organisation and social relations may be partially true in a few cases, but social enterprises led by the new breed of social entrepreneurs are almost certain to mirror business practice and commercial values.

Ideological confusion is rampant, for example, *"...third sector organisations are not-the-state and they are not-the-market"* (Alcock, 2010). The idea that large voluntary organisations and social enterprises delivering public services exist 'in between' the state and the market and sometimes 'overlap with them' but are not part of the market, is delusional and misleading.

Markets and capital are never static, so the middle ground of a mixed economy is illusionary – once that is reached, capital will seek further marketisation and public provision will face even stronger political and economic opposition.

Social enterprises may be considered to be a potential alternative provider, where in-house provision is rejected at options appraisal stage, and/or an in-house bid is not sanctioned. But this is quite different from advocating and campaigning for social enterprises as a mainstream choice. It is not prudent to promote alternative means of provision, ownership or tenure in a capitalist economy, without clarity of their function, employment relations and governance. Capital will always exploit their role, set them against direct public provision and cherry pick successful ones by takeover and privatisation. Claims that the 'market' is big enough for a range of providers is politically and economically naive. The lack of in-depth strategy is stark. To contemplate alternative provision without considering the implications for the future of in-house provision in local and central government, the NHS and other public bodies, is a grave mistake.

Misinformation about social enterprises is rife. For example, the Department of Health announced the creation of 61 social enterprises providing £900m of NHS services, but they represented just 0.009% of the NHS budget (eGov Monitor, 2010). The cost of the department's £100m Social Enterprise Investment Fund is rarely mentioned. However, the 'non-profit' element and sense of 'choice' provided by social enterprises is assumed to legitimate market mechanisms, even though they represent a fraction of each market. Social enterprise and the voluntary sector will not *"...displace market forces and capital accumulation as the basis for organising production and distribution"* (Harvey, 2010).

Social enterprises will be able to determine employee terms and conditions, but they will be bound by market forces and the organisation's performance. Social enterprises will, therefore, be hard pressed to be good employers and create a surplus for community investment. Many will be stretched to create a surplus for reinvestment in the enterprise, thus making 'contractor empowerment' a much more limited concept than people are led to believe. 'Becoming your own boss' and 'taking control of your own destiny' are grossly exaggerated to generate myths and to avoid the reality that most employees will be working to a contract in which they have little or no input.

The ability of social enterprises to adopt good quality employment policies such as TUPE Plus (and secondment when this is an option) and pensions is very limited and usually ruled out on cost grounds. The withdrawal of the Code of Practice to prevent two-tier workforces and potential restrictive access to the Local Government Pension Scheme are designed to assist private and social enterprise contractors, at the expense of terms and conditions of transferred and new staff. They are facilitating a 'race to the bottom' (Cunningham, 2008).

An inquiry into employee ownership in public service delivery painted a very rosy picture of mutuals and social enterprises. It focused on the challenges and solutions required to increase and sustain employee ownership, hardly surprising since the All Party Parliamentary Group (APPG) on Employee Ownership is funded by the Employee Ownership Association (APPG, 2011).

More secrecy, less scrutiny

There are few references to the need to revolutionise transparency and disclosure. Quite the opposite is happening, as commissioning is mainstreamed across the public sector and 'commercial confidentiality' is used to prevent disclosure of basic information on projects, options appraisal, business cases and bids. The procurement process is not designed to be participatory. And the more that the voluntary and community organisations engage in procurement, they too will be constrained by the same level of secrecy in communicating with their members and the public. Both the public and private sectors use the blanket of 'commercial confidentiality' to protect competitive advantage over other contractors, at the expense of the public interest and community participation. Local authorities will have a constant flow of Official Journal of the European Union notices that effectively stifle debate and exclude the public from the decision making process.

This will make meaningful participation increasingly difficult. By getting people engaged now, it is hoped to involve them in a compromise. Individual service users will increasingly be sandwiched between the collective and highly organised interests of the state, private contractors and voluntary organisations and social enterprises.

Decline and fall of mutuals and social enterprises

The success of mutual and social enterprises is heavily promoted, but their failure is rarely mentioned, leading to risks being understated. Recent history is instructive. The de-mutualisation of building societies was driven by a combination of carpet-baggers seeking windfalls and deregulation of financial markets, which led to building societies diversifying into banking services.

Mutually-owned building societies have a long history of providing savings and mortgages in the UK. However, ten large building societies were demutualised, either via stock market flotation or takeover by banks, commencing with Abbey National in 1989 and culminating in a frenzy of carpet-bagger and investment bank activity between 1995-2000 in search of windfalls. All ten have subsequently lost their independence. Three are foreign owned, two exist only as trading names, three were rebranded, and two were nationalised in the bank bailouts of 2008.

Social enterprises will endure the same commercial pressures as other companies. Ealing Community Transport (ECT) was regarded as a flagship venture, but had to be rescued by private contractor May

Gurney in 2008. ECT's diversified growth into waste management, rail and healthcare recycling was financed through borrowing. Losses within the rail business put a severe strain on resources and the withdrawal of bank credit facilities (Ealing Community Transport, 2009). Four leisure trusts have failed to date and many trusts were not performing as well as in-house services (ESSU, 2010d).

By the mid 1990s there had been about forty management buy-outs of local authority services but two failed with large debts, two returned to in-house provision following a critical audit report of illegalities in their establishment, and the remainder were taken over by larger contractors. The number of management buy-outs from local and central governments was virtually zero between 2000-09 (ibid).

Secure Healthcare had a £5m NHS contract to provide care for prisoners in 2007 and received about £500,000 start-up funding under the Department of Health's social enterprise pathfinder scheme, but a year later went into liquidation with debts of over £1m.

Eaga began in Newcastle upon Tyne in 1990 and expanded to become a national organisation using government grants to improve home energy efficiency. It became a 100% employee owned company in 2000, modelled on the John Lewis Partnership, but seven years later floated on the London Stock Exchange with an employee trust having a 37% shareholding. In March 2011 shareholders voted 99.95% to accept a £306.5m bid from Carillion plc, one of Britain's largest construction companies. The employee trust shareholding reduced to 6.59% (Carillion plc, 2011).

A partnership of clinicians owns 49.9% of Circle Health, claiming to improve healthcare delivery in six hospital/clinics. But it is just one subsidiary in a complex corporate structure of parent company Circle Holdings. Circle Health reported £27.4 losses in 2010. Two shareholders, Lansdowne Holdings, a property investment company and Odey Asset Management, control 40.3% of Circle Holdings (Bureau of Investigative Journalism, 2011c).

Employee-owned bus companies were subjected to intense competition from large national private companies intent on driving them into selling out. Employee ownership of bus companies mushroomed following the 1986 deregulation and privatisation of municipal bus companies. Some were owned via Employee Share Ownership Plans (ESOPs), with an employee benefit trust that purchased shares in the new company via an external loan. Other employee bus companies directly purchased shares. Employee share ownership ranged from 49% to 100%. Twenty-three bus companies had substantial employee ownership by 1993.

However, intense competition with 'bus wars' led to rapid concentration as a few companies, First Bus and Stagecoach in particular, used their commercial power to compete against and takeover bus companies. By 1997, one of the four Empolyees Share Ownership Plan (ESOP) controlled bus companies had been sold, employee ownership continued in 15 companies (18.7%) but employee ownership in 16 other companies had been eliminated (Spear, 1999). Tendering of bus services, declining passenger numbers, and bus wars resulted in a decline in the average earnings of bus drivers, falling from 98% to 80% of average manual wages between 1986-94 (House of Commons Library, 1995).

Preston Bus, the last employee-owned bus company, was sold to Stagecoach in 2009 after a prolonged bus war that resulted in losses leaving it with little option but to sell the company. Stagecoach had previously been accused of *"...predatory and deplorable"* action by the Monopolies and Mergers Commission in the collapse of the Darlington municipal bus company (Herald Scotland, 2011). In November 2009, the Competition Commission ordered Stagecoach to divest Preston Bus, which was eventually sold to Rotala plc in February 2011. The sixty subsidiaries of the National Bus Company were sold off to separate buyers, 35 to management and two to a joint management and employee buyout. Only three management teams remain, the rest sold out to other bus companies (Centre Forum, 2011).

The current promotion of the mutual/social enterprise 'solution' is a repetition of earlier initiatives, albeit under different economic conditions. However, the outcome is almost certain to be the same mixture of success and failure.

Growth of social enterprises into national organisations
Does the growth of large national housing associations, through takeover and merger of local associations, provide a model? The housing association sector has changed radically in the last 30 years, since the 1974-79 Labour Government expanded their role and redirected public spending from local authorities on spurious grounds of efficiency. The sector is dominated by national and regional housing associations, many having diversified into the provision of social care and regeneration partnerships with private developers.

Lessons can be drawn from Australia, where Federal and State governments have developed contractual and quasi-contractual relationships with the voluntary sector for some time. Larger voluntary organisations have tended to capture the bulk of contracts, although they represent a minority of voluntary organisations. This is resulting in *"... an increasing polarisation within the sector between the majority consisting of smaller, voluntaristic and less sophisticated organisations, and the minority of wealthy, professionalised, corporate, employing organisations"* (Butcher, 2005).

It often suits governments to *"...laud the contributions"* of voluntary organisations, which can exaggerate the ability and value of the voluntary sector. Butcher concludes that these attributes often contain 'elements of myth' which, in turn, are used to legitimate the sector's role and *"...reinforce the notion that a mixed economy of service delivery is reliant on it"'* (ibid).

Some public sector managers promote social enterprises because they believe there is kudos that will help their career progression, if they can demonstrate that they have helped to implement big society policies.

The provision of public services by social enterprises might change social expectations, for example, service users expecting a step change in how they are treated, in the outcome of their claim, or they might expect a social enterprise to be an advocate on their behalf. In practice, social enterprises will be like any other contractor, regulated by a contract, employing basically the same staff, acting as an agent of local or central government.

Myth of empowerment

Increased contestability and competition, thus widening the role of procurement and commercial confidentiality in public management, will lead to less disclosure and reduced transparency, which makes participation more difficult. But by getting people engaged now, it is hoped to lock them into a consumer orientated consultative relationship. There is a fundamental contradiction in encouraging participation in a transformation process that is designed to constrain and limit options and to channel decision-making into markets, opting out of public provision, whilst promoting a community 'do-it-yourself' take over of responsibility for local facilities and services. Big society and the new-found faith in community engagement and empowerment is simply another stage in the neoliberal approach to further embed marketisation in public services. It has five functions.

Firstly, participation of voluntary and social enterprises is a diversion to try to make commissioning, contestability and outsourcing politically acceptable. It is a big business agenda, as discussed in Chapter 3. Best Value was a means of extending competition to all local authority services. Now, competition is demanded in all public bodies. Engaging civil society in this process helps to diffuse and confuse opposition and unleashes 'entrepreneurs' who see opportunities for empire building. It is a market agenda, creating the illusion that community and civil society organisations will somehow not be part of the market or affected by market forces.

Secondly, choice mechanisms encourage individual participation and decision-making. Consumers thus share a degree of responsibility if, or when, markets or contracts fail. So the policy, market structures or principles are not wrong, but rather the way that people have exercised choice and engaged in the market.

Thirdly, neoliberalism requires people to participate in markets and accept the ideology of market forces, for example, to accept and exercise choice in schools and hospitals. Therefore, participation has an ideological motive. Whether participation will be sustainable once public service markets become 'mature' is another matter. The private sector will not want anything other than superficial participation. The lack of community participation in private schools and private health care are indicative of their approach.

Fourthly, community engagement is viewed in a one-dimensional perspective, in which class, community, political, economic and other interests are ignored. It assumes a class and conflict-free uniformity that does not exist in reality. Neighbourhoods are not homogenous and have different needs, aspirations and economic and social interests. No reference is made to joint community and trade union participation, as this is considered to be two separate and distinct types of 'participation'. Significantly, there are no proposals for radical reform of local democratic governance, accountability and participation in the public policy-making process (see Chapter 5).

Finally, participation in big society and the neoliberal transformation of public services strategy require accepting that there is no alternative.

Right-wing interests, masquerading as promoters of shared ownership, co-production and local control are taking advantage of the community, voluntary organisations and social enterprise 'agenda' to promote 'new models' of employee and community-owned 'civil companies' to deliver services, *"...governed neither by the public state or the private market"* and have full budgetary control with no commissioning or contracting (Respublica and NESTA, 2009). Antidemocratic, anti-collective and anti-trade union views underpin the verbiage glorifying innovation, civil society and localism in the media and think tank reports. They assiduously avoid the public interest and social justice agenda. It is localism run riot, whilst being eerily quiet about the state and transnational capital!

The Coalition's version of participation is designed as a mechanism to embed the ideology of neoliberal transformation of public services, which serves to reinforce the belief that there is no feasible alternative to marketisation and privatisation. Real engagement and 'empowerment' remains a fantasy concept. The Coalition promotes a form of 'social action' in which individuals, volunteers, charities, community groups and voluntary organisations act as 'change agents' to change individual or group behaviour and to lobby for local policies. It is far removed from grassroots organising, education and action. There is a fundamental contradiction in expecting and encouraging participation in a transformation process that is designed to constrain and limit the options and to channel decision making into transfers, markets, opting out of public provision and community taking over responsibility for local facilities and services.

Participation in 'place making' is another new meaningless phrase. Local authorities have had responsibility for planning and regulating their area for decades. How is participation in place making going to be any different? It is over 40 years since the Skeffington Report on Participation in Planning (Skeffington, 1969). Apart from some good practice, where participation has been significant and effective, it is questionable whether communities are more involved in the decision-making process about what happens to their neighbourhood?

Genuine and sustainable participation requires other fundamental changes, such as a commitment to transparency and disclosure of policies, analysis, reviews, plans, projects and participation, and engagement in the design and planning process. The democratisation of the planning, transformation and procurement processes – service reviews, options appraisals, business cases, procurement and contract management – is a prerequisite, but it is not even on the agenda! Information and communications technology has rapidly increased the expression of opinions in blogs, and social networks, but methods of communication should not be confused with methods of participation or engagement.

Proposals for radical changes in democratic governance were set out in Chapters 4 - 6. Participation in the public policy decision-making process serves to strengthen democratic accountability, to identify social, economic and environmental needs and aspirations, and to improve the various stages of the policy-making process. It can strengthen community identity, cohesion and participation in community, trade union and civil society organisations. This is a prerequisite for social justice campaigns for rights, resources and policies. Meaningful participation should include face-to-face deliberation of options, assessing costs and benefits, discussion of advantages and disadvantages to particular groups, and collective interests and strategic planning.

The empowerment debate demonstrates a lack of understanding of power relations and the conditions and processes required in which different types and degrees of empowerment may take place. Empowerment doesn't just happen, because it is decreed by politicians or policy advisers. It is not given, but won through organising and action. Nor does it necessarily lead to a permanent shift in power. *"Community empowerment is the outcome of engagement and other activities. Power, influence and responsibility are shifted away from existing centres of power and into the hands of communities and individual citizens"* (Local Government Improvement & Development, 2011). If this is limited to contractor and employer roles, then little, if any, political empowerment will occur. The extent to which devolution brings decision-making and government 'closer to the people' is questionable since there is no natural link between devolution and empowerment.

The government views community engagement from a one-dimensional perspective in which class, community, political, economic and other interests are ignored. It assumes a class and conflict-free uniformity, which does not exist in practice, except, perhaps, in a few small settlements. They yearn for depoliticised forms of participation, which are sanitised, clinical and conflict free. This assumes a high degree of consensus within the community, minimal conflict with the state and its agents (increasingly transnational companies and consultants), and a symbiosis of interests between community and transnational capital for the delivery of 'world class' public services, or that one can be engineered!

Scant reference is made to collective organisation, but limited to individuals and citizens or to 'communities' or 'non-profit organisations', by which they mean voluntary organisations and social enterprises. They do not believe there is a shortage of campaigns but the state and private sector do not want to recognise collective power, that could oppose market 'reforms'. Their version of empowerment is not political empowerment, because they want to minimise collective power. Not surprisingly, they never refer to increasing the power of the workers. Also, theirs is a form of 'empowerment' created by participation in market mechanisms, in effect, limited to a degree of consumer power. Markets are designed to engage individuals, not collective organisations.

The procurement of larger, multi-service, longer-term contracts will further limit the scope of local decision-making, because virtually all the important decisions will have been made in the procurement process and contract negotiations. The contract culture will be pervasive. Services users will get the stock answer that the Council is constrained by the contract and trade unionists will be told the Council is no longer the employer and their only concern is the quality of the service. Each local authority arms length company has responsibility for participation and workplace industrial relations. They are usually no more receptive to user/community organisation and staff/trade union participation than local authorities or other public bodies. Community and trade union representatives are in a minority on boards and are often appointed rather than elected. Boards of directors are legally obligated to prioritise the interests of the company, not the authority or organisation which they represent. Board members are bound by commercial confidentiality and, therefore, unable to share policy and contractual information with their own organisations.

Co-production?

Citizens, service users and staff must be involved in the design, planning and delivery of public services and infrastructure projects. Tenants and residents have demanded involvement in renewal and regeneration projects since the 1950s and have been closely involved in area planning and the design of housing. However, these projects were crucially dependent on the organised power of those communities, arising from earlier campaigns, and to committed architects and planners.

The concept of 'co-production' has become a popular cause (Compass 2008, NEF 2009, Needham and Carr 2009, Bovaird and Downe, 2008). There would be wide agreement if co-production simply meant citizen, service user and staff having in-depth involvement and collaboration in the design, planning and delivery process. However, those who advocate this concept also promote 'social capital' and the 'new social economy' (see chapter 2). Service users cannot 'co-produce' because they do not have an economic role in the production of services in the sense of financial, employment, management, statutory and democratic responsibility. Service users must be organised and have a degree of political power to influence public policy, but they do not have economic power, legal and statutory powers, nor do they have a political mandate. Service users must participate and be engaged in the design and delivery process but this is not 'co-production'.

Despite workforce involvement in the NHS being 'on the agenda' for more than a decade, exhortation and guidance *"...have yet to be translated into practice on a consistent basis"* (Ellins and Ham, 2009). This creates conditions in which alternative solutions, at least superficially, give workers more engagement. However, simply replicating current public management practice in a social enterprise, will not achieve a step change in workforce involvement.

The ideology of co-production and charter schools is, not surprisingly, now being extended to 'co-produced communities' and 'charter cities'. A 'co-produced community' is about *"...how the community and the 'social sector' more broadly, connects with public and commercial sectors, including new service behaviours, different types of interrelationships and a more direct bond between local commerce and local people"* (McInroy and Blume, 2011). 'Charter cities' in developing countries could be *"...special reform zones that allow governments to quickly adopt innovative new systems of rules, rules that can be markedly different from those in the rest of the country"* (Romer, 2010). The charter city infrastructure could be financed by private investors who would collect fees for the services they provide. Both should be classified as 'all in it together PPP models'.

Future of advocacy and organising

Voluntary organisations and social enterprises could replace community action membership organisations in the delivery of public services. A big increase in non-profit service agencies in the US *"...inadvertently created major obstacles to citizen engagement because the community 'space' previously occupied by membership organisations is now populated with service agencies"* (Smith, 2010). The formalisation and increasing professionalisation of community organisations, driven by trying to retain contracts and grants, *"...tended to channel citizen participation into board governance"* (ibid).

The National Survey of Charities and Social Enterprises places significant importance on the relationship between local government and voluntary organisations. Local authorities benchmark their performance using the 'N17 score' – *"[t]aking everything into account, overall, how do the statutory bodies in your local area influence your organisation's success?"* (Cabinet Office (2011d). The possibility that a voluntary organisation may have a strained relationship with the local authority because of its strident advocacy and organising activities, (and thus a low N17 score), but be providing its members with significant benefits and strengthening community cohesion, is not taken into account.

Voluntary organisations and social enterprises will be reluctant to challenge the dominant state/capital interests when they compete for contracts, and thus reduce their advocacy and campaigning work. Senior managers of these organisations (the 'entrepreneurs'), directors on Boards, and trustees, are likely to adopt more commercial attitudes putting the 'success' of the organisation before social and community and public interest. Thus neoliberalism is more deeply embedded in this sector.

The reality could be 'less for more' as public and charitable money and skills are diverted into contracting. The contract culture will deepen within these organisations as they become more and more reliant on winning and retaining contracts. Voluntary organisations and social enterprises will be under pressure to participate and 'deliver', although many organisations will be reticent, wary of the charge that they are the 'respectable face of capitalism' to deliver savings and lower the cost of public services. More organisations may adopt anti-trade union attitudes, as they conflict with trade unions over staffing levels, terms and conditions and pensions, as they adopt private sector employment practices to 'compete'.

Clear evidence of ideological and operational shifts are evident in other countries, such as the US and Australia, which have adopted similar policies.

"Leaders used to understand that they have to change the relations of power in order to effectively pursue their values and interests. Politically, that involves building support both at the base and among elected officials. Economically, that involves strategies and tactics that affect profits in order to compel owners and managers to engage in good faith negotiations. For bureaucracies, it means disrupting business as usual. In people power organizations, leaders learn that whatever the particular issue might be they will be unable to do much about it without power. But now their perspective has shifted from one of building people power to building innovative programs that will be 'models' or 'pilot projects' to demonstrate what could be done if the political will was there to do it, and to empowering individuals" (Miller, 2010).

This view is supported by others. *"What also distinguishes the expansion of social-service non-profits is that increasingly their role is to take responsibility for persons who are in the throes of abandonment rather than responsibility for persons progressing toward full incorporation into the body politic"* (Gilmore, 2007).

New services, innovative delivery methods and the application of new technologies such as telemedicine are likely to be 'engineered' to be delivered by private contractors or social enterprises rather than the public sector. This has grave implications for the reputation and relevance of public sector in-house service delivery, as it will be portrayed as 'bog standard', whilst other providers will be 'new' and 'forward-looking'. Thus the developmental aspect of in-house services will be stultified. Voluntary organisations and social enterprises are likely to promote the integration of health and social care; environmental, recycling and employment; but the substance of the service and employment content of these contracts would need rigorous scrutiny.

The discussion of empowerment and localism inevitably includes references to 'social capital', defined as *"...any aspect of the social that cannot be deemed to be economic but which can be deemed to be an asset"* (Fine, 2010). It ranges from relationships and bonds between family, friends and within communities, to networks of contacts and to community activity, identity and trust in institutions and organisations, the police and political representatives. Fine sets out a comprehensive case for why this term should be discarded. It often describes everything 'social' and is widely misused. Social ownership or social capital could readily become the launch pad to promote 'community capital' as the new asset base.

Instead of celebrating the sector's role as a 'partner' in a growing mixed economy welfare state, we need to challenge this neoliberal construct and draw up an alternative role for voluntary organisations and social enterprises.

CHAPTER 10

Why markets fail

The last three decades have seen a concerted effort by governments and business interests to marketise public services, despite the fact that a succession of economic crises have been caused by the failure of markets. The economic and social consequences of the 2008/09 financial crisis continue to reverberate with continuing foreclosures, bankruptcy and negative equity in the mortgage and real estate markets, recession and mass unemployment. This chapter examines the structure of markets and their internal flaws, market and contract performance, and the myth of the perfect market.

People's experience of markets is mainly in the purchase of household goods, clothing, food and utilities and, less frequently, in house rental/mortgage, insurance, financial services, car purchase and travel markets. The scale of European welfare state and public service provision means that people have limited experience of education and health markets.

Market failure occurs when demand and supply is manipulated to create shortages and price rises and when asset bubbles form and burst, usually fuelled by speculation. Market participants may fail financially (for example, going into liquidation or a financial crisis forces sale of the company) or have contracts terminated because of poor performance (see Chapter 8 in Whitfield, 2010a).

Recurring crises
The history of manias, panics and crashes in real estate, currency trading, and stocks and shares are systematically related (Kindleberger and Alber, 2005). Before the current financial crisis there had been *"… more asset price bubbles between 1980 and 2000 than in any earlier period"* (ibid). The causes of financial crises are systemic, although certain individuals and firms had prominent roles. They were rarely caused by recent policies and developments but had been evident for a decade or more. Off-balance sheet financing, risk aversion techniques, deception about company performance, greed and profiteering were common. Deregulation, the failure to monitor and enforce regulations, and concerted opposition to new regulations were common factors.

Crises were consistently caused by the growth and bursting of asset bubbles in property, shares and currency trading. The Stern Review concluded that climate change *"...must be regarded as market failure on the greatest scale the world has seen"* (Stern, 2007). Climate change is an externality that is global in its causes and consequences, impacts that are persistent, and despite uncertainties about the scale, type and timing of impacts, are likely to have a profound effect on the global economy without policy changes. *"...[H]uman induced climate change is an externality, one that is not 'corrected' through any institution or market, unless policy intervenes"* (ibid).

The responses to crises have common features. Governments bail out companies, provide guarantees and financial support, and launch fiscal stimulus measures in the economy. Calls for stronger and more comprehensive regulations are met with strident opposition from business interests and neoliberals. The financial consequences and 'solutions' are usually targeted austerity, with cuts in public expenditure and welfare benefits, and tax increases imposed on working families. The need to understand the causes of crises, to attribute responsibility and liability, and to learn lessons are systematically sidelined by focusing on the effects of economic recession, rising unemployment and public spending cuts.

The structure of markets

Markets require structures and conditions, a set of values and ideology, which determine the relationships between participants, plus a mechanism for setting prices for goods and services, with risk and reward (profit) for service providers. Markets are claimed to distribute resources efficiently, and market relationships are said to provide a framework for social relations that is supposed to be beneficial to society.

Markets are not created overnight, nor simply by legislation and regulation. They must be constructed and have willing participants. They require continuity of demand, profitability and regulations to govern participants and the easy entry and exit of providers. Public service principles and values have to be downgraded or replaced by competition, economic efficiency and profit making. Most public service markets are financed by the state and thus require, from a private sector perspective, a contracting process with low transaction costs and minimal cost of environmental and social regulation. A legal environment is needed to give authority and legitimacy for contracts, transactions, and the protection of property and intellectual rights.

Information is not symmetrical because users and potential users do not have the same information, access, time, experience, knowledge and negotiating skills to make use of market information.

Markets require excess provision or supply over demand, so that there is spare capacity to allow market forces to operate. The proper functioning of markets relies on maintaining good contractual relationships between client and contractor, between contractors, subcontractors and suppliers, and between contractors and service users. However, markets are often slow to react to new or changed demands thus creating a lag or gap between people's needs and the supply of services or products.

Markets tend to focus on short-term interests and marginalise or ignore longer-term interests. Subprime mortgages and securitisation led financial institutions to focus on ramping up the flow of mortgages and fees and the refinancing of existing mortgages as homeowners extracted equity for consumer spending. Meanwhile the annual income multiplier required by new homeowners continued to increase as house prices soared. It was unsustainable, yet 'the market' did nothing, despite warnings of an impending implosion.

A 'free market' is a theoretical concept, where markets operate without government intervention or regulation. Goods, services and labour are voluntarily exchanged at prices agreed by participants. Right-wing 'free marketeers' want state intervention to enforce private contracts and property ownership. They believe any other form of state intervention, for social, environmental or public interest objectives, makes markets 'inefficient'.

Most public service contracts are 'incomplete' because no contract can precisely predict future demand, legislation and socio-economic conditions. Some services are difficult to specify and the public sector has to respond to changes in demand and maintain a degree of flexibility to respond to crises and changed circumstances. In fact, the trend is towards more and more incomplete contracts because of the switch from specifications detailing inputs, processes and outputs, to contracts that focus on outcomes, despite the difficulty identifying cause and effect in service delivery. These contracts exhibit more flexibility than traditional highly specified contracts, but this is limited to the defined scope of, and demand for, the service.

Markets require regulatory frameworks to govern market access, the rights of users and service providers, and redress in cases of market abuse. The failures that caused the current financial crisis should have exposed as myth the idea that markets can 'self-regulate' or 'self-monitor'.

Securitisation and secondary markets
Secondary markets frequently emerge, such as brokers and agents to

advise individual budget holders and users receiving direct payments, on how to use their budget/payment to maximum effect, supply information and advise on providers and markets.

Banks, building societies and mortgage brokers may re-sell mortgage loans, either as a whole loan, or through the pooling of loans to investment banks. It is common practice to bundle or pool thousands of individual loans into a Mortgage-Backed Security (MBS) that is sold via special purpose companies using off-balance sheet accounting. Loans may be sliced and diced and elements re-sold many times. This secondary market led to major problems in recording property rights, highlighted by the US foreclosure crisis and 'robo-signing' of legal documents, exposing flawed ownership information (Congressional Oversight Panel, 2010).

A PPP secondary market has been developed in Britain, and is emerging in other countries such as Canada and Australia, as construction companies and banks sell equity in PPP companies to investment companies and infrastructure funds (see Chapter 8).

The carbon trading market has created a secondary market. The European Union's emission trading scheme *".....is now witnessing the development of more complex carbon market products, which package together credits from several installations, then slice these up and resell them. In essence, this is the same structure that brought the derivatives market to its knees, and the same problem; carbon markets involve the selling of a product that has no clear underlying asset – fertile conditions for the creation of a new 'bubble'"* (Reyes, 2009). Governments and international bodies issue licences or carbon permits to companies, which can reduce emissions, or trade the permits with other companies. Instead of cutting emissions at source, carbon offsets enable companies and organisations to finance emission-saving projects in other regions. But the carbon trading and offset system are failing – no emissions reductions, no fundamental 'overhaul of energy systems', and offsets under the UN carbon market only reinforce fossil dependency in developing countries (Lohmann, 2009).

Internal flaws

Choice

The provision of choice in public services is consciously and consistently exaggerated or overstated. Most service users want good quality local services, schools and hospitals that will be their first choice in the vast majority of decisions. They want a degree of flexibility and involvement in planning and designing services, but they do not want a multiple choice. Sometimes patients want a second opinion, sometimes parent/pupils and patients want to transfer to another local school or doctor, and public services should have such options as a core part of their design and provision. With proper accountability and user involvement, they should be able to exercise these changes as a right. But this is fundamentally different from establishing market-driven choice.

Some choice is uneconomical, for example allowing each household or neighbourhood to choose who provides waste and recycling collection services. The division of these services into small contracts to allow competition to drive efficiencies would be costly and ultimately lead to contractor collusion. Larger companies would acquire smaller companies that won contracts in order to consolidate collection rounds. In other words, they would seek to secure most of the financial benefits from economies of scale. Ideological dogma would override value for money and fiduciary duty. It is important that choice is real and fulfils economic and social needs and is based on genuine participation.

The effectiveness of choice is frequently overstated: *"....it is important not to overestimate the ability of user choice to drive better outcomes. Enabling choice in itself is not a guarantee of effective competition between providers – just as in private markets the fact that consumers are able to make choices does not always mean that the market works effectively or that desired outcomes are achieved"* (OFT, 2010).

It is important to avoid simplistic comparisons of the production and sale of retail goods with the complex and costly provision of public services. A choice of service provision comes at a price.

Firstly, choice in service provision requires duplication of services and spare capacity, increased administration and the extraction of profits by private contractors. This translates into higher taxes or insurance payments than would otherwise be the case.

Secondly, the exercise of choice often means higher personal costs for users, for example, travel to other cities for health care or longer home-school travel. Additional time and transport costs can mount up, when assessed on an annual basis. The reality of choice is tempered by pricing and affordability (fees and charges may be designed to exclude certain users); access requirements may exclude potential applicants; the location of services may require transport and accommodation costs that make the choice uneconomic; and supplemental costs for so-called 'added value' services may be prohibitive.

Thirdly, many people in need are excluded from exercising choice and this leads to a two-tier system of private services, with state-provided residual services for those who cannot afford insurance and/or a personal contribution towards costs.

Fourthly, there are economic, social and environmental costs arising from duplication of services and increased travel, particularly by car. Activity between providers may appear to be economic growth, but for the most part it is simply transfers between sectors of the economy.

Producers and contractors seek to maximise their market share through organic growth and by takeover/merger of competing companies. A significant market share enables a company to wield more influence in determining prices, pay rates, regulations and policy. On the other hand, a natural monopoly may exist when a service can only be supplied at the lowest cost by limiting delivery by a single provider.

The Office of Fair Trading and the Cabinet Office are exploring how 'choice-tools' can evolve to help 'consumers' make health care and education choices in public service markets. Markets, empowered consumers and open competition drive innovation and productivity, thus generating long-term economic 'growth', the new mantra. So what are choice-tools? They consist of comparison websites (which already exist for insurance, energy and travel), consumer feedback sites, and online marketing techniques used by Amazon and Google! And, of course, there must be a self-regulated competitively neutral market in the provision of choice-tools (OFT, 2011a).

Competition – the reality

The introduction of competition into the provision of public services is claimed to improve efficiency and reduce costs whilst maintaining quality. Private contractors, business groups, right-wing think tanks and their academic allies, constantly use selective evidence to advocate marketisation and privatisation. They ignore the high transaction costs involved in competitive tendering, as well as the wider public sector costs and public interest issues arising with the regulation of markets. Less surprising, they ignore the high level of cost overruns, failures, delays and poor quality of private contractors, and the inferior quality of employment conditions in private sector contracting. But they try to 'legitimise' profits from the private delivery of public services (Grout, 2009).

Competitive markets are promoted as the means of imposing discipline in the public sector to make it more efficient. Competition is supposed to force a 'race to the top' for quality and innovation and impose sanctions on inefficient providers, by forcing them to either restructure or face closure. More often, this is overtaken by a race to the bottom by eliminating jobs and cutting pay and conditions.

Four competition themes - tackling barriers to entry and to exit, achieving genuine choice and aligning incentives were identified by the OFT. They claim that commissioners have responsibility to ensure that users *"…have sufficient tools and information to exercise effective choice to drive competition"* (OFT, 2011b). They effectively recommend 'dumbing down' the procurement process by streamlining *"…not to go beyond the minimum required under EC regulation"*; consider disaggregating contracts for different services *"…to encourage greater supplier participation"*; design framework contracts to allow additional firms to be added during the life of the framework; *"…the cost of failure by public sector suppliers"* should be taken into account in tender evaluation but no mention of the cost of private sector failure or questionable private sector compensation clauses, designed to deter the authority from terminating the contract.

Their basic premise is that the commissioner (i.e. the state) incurs all the costs of the market mechanisms, competition regimes, transaction costs, and the private sector only bears responsibility for delivering the contract, even in fully-fledged markets.

The OFT claim that the transfer of risk from the public sector to the private or voluntary sector *"…may constitute additional barriers to entry to certain types of suppliers in public services markets, such as the transfer of pension liabilities, the transfer of undertakings on protection of employment (TUPE) and liability for health and safety. As these liabilities are transferred to the private and third sector from the public sector, they can raise these suppliers' costs and lead to bids from the private and third sector appearing more expensive than in-house supply. This may lead to procurers favouring in-house supply, where because such liabilities do not need to be transferred as part of the procurement exercise these costs are effectively hidden, causing the in-house supplier to be chosen even when it does not offer the best value for money"* (OFT, 2011b).

Competition incurs a range of additional costs, such as financing, managing markets and the contracting process. The costs of outsourcing are divided into three categories: annual costs, reduction in the proportion of the budget spent on service delivery, and one-off transaction costs.

Annual costs
Public bodies retain the client function required to identify community needs and plan service requirements. NHS commissioning in Wales resulted in cost increases in real terms of 18.9% and 10.8% in 2003/4

and 2004/5 as a direct result of the introduction of commissioning (Lane and Jenkins, 2006). NHS Choices is funded by the Department of Health and costs about £25m annually.

Costs of contract monitoring includes the additional costs of regulating and enforcing rules for market mechanisms. Contract monitoring costs that are borne by the contracting authority are usually between 1% - 3% of the contract value. The cost of regulatory bodies is substantial, despite some being funded by licence fees and levies on service providers. For example, the combined running costs of the Care Quality Commission, healthcare regulator Monitor, the Financial Services Authority, Tenant Services Authority, Office of Fair Trading and part funding of the communications regulator OFCOM, was over £750m in 2009/10 (annual reports).

Pension costs could increase if contractors do not offer continued membership of local authority pension schemes for transferred and new staff via Admitted Body Status. If new staff opt out, or are not permitted to join the local government pension scheme, particularly where authorities have embarked on large-scale outsourcing, the scheme could potentially require increased contributions by local authorities and members in order to maintain a positive cash flow.

Savings from competition are exaggerated and often disappear when the full public cost of outsourcing is taken into account. Savings in fourteen strategic partnerships were between 1.0% and 15.4% of the contract value with a mean of 8.3% (Audit Commission, 2008). Only £3.3m of the planned £200m savings had been achieved three years into Somerset County Council's flagship ten-year strategic partnership with IBM (Audit Commission, 2010b). The contract is being renegotiated with several services, including finance and up to 50% of staff, expected to be transferred back to the Council. The joint venture has failed to win new work from authorities in the South-West.

A review of Liverpool's strategic partnership with BT revealed the Council was overcharged by £19m over a nine-year period by the excessive mark-up of the cost of equipment, support charges, software, hardware and training. Some desktop and laptop prices were marked up between 93% - 143% compared to the cost of alternative suppliers. It concluded in-house provision would save £82m up to 2016/17 with annual savings of £23m for 2017/18 and beyond. The review was unable to verify the planned £100m investment, financed by the City Council, because of a systemic lack of transparency (Liverpool City Council, 2010).

Research evidence revealed that savings for Compulsory Competitive Tendering (CCT) between 1985-95 were less than a quarter of those claimed. Two detailed studies found savings averaged 6.5% and just over 8% (Department of the Environment, 1993 and 1997). A study of market testing in the civil service concluded that *"...any activity where potential savings are less than 10% is not likely to be worth putting to competition on cost grounds alone"* (Cabinet Office, 1996).

A comprehensive study for the Equal Opportunities Commission found 'savings' of £124m in 39 authorities, but the full social and tendering costs totalled £250.1m, leaving a net cost of £126m per annum – equivalent to a 16% cost (Escott and Whitfield, 1995). The Government was, in effect, subsidising outsourcing, since it was responsible for 97% of the costs. In other words, for every £1m of 'savings' claimed, it cost the Government and the public purse £2m. And if this seems to be relying on 'old' evidence, the Department of Health's evidence for the impact assessment of the Coalition Government's 'Liberating the NHS' proposals were based on 1990 and 1995 studies of competitive tendering in refuse collection and bus services (Department of Health, 2011c) and a market study of international phone calls, passenger flights in Europe, new cars and replica football kits (Department of Trade & Industry, 2004). All other evidence, including government studies, was ignored.

Savings are usually rolled up over ten years, for example an annual £1m in year one will be assumed to be £10m. Figures are rounded up, for example, £1.7m becomes £2m per annum but makes a difference of £3m spread over ten years.

Public costs arise from the direct and indirect consequences of competition and outsourcing, such as increased unemployment, losses/gains in tax/National Insurance and VAT revenue, the cost of income support paid to low-waged staff, the increased cost of housing benefits and council tax rebates, plus the rising cost of increased use of health and social services. They represent a 16% cost, primarily to central government (Centre for Public Services, 1995).

One-off transaction costs

Transaction costs include the costs of the procurement process (the preparation of options appraisals, business cases; preparing for, and managing, the procurement process); consultants, lawyers and advisers fees; contract management and monitoring costs and civil service or public staff time, because this is an opportunity cost, as they could be working on other projects. Transaction costs are a minimum 2%-3% of the contract value, or up to 5%-6% with a competitive dialogue procurement process (HM Treasury, 2010b). The purchaser/provider split in the NHS led to increased administration costs, rising from about 5% of health service expenditure in the 1980s to 12% by 1997 and rising again to 13.5% by 2005 (House of Commons Health Committee, 2010).

The cost of the contract is usually assumed, wrongly, to be the contract price. But this ignores the estimated cost of contract variations over the contract period and contract-related governance arrangements, such as strategic, management and operational boards. There may be knock-on costs arising from the corporate impact on the authority (such as reduced volume/higher cost of services borne by other directorates).

Market support costs of choice, competition and contestability mechanisms and the transfer of organisations and assets are substantial. New Labour's market initiatives had incurred one-off costs of £8.4bn by 2006 with annual costs of £3.1bn (Whitfield, 2006a).

Public subsidies are required in some markets, for example, the privatised railway system receives an annual subsidy, £4bn in 2010-11, yet fares are over 30% higher than comparator European railways. *"The higher whole-system costs appear to result in significantly higher subsidies per passenger-km"* (McNulty Review, 2011).

Secondary market costs: the cost of brokers and agents to advise on personal budgets and direct payments will be significant. Back-office administration costs are expected to decline, but the cost of administering large numbers of individual contracts is likely to be higher than expectations. Start-up costs, double running costs (continued availability of services to non-budget holders), monitoring, dealing with complaints and legal challenges, and ensuring equity of access, will be significant. Some back office costs may be transferred to the secondary market, but there is considerable uncertainty over who will bear the cost of advisers and agents. The secondary market may initially comprise mainly small and medium-sized enterprises, but this sector is likely to consolidate into provision by a handful of national or transnational companies.

One-off transaction costs vary between 6.5% and 9.5% of the contract value (see Table 10). In summary, annual retained client costs are between 7% and 13% of the contract value. Total contract operational costs, taking account of monitoring, average savings, other operational and public sector costs are between 9.5% and 40.7% of the contract value. In addition, between 6% - 12% of the contract value is redirected to the company as profit. One-off transaction costs incurred in the procurement process will be between 6.5% and 11.0% of the contract value.

Reduction in spending on service delivery
The contractor's profit, ranging between 6% and 12% of the contract value, is a reduction in the proportion of the budget spent on service delivery (see Table 10).

In summary, the annual contract costs range between 9.5% and 40.7% of the contract value, plus one-off transaction costs of 6.5% - 9.5% of the contract value. The total cost of outsourcing is between 10.3% - 42.2% taking account of savings and spreading the transaction costs over an eight-year contract period. It should be noted that this does not include the retained client costs, nor the fact that 6%-12% of the contract value will be diverted from service delivery into the contractor's profit.

The Society of Information Technology Management (SOCITM), the membership association for public sector ICT professionals, *"...has tracked costs and user satisfaction in both in-house and out-sourced operations for over a decade. On a like-for-like basis, the outsourced operations are always more expensive"* (SOCITM, 2011).

An analysis of annual billing rates for US federal government contractor employees across 35 occupational classifications covering over 550 service activities of US federal government outsourced

Table 10: The cost of outsourcing*

Additional costs incurred by public sector	Additional Costs as a % of Contract Value
ANNUAL RETAINED CLIENT COSTS	
Identify needs, plan service requirements, governance	7% – 13%
ANNUAL CONTRACT COSTS	
Contract management and monitoring (1) *(or monitoring complex ICT contracts)* (1)	1% – 3% (up to 7%)

Dexter Whitfield

Table 10: The cost of outsourcing* (continued)

Additional costs incurred by public sector	Additional Costs as a % of Contract Value
Additional Annual Operational Costs	
Delays, cost overruns, variations for additional work – variable 5% - 30% (2)	5% – 30%
Potential additional contribution to public sector pension fund because transferred/new staff do not join	n/a
Risk of poor performance and other risks (variable)	n/a
Average savings in outsourcing (3)	-6.5% – -8.3%
Additional public sector costs (loss of tax revenue, cost of benefits) (4)	10% – 16%
Total Annual Contract Costs	**9.5% – 40.7%**
ONE-OFF TRANSACTION COSTS IN AWARDING CONTRACT	
Options appraisal and business case	0.2% – 0.5%
Procurement process via Competitive Dialogue, inclusive of consultants and lawyers (5)	5% – 6%
(or procurement via negotiated tender, inclusive of consultants and lawyers) (5)	2% – 3%
Officer time and on-costs (frequently not assessed)	0.3% – 1.5%
Cost of related work financed by public sector (variable)	n/a
Contract renegotiation/termination costs (6)	1% – 3%
Total Transaction Costs	**6.5% – 9.5%**
Total Contract Costs (one-off transaction cost spread over 8 year contract period) but excluding retained client costs	**10.3% – 42.2%**
REDUCTION IN SPENDING ON SERVICE DELIVERY	
Contractor's Profit (7) In addition, the contractor will add the cost of risk premiums, bidding costs, and the increased cost of private capital compared to that of the public sector.	6% – 12%

Notes: *Based on minimum total contract value of £10m. Source: (1) Audit Commission 2008. (2) Based on ESSU, 2007. (3) Audit Commission 2008, Department of the Environment 1993 and 1997, Centre for Public Services 1995, Escott and Whitfield 1995. (4) Centre for Public Services, 1995. (5) HM Treasury Competitive Dialogue, 2010. (6) Based on sample of contract termination costs. (7) Pre-tax operating profit based on sample of major outsourcing companies.

contracts concluded "*...the government pays billions more annually in taxpayers dollars to hire contractors than it would to hire federal employees to perform comparable services*" (Project on Government Oversight, 2011). The federal government pays "*...contractors 1.83 times more than the government pays federal employees in total compensation, and more than 2 times the total compensation paid in the private sector for comparable services*" (ibid).

Contestable markets

A contestable market is one in which providers face a credible threat of competition with keen competition on prices having low barriers of entry and exit. Much of the concern about achieving 'contestability' is not from a technical economic perspective, but has a political objective to maximise private sector interest and to minimise the likelihood of in-house provision. There are many examples where options appraisals reduce competition by excluding the in-house option, or using a status-quo option that is designed to fail. Private contractors don't like competing against in-house bids because they believe the publc sector has unfair advantage with local knowledge and political support. Competitive neutrality or a 'level playing field', a favourite demand from private contractors and their trade organisations, is intended to ensure that bidders are treated equally and fairly. In reality, it is tilted towards the private sector, because of the constraints imposed on public sector organisations, such as trading restrictions, raising capital investment, economies of scale, ability to diversify and accountability and disclosure requirements (Whitfield, 1992).

Markets consolidate via takeovers, mergers, diversification, and by firms exiting the market. For example, five companies, Arriva (Deutsche Bahn), First Group, Go-Ahead Group, National Express and Stagecoach Group, dominate the provision of local bus services following deregulation in 1986. Public sector auditing and management consultancy is dominated by four global companies - Pricewaterhouse Coopers, KPMG, Deloitte, and Ernst and Young. Four companies, Veolia (France), Biffa, Sita (France) and FCC (Spain) had 43% of the waste management market in 2008. The collection and treatment of waste (recycling, reuse and disposal) market was valued at £8.9bn in 2009 (Key Note, 2010). Three companies, BT, Capita and Mouchel, have a 61.4% market share by value of local government strategic partnership contracts. Six of the ten companies with SSP contracts are foreign-owned with 32.5% market share by contract value (Whitfield, 2010b).

The embeddedness of competition and markets

Neoliberal transformation is more uneven than is usually acknowledged. The legal 'lock-in' built into the system is one indicator, for example, through regulatory frameworks or penalties payable for contract termination, or through externally imposed controls such as Free Trade Agreements or EU regulation. Others include the extent of cultural change that has been introduced (for example, the erosion of public service principles, or acceptance of commercial values); the operational scope of market mechanisms and new institutional forms; the success or otherwise of changes introduced (such as savings, performance improvement, innovation); the nature of changes in the organisation of work and jobs; changes in power relations with new user organisations that would defend the arrangements; and an attempted weakening of trade union opposition.

The erosion of public service principles and values and their replacement by business values and individual responsibility, has been significantly slowed because of a gulf between rhetoric and reality. Some senior and middle public sector managers avidly promote commissioning and partnerships, in the belief that there is 'no viable alternative'. However, a large proportion of public sector staff remain committed to public service principles, despite the confusing language of neoliberal transformation.

Irrespective of the degree of lock-in, the elements of embeddedness are reversible with the appropriate level of political commitment and public sector capability, although the speed of reversal will inevitably vary.

Market games

Markets and competitive regimes encourage contractors to maximise their income. To do this, they resort to 'gaming' techniques that exploit loopholes in payment systems, ineffective monitoring and inspection, contract variations, and focus on high-income activities. Construction companies are adept at submitting claims for additional costs caused by client delays, adverse weather and additional work. Service companies are adept at submitting claims for what they perceive to be changes in the scope of the contract and/or out-of-hours service provision.

Gaming in the health market includes up-coding (recording additional unnecessary diagnoses and procedures, or selecting the most expensive diagnoses); the discharge and readmission of patients to attract additional payments for a single treatment; inappropriate admissions (for example, from accident and emergency); deliberately keeping patients in hospital for more than 48 hours to attract the full tariff; misclassifying patients into specialist healthcare resource groups that are funded through separate arrangements; and patient dumping, by not accepting severely ill patients or 'under-treating' them, by limiting or withholding more expensive treatments, are other techniques used (Whitfield, 2006).

Techniques used in other services include deliberately failing to carry out functions that incur low financial penalties, because it is often cheaper for contractors to bear the financial penalties imposed for poor service than it is to employ staff to maintain quality standards. 'Cream-skimming', 'cherry picking' and focusing on the 'low hanging fruit' describe contractor's selecting high value or low-cost customers, who are more profitable to serve. This is similar to 'parking', which is the ruthless non-treatment of harder-to-help clients.

Inefficiencies in markets

Efficiency is a means to an end, not an end itself: *"...it is not a goal, but an instrument to achieve other goals. It is not a value, but a way to achieve other values"* (Stein, 2001). Efficiency has no inherent value. Yet minimising the cost of administration is often cited as an objective, an end in itself, and becomes a target with percentage reductions (often justified by claiming to transfer 'savings' to 'frontline services'). But efficient at what, for whom, and how does 'increased efficiency' impact on the quality of service and strategic objectives? On this basis, perish the thought, health and education could be made more efficient by excluding patients with long-term illness and pupils with special needs.

Government and public services are often branded as being inefficient whilst the private sector is considered efficient, despite evidence to the contrary. Efficiency should only be considered in the context of the overall objectives and strategy of a service. The cost of administration and use/allocation of resources (the 'cost of doing business' in the private sector) should only be assessed in the context of these objectives and strategy.

Several efficiency drives have been launched by governments in the last two decades, for example, the Gershon Review with £21.5bn savings by 2007/08 built into the Spending Review 2004 (HM Treasury 2004). More recently, the now-abandoned Regional Efficiency and Improvement Programme focused on improving efficiency through joint purchasing, shared services and rationalisation. However, efficiency programmes frequently focus on productivity and costs, and do not address team working and managerial delayering, innovative ideas from staff and trade unions, joint public sector or shared service delivery. Public sector managers look to copy private sector organisational structures, business values and working practices to achieve 'efficiency' gains. This further erodes public sector values and priorities and makes productivity and savings targets the focus of performance management. Despite the 'freedom and flexibility', 'localism' and sustainable development rhetoric, efficiency initiatives usually emphasize making better use of national buying power, rather than local or regional supply of goods and services.

Markets are never static. Vouchers, savings accounts and other mechanisms are promoted to extend competitive forces and consumer choice, whilst increasing the scope for user charges through 'added value' contributions to widen 'choice'. The transaction, regulation and financial cost of operating competitive regimes are rarely quantified let alone taken into account. Nor are the public costs of labour market impacts, accountability and increasing inequality fully considered.

Marketisation drives privatisation into other services, in particular, by arms length companies seeking independence and diversification. It leads to the growth of brokers and agents to advise service users on how they can gain maximum advantage from the market. Twenty Premier League football clubs spent £67m on agents' fees in the financial year ending September 2010. This may be an extreme example of the broker/agent role but demonstrates how they syphon resources and who ultimately pays. Public and private providers will be increasingly forced into advertising and marketing to attract pupils and patients. Promoting a brand, differentiating the 'offer', cultivating niche markets will require a marketing strategy, management responsibility, the production of advertising and marketing materials and a marketing budget. There are likely to be restructuring and organisational costs further down the line, as public and private providers withdraw from some services and start up new ones.

How markets deal with risk

Chapter 1 described the role of securitisation, a form of financial engineering, in which financial institutions seek to spread the risk of investments by transferring them to other financial institutions or to special purpose companies (with off-balance sheet financing so that the debt does not appear in the accounts). The commodification and transfer of risk was examined in Chapter 3. Risks in outsourcing and PPP projects should be identified and priced at an early stage but are often not. The price of risk transfer is often adjusted in PPP cost assessments because it is a variable estimate and can take account of changing contractual responsibilities, economic conditions and comparative costs of other alternatives (Whitfield, 2010a).

Another tactic is to spread share ownership across a number of different investment funds. 'Portfolio management' often involves the acquisition of assets, followed by the sale of small share stakes and is, in essence, another type of securitisation. For example, Global Infrastructure Partners acquired Gatwick Airport from BAA (Ferrovial, Spain) in 2010 and subsequently sold a 15% stake to the Abu Dhabi Investment Authority, a sovereign wealth fund, and a 12% stake to South Korea's National Pension Service.

Commissioning and economic growth

Apparently, competition in public service markets *"...can result in increased economic growth and greater prosperity"* (OFT, 2011b). It is claimed that 'dynamic markets' drive effective competition between suppliers who either make efficiency savings, improve quality and innovate or risk losing market share. Greater efficiency leads to improved productivity that in turn leads to *"growth and wealth creation"* (ibid). There are many flaws in the application of this ideology. Firstly, most of the evidence is based on research in manufacturing industry or retail sectors. Secondly, there are tenuous links between how improved efficiency and productivity in public service contracts leads to growth in the economy. Thirdly, prosperity and wealth creation for whom? The shareholders and senior management of the large national and transnational companies will be the prime beneficiaries of 'efficiency savings'. Fourthly, the performance of the private sector in delivering public services is completely missing from the OFT and consultants' studies. Fifthly, there is an assumption that all innovation is positive and in the public interest. The evidence of financial innovation over the last decade proves that this is a crass assumption. Finally, the quality of jobs for the people delivering public services is consistently ignored.

Opacity of markets

The securitisation of assets and debts is a classic opaque market, where trading operations, special purpose companies and off-balance sheet accounting methods mean that the whole process is carried out in secret. Mortgage holders had no knowledge that their mortgages were being sliced and diced, packaged with other mortgages and sold to third parties. Banks and financial institutions were ignorant of, or mis-assessed, the risks they retained in this process. Regulators, and others, once they were aware of the failures, made little or no effort to remedy the situation.

The lack of market transparency in the US subprime mortgage industry accelerated the crisis (interest rates were rarely advertised, hidden restrictions, complicated hybrid, adjustable-rate loans had initial teaser rates, with sharp increases after a few years) and brokers were frequently paid kickbacks by lenders, to steer borrowers into over-priced loans (Center for Responsible Lending, 2008). Sixty-one per cent of subprime loans that originated in 2006 *"...went to people with credit scores high enough to often qualify for conventional loans with far better terms"* (Brooks and Simon, 2007).

The PPP secondary market operated by PPP contractors, banks and financial institutions is very opaque and hypocritical. It operates on a need-to-know basis that assumes those without a direct financial stake do not have a right to know and, therefore, there is no obligation to publicise transactions. The overuse of 'commercial confidentiality', particularly in the public sector, conceals major matters of public interest, but is deemed necessary to 'protect' the commercial interests of companies.

Role of the state in markets

The public-versus-private debate is often defined as 'government versus markets' but this masks the wide ranging role of the state in developing markets. The state legitimates, creates, finances or subsidises, regulates and polices markets (to prevent collusion, bid rigging and Ponzi finance schemes). It controls demand, manages competition and procurement, reduces entry/exit barriers, controls or influences prices, and intervenes to prevent market failure. These roles vary widely between different types of markets and sectors and they undertake most of these roles in emerging markets, in particular the marketisation of public services. The state influences markets via public health policies that seek to change living patterns, such as eating and smoking. It may involve punitive taxation. State 'intervention' in public service markets starts from a different position than in commercial markets, because the state is creating, transferring and financing marketised services previously publicly provided and funded.

Local and central government, the European Union and international bodies have an influential role in shaping how markets operate. Individualisation and personalisation of public services leads to the growth of markets, brokers and other sub-markets. National and international standards and legislation establish regulatory frameworks for markets, including labour markets, such as the minimum wage, pensions and rights of staff transferred between employers. The inspection of performance is another regulatory control, for example care homes, which set broad parameters within which market participants operate. Facilities can be closed for consistent poor performance.

Market access may be directly or indirectly regulated by the state. For example, private contractors seeking access to the distribution and/or delivery of mail and parcels are regulated by the Postal Services Commission, implementing EU and UK liberalisation policies, which impose restrictions on both public and private providers.

Market prices in regulated industries – gas, electricity, telephone and water – are determined by negotiations on investment, maximum prices and profits between the state appointed regulator and industry representatives. The state also imposes regulations and procedures to protect citizens in terms of the quality of goods (recalls), treatment and rights of redress. It regulates labour markets to set minimum health and safety standards to prevent ill-treatment of workers.

State intervention to prevent market failure was evident in the bailout of banks in the US, UK, Germany and Ireland. The objectives of fiscal stimulus are to maintain or sustain economic stability and may support particular markets, for example, increased infrastructure spending will support the construction market and supply sectors, such as building materials and rapid transit or rail manufacturing.

Changing values and market language
Governments impose market rules and regulations to try to protect the public and service users from market abuse, exploitative prices, private monopoly and corporate greed. The advocates of marketisation and privatisation have a problem. So they resort to denials, half-truths and lies. Some go to inordinate lengths to try to set out a case as to how their 'reforms' or 'modernisation' will produce benefits for all, and claim they are 'not creating markets or privatising services'. A whole new body of words and phrases has been hijacked and used to mask and conceal true intentions or impose new business values. They now resort to invoking memories of the co-operative movement and mutualism in a desperate attempt to sell their policies. And when all else fails, just say 'sorry' the service failed, the bank went bust, or for centuries of discrimination and exploitation.

'Linguistic engineering' is practised both by the state and transnational companies. The latter use corporate rhetoric designed to create a specific view of corporate reality and *"...to present themselves in a benevolent and self-endorsing light"* (Alexander, 2003).

The four 'C's of challenge, compare, consult and competition, as the four elements of service reviews were introduced with 'best value' in 1998. The first three have been marginalised by the marketisation agenda in which 'choice', 'individual budgets', 'personalisation', 'direct payments', 'care brokers', 'personal advisers' and 'charging' are part of the neo-speak language. Contractors are now called 'providers' in an attempt to neutralise their position. Outsourcing and insourcing, off-shoring and near-shoring, *de facto* accept the ideology of commissioning instead of in-house provision. Service delivery, described as the 'offer', is another term with unacceptable commercial ideology. The procurement process has its own language of 'clients', 'commissioning', 'competition', 'contestability', 'contracts', 'consultants', 'Community Interest Companies' and 'co-production'. The government now encourages 'community action'! But there is one 'c' word which is missing – class.

The so-called 'independent' sector is dominated by private companies. The mask of 'independent' status is often used to try to 'neutralise' the transfer of services and assets to the private sector. Management consultants are not 'independent' or neutral. The current fad for 'independent' budget reviews by 'business leaders' and business-minded academics (Scotland and Ireland), is another manifestation of attempts to provide cover for more rampant neoliberal transformation of public services, and to bolster the claim that *"...there is no alternative"*.

Public Private Partnerships have their own jargon, such as bankability and public sector comparator, which are used to confuse, conceal, and maintain a barrier between the political and business interests promoting PPPs and service users and the public.

Statements such as the 'NHS free at the point of use' are meaningless because the health service could be entirely provided by the private sector and remain funded by the state, with the basic service free at the point of use. But once the private sector had a powerful role in service delivery, it would ensure that 'free at the point of use' would have less and less meaning or truth. The service that is free becomes more proscribed by stealth.

Advocates of contestability, competition, markets, public-private partnerships and outsourcing often claim that these policies are 'not privatisation'. This is a denial of theory and reality. For example, strategic service-delivery partnerships are claimed not to be privatisation when it is patently obvious that work previously carried out by the public sector is outsourced to private firms, with long-term contracts requiring the transfer or secondment of staff, equipment and intellectual property.

Privatisation is not limited to the transfer of economic and physical assets from the public to the private sector (see Chapter 3). It is 'playing with words' to argue otherwise. In other circumstances this is usually called deception.

Harold Pinter referred to 'political language' in his 2005 Nobel acceptance speech. Politicians *"...are interested not in truth but in power and in the maintenance of that power. To maintain that power it is essential that people remain in ignorance, they live in ignorance of the truth, even the truth of their own lives. What surrounds us therefore is a vast tapestry of lies, upon which we feed"* (Pinter, 2005).

Market and contract performance

Externalities or social costs and benefits

Externalities, or impacts, occur when companies, organisations and users do not bear the full costs or benefits of an activity. The costs or benefits are borne by other users, contractors, the state or society as a whole. For example, education at all levels benefits society by developing skills, attitudes, knowledge and research ability. Alternatively, manufacturing plants or farmers may pollute a river and damage the environment, yet they do not bear the costs. However, social, economic and environmental costs and benefits are rarely quantified, let alone taken into account, at the options appraisal or procurement stage. The contract price and budget are usually the only concern. The state has a crucial role in minimising negative externalities and promoting positive externalities through taxation, regulation, monitoring and inspection, planning and the provision of services.

The financial crisis and subsequent recession and the effects of climate change, are examples of externalities caused by market failure. US real estate failure resulted in persistent and negative shocks to housing demand with a decline in house prices and wealth much more severe than the metropolitan average. The future viability of some neighbourhoods has been questioned, where recovery will be protracted (Follain, 2010). The banks have no intention of admitting responsibility for the multi-billion economic and social costs of neighbourhood and city decline.

Externalities or market impacts include environmental (the cost of pollution or congestion), financial (public sector costs and benefits), health (effect of increased unemployment or changes in health and safety), economic (the effect of changes in production and supply chains on local firms), employment (public sector conditions and industrial relations influence the local labour market), and social (equalities and participation). The 'logic' of the market extends to jobs, terms and conditions. Private contractors are required to operate within the European Acquired Rights Directive (TUPE regulations in the UK) but the imposition of 'market discipline' mostly results in the loss of jobs and reductions in terms and conditions.

Market and contract failure

Market failure can occur from inadequate or asymmetric information. This may be due to market participants and can lead to inefficient resource allocation. Market access may be limited for particular contractors or to groups of users. Low income households are disadvantaged in both the supply and demand side of markets in terms of prices, quality of services and products, and ease of access. For example, lone parent households, social housing tenants and people with disabilities suffer significant disadvantages in energy, transport, food, financial services and the internet (OFT, 2010).

Bus services were deregulated in the name of competition in 1986 that led to a ruthless free-for-all, takeovers and mergers, and worse terms and conditions for drivers. Bus services continued to receive subsidies, now running at £2.6bn per annum. By 2011, 69% of local bus services are provided by five large operators – Arriva (Deutsche Bahn), First Group, Go-Ahead, National Express and Stagecoach – with only eleven municipal operators remaining. An inquiry into the bus market (excluding London and Northern Ireland) concluded *"...there are features of local markets for the supply of local bus services which in combination prevent, restrict or distort competition"* (Competition Commission, 2011). Bus operators in local markets faced limited head-to-head competition and a reduced threat from potential competitors and new entrants. *"The competitive process does not necessarily lead to the most efficient operator running the route and the surviving operator is not necessarily exposed to an ongoing discipline following the exit of its rival"* (ibid). The annual average return on capital employed for the five large operators was 13.6% for the five-year period between 2005/06 and 2010/11. This was yet another predictable outcome of 'market competition' in public services.

Identifying the full scale of market and contract failure is a book in itself. Many public sector contracts perform as required but a significant number do not. And when this is concentrated in particular services it is market failure. The termination, reduction in scope or renegotiation of contracts can arise from poorly constructed bids, mis-pricing the bid, a contractor failing to understand the complexity of a service, inflated demand, income and/or savings forecasts, equipment failure or inadequate specification.

This has certainly been the case with information and communications technology (ICT) contracts. A detailed analysis of 105 public sector ICT contracts, valued at £29.5bn, in central government, NHS, local authorities, public bodies and agencies outsourced in the previous decade, revealed cost overruns averaging 30.5% (£9bn). Of these, 57% of contracts experienced cost overruns that averaged 30.5%, major delays in 33% of projects, and 30% of contracts were terminated (Whitfield, 2007b).

The track record of strategic partnerships in the UK includes three contract terminations, two other contracts significantly reduced in scope, a further three with major problems and another being renegotiated – nine out of 44 contracts (Whitfield, 2010b). Globally, over 960 PPP projects, valued at over US$510bn, have been terminated, or were in major distress by 2009 (Whitfield, 2010a).

The NHS market-testing programme led to a series of contract failures and reduction in cleaning standards between 1983-2000 (Public Service Action, 1983-1997). By 2002 some 52% of domestic services contracts were outsourced, with an estimated value of £94m according to an unpublished NHS study. However, standards had declined to such an extent that the government allocated £31m to improve the quality of cleaning, combined with a Patient Environment Action Team (PEAT), to visit every hospital to inspect standards. Additional investment, specifically to improve cleaning, had risen to £68m by 2004. A new campaign began in 2004 to control infection, particularly MRSA, with a new specification (Department of Health, 2004). Local authorities' in-house care services have a significantly higher proportion rated good and excellent compared to privately-run services (Care Quality Commission, 2011).

The performance of private employment training was poor. In 2008–09, £94m (38%) of Pathways to Work programme expenditure on employment support did not deliver additional jobs. Between 2005-10 the Pathways programme cost £793m but did not provide a net return to the Exchequer. *"Although there has been a reduction of 125,000 claimants in receipt of incapacity benefits between February 2005 and*

August 2009, the Department accepted that Pathways will have contributed only modestly to this reduction, and cannot determine precisely its contribution" (House of Commons Committee of Public Accounts, 2010).

Markets frequently do not quickly rebound, which leads to further market failures. For example, the credit crunch has led to a continuing crisis in the US mortgage industry with one in four homes with mortgages classified as 'under water' (over three months behind on mortgage payments or in foreclosure). That accounts for $766bn negative equity debt. There is further crisis in the foreclosure process.

Crime and corruption

Major firms or contractors, acting alone or in consort, can exercise market power by reducing production in order to keep prices artificially high and thus produce higher profits. Contractors sometimes try to fix contract prices and/or win bids by collusion. Companies may wield market power through political connections, financing policy think tanks, promoting weak regulatory regimes and other corporate welfare strategies (see Chapter 3). Bribery and corruption are sometimes used to win contracts and to deter new market entrants.

Collusion with competing firms in bidding for contracts or fixing the price of products, in effect rigging the market, is illegal. The Office of Fair Trading imposed £129.2m fines on 103 building companies for collusion in bidding for construction contracts between 2000-05 (Office of Fair Trading, 2009b). The companies ranged from small to large including Kier (£17.9m fine), Interserve (£11.6m) and Galliford Try (£8.3m). In addition, six recruitment agencies were fined £39.3m for operating a cartel, the 'Construction Recruitment Forum', which fixed prices for the supply of professional, managerial, trade and labour skills to the construction industry (Office of Fair trading, 2009c).

Rogue traders and criminal networks subvert markets and exploit regulatory loopholes, for example, the supply of cheap labour, illegal sourcing of materials (often cheap imports that break sustainability guidelines and export/import regulations) and tax evasion, which may reduce prices and enable them to undercut legitimate suppliers. Regulatory bodies often fail to monitor the effectiveness of regulations and contract performance because of a lack of resources, powers and/or political commitment.

Financial donations to political campaigns are often made in the expectation of voting for weak regulatory regimes, tax breaks, outsourcing and privatisation. In addition, major companies spend large sums employing lobbyists to promote existing regulatory regimes or to advocate stringent controls on trade unions. This shadow activity, on the edge of legality, is another characteristic of market forces.

Markets increase corporate welfare as contractors, business interests and trade bodies campaign for light regulation, deregulation, tax cuts, and subsidies, and constantly seek to embed market discipline throughout the public sector. For example, the Bankruptcy Coalition, which included the American Bankers Association, the Mortgage Bankers Association, Citigroup and Bank of America spent $65.7m in 2007/08 in lobbying and campaign contributions to make the case against stronger regulation of the industry and against giving bankruptcy judges the power to modify the terms of mortgages.

In reality the drive to marketise and privatise public services and the welfare state means that service users will be forced to deal with global financial institutions and transnational companies for these services on a daily basis.

Conclusion

Continuing financial crises, market and public service contract failures reflect the political and corporate commitment to neoliberalism, irrespective of the consequences for service users, public employees, social justice, and local and regional economies.

Austerity and spending cuts create the conditions under which the financialisation, personalisation, marketisation and privatisation of public services and the welfare state will be accelerated.

Who delivers public services and who owns the public infrastructure are vitally important, but they are only part of the agenda. Coalition policies are designed to dispossess, disinvest, destabilise, depoliticise and disempower, amounting to the deconstruction of democracy.

Their policies are designed to radically change the design, scope and quality of public services. Once services are financialised and individualised, the principles of solidarity and social justice will be permanently eroded. Contractors, consultants and business and trade organisations do not just have a vested interest in obtaining more public service contracts. They are committed to the neoliberal transformation of public services and a corporate welfare state. The commodification of children and the elderly; the break up and fragmentation of public networks of schools and hospitals; deregulation; the imposition of market forces; the sale of universal services; and vast profits from privately financed infrastructure and services, are all designed to spur the growth of private health, private education and private care.

We should not be distracted by the rhetoric of localism and social enterprise. The idea that a 'new social economy' can challenge, or even be an alternative to, capitalism, is unfounded. It is a diversion and a delusion. We need to harness the innovation and skills that already exist in the public sector, instead of trying to advance the self-interest of entrepreneurs. The energy and public money put into building an alternative sector will ultimately reduce and undermine the public sector.

Instead, we must reconstruct the economy, state and public services. Reconstruction has three inter-connected parts – new economic policies, alternative policies for public services and the welfare state, and a new public service management.

The deconstruction of democracy will not be defeated by trade unions, community organisations, civil society organisations or political groups acting alone.

We must organise in the workplace and community, forge coalitions and public service alliances, and build political support for alternative policies and plans. We have to organise industrial, civil and community action, intervene in the transformation and procurement processes, and challenge the vested interests of business and their political allies.

References

Airbus Future Projects Office (2008) *Boeing 787 Lessons Learnt*, October, Bristol.

Alcock, P. (2010) *What are our Future Sources of Welfare: A new role for the third sector?* In *Supply Side Futures for Public Services*, 2020 Public Services Trust, London, http://www.2020publicservicestrust.org/publications/

Alexander, R. (2003) *Environmental Issues, Third World Agriculture and Multinationals: Who Pays the Price?* TRANS, Internet-Zeitschrift für Kulturwissenschaften, No. 15, http://www.inst.at/trans/15Nr/06_4/alexander15.htm

Allen Report (2011a) *Early Intervention: The Next Steps, An Independent Report to the Government*, Graham Allen MP, January, London, http://grahamallenmp.wordpress.com

Allen Report (2011b) *Early Intervention: Small Investment, Massive Savings, Second Independent Report to the Government*, Graham Allen MP, July, London, http://grahamallenmp.wordpress.com

All Party Parliamentary Group on Employee Ownership (2011) Sharing Ownership: *The Role of Employee Ownership in Public Service Delivery*, June, London.

Amato, G. and Verhostadt, G. (2011) A Plan to save the euro and curb speculators, *Financial Times*, 3 July, http://www.ft.com/intl/cms/s/0/1c6c3d0c-a59c-11e0-83b2-00144feabdc0.html#axzz1Ykwwrvlb

American Institute of Architects and Associated General Contractors of America (2004) *Primer on Project Delivery*, Washington DC, www.aia.org

American International Group (2011) *Understanding AIG's Relationship with the U.S. Government*, June, (accessed 8 September, 2011) http://www.aigcorporate.com/GIinAIG/owedtoUS_gov_new.html

Anti-Academies Alliance (2011) *Free Schools and Why would a school want to become an Academy?* Birmingham, http://www.antiacademiesalliance.org.uk

Apollo Group (2009) Apollo Group Inc. Resolves University of Phoenix False Claims Act Case, News Release, 14 December, Phoenix, http://www.apollogrp.edu

Apollo Group (2010) Ninth Circuit Court of Appeals Reverses Lower Court Ruling in Apollo Group Inc. Securities Lawsuit, News Release, 23 June, http://www.apollogrp.edu

Apollo Group (2011a) Apollo Group Inc. *Reports Fiscal 2011 Third Quarter Results*, News Release, 30 June, Phoenix, http://www.apollogrp.edu

Apollo Group (2011b) *Annual Report 2010*, http://www.apollogrp.edu/Annual-Reports/Apollo2010AR.pdf

Arvidson, M., Lyon, F., McKay, S. and Moro, D. (2010) *The ambitions and challenges of SROI*, Working Paper 49, Third Sector Research Centre,

Birmingham, www.tsrc.ac.uk

Audit Commission (2008) *For better, for worse: Value for money in strategic service-delivery partnerships*, January, London. http://www.auditcommission.gov.uk

Audit Commissions (2010a) *Financial Management of Personal Budgets*, October, London, http://www.audit-commission.gov.uk

Audit Commission (2010b) Annual Audit Letter: Somerset County Council, 2009/10, November, London, http://www1.somerset.gov.uk/council/board9/2010%20December%209%20Item%2013%20Somerset%20County%20Council%20Annual%20Audit%20Letter%202009-10%20Appendix%20A.pdf

Audit Commission (2011) *Procurement Strategy*, September, London, http://www.audit-commission.gov.uk

Bellofiore, R. (2011) A crisis of capitalism, *The Guardian*, 22 September, http://www.guardian.co.uk/commentisfree/2011/sep/21/crisis-of-capitalism?INTCMP=SRCH

Big Society Capital (2011) Big Society Capital Launch, Press Release, September, London, http://www.bigsocietycapital.com/pdfs/BSC%20Launch%20Press%20Release.pdf

Bland, J. (2011) *Time to get serious: International lessons for developing public service mutuals*, Cooperatives UK, http://www.uk.coop

Blejer, M. (2011) Europe is running a giant Ponzi scheme, *Financial Times*, 5 May, http://www.ft.com/intl/cms/s/0/ee728cb6-773e-11e0-aed6-00144feabdc0.html #axzz1Ykwwrvlb

Bloomberg News (2011) *Whitney Municipal-Bond Apocalypse Short on Specifics*, 1 February, http://www.bloomberg.com/news/print/2011-02-01/whitney -municipal-bond apocalypse-is-short-on-default-specifics.html

Bovaird, T. and Downe, J. (2008) *Innovation in Public Engagement and Co-production of Services*, Meta-Evaluation of the Local Government Modernisation Agenda, University of Birmingham.

Boyle, D. and Harris, M. (2009) *The Challenge of Co-Production*, NESTA and New Economic Foundation, December, London.

Brooks, R. and Simon, R. (2007) Subprime Debacle Traps Even Very Credit-Worthy, *Wall Street Journal*, 3 December, http://online.wsj.com/article/SB119662974358911035.html

Browne Review (2010) *Securing a Sustainable Future for Higher Education*, The Independent Review of Higher Education Funding and Student Finance, London, http://webarchive.nationalarchives.gov.uk/+/hereview.independent.gov.uk/hereview

Buiter, W. (2008) Blockade the tax havens, *Financial Times*, 20 February, http://blogs.ft.com/maverecon/2008/02/blockade-the-tax-havens/

Bureau of Investigative Journalism (2011a) *£500m paid in botched NHS contracts*

to private companies, 25 May, http://www.thebureauinvestigates.com/2011/05/
25/500m-sweetener-paid-to-private-companies-to-treat-nhs-patients/

Bureau of Investigative Journalism (2011b) *Get the data: NHS spent £60m on
cancelled healthcare contracts*, 25 May, http://www.thebureauinvestigates.com/
2011/ 05/25/get-the-data-60m-spent-on-cancelled-healthcare-contracts/

Bureau of Investigative Journalism (2011c) *Analysis: Should we be wary of private
companies' involvement in healthcare?* 27 May, http://www.thebureau
investigates.com/2011/05/27/should-we-be-wary-of-private-companies-
involvement -in-healthcare/

Burke, M. (2010) Investment in Education would cut the Deficit, *Socialist
Economic Bulletin*, 16 December, http://socialisteconomicbulletin.blogspot.com/
2010/12/investment-in-education-would-cut.html

Burke, M. (2011) The attack on the NHS, *Socialist Economic Bulletin*, 7 April,
London.

Burke, M., Irvin, G. and Weeks, J. (2011) *A Brighter Future for the British
Economy*, September, London, http://falseeconomy.org.uk/files/brighter.pdf

Burnham, P. (2001) New Labour and the politics of depoliticisation, *British
Journal of Politics and International Relations*, Vol 3, No 2, June, pp 127-149.

Bush, J. and Gingrich, N. (2011) Better off Bankrupt, *Los Angeles Times*, 27
January, http://www.latimes.com/news/opinion/commentary/la-oe-gingrich
-bankruptcy-2110127,0,4958969.story

Butcher, J. (2005) Government, *The Third Sector and the Rise of Social Capital*,
Centre for Research in Public Sector Management, October, University of
Canberra, Canberra.

Cabinet Office (1996) *Competing for Quality Policy Review*, London.

Cabinet Office (2010) *Building a Stronger Civil Society*, October, London,
www.cabinetoffice.gov.uk

Cabinet Office (2011a) *Growing the Social Investment Market: A vision and
strategy*, February, London.

Cabinet Office (2011b) *Big Society innovation aims to get families out of
deprivation*, Press Release, 26 August, London, http://www.cabinetoffice.gov.uk/
news/big-society-innovation-aims-get-families-out-deprivation

Cabinet Office (2011c) *Procurement policy Note – Modernising the EU Public
Procurement Rules: Update on UK Influencing Activity*, Information Note
05/11, August, London.

Cabinet Office (2011d) *Data Centre Strategy, G-Cloud and Government
Applications Store Programme Phase 2*, February, London, http://www.cabinet
office.gov.uk/sites/default/files/resources/01-G-CloudVision.pdf

Cabinet Office (2011e) *National Survey of Charities and Social Enterprises 2010*,
June, London, http://www.nscsesurvey.com/download/2010/Overall.pdf

Callinicos, A. (2010) *Bonfire of Illusions: The Twin Crises of the Liberal World*, Polity Press, Cambridge.

Campaign Against Climate Change (2010) *One Million Climate Jobs: Solving the economic and environmental crises*, London, www.climate-change-jobs.org/node/14

Campaign for State Education (2011) *A Good Local Education Authority*, June, London, http://www.campaignforstateeducation.org.uk

Care Quality Commission (2011) *The state of health care and adult social care in England*, London, http://www.cqc.org.uk/_db/_documents/6227_CQC_SoC2009-10_TAG.pdf

Carillion plc (2011) Completion of the Acquisition of Eaga plc by Carillion plc, 21 April, Stock Exchange Announcement, http://www.carillionplc.com/investors/SEA%20-%2021st%20April%202011.asp

Center for American Progress (2011) *Social Impact Bonds: A promising new financing model to accelerate social innovation and improve government performance*, February, Washington DC.

Center for Responsible Lending (2008) *Turmoil in the U.S. Credit Markets: The Genesis of the Current Economic Crisis, Testimony of Eric Stein*, U.S. Senate Committee on Banking, Housing and Urban Affairs, 16 October, Washington DC, http://www.responsiblelending.org/mortgage-lending/policy-legislation/congress/senate-testimony-10-16-08-hearing-stein-final.pdf

Centre for Public Services (1995) *Calculation of the National Costs & Savings of CCT*, Research Paper, Sheffield, http://www.european-services-strategy.org.uk/outsourcing-library/public-costs/calculation-of-the-national-costs-and-savings/

Centre for Public Services (1999) *The Future of Tameside Care Group*, http://www.european-services-strategy.org.uk/outsourcing-library/transfers-and-externalisation/

Centre for Public Services (2004) *The Case for the 4th Option for Council Housing: and a Critique of Arms Length Management Organisations*, May, Sheffield, www.european-services-strategy.org.uk/publications

Centre for Public Services (2005) *Strategic Partnership in Crisis*, Bedfordshire UNISON, March, Sheffield, www.european-services-strategy.org.uk/publications

Centre for Research and Information on the Public, Social and Cooperative Economy, (2007) *The Social Economy in the European Union*, European Economic and Social Committee, http://www.eesc.europa.eu/?i=portal.en.social-economy-category-documents.3167

Centre for Research in Socio-Cultural Change (2011) *Knowing What To Do: How not to build trains*, July, http://www.cresc.ac.uk/publications/knowing-what-to-do-how-not-to-buildtrains

Centre for Research on Education Outcomes (2009) *Multiple Choice: Charter School Performance in 16 States*, June, Stanford University, http://credo.stanford.edu/reports

Centre for Research on Education Outcomes (2011) *Charter School Performance in Pennsylvania*, April, Stanford University, http://credo.stanford.edu/reports/PA%20State%20Report _20110404_FINAL.pdf

Centre Forum (2011) *Your Choice: how to get better public services*, London, http://www.centreforum.org/assets/pubs/your-choice-web.pdf

Civitas (2010) *Refusing Treatment: The NHS and market-based reform*, October, London.

Clarke, L. (2010) Why are we so bad at construction training, *The Guardian*, 26 October, http://www.guardian.co.uk/education/2010/oct/26/construction -training-green-building

Cohen, R. (2011) Motown Blues: Foundations and Government Struggle for Solutions and With Each Other, *The Nonprofit Quarterly*, 17 July, http://www.nonprofitquarterly.org

College Results Online (2011) University of Phoenix-Online Campus, (accessed 31 July 2011), http://www.collegeresults.org

Compass (2009) *Co-production: The modernisation of public services by staff and users*, Gannon, Z. and Lawson, N. http://www,compasonline.org.uk

Community Sector Coalition (2011) *Unseen, Unequal, Untapped, Unleashed, The potential for community action at the grassroots*, London, http://www.e-c-a.ac.uk/media/uploaded_files/CSC_policy_paper_Unleashing_the_Potential.pdf

Competition Commission (2011) *Local Bus Market Investigations: Provisional Findings*, London, http://www.competition-commission.org.uk/inquiries/ref2010/localbus/ provisional_findings.htm

Confederation of British Industry (2010) *Tackling congestion, driving growth: A new approach to roads policy*, London, http://www.cbi.org.uk/pdf/ -cbi-tackling-congestion.pdf

Conference for Socialist Economists London Working Group (1980) *The Alternative Economic Strategy: A Labour Movement Response to the Economic Crisis*, London.

Congressional Budget Office (2011a) *Report of the Troubled Asset Relief Program*, March, Washington DC, http://cbo.gov/doc.cfm?index=12118&zzz=41633

Congressional Budget Office (2011b) *Long-Term Analysis of a Budget Proposal by Chairman Ryan*, April, Washington DC, http://www.cbo.gov/ftpdocs/121xx/doc12128/04-05-Ryan_Letter.pdf

Congressional Oversight Panel (2010) *November Report: Examining the Consequences of Mortgage Irregularities for Financial Stability and Foreclosure Mitigation*, http://cybercemetery.unt.edu/archive/cop/20110402010313/ http://cop.senate.gov/documents/cop-111610-report.pdf

Cook, C. (2011) Education: Lesson in Progress, *Financial Times*, 1 September, http://www.ft.com

Corporate Europe Observatory (2010) *The Battle to Protect Corporate Investment Rights*, July, Brussels.

Cragg, S. (2011) *In the Matter of the Health and Social Care Bill 2011: and in the matter of the duty of the Secretary of State for Health to provide a National Health Service*, Doughty Street Chambers, July, London.

Cunningham, I. (2008) A Race to the Bottom: Exploring Variations in Employment Conditions in the Voluntary Sector, *Public Administration*, December, Vol. 86, Issue 4, p1033-1053.

Davies, W. (2010) *Bringing mutualism back into business*, Policy Network, December, London, http://www.policy-network.net

Deber, R. Forget, E. and Roos, L. (2004) Medical savings accounts in a universal system: wishful thinking meets evidence, *Health Policy 70*, pp49–66.

Deber, R. (2011) *Medical Savings Accounts in Financing Healthcare, Canadian Health Services Research Foundation, Financing Models*, Paper 3, Ottawa, www.chsrf.ca

Department for Communities and Local Government (2011a) *Enterprise Zone Prospectus*, London, http://www.communities.gov.uk/documents/localgovernment/pdf/1872724.pdf

Department for Communities and Local Government (2011b) *Eric Pickles predicts public service shake up - as Community Budgets begin*, Press Release, 29 March, London, http://www.communities.gov.uk/news/newsroom/187561

Department for Education and Skills (2004) *Scoping the market for children's services*, PricewaterhouseCoopers, October, London.

Department for Work and Pensions (2011) *The Work Programme*, August, London, http://www.dwp.gov.uk

Department of Business, Innovation and Skills, (2009) *Research to improve the assessment of additionality*, October, London, http://www.bis.gov.uk

Department of Education (2011) *Government Response to Judicial Review hearings on Building Schools for the Future*, 24 January, London, http://www.education.gov.uk

Department of Health (2004) *Towards cleaner hospitals and lower rates of infection*, London, http://www.dh.gov.uk/en/Publicationsandstatistics/Publications/PublicationsPolicyAndGuidance/Browsable/DH_4096315

Department of Health (2006) *Independent Sector Treatment Centres*, Report from Commercial Director, February, London.

Department of Health (2010a) *A Vision for Adult Social Care*, November, London, http://www.dh.gov.uk/prod_consum_dh/groups/dh_digitalassets/@dh/@en/@ps/documents/digitalasset/dh_121971.pdf

Department of Health (2010b) *The NHS Constitution*, London,

http://www.dh.gov.uk/prod_consum_dh/groups/dh_digitalassets/@dh/@en/
@ps/documents/digitalasset/dh_113645.pdf

Department of Health (2011a) Dismantling the NHS National programme for
IT, Press Release, 22 September, London, http://mediacentre.dh.gov.uk/2011/
09/22/dismantling-the-nhs-national-programme-for-it/

Department of Health (2011b) *Government response to the NHS Future Forum
report: Briefing notes on amendments to the Health and Social Care Bill*, June,
London, http://www.dh.gov.uk/prod_consum_dh/groups/dh_digitalassets/
documents/digitalasset/dh_127880.pdf

Department of Health (2011c) *Health and Social Care Bill 2011: Impact
Assessments*, London, http://www.dh.gov.uk/prod_consum_dh/groups/
dh_digitalassets/documents/digitalasset/dh_123582.pdf

Department of the Environment (1993) *Competition and Service: The Impact of
the Local Government Act 1988*, HMSO, London.

Department of the Environment (1997) *CCT and Local Authority Blue-Collar
Services*, London.

Dervereux, M. and Loretz, S. (2011) *Corporation Tax in the United Kingdom*,
University of Oxford.

Detroit Regional Workforce Fund (2011) *Addressing Detroit's Basic Skills Crisis*,
www.detroitregionalworkforcefund.org

Dolphin, T. (2010) *Financial Sector Taxes*, Institute for Public Policy Research,
June, London, http://www.ippr.org.uk

Dolphin, T. (2011) quoted in Ministers admit family debt burden is set to soar,
The Guardian, 2 April, http://www.guardian.co.uk/politics/2011/apr/02/
family-debt-burden-government-figures

Downes, P. (2011) The scandal of the cost of Gove's cash 'bribe', Anti-Academies
Autumn Newspaper, September, Birmingham, http://antiacademies.org.uk/
2011/09/anti-academies-autumn-newspaper

Economic Policy Institute (2011) *Abandoning What Works: Expansionary fiscal
policy is still the best tool for boosting jobs*, Briefing Paper 304, April,
Washington DC, http://www.epi.org/page/-
/old/briefingpapers/BriefingPaper304%20(4).pdf

eGov Monitor (2010) *61 Health Service Projects Worth £900 Million To Become
Social Enterprises Run By NHS Staff Says Andrew Lansley*, 17 November,
http://www.egovmonitor.com/node/39468/print

Ellins, J. and Ham, C. (2009) *NHS Mutual: Engaging staff and aligning incentives
to achieve higher levels of performance*, Nuffield Trust, London,
www.nuffieldtrust.org.uk

Elliott, L. and Atkinson, D. (2008) *The Gods that Failed: How Blind Faith in
Markets Has Cost us Our Future*, Bodley Head, London.

Erturk, I, Froud, J, Johal, S, Leaver, A, Moran, M, Williams, K. (2011) *City State against national settlement: UK economic policy and politics after the financial crisis*, Working Paper No 101, Centre for Research on Socio-Cultural Change, Milton Keynes.

Escott, K. and Whitfield, D. (1995) *The Gender Impact of CCT in Local Government*, for Equal Opportunities Commission, Manchester.

EuroMemo Group (2011) *Confronting the Crisis: Austerity or Solidarity*, http://www.euromemo.eu

European Commission (2011) *Reflections Paper on Services of General Interest in Bilateral FTAs (Applicable to both Positive and Negative Lists)*, Directorate-General for Trade, 28 February, Brussels.

European Commission (2011) *Green Paper on the modernisation of EU public procurement policy Towards a more efficient European Procurement Market*, COM(2011) 15 final, January, Brussels, http://ec.europa.eu/internal_market/consultations/docs/2011/public_procurement/20110127_COM_en.pdf

European Services Strategy Unit (2006) *North Tyneside – A Commissioning Council? Evidence Base for the Alternative polices, for UNISON Northern.* www.european-services-strategy.org.uk/outsourcing-library/public-costs/north-tyneside-a-commissioning-council-evide

European Services Strategy Unit (2007a) *Cost Overruns, Delays and Terminations: 105 outsourced public sector ICT projects*, Research Report No 2: www.european-services-strategy.org.uk/publications

European Services Strategy Unit (2007b) *Does Excelcare Really? An investigation into the transfer of 10 residential care homes by Essex County Council to Excelcare Holdings PLC*, Essex UNISON, www.european-services-strategy.org.uk/publications

European Services Strategy Unit (2008a) *Commissioning and Procurement Toolkit: Local Government and Health, UNISON Northern Region*, http://www.european-services-strategy.org.uk/outsourcing-library/procurement-and-commissioning-best-practice

European Services Strategy Unit (2008b) *The Case Against Leisure Trusts*, www.european-services-strategy.org.uk/outsourcing-library.

European Services Strategy Unit (2008) *PPP Briefing: Strategic Service-delivery Partnerships and Outsourced Shared Services Projects*, http://www.european-services-strategy.org.uk/news/2008/ppp-briefing-strategic-service-delivery-partne

European Services Strategy Unit (2009) *Future of Hendon Cemetery and Crematorium Implications for Future Shape*, April, Barnet UNISON, http://www.european-services-strategy.org.uk/publications/public-bodies/transformation-and-public-service-reform/

European Services Strategy Unit (2010a) *Employment Risk Matrix*, www.european-services-strategy.org.uk/outsourcing-library.

European Services Strategy Unit (2010b) *Critique of Barnet Council's Options Appraisal of Adult Social Care In-House Provider Services*, Barnet UNISON, http://www.european-services-strategy.org.uk/news/critique-of-barnet-councils -options-appraisal

European Services Strategy Unit (2010c) *Good Practice Transformation Toolkit*, Barnet UNISON, http://www.european-services-strategy.org.uk/news/ good-practice-transformation-toolkit-for-barne

European Services Strategy Unit (2010d) *The impact and performance of management buyouts, social enterprises and mutual model*, Briefing No. 7, Future Shape of the Council Programme, Barnet UNISON, http://www.european-services-strategy.org.uk/news/2008/future-shape-of -the-council-london-borough-of

European Services Strategy Unit (2010e) *Economic Case for In-House Options and Bids*, http://www.european-services-strategy.org.uk/news/the-economic-case -for-in-house-options-and-bid

European Services Strategy Unit (2011a) *Analysis of Development and Regulatory Services Business Case*, London Borough of Barnet, Barnet UNISON, http://www.european-services-strategy.org.uk/news/analysis-of-development -and-regulatory-service

European Trade Union Confederation (2006) *The European Social Model*, 21 March, Brussels, http://www.etuc.org/a/2771

European Union (2007) Treaty of Lisbon, *Official Journal of the European Union*, 2007/C 306/01, 17 December, Brussels.

Farnsworth, K. (2004) *Corporate Power and Social Policy in a Global Economy: British Welfare Under the Influence*, The Policy Press, Bristol.

Ferguson, I. (2008) *Reclaiming Social Work: Challenging Neoliberalism and Promoting Social Justice*, Sage, London.

Financial Crisis Inquiry Commission (2011) *The Financial Crisis Inquiry Report: Final Report of the National Commission on the Causes of the Financial and Economic Crisis in the United States*, January, Washington DC, http://www.gpoaccess.gov/fcic/fcic.pdf

Financial Times (2011) CBI rethinks stance on education, 26 August, http://www.ft .com/ intl/cms/s/0/bcca2362-d013-11e0-81e2-00144feabdc0.html#axzz1XigkfafV

Fine, B. (2010) *Theories of Social Capital: Researchers Behaving Badly*, Pluto Press, London.

Finlayson, A. (2008) *Characterizing New Labour: The Case of the Child Trust Fund*, Public Administration, Vol. 86, No. 1, p95-110.

Flinders, M. and Buller, J. (2005) *Depoliticisation, Democracy and Arena-Shifting*, paper to 'Autonomization of the state' conference, April, Stanford University.

Follain, J.R. (2010) *A Study of Real Estate Markets in Declining Cities*, Research Institute for Housing America and Mortgage Bankers Association, December, Washington DC.

Frege, C., Heery, E and Turner, L. (2004). "The New Solidarity? Trade Union Coalition-Building in Five Countries." in C. Frege and J. Kelly eds. *Varieties of Unionism: Strategies for Union Revitalisation in a Globalizing Economy*, Oxford, Oxford University Press: 137-158.

Gilmore, R. (2007) *In the Shadow of the Shadow State, in The Revolution Will Not Be Funded: Beyond the non-profit industrial complex*, South End Press, Cambridge, Mass.

Government Accountability Office (2010) *Higher Education: Stronger Federal Oversight Needed to Enforce Ban on Incentive Payments to School Recruiters*, GAO-11-10, Washington DC, http://www.gao.gov/

Government Accountability Office (2011) *Federal Reserve System: Opportunities Exist to Strengthen Policies and Processes for Managing Emergency Assistance*, GAO-11-696, July, Washington DC, http://www.gao.gov/new.items/d11696.pdf

Grout, P. (2009) *Private Delivery of Public Services, Centre for Market and Public Organisation*, University of Bristol, Bristol.

Hall, D. (2010) *Why we need Public Spending*, Public Services International Research Unit, London, http://www.psiru.org/sites/default/files/2010-10-QPS-pubspend.pdf

Ha-Joon Chang and Green, D. (2011) Robin Hood: a tax whose time has come, 18 April, *The Guardian*, http://www.guardian.co.uk/commentisfree/2011/apr/18/robin-hood-tax-financial-transactions

Hart-Smith, L. (2001) *Outsourced Profits: The Cornerstone of Successful Subcontracting*, Boeing, Long Beach, California.

Harvey, D. (2010) *The Enigma of Capital and the Crises of Capitalism*, Profile Books, London.

Health Service Journal (2011) DH in talks for 'international players' to take on struggling hospitals, 5 September, http://www.hsj.co.uk/news/acute-care/dh-in-talks-for-international-players-to-take-on-struggling-hospitals/5034587.article

Hems. L. (2011) *Social Impact Bonds: Can This New Asset Class Create More Than a Win-Win? In Knowledge@Australian School of Business*, 15 March, http://knowledge.asb.unsw.edu.au/printer_friendly.cfm?articleid=1359

Herald Scotland (2009) *Stagecoach facing forced sell-off of town bus operations*, 4 September, www.hearaldscotland.com

Herlofson, K. Hagestad, G. and Slagsvold, B. (2011) *Intergenerational family responsibility and solidarity in Europe*, Norwegian Social Research, Oslo.

HM Government (2010) *Securing Britain in an Age of Uncertainty: The National Security Strategy*, October, London.

HM Treasury (2004) *Releasing Resources to the Frontline: Independent Review of Public Sector Efficiency*, Sir Peter Gershon, July, London.

HM Treasury (2009) Operational Efficiency Programme, April, London, http://www.bis.gov.uk/assets/biscore/shex/files/oep_final_report_210409_pu728.pdf

HM Treasury (2010a) *National Infrastructure Plan 2010*, London, http://www.hm-treasury.gov.uk/d/nationalinfrastructureplan251010.pdf

HM Treasury (2010b) *HM Treasury Review of Competitive Dialogue*, November, London, http://www.hm-treasury.gov.uk/d/ppp_competitive_dialogue.pdf

HM Treasury (2011a) *Making Savings in Operational PFI Contracts*, July, London, http://www.hm-Treasury.gov.uk/d/iuk_making_savings.pdf

HM Treasury (2011b) *UK Private Finance Initiative Projects: summary data*, March, London, http://www.hm-Treasury.gov.uk/ppp_pfi_stats.htm

HM Treasury (2011c) *Budget 2011*, HC 836, March, London, http://cdn.hm-treasury.gov.uk/2011budget_complete.pdf

HM Treasury and Department for Business, Innovation & Skills (2011) *The Plan for Growth*, March, London.

Higher Education Funding Council for England (2011) Teaching Funding and Student Number Controls, Consultation, June, London

Hiltzik, M. (2011) 787 Dreamliner teaches Boeing costly lesson on outsourcing, *Los Angeles Times*, 15 February.

Hines, C. and Murphy, R. (2010) *Green Quantitative Easing, Paying for the economy we need*, http://www.financeforthefuture.com/GreenQuEasing.pdf

Holland, S. (2011) New Deal for Europe, *The Spokesman*, No 113, Spokesman Books, Nottingham, http://www.spokesmanbooks.com

Holliday, I. (2000) Is the British State Hollowing Out? *Political Quarterly*, Vol. 71, Issue 2, p167-176.

Holtham, G. (2011) Essential investment requires state enterprise, in Straw, W., *Going for Growth*, Left Foot Forward, Friedrich Ebert Stiftung and Institute for Public Policy Research, London.

House of Commons Health Committee (2010) *Commissioning, Vol 1*, HC 268-1, Session 2009-2010, March, London.

House of Commons Library (1995) *Deregulation of the Buses*, Research Paper 95/57, April, London, http://www.parliament.uk/briefing-papers/RP95-57

House of Commons Library (2011) *Government borrowing, debt and debt interest payments: historical statistics and forecasts*, Standard Note SN/EP/5745, 1 June, London, http://www.parliament.uk/briefing-papers/SN05745

House of Commons Committee of Public Accounts (2010) *Support to incapacity benefits claimants through Pathways to Work*, HC 404, September, London, www.publications.parliament.uk/pa/cm201011/cmselect/cmpubacc/404/404.pdf

House of Commons Public Accounts Committee (2011a) *Lessons from PFI and other projects*, HC 1201, September, London, http://www.publications .parliament.uk/pa/cm201012/cmselect/cmpubacc/1201/1201.pdf

House of Commons Public Accounts Committee (2011b) *The National Programme for IT in the NHS: an update on the delivery of detailed care records systems*, HC1070, August, London, http://www.publications.parliament.uk/ pa/cm201012/cmselect/cmpubacc/1070/1070.pdf

House of Commons Public Administration Select Committee (2011) *Government and IT - "a recipe for rip-offs": time for a new approach*, HC715-1, July, London. http://www.publications.parliament.uk/pa/cm201012/cmselect/cmpubadm/ 715/715i.pdf

House of Commons Treasury Committee (2011) *Private Finance Initiative,* HC1146, August, London, http://www.publications.parliament.uk/pa/ cm201012/cmselect/cmtreasy/1146/1146.pdf

House of Lords Select Committee on Economic Affairs (2010) *Private Finance Projects and off-balance sheet debt*, HL Paper 63-1, March, London.

Hunt, B. (2011) *Sitting on a heap: fund strategy*, 18 April, http://www.fundweb.co.uk/ fund-strategy/issues/18th-april-2011/sitting-on-a-heap/1029656.article

Hurley, J., Guindon, E., Rynard, V. and Morgan, S. (2008) *Publicly Funded Medical Savings Accounts: Expenditure and Distributional Impacts in Ontario, Canada*, Health Economics 17, pp1129-1151.

Independent Commission on Banking (2011) *Final Report: Recommendations,* September, London, http://bankingcommission.s3.amazonaws.com/ wp-content/uploads/2010/07/ICB-Final-Report.pdf

International Monetary Fund (2004) *Public Private Partnerships*, Washington DC, www.imf.org

International Monetary Fund (2010a) *Fiscal Monitor*, May, Washington DC, www.imf.org

International Monetary Fund (2010b) *Long-Term Trends in Public Finances in the G-7 Economies*, September, Washington DC, www.imf.org

International Monetary Fund (2011) *World Economic Outlook: Slowing Growth, Rising Risks*, September, Washington DC, http://www.imf.org/external/pubs/ft/ weo/2011/02/pdf/text.pdf

INTO (2011) *UEA London Prospectus 2011-2012*, London, http://www.intohigher.com/uea-london

Institute for America's Future (2010) *Big Bank Takeover: How Too-Big-To-Fail's Army of Lobbyists Has Captured Washington*, Washington DC, http://www .ourfuture.org/files/documents/big-bank-takeover-final.pdf

Institute for Fiscal Studies (2011) *The Spending Patterns and Inflation Experience of Low-Income Households over the Past Decade,* IFS Commentary C119, London, http://www.ifs.org.uk/comms/comm119.pdf

Institute for Policy Studies (2011) *Executive Excess 2011: The Massive CEO Rewards for Tax Dodging,* August, Washington DC, www.ips-dc.org

Jackson, A. (2011) Public Sector Austerity: Why Canada is Leading the Way? Socialist Project, *E-Bulletin No 531,* Canada.

James Review (2011) *Review of Education Capital,* Department of Education, London, http://media.education.gov.uk/assets/files/pdf/c/capital%20review %20final%20report%20april%202011.pdf

Jones, R. (2011) There's big money to be made under Dilnot's plan, *The Guardian,* 6 June, London.

Joye, C. (2011) The taste of cannibal capitalism, *Business Spectator,* 21 July.

J.P.Morgan Global Research (2010) *Impact Investments: An emerging asset class,* New York.

Judt, T. (2010) *Ill Fares The Land,* Penguin, London.

Julius Review (2008) *Public Services Industry Review,* for Department for Business Enterprise and Regulatory Reform, July, London, http://www.bis.gov.uk/files/file46965.pdf

Kaul, I., Conceicao, P, Le Goulven, K. and Mendoza, R. (2003) *Providing Global Public Goods,* Oxford University Press, Oxford.

Kindleberger, C. and Aliber, R. (2005) *Manias, Panics and Crashes: A History of Financial Crises,* Palgrave MacMillan, Basingstoke.

King, R. and Sweetman, C. (2010) *Gender Perspectives on the Global Economic Crisis,* Oxfam International Discussion Paper, February, www.oxfam.org

Kirchner, S. (2011) Why Does Government Grow? *Policy Monograph 117,* Centre for Independent Studies, St Leonards, Australia.

KPMG (2010) *Payment for Success – How to shift power from Whitehall to public service customers,* London.

Krajewski, M. (2011) *Public services in the Draft Canada-European Union Economic and Trade Agreement (CETA),* for European Federation of Public Service Unions and the Austrian Federal Chamber of Labour (AK), September, http://www.epsu.org

Krugman, P. (2009) *A Country is not a Company,* Harvard Business Review Classics, Boston.

Kyrili, K. and Martin, M. (2010) *The Impact of the Global Economic Crisis on the Budgets of Low-Income Countries,* Development Finance International for Oxfam International.

Labor Notes (2010) *Who Pays Taxes,* October, Detroit, http://www.labornotes.org/2010/10/who-pays-taxes

Laing and Buisson (2005) *Children's Nurseries 2005,* London.

Lane, A. and Jenkins, E. (2006) The Impact of NHS Re-Organisation on Service Commissioning Costs: A Welsh Case Study, *Journal of Finance and Management in Public Services*, Volume 6, Number 2.

Lapavitsas, C. (2008) *Financialised Capitalism: Direct Exploitation and Periodic Bubbles*, May, Department of Economics, SOAS, University of London.

Levin, Y. (2011) *Beyond the Welfare State*, National Affairs, Spring No 7, http://www.nationalaffairs.com/docLib/20110318_Spring2011web.pdf

Leys, C. and Player, S. (2011) *The Plot Against the NHS*, Merlin Press, Pontypool.

Liverpool City Council (2010) *Improving the LDL Relationship*, June, Liverpool.

Local Better Regulation Office (2011) *Local Authority Regulatory Services Budgets 2011-12*, September, http://www.lbro.org.uk/resources/docs/lars-budgets-2011-12-overview.pdf

Local Government Improvement & Development (2011) *Community empowerment – definition*, http://www.idea.gov.uk/idk/core/page.do?pageId=9396818

Lohmann, L. (2009 *Climate Crisis: Social Science Crisis*, Cornerhouse, www.thecornerhouse.org.uk

London Borough of Barnet (2006) Edgware, Burnt Oak & Mill Hill Area Forum, 26 October, Forum Officers' Action Notes, London, http://www.barnet.gov.uk

London Borough of Barnet (2011a) *MetPro Rapid Response Internal Audit Report*, Report to Audit Committee, 16 June, London, http://www.barnet.gov.uk

London Borough of Barnet (2011b) *Care Home Contract – Final Decision of Catalyst Housing Arbitration*, Report to Cabinet Resources Committee, 2 March, London, http://www.barnet.gov.uk

London Borough of Barnet (2011c) *Update on admitted body organisations issues and revised monitoring arrangements*, Report to Pension Fund Committee, 22 June, London. http://www.barnet.gov.uk

London Borough of Barnet (2011d) *Leisure Contract Review, Report to Cabinet resources Committee*, 27 September, London, http://www.barnet.gov.uk

London Borough of Barnet (2011e) *Replacement of cremators, building works, renovations and compliance with mercury abatement legislation at Hendon Cemetery and Crematorium*, Report to Cabinet Resources Committee, 27 September, London, http://www.barnet.gov.uk

McCarthy Review (2011) *Report of the Review Group on State Assets and Liabilities*, Department of Finance, Dublin, http://www.finance.gov.ie/viewdoc.asp?fn=/documents/Publications/Reports/2011/revgrpstatassets.pdf

McInroy, N. and Blume, T. (2011) *A Quest for Co-produced Communities*, Local Government Chronicle, 19 July.

McLean, B. and Nocera, J. (2010) *All The Devils Are Here: The hidden history of the financial crisis*, Penguin, London.

McNally, D. (2011a) Follow the Money: Behind the European Debt Crisis Lie

More Bank Bailouts, *Socialist Project No. 547*, 23 September, http://www.socialistproject.ca/bullet/547.php

Mcnally, D. (2011b) *Global Slump: The Economic and Politics of Crisis and Resistance*, Merlin Press, Pontypool.

McNulty Review (2011) *Realising the Potential of GB Rail: Final Independent Report of the Rail Value for Money Study*, Department for Transport and Office of Rail Regulation, London.

Marchand, Y. and Meffre, R. (2011) Detroit in Ruins, *The Observer*, 2 January, http://www.guardian.co.uk/artanddesign/gallery/2011/jan/02/photography -detroit#/?picture=370173058&index=13

Miller, M. (2011) *The Plague of the Nonprofits*, Shelterforce, February, http://www.shelterforce.org/article/2113/the_plague_of_the_nonprofits1

Ministry of Justice (2011) *Competition Strategy for Offender Services*, July, London, www.justice.gov.uk

Mirrlees Review (2010) *Reforming the Tax System for the 21st Century*, Interim Report, Institute for Fiscal Studies, London, http://www.ifs.org.uk/mirrleesReview

Mott, A. (2010) *Community Learning Partnerships: Introduction and Framing*, Washington DC, http://www.communitylearningpartnership.org/work_papers.php

Murray, R. (2009) *Danger and Opportunity: Crisis and the New Social Economy*, Young Foundation and NESTA, September, London.

Murphy, R. (2009) *Country-by-Country Reporting: Holding Multinational Corporations to Account Wherever They Are, Task Force on Financial Integrity & Economic Development*, June, Washington DC www.financialtaskforce.org

NASUWT (2010) *Charter Schools Briefing*, London, http://www.nasuwt.org.uk

National Audit Office (2008) *Shared Services in the Department of Transport and its Agencies*, HC 481, Session 2007-2008, May, London. http://web.nao.org.uk/ search/search.aspx?Schema=&terms=DVLA+2008

National Audit Office (2009a) *Maintaining financial stability across the United Kingdom's banking system*, HC 91 Session 2009-2010, December, London, http://www.nao.gov.uk

National Audit Office (2009b) *Performance of PFI Construction*, October, London, http://web.nao.org.uk/search/search.aspx?Para=2009%7CPARAYEAR

National Audit Office (2010a) *The Academies Programme*, HC 288, Session 2010-2011, London, http://www.nao.gov.uk

National Audit Office (2010b) *Maintaining the financial stability of UK banks: update on the support schemes*, HC 676 Session 2010-2011, London, http://www.nao.gov.uk

National Audit Office (2011a) *The National Programme for IT in the NHS: an update on the delivery of detailed care records systems*, HC 888, Session 2010–2012, May, London, http://www.nao.gov.uk

National Audit Office (2011b) *Regulating financial sustainability in higher education*, HC 816, Session 2010-2011, March, London, http://www.nao.gov.uk

National Audit Office (2011c) *Establishing Social Enterprises under the Right to Request Programme*, June, London, http://www.nao.gov.uk

National Centre for Health Outcomes Development (2005) *ISTC Performance Management Analysis Service*, Preliminary Overview Report for GSU1C, OC123, LP4 and LP5, October, London.

National Centre for Vocational Education Research (2006) *Trading Places: The Impact and Outcomes of Market reforms in Vocational Education and Training*, Adelaide.

National Commission on Fiscal Responsibility and Reform (2010) *The Moment of Truth*, December, The White House, Washington DC, http://www.fiscal commission.gov

National Council for Independent Action (2011) *Voluntary Action under threat: what privatisation means for charities and community groups*, http://www.independentaction.net

National Offender Management Service (2005) *The NOMS Offender Management Model*, London.

National Statistics (2010a) *Wider measures of public sector debt: A broader approach to the public sector balance sheet, July*, London, www.statistics.gov.uk/cci/article.asp?ID=2463

National Statistics (2010b) *United Kingdom National Accounts: The Blue Book*, 2010 Edition, July, London

National Statistics (2010c) *Share ownership Survey 2008*, January, www.statistics.gov.uk

National Union of Public Employees and Services to Community Action and Tenants (1978) *Up Against a Brick Wall: The dead-end in housing policy*, London.

Needham, C. and Carr, S. (2009) *Co-production: an emerging evidence base for adult social care transformation*, Social Care Institute for Excellence, March, London.

Network for the Post-Bureaucratic Age (2010) *Better for Less: How to make Government IT deliver savings*, September, http://postbureaucraticage.wordpress.com

Newcastle City Council (2006) *Building Schools for the Future – Evaluation of bid for Soft FM Services* and *Building Schools for the Future - Evaluation of bid for ICT Managed Services*, Report to Procurement Committee, 19 January, Newcastle upon Tyne.

Newcastle City Council (2011) *Byker Investment Task Force Report*, http://www.newcastle.gov.uk/planning-and-buildings/regeneration/byker-investment-task-force-report

New Economic Foundation (2009) *The Challenge of Co-production: How equal partnerships between professionals and the public are crucial to improving public services*, London, http://www.neweconomics.org

New Local Government Network (2011) *Changing Behaviours: Opening a new conversation with the citizen*, London.

New York Times (2011) *For-Profit College Group Sued as US Lays Out Wide Fraud*, 8 August, http://www.nytimes.com/2011/08/09/education/09forprofit.html?_r=1&emc=eta1

Nuffield Trust (2009) *Beyond Practice-Based Commissioning: the local clinical partnership*, November, London, http://www.nuffieldtrust.org.uk/publications/beyond-practice-based-commissioning-local-clinical-partnership

Nuffield Trust (2010) *Giving GPs budgets for commissioning: what needs to be done?* June, London, http://www.nuffieldtrust.org.uk/publications/giving-gps-budgets-commissioning-what-needs-be-done

Office for Budget Responsibility (2010) *Budget 2010: The economy & public finances – supplementary material*, June, London, http://budgetresponsibility.independent.gov.uk/wordpress/docs/junebudget_supplementary_material.pdf

Office for Budget Responsibility (2011) *Fiscal Responsibility Report*, July, London. http://budgetresponsibility.independent.gov.uk

Office of Fair Trading (2009a) *Local bus services: Report on the market study and proposed decision to make a market investigation reference*, August, London, http://www.oft.gov.uk

Office of Fair Trading (2009b) *Bid rigging in the construction industry in England*, No. CE/4327-04, London, http://www.oft.gov.uk/OFTwork/competition-act-and-cartels/ca98/decisions/bid_rigging_construction

Office of Fair Trading (2009c) *OFT fines recruitment agencies for a collective boycott and price fixing cartel*, Press Release 119/09, London, http://www.oft.gov.uk/news-and-updates/press/2009/119-09

Office of Fair Trading (2010) *Choice and Competition in Public Services: A guide for policy makers*, Frontier Economics, March, London, http://www.oft.gov.uk

Office of Fair Trading (2011a) *Empowering consumers of public services through choice tools*, April, London, http://www.oft.gov.uk

Office of Fair Trading (2011b) *Commissioning and competition in the public sector*, March, London, http://www.oft.gov.uk

Office of Government Commerce (2009) *Contract Management – Checklist*, London, http://www.ogc.gov.uk/documents/contract_management_checklist.pdf

Organisation for Economic Co-operation and Development (2011a) *OECD Economic Outlook 2011*, Vol. 1, September, Paris, http://www.oecd.org

Organisation for Economic Co-operation and Development (2011b) *Health Sector Innovation and Partnership: Policy Responses to the New Economic*

Context, DELSA/HEA(2011)17, June, Paris, http://www.oecd.org

O'Toole, F. (2010) *Ship of Fools: How stupidity and corruption sank the Celtic Tiger*, Faber and Faber, London.

Oxford Economics (2008) *The Public Services Industry in the UK*, July, Oxford, http://www.oxfordeconomics.com

Palley, T. (2005) From Keynesianism to Neoliberalism: Shifting Paradigms in Economics, in Saad-Filho and Johnstone, *Neoliberalism: A Critical Reader*, Pluto Press, London.

Panitch, L. (2011) The Left's Crisis, *The Bullet*, 15 August, http://www.socialist project.ca/bullet/536.php

Pawson, H. (2010) Transfer programme delivered 1.4 million units over 20 years but now faces wind-down, *Social Housing*, January.

Pinter, Harold (2005) 'Pinter v the US, Nobel acceptance speech', *The Guardian*, 8 December.

Plimmer, G. (2011) Privatisation fever takes grip, *Financial Times*, 26 June, http://www.ft.com/intl/cms/s/0/04a8c0b8-a020-11e0-a115-00144feabdc0 .html#axzz1YNhJVUJk

Policy Exchange (2009) *Delivering a 21st Century Infrastructure for Britain*, London, http:// www.policyexchange.org.uk

Pollock, A., Price, D. and Player, S. (2007) *An Examination of the UK Treasury's Evidence Base for Cost and Time Overrun Data in UK Value-for Money Policy and Appraisal*, Public Money & Management, April, 127-133.

Pollock, A. (2004) *NHS plc: The Privatisation of our Health Care*, Verso, London.

Postal Services Commission (2004) *Postcomm and Postal Services*, London.

PricewaterhouseCoopers (2011) *Understanding Commissioning Behaviours: Commissioning and Competition in the Public Sector*, March, London.

Privatization Barometer (2011) *The PB Report 2010*, Milan, http://www.privatizationbarometer.net

Project on Government Oversight (2011) B*ad Business: Billions of Taxpayer Dollars Wasted on Hiring Contractors*, Washington DC, http://www.pogo.org/ pogo-files/alerts/contract-oversight/co-gp-20110913.html

Public Service Europe (2011) *Polish presidency wants EU rating agency*, 14 July, http://www.publicserviceeurope.com/article/612/polish-presidency-wants -eu-rating-agency

Pulse (2011) *PCTs clamour to put entire care pathways out for tender*, 10 August, http://www.pulsetoday.co.uk/newsarticle-content/-/article_display_list/ 12511685/pcts-clamour-to-put-entire-care-pathways-out-for-tender#

Respublica and NESTA (2009) *The Ownership State: Restoring excellence, innovation and ethos to the public services*, October, London, http://www.nesta.org.uk

Reyes, O. (2009) Climate Crunch, *Red Pepper*, April/May, p24-25.

Rivlin, A. (2011) *Making Medicare, Medicaid and Social Security Sustainable for the Long Run*, Testimony to US House of Representatives Committee on the Budget, March, Washington DC, http://www.brookings.edu/testimony/2011/0317_house_budget_rivlin.aspx

Romer, P. (2010) For richer, for poorer, *Prospect*, Issue 167, January.

Rosenbloom, S. (2009) The Equity Implications of Financing the Nation's Surface Transportation System, *Transportation Research News 261*, March-April, http://onlinepubs.trb.org/onlinepubs/trnews/trnews261equity.pdf

Royal Town Planning Institute (2011) *Top Five Planning Myths*, September, London, http://www.rtpi.org.uk/download/12742/Planning-Myths.pdf

RTE News (2011) *Banks borrowed more from Central Bank*, 12 August, Dublin.

Sadowski. R. (2011) *A Cash Build-up and Business Investment*, January, Federal Reserve Bank of Cleveland, http://www.clevelandfed.org/research/trends/2011/0111/01regact.cfm

Scotland's Independent Budget Review Panel (2010) *Independent Budget Review*, July, http://www.independentbudgetreview.org

Secretary of State for Health (2011) *Government response to the NHS Future Forum report*, Cm 8113, June, London.

SCAT Publications (1980) *The Great Sales Robbery: Sale of Council Housing*, London.

Schlosser, E. (1998) The Prison Industrial Complex, *Atlantic Magazine*, December, http://www.theatlantic.com/magazine/archive/1998/12/the-prison-industrial-complex/4669/

Schmidt, E. (2005) Coalition Building: Trade Union Dialogues with Civil Society, *Transfer*, 3/05 p449-456.

Shepherd, J. (2011) Private firm in talks to run 10 universities for profit, *The Guardian*, 22 June, http://www.guardian.co.uk/education/2011/jun/21/bpp-private-bid-run-public-universities?INTCMP=SRCH

Skeffington, A. (1969) *People and Planning. Report of the Committee on Public Participation in Planning* ('Skeffington Report'). HMSO, London.

Smith, S. (2010) Nonprofits and Public Administration: Reconciling Performance Management and Citizen Engagement, *The American Review of Public Administration, Vol. 40*, No. 2, p129-152.

Social Enterprise Coalition (2011) *Fightback Britain: the State of Social Enterprise Survey 2011*, London, http://www.socialenterprise.org.uk

Social Finance (2009) *Social Impact Bonds: Rethinking finance for social outcomes*, August, London, http://www.socialfinance.org.uk

Social Finance (2010) *Towards a new social economy: Blended value creation through Social Impact Bonds*, London, http://www.socialfinance.org.uk

243

Social Market Foundation (2010) *Roads to Recovery: Reducing congestion through shared ownership,* London, http://www.smf.co.uk/assets/files/ Roads_to_recovery.pdf

Social Work Action Network (2010) *Social work and social justice: a manifesto for a new engaged practice,* http://www.socialworkfuture.org/index.php/ swan-organisation/manifesto

Society of Information Technology Management (2011) Costs of outsourcing – uncovering the real risks, *Briefing No. 28,* April, http://www.socitm.gov.uk/

Somerset County Council (2010) *Southwest One Review,* June, Taunton, http://www.somerset.gov.uk/irj/go/km/docs/CouncilDocuments/SCC/ Documents/Resources/Communications/SouthwestOneReview.pdf

Spear, R. (1999) The Rise and Fall of Employee-Owned UK Bus Companies, *Economic and Industrial Democracy, Vol. 20,* p253-268.

Standard & Poor's (2011a) *United States of America Long-Term Rating Lowered to AA+ on Political Risks and Rising debt Burden: Outlook Negative,* 5 August, New York, http:///www.standardandpoors.com/ratingsdirect

Standard & Poor's (2011b) *Cross-Market Commentary: The Largest Corporate Cash Holdings Are All Over the Map,* 19 January, http://www.standardand poors/products-services/articles/en/us/?assetID=1245282374054

Standard & Poor's (2011c) *Cross-Market Commentary: Cash Holdings Exceed Market Value for 22 Non-financial Issuers,* 25 April, http://www.standardand poors/products-services/articles/en/eu/?assetID1245303599198

Standing, G. (2011) *The Precariat: The New dangerous Class,* Bloomsbury, London.

Stein, J.G. (2001) *The Cult of Efficiency,* CBC Massey Lectures Series, Anansi Press, Toronto.

Stern Review (2007) *The Economics of Climate Change,* HM Treasury, London.

Stichele, M. (2008) How Trade, the WTO and the Financial Crisis Reinforce Each Other, Centre for Research on Multinational Corporations, www.tni.org/archives/ stichele/tradewtofinancialcrisis.pdf?

Stiglitz, J. (2010) *Freefall: Free Markets and the Sinking of the Global Economy,* Penguin, London.

Sustainable Development Commission (2011) *Looking back, looking forward: Sustainability and UK food policy 2000-2011,* London.

Tattersall, A, (2011) Coalitions of the Willing, *Red Pepper, No 177,* April/May.

Tax Research UK (2009) *The direct tax cost of tax havens to the UK,* http://www.taxresearch.org.uk/blog

Tax Research UK (2010) *Why HM Revenue & Customs have got the Tax Gap wrong,* Tax Briefing, June, http://www.taxresearch.org.uk/blog

The Economist (2011) *Nightmareliner: Boeing's new 787 has been cleared for take-off but its troubles continue,* 3 September, London.

Thiemann, M. (2011) *Regulating the off-balance sheet exposure of banks*, Foundation for European Progressive Studies, Brussels, http://www.fepseurope.eu/ fileadmin/ downloads/political_economy/1106_OffBalanceSheetExposure_Thiemann.pdf

Timmins, N. (2011) Public Finances: A divisive initiative, *Financial Times*, 7 August, http:// www.ft.com/intl/cms/s/0/fdb098aa-c138-11e0-b8c2 -00144feabdc0.html#axzz1XigkfafV

Trade Union Congress (2008) *The Missing Billions: The UK Tax Gap*, Touchstone Pamphlet No. 1, London, http://www.tuc.org.uk

Trade Union Congress (2011a) *TUC Budget Submission 2011: A Budget for economic growth and social cohesion*, London.

Trades Union Congress (2011b) Congress 2011 Decisions, No. 70 (accessed 4 October 2011), http://www.tuc.org.uk/the_tuc/tuc-20038-f0.cfm

UNISON (2010) *Alternative Budget: we can afford a fairer society*, September, London, http://www.unison.org.uk/acrobat/18887.pdf

Universities UK (2010) *The Growth of Private and For-Profit Higher Education Providers in the UK*, March, London.

University and College Union (2010) *Privatising Our Universities*, February, London.

University and College Union (2011) *For-Profit Education: A Step Too Far?* May, London.

University and College Union (2011a) *Fighting Privatisation: A Branch Activists' Guide*, May, London.

US Chamber of Commerce (2011) *Open Letter to Congress and the President of the United States*, 5 September, Washington DC, http://www.uschamber.com/sites/default/files/110905_jobs_letter.pdf

US Senate Permanent Subcommittee on Investigations (2008) *Tax Haven Banks and US Tax Compliance*, July, Washington DC, http:// hsgac.senate.gov/public/ _files/071708PSIReport.pdf

US Senate Permanent Subcommittee on Investigations (2011) *Wall Street and the Financial Crisis: Anatomy of a Financial Collapse*, April, Washington DC, http://hsgac.senate.gov/public/_files/Financial_Crisis/FinancialCrisisReport.pdf

Wainwright, H. and Little, M (2009) *Public Service Reform – But not as you know it: How Democracy can transform public services*, Picnic Publishing, Hove.

Wall Street Journal (2011a) *Detroit and Decay*, 15 January, www.wsj.com

Wall Street Journal (2011b) *Public Schools Charge Kids for Basics*, Frills, 25 May, www.wsj.com

Weldon, D. (2010) There is an alternative – unlock the surplus, *Red Pepper*, December, http://www.redpepper.co.uk/there-is-an-alternative-unlock-the-surplus

Westlake, S. (2011) Encouraging growth through innovation, in Straw, W., *Going for Growth*, Left Foot Forward, Friedrich Ebert Stiftung and Institute for Public Policy Research, London.

White, L. (2010) The Credit Rating Agencies, *Journal of Economic Perspectives, Vol. 24*, No. 2, Spring, pp211-226.

Whitfield, D. (1983) *Making It Public: Evidence and action against privatisation,* Pluto Press, London.

Whitfield, D. (1992) *The Welfare State: Privatisation, Deregulation and Commercialisation of Public Services,* Pluto Press, London.

Whitfield, D. (2001) *Public Services or Corporate Welfare: Rethinking the Nation State in the Global Economy,* Pluto Press, London.

Whitfield, D. (2002) 'Impact of Privatisation and Commercialisation on Municipal Services in the UK', *Transfer – Journal of the European Federation of Public Service Unions,* Brussels.

Whitfield, D. (2006a) *New Labour's Attack on Public Services: Modernisation by Marketisation,* Spokesman Books, Nottingham.

Whitfield, D. (2006) The Marketisation of Teaching, *PFI Journal No 52,* April, London. www.european-services-strategy.org.uk/outsourcing-library

Whitfield, D. (2006) 'Articles of Faith', Education Supplement, *Red Pepper, No 138,* February.

Whitfield, D. (2006) *A Typology of Privatisation and Marketisation,* Research Report No 1, European Services Strategy Unit www.european-services-strategy.org.uk/publications

Whitfield, D. (2007a) *Options Appraisal Criteria Matrix,* European Services Strategy Unit, Research Report No. 2, www.european-services-strategy.org.uk/publications

Whitfield, D. (2007b) *Cost Overruns, Delays and Terminations: 105 outsourced public sector ICT projects, European Services Strategy Unit,* Research Report No 3. www.european-services-strategy.org.uk/publications

Whitfield, D. (2008a) *Economic Impact of Prisons in Rural Areas: A Review of the Issues, for Public Service Association & Australian Institute for Social Research (AISR),* University of Adelaide, http://www.european-services-strategy.org.uk/ news/2008/economic-impact-of-prisons-in-rural-areas-a-re

Whitfield, D. (2008b) *Public Private Partnerships: Confidential 'Research', A Critique of the Audit Commission's study of Strategic Service-delivery Partnerships.* www.european-services-strategy.org.uk/news/2008/ppp-research-critique

Whitfield, D. (2010a) *Global Auction of Public Assets: Public sector alternatives to the infrastructure market and Public Private Partnerships,* Spokesman Books, Nottingham.

Whitfield, D. (2010b) *PPP Database: Strategic Service-delivery Partnerships,* November, www.european-services-strategy.org.uk

Whitfield, D. (2011a) *The £10bn Sale of Shares in PPP Companies: European Services Strategy Research Report No. 4,* www.european-services-strategy.org.uk/publications

Whitfield, D. (2011b) Is Commissioning the Way Forward? *Local Government Chronicle,* 9 June, www.lgcplus.com

Wiborg, D. (2010) *Swedish Free Schools: Do they Work?* Centre for Learning and Life Chances in Knowledge Economies and Societies, http://www.llakes.org

World Commission on Environment and Development: Our Common Future (1987) *From One Earth to One World: An Overview,* United Nations, New York.

World Economy, Ecology and Development (2011) *Towards a Global Finance System at the Service of Sustainable Development,* Berlin, http://somo.nl/ publications-en/Publication_3640/at_download/fullfile

Wyler, S. and Blond, P. (2010) *To Buy, to bid , to build: Community Rights for an Asset Owning Democracy,* November, NESTA and ResPublica, London.

Youth Today (2011) *For-Profit Colleges, Allies Spend $4.5 million Lobbying Against Gainful Employment,* 27 April, http://www.youthtoday.org.view _article.cfm?article_id=4755

Young Foundation (2011) *Social Impact Investment: the challenge and opportunity of Social Impact Bonds,* London.

About the Author

Dexter Whitfield is Director of the European Services Strategy Unit (continuing the work of the Centre for Public Services founded in 1973) and Adjunct Associate Professor, Australian Institute for Social Research, University of Adelaide.

He has carried out extensive research and policy analysis of regional/city economies and public sector provision, jobs and employment strategies, impact assessment and evaluation, marketisation and privatisation, public private partnerships, modernisation and public management (www.european-services-strategy.org.uk).

He has undertaken commissioned work for a wide range of public sector organisations, local authorities and agencies and worked extensively with trade unions in the UK at branch, regional and national levels, and internationally. He has advised tenants and community organisations on housing, planning and regeneration policies.

Dexter is the author of Global Auction of Public Assets: Public sector alternatives to the infrastructure market & Public Private Partnerships (2010); New Labour's Attack on Public Services: Modernisation by Marketisation (2006), Public Services or Corporate Welfare: The Future of the Nation State in the Global Economy (2001), The Welfare State: Privatisation, Deregulation & Commercialisation (1992) and Making it Public: Evidence and Action against Privatisation (1983). He was one of the founding members of Community Action Magazine (1972-1995) and Public Service Action (1983-1998). He has published articles in journals and delivered papers and advised public bodies and trade unions in Europe, US, Canada, Australia and New Zealand.

Index

Conservative 11, 34, 129, 137, 171, 181
Construction Management At-Risk 112
Consultants 13, 35, 36, 44, 60, 54, 72, 90, 104, 155, 171, 207, 209, 223
Consumerism 4, 17, 39, 46, 82, 142, 144, 183
Contestable markets 43, 210
Contract culture 17, 29, 54, 100, 143, 173, 185, 194, 196
Contract failure 14, 28, 30, 56, 61-2, 123, 129, 171, 187, 189, 198, 200, 203-204, 215, 219-221, 223
Contract management 13, 21, 23, 29, 44, 54, 57, 60, 75, 100, 104, 109, 112, 128-129, 138-139, 159, 171, 179, 183-184, 189, 207-208, 210, 214
Contract termination 54, 96, 100, 104, 112, 113, 114, 117, 128, 149, 209, 211, 220
Co-operatives 25, 75, 173
Co-production 194-195, 178, 191, 217
Corporate citizen 43, 48, 55
Corporate greed 4, 216
Corporate policies 30, 108
Corporate power 2, 13, 43, 55, 217, 221
Corporate Social Responsibility 48, 55, 95, 124
Corporate welfare 2, 13, 16, 44, 50-63, 89, 222, 223
Corporatisation 54
Corruption 6, 13, 30, 41, 51, 54, 80, 81, 84, 101, 118, 221
Cost of marketisation 180, 204-210
Cost overruns 62-63, 105, 203, 209, 220
Countrywide Financial 4
Credit Suisse 5
Criminal justice 32, 39, 50, 87, 132, 156, 165, 166
Decent Homes 97, 163, 164

Defend Council Housing 125
Deficit 1, 5, 7, 8, 9, 10, 20, 69, 82, 107, 115, 136, 162, 227
Deloitte 167, 210
Democratic accountability 4, 17, 29, 30, 31, 36, 42, 44, 45, 48, 67, 84-85, 88, 90, 95, 96, 98, 100, 103, 105, 107, 108, 118, 134, 135, 150, 169-170, 171, 179, 191, 192
Democratic control 29, 31, 32, 33, 36, 44, 67, 96, 100, 134, 150, 169, 171, 172, 179, 191
Department of Health 142-144, 174, 186, 188, 205, 206
Depoliticisation 17, 37-38, 115, 119, 121, 145, 171
Deregulation 2, 4, 16, 30, 43, 48, 53, 72, 142, 165, 180, 187, 188, 198, 210, 222, 223
Design, Build Finance and Operate 33, 39, 42, 51, 68, 71, 156
Destabilisation 17, 36-37, 115, 145, 149
Detroit 10, 99,
Deutsche Bahn 131, 210, 219
Deutsche Bank 5
Developing countries 81, 195, 201
Diagnostics 145
Direct payments 18, 19, 26-27, 31, 40, 43, 56, 62, 89, 92-93, 97, 107, 184, 201, 207
Disempowerment 17, 38, 115, 119, 121, 145
Disinvestment 17, 35-6, 62, 115
Dispossession 17, 34, 115, 119
Ealing Community Transport 187
Early Intervention 24, 121, 146-147, 151
East Coast rail 34, 75, 170
easyCouncil 14, 137
EBS Building Society 6

INTO University Partnerships 140
Ireland 5, 6, 7, 9, 10, 18, 50, 60, 158,
161, 175, 216, 217
Irish Life and Permanent 6
Irish Nationwide 6
Italy 6, 7, 8, 158, 174, 175
Isle of Skye Bridge 131
Japan 6, 7, 8, 12
Joint venture company 137, 159
JP Morgan 4, 18, 22, 23, 51
Kaplan International Colleges 140
KfW Bankengruppe 68
KPMG 56, 138, 210
Land Value Tax 79
Large Scale Voluntary Transfer 163-164
Lawson, N. 78
Leeds 150
Lehman Brothers 4
Leisure 33, 45, 75, 99, 115, 120, 138,
170, 176, 179, 180-181, 188
Leicestershire 23
Liberalisation 29, 42, 43, 48, 55, 58, 59,
80, 216
Lisbon Treaty 53, 59, 79
Liverpool 205-206
Lloyds Banking Group 5, 6, 91, 164
Local Asset Backed Vehicle 171
Local Authority Trading Company 32,
138
Local Enterprise Partnership 165, 170,
171
Localism 13, 166, 171-172, 173, 189,
192, 197, 213, 223
London Borough of Barnet 14, 28, 32,
33, 41, 137, 138-139, 154
Los Angeles 99
Maastricht Treaty 8
Managed services 44, 60
Manchester 157
Market failure 3, 4, 16, 28, 30, 46, 56,

62, 84, 134, 145, 171, 187, 198-204,
215-216, 218-223
Market games 212-213
Market mechanisms 17, 27, 29, 32, 39,
42, 43, 46, 54, 62, 75, 91, 104, 109,
145, 186, 191, 194, 204, 205, 207,
211, 213
Marketisation 1, 3, 4, 14, 15, 16, 17, 24,
28, 29, 31, 32, 33, 34, 39, 40-49, 50,
55, 65, 69, 80, 102, 115, 117, 120,
124, 130, 133, 142, 143, 153, 180,
182, 183, 185, 190, 192, 203, 213,
215, 216, 217, 223
Medicare 35, 37
Merrill Lynch 4
Minneapolis 99
Mitigation 61
Mixed economy 32, 152, 185, 190, 197
Modernisation 32, 72, 102, 216, 248
Morgan Stanley 51, 146
Mouchel plc 210
Multipliers 92, 106, 108
Mutation 31, 32, 115
Mutuals 2, 16, 32, 71-72, 98, 117, 161,
164, 173, 175-179, 186-187, 189, 216
NASUWT 151
National Audit Office 6, 155, 156, 164,
National Climate Service 68
National Commission on Fiscal
Responsibility and Reform 53
National debt 5, 11, 92
National Endowment for Science,
Technology and the Arts 22, 191
National Express 34, 170, 210, 219
National Health Service 19, 21, 33, 37,
54, 58, 61, 94, 96, 102, 137, 142-145,
155, 174, 176, 179, 180, 186, 188,
195, 204, 205, 206, 207, 217, 220
National Infrastructure Plan 68, 105,
111, 158

FAREBROTHER

1799–1999

Charles Farebrother

FAREBROTHER

A Property Business over
Two Hundred Years

1799–1999

by

John Butland Smith

Published for Farebrother by

SHAUN TYAS
STAMFORD
1999

.

Published for
FAREBROTHER
1, Pemberton Row
Fetter Lane, London
EC4A 3ET

by

SHAUN TYAS
(an imprint of 'Paul Watkins')
18 Adelaide Street
Stamford, Lincolnshire
PE9 2EN

ISBN

1 900289 23 7

Printed and bound by Woolnoughs of Irthlingborough

CONTENTS

v

ACKNOWLEDGEMENTS

I should like to record my thanks to the many people who helped to make this book possible. At Farebrother, Huw Colwyn Foulkes, from whom the idea of a history originated, was endlessly helpful in acting as my main contact with the practice. Without his patient and constructive involvement the book could not have been written. The present senior partner, Christopher Woodbridge, and his predecessor, Michael Bridges Webb, both gave generously of their time and provided very helpful discussion. George Davies, formerly Chief Cashier of Farebrother and an employee for more than fifty years, gave very perceptive and entertaining accounts of life within the practice from the 1930s onwards. Other staff were unfailingly helpful and welcoming. I hope that they find something of interest in this history of their company.

The staff of Guildhall Library (Corporation of London) have, as always, been most helpful. I should like to thank the City Archivist, Stephen Freeth, and especially Sophie Bridges, for essential help with the Farebrother archives. Other libraries which gave valuable assistance included the Corporation of London Records Office at Guildhall, the Newspaper Library at Colindale, North London, the London University Library at Senate House, and the Librarians of the Royal Institution of Chartered Surveyors in George Street, Westminster. The staff of the Local Studies Collection at Richmond Old Town Hall provided much useful information regarding Sir John Whittaker Ellis. The staff of the Minet Library, Lambeth Archives Department, were likewise very helpful concerning Charles Farebrother.

My thanks are due to many individuals who helped in a variety of ways. I would particularly mention Don Bennett, Peta Buckland and Robin Forrest. I am also grateful to Heidi Jackson at Newstead Abbey, who was most helpful regarding Lord Byron.

The staff at Leicester University were very helpful in all aspects of the work. I would particularly like to thank Gillian Austen, who not only typed the manuscript but also made many constructive suggestions.

Finally, I should like to thank my wife, Diana, who bore kindly and patiently with my frequent absence and distracted presence during the summer of '98.

John Butland Smith
October, 1998

PREFACE

This book was written to commemorate the 200th anniversary of Farebrother, Chartered Surveyors. Although the company has always been regarded as having been founded in 1799, its actual origins are obscure. Therefore the first task was to explore the history of Charles Farebrother himself and to examine how he rose to become the founder of the business and Lord Mayor of London.

It is impossible and indeed unhelpful to describe the history of Farebrother and his company without setting them in the context of the City of London. The story can only be appreciated fully within the framework of the social and economic history of London and this approach has been followed throughout. As far as possible events concerning Farebrother and his successors have been related to the development of London and also to the development of surveying, auctioneering and the professions associated with property.

The story is remarkable in many ways. Farebrother today is a successful private company which, within its long and varied history, has produced three Lord Mayors of London. The company has adapted continually to external change and yet retains to the full Charles Farebrother's unusual ability to provide a total service dealing with all aspects of property. Moreover it is appropriate that the company today concentrates on property in "Midtown" which is in effect the area in which Charles Farebrother began his work 200 years ago.

John Butland Smith

FOREWORD

My partners and I are proud to be part of a practice that has flourished for so many years and we have been planning ways to celebrate the 200th anniversary of Charles Farebrother starting his career.

While undoubtedly we had many historical connections no-one had ever researched the history of the practice and this seemed an ideal way to mark our bi-centenary. John Smith was approached and undertook this task with great skill and enthusiasm and produced a book that I hope the reader will find both fascinating and illuminating as to the changes in the world of property over two hundred years.

The story particularly re-affirms the dedication of the partners to their clients personally and their passion for property generally.

Christopher J. Woodbridge
1, Pemberton Row
September, 1998

CHAPTER 1
CHARLES FAREBROTHER
HIS LIFE AND TIMES

1.1 *Early Years and Apprenticeship*

Charles Farebrother began his working life on 6 February 1799. Vintners' Company records show that on that day Farebrother signed the deed of apprenticeship and paid the required two shillings and sixpence, to be used in aid of the Orphans Fund. He was apprenticed to Joseph Brasbridge, a silversmith and cutler of 98 Fleet Street, in consideration of £210 paid over seven years. Over the course of the next seven years, Farebrother completed his apprenticeship and was recommended by Brasbridge to become a freeman of the Vintners' Company by servitude on 2 July 1806. Farebrother is recorded as having paid twenty-six pounds and five shillings plus a fine of one guinea to the poor box: he was then duly admitted and clothed in the livery.[1]

When Farebrother became free of the Vintners' Company in 1806 he was living at 7 Beaufort Buildings, Strand, and had been acting as an auctioneer from that address since 1804. Moreover, in 1803, in the fourth year of his apprenticeship, he was practising as an auctioneer from 16 Old Bond Street.

---

[1] Vintners' Company: Apprentice Bindings and account of orphans duty 1722–1835 MS 15221-2, and Register of Freedom Admissions 1768–1882 MSS 15212-2 and 15213-2 p. 90, Guildhall Library Ms. See also *Estates Gazette*, Centenary Supplement (3 May 1958).

1

Farebrother's earliest recorded auction was in April
1802 when he was living at 5 College Street, Westminster.
The advertisement in *The Times* announces the sale on
Tuesday 13 April at Messrs Blades and Hermon's Great
Room, No. 25 Conduit Street, Bond Street, of "the most
valuable assemblage of Ancient Dutch and Flemish
STAINED GLASS ever submitted, the whole selected by an
AMATEUR, at an unbounded expence [sic], consigned
from the continent within a month".[1]

The second occasion on which Farebrother held an
auction was on Wednesday, 11 August 1802, advertised in
The Times from July onwards. He was still living at 5
College Street, Westminster, from which address all details
were available. The auction, which was held in Wych Street,
Temple Bar, was in two parts. At 10.00 a.m. Farebrother
was selling a collection of building materials derived from
the salvage of "a large and substantial mansion known by
the name of BOHEMIA HOUSE". The products offered
included brickwork, lead, timber, doors, joists, panelling,
wainscoting, etc. Immediately afterwards, at 12.00 noon,
Farebrother was to sell at the 'Queen of Bohemia Inn' in
Wych Street an adjacent plot of freehold land between
Wych Street and Little Stanhope Street, Temple Bar,
described as "well adapted for erecting a brewery, distillery,
warehouses, etc. of which immediate possession will be
given". This latter sale also included a number of buildings,
"one of them the King of Prussia Public-house, now in full
trade".[2]

---

[1]   *The Times*, 10 April 1802.
[2]   Ibid., 31 July 1802.

2

Thus it appears that Charles Farebrother, during the
time of his nominal apprenticeship to Joseph Brasbridge,
had already begun his career as an auctioneer and by the end
of 1802 had diversified from the sale of chattels into selling
buildings and land. Although this shows a high degree of
enterprise, it is not an entirely unusual combination of
activities. In 1800 a young man engaged in trade or craft in
the City of London would have considered it an accepted
and conventional step towards becoming a freeman of a
livery company. What is unusual is that Farebrother
became free of the Vintners by servitude. From 1750
onwards a decreasing proportion of freemen achieved this
status by serving an apprenticeship; the freedom was more
commonly achieved either by patrimony (father's membership) or by redemption (payment of a fee). This suggests
that Farebrother's origins were not privileged and he in fact
went some way towards confirming this in his remarks on
becoming Lord Mayor of London in 1833. He disclaimed

any privilege of birth but spoke highly of his parents for instilling in him the virtues of honesty and the rewards of a clear conscience.[1]

Charles Farebrother's choice of livery company, the Vintners, was probably decided by his apprenticeship to Joseph Brasbridge, who was an active member of that company and indeed silversmith to it. From the early 1700s onwards it had become increasingly unlikely that young men would serve an apprenticeship in a livery company directly connected with their own occupation. The attraction for a young apprentice was that freedom of the livery company would lead on to freedom of the City.

The livery companies have a long history, extending in some cases back to the 12th century. From the 15th century onwards they were incorporated by royal Charter. In the middle of the 18th century, the total number of liverymen was about 8,000, which rose to 12,000 in 1832 but declined in the mid-Victorian period to 5,500 in 1855. Certainly, in 1800 the livery companies were able to exert a powerful influence on the political and working life of the City of London.[2]

Through the medium of their exclusive court, Common Hall, the liverymen of the City, who like Charles Farebrother had been made free and invested in the livery of a company, nominated and elected officers, including the Lord Mayor and one of the two Sheriffs. Originally the overwhelming advantage, and indeed necessity, of becoming a liveryman free of the City was that only those belonging to this group were permitted to buy or sell goods within the square mile of the City. The last traces of this regulation were not totally removed until 1856.[3]

[1] Ibid., 11 November 1833.
[2] I. G. Doolittle, *The City of London and its Livery Companies* (Dorchester, 1982), pp. 89–90ff.
[3] Ibid. See also V. Hope, C. Birch, G. Tarry, *The Freedom, The Past and Present of the Livery, Guilds and the City of London*

For the young Charles Farebrother, becoming free of the Vintners' Company in 1806, the livery was both a validation of the right to trade and a necessary first step on the road to high civic office. Farebrother was later to become Master of the Vintners' Company three times – in 1835, 1852 and 1856.

The world in which Joseph Brasbridge lived and traded and in which Charles Farebrother served seven years of apprenticeship has been clearly described and is of particular interest in throwing light on the remarkable networks and business relationships which the young Farebrother must have encountered. Fortunately, Brasbridge left an account of these circumstances in his autobiography, *The Fruits of Experience*, written in his eightieth year and published in 1824.[1] The book was intended as a warning to others that they should avoid the diversions and temptations which led Brasbridge down from the possession of a successful business into bankruptcy.

Brasbridge began his career as a silversmith and cutler in 1770 and married the sister of his partner, "a most lovely and amiable woman with a portion of two thousand pounds". After his wife died in childbirth and his young son died prematurely, Brasbridge remarried. Thereafter he built up a very successful business with many wealthy and aristocratic customers. Orders received for plate included, for example, one from Lady Stanhope valued at £300.

Unfortunately, Brasbridge dissipated his wealth in the pursuit of pleasure with like-minded companions. His ruinous tastes included cards and gambling at various houses: the Crown and Rolls in Chancery Lane, the Queen's Arms in St. Paul's Churchyard, and the Highflyer Club. The last was held at the Turf Coffee House founded

(Buckingham, 1982).

[1] Joseph Brasbridge, *The Fruits of Experience*, Red Lion Court, Fleet Street (1824). Brasbridge's Memoirs are reviewed in *Blackwood's Edinburgh Magazine*, xvi, 428 (1824).

by Mr Tattersall, grandfather of the well-known racing personality. Other entertainments which drained Brasbridge's finances included riding, hunting and following prize fighting. His favoured drinking places included the Cider Cellar in Maiden Lane (noted for political debate) and the Spread Eagle in the Strand.

When the inevitable bankruptcy ensued, Brasbridge was rescued by the remarkable generosity of friends who contributed £2,000 to re-establish him in business at 98 Fleet Street. Needless to say, these friends did not include his erstwhile drinking and gambling companions. However, once re-established, his later circle of acquaintances is remarkable and shows a high degree of wealthy networking for the business. For example, Matthew Boulton of Soho gave him commercial advice; Sir Robert Peel was a friend. Mrs Thrale visited his shop on her way to see Dr Johnson who lived nearby. Customers included the Dukes of Argyll and of Marlborough, the Duchess of Buccleuch, Lord Bath, Lady Hamilton and many others, bishops, MPs, government ministers and officials. This was the well-connected environment into which the young Charles Farebrother entered upon his working life.

1.2 The Development of the Auction Sale

The auction sale originated and evolved from the sales of chattels which were frequently conducted in London coffee houses and public houses from the end of the 17th century. The principal auctioneers at that time were Mr Gillieflower and Mr Millington. The latter gave a summary of his guiding principles in a foreword to the catalogue for a sale of paintings at the Barbadoes Coffee House in February 1689 or 1690. Mr Millington concludes:

> When I first essay'd this way of Selling Paintings and Limnings by Auction, I propounded to myself the obliging of the Gentry, Citizens, etc. and to bring it into Esteem and Reputation, to

make it familiar and acceptable, and withal an honest gain to myself. And as I am bound publickly [sic] to own, so I will upon all opportunities freely acknowledge that the worthy Gentlemen etc. the Buyers, have both by their presence and custom, promoted and incouraged [sic] it. And that I may remove the Prejudices of some, and the Misapprehensions of others, as to the sincerity of the management, I have printed the Conditions of Sale with an additional one, that no Person or Persons shall be admitted to bid for his, or their own Pictures etc. for I will and cannot omit to aver, that the Gratifying of my Customers with moderate Pennyworths in the things I sell, was one of the Principal motives that gave rise to the attempt, and is the most probable way to continue it, which having (without vanity be it said) in some measures effected, I do not in the least repent, (that for your sakes, Gentlemen) I have hitherto extended and exercised my lungs.[1]

Another contemporary catalogue from the end of the 17th century is marked "Pray read me, but do not take me from the Table", and announces that:

[The goods] will be exposed to sale, by way of Mineing on Thursday 12th. Friday 13th. and Saturday 14th. of this instant *March* at Mrs Smythers Coffee House in Thames Street, by the Custom House: the sale beginning each Morning precisely at Nine of the Clock. The said paintings are to be viewed from this day forward until all be sold. Catalogues may be had at the place of sale.[2]

The technique of "mineing" was for the auctioneer to offer each lot at a high price and to lower the price in stages

---

[1]   P. Ash, Centenary Supplement to *Estates Gazette*, 3 May 1958.
[2]   Ibid.

until someone shouted "mine". Other bidders were then free to offer more until eventually a final price was reached.

There were other methods of arriving at a final price. The technique of sale by candle was very commonly used. Bids were encouraged by lighting a candle. When the candle went out, the last man to bid the highest figure took the lot on offer. Samuel Pepys gives an account of this method being used to sell three ships:

> Sepr. 3rd. 1662. After dinner, we met and sold the Weymouth Successe and Fellowship Hulkes where pleasant to see how backward men are at first to bid, and yet, when the candle is going out, how they bawl, and dispute afterwards who bid the most first. And here I observed one man cunninger than the rest, that was sure to bid the last man, and carry it: and enquiring the reason, he told me that just as the flame goes out, the smoke descends, which is a thing I never observed before, and by that he do know the instant when to bid last.[1]

The novel *Moonfleet*, published in 1898 and set in a Dorset fishing village in 1757, describes a variant of the technique:

> The custom ran in Moonfleet when either land or lease was put up to bidding, to stick a pin in a candle; and so long as the pin held firm, it was open to any to make a better offer, but when the flame burnt down and the pin fell out, then land or lease fell to the last bidder.[2]

Sale by candle was still used in London coffee houses, including Garraways, at the end of the 18th century but then died out.

---

[1] *Pepys Diary*, 3 September 1662, quoted by P. Ash.
[2] J. Meade Falkner, *Moonfleet* (Harmondsworth, 1995), p. 80.

2 D.c.f.

FOR
SALE
BY THE
CANDLE,
AT

GARRAWAY'S Coffee-Houfe, in *Ex-
change-alley, Cornhill,*

On *Thurfday* the 5th of *December*, 1765, at
Five o'Clock in the Afternoon, the following
Goods, *viz.*

54 Barrels Rice, garbled and feparated from the Damag'd
18 Ditto garbling Duft
35 Ditto total Damaged

54 Barrels Rice, garbled and feparated from the Damag'd
in 8 Lots, Tare as on the Cafks, with cuftomary
Allowances, at   per ℔, to advance 3d.

	Lot	Barrels
16	1	13 Barrels
1 6 4	2	9
16 1	3	4
1 5 1 1	4	1

Sale by candle auction at Garraway's in 1765.

The demise of sale by candle is not surprising because of
the length of time the process must have taken. The usual
length of candle used was one inch and this would take a
long time, perhaps an hour, to burn down.[1] There is
reference in *Moonfleet* that "the men fell to smoking to pass
the time, till there could not have been more than ten

---

[1] Some sales by candle survived in the provinces to a much
later date. In Lincolnshire the technique was used in sales of
land as late as the 1920s and '30s: see M. Sutton, *A
Lincolnshire Calendar* (Stamford, 1997), pp. 204–5. *The Times*,
20 March 1873.

minutes' candle to burn." Although the final moments were tense, the process was much too lengthy for the quickening pace of trade in the early 19th century.

Although the sale of chattels had been the original objective of most auctions, the sale of land, estates and buildings became well established during the 18th century. Sales of chattels can be dated back to the late 17th century. The first land auction has been claimed to date from about 1740 when Christopher Cock of Covent Garden sold two houses as part of the stock of a bankrupt. By the end of the 18th century, property sales by auction were so widespread that announcements were grouped in *The Times* under the new heading 'Sales by Auction', covering all categories of chattels and real estate being offered.

It has been claimed, reasonably, that the profession of estate agent developed from that of land auctioneer. The description 'estate agent' originated around 1820–30 to describe those who issued private treaty sales advertisements, often in conjunction with their announcements of auctions.[1]

The atmosphere at an early Victorian London auction has been well described by Thackeray in *Vanity Fair*[2]:

> If there is any exhibition in all Vanity Fair which Satire and Sentiment can visit arm-in-arm together; where you light on the strangest contrasts laughable and tearful: where you may be gentle and pathetic, or savage and cynical, with perfect propriety: it is at one of those public assemblies, a crowd of which are

[1] Ash, op. cit.

[2] W. M. Thackeray, *Vanity Fair*, chapter XVII (1847). Mr Robins was noted for auctioneer's oratory: shortly before he died at the age of 70, he rejected an offer of 2,000 guineas to conduct an auction in New York: see Jeremy Cooper, *Under the Hammer: the Auctions and Auctioneers of London* (London, 1977), pp. 51–2.

advertised every day in the last pages of *The Times* newspaper, and over which the late Mr George Robins used to preside with so much dignity. There are very few London people, as I fancy, who have not attended at these meetings...

George Robins, who died in 1847, was a well known auctioneer and a contemporary of Charles Farebrother. Their advertisements frequently appeared in adjacent spaces on the last page of *The Times*.

1.3 *Garraway's Coffee House*

Coffee houses had been established in London since the middle of the 17th century. A manuscript of 1659 refers to the sale in almost every street of "a Turkish drink called Coffee and another kind of drink called Tee, and also a drink called Chocolate, which was a very harty drink".[1] Coffee became much more popular than tea. Coffee houses were at their most frequented and influential in the first half of the 18th century. In addition to providing refreshment they acted as social centres and meeting places for people of varied classes and occupations.[2] They represented addresses to and from which letters could be sent and acted as offices when such facilities were rare. Because people of similar occupations and interests tended to congregate together

[1] G. L. Apperson, 'The Old London Coffee Houses' in P. H. Ditchfield (ed.), *Memorials of Old London*, vol. II, p. 135.

[2] B. Lillywhite, *London Coffee Houses* (London, 1963) This excellent and comprehensive book includes an advertisement from the *Public Advertiser*, 1 Jan. 1761 which shows that coffee houses were venues for possible romance, thus: "a tall young gentleman ... was narrowly observed and much approved of by a certain young lady at the last ridotto ... if his heart is entirely disengaged, that if he will apply to A. B. at Garraway's Coffee House ... he may be directed to have an interview with the young lady, which may prove greatly to his advantage", p. 221.

Garraway's Coffee House, Cornhill, *Estates Gazette.*

certain coffee houses became the recognised centres for the business and social activity of specific groups. The Stock Exchange evolved via Jonathan's Coffee House in Exchange Alley. Lloyd's Coffee House, which moved to Lombard Street in 1691, and where individuals raised the money needed to insure merchant shipping, eventually developed into the familiar world-wide insurance company.

In the same way that Lloyd's Coffee House was for insurance brokers, Garraway's, in Exchange Alley, off Cornhill, was the recognised centre for the sale of stocks, bonds and indeed "merchandise of all types". Furthermore Garraway's was the principal venue for auction sales and remained so for a long time, even after the specially-built London Auction Mart in St Bartholomew's Lane was opened in 1808.

Garraway's had a very long history.[1] The original house was destroyed in the Great Fire of London, rebuilt, burnt down in 1748 and was back in business by 1752. It was a very active commercial centre at the time of the collapsed speculation known as the South Sea Bubble in 1721, and was described by Jonathan Swift as "a place of resort for reckless adventurers". Thomas Garway, "a tobacconist and coffee man", was said to have been the original proprietor; the name was later corrupted to Garraway's. He was the first man in England to sell tea which he recommended "for the cure of all disorders".[2]

Garraway's was well known to Charles Dickens and is mentioned in *Pickwick Papers*, *Martin Chuzzlewit*, *Little Dorrit* and *The Uncommercial Traveller*.[3]

The atmosphere in Garraway's when Charles Farebrother was conducting auctions from 1803 onwards was both conducive to business and very convivial. The owner provided a wide range of newspapers, journals and pamphlets giving the latest financial information. In common with other coffee houses, Garraway's had widened the choice of beverages to include ales, wines and spirits and the very popular "laced coffee" or coffee dashed with brandy. There were "large trays of ham, beef and tongue sandwiches, cut in a most substantial manner ... ranged on the bar". "Fruit women" came in selling oranges and nuts.[4]

---

[1]   See Lillywhite, op. cit.; also *The London Encyclopedia*, p. 303.

[2]   *The Times*, 20 March 1873.

[3]   E. Beresford Chancellor, *The London of Charles Dickens, being an Account of the Haunts of his Characters and the Topographical Settings of his Novels* (London, 1924), pp. 103, 162, 226–7, 289.

[4]   D. Kynaston, *The City of London, a World of its Own, 1815–1890* (London, 1994), p. 144.

The auction room where "estates and houses of enormous value are daily put up to sale"[1] was "an old-fashioned apartment on the first floor, with a little rostrum for the auctioneer and a few long 'settles' for the buyers".[2] Selling continued late into the night: Garraway's was "always the place of resort for the 'late' men" who would refresh themselves with champagne and anchovies.[3]

The tradition and versatility of Garraway's kept the house in business long after the coffee house fashion had declined in the years leading up to 1830. The items sold at Garraway's by Charles Farebrother varied widely and included great estates, more modest houses, stained glass, building materials and plots, silver plate, jewellery, furniture, wines, cotton and linen, wharfs on the river, rental reversions, annuities, etc. In May 1811 Farebrother auctioned at Garraway's a number of lots including the Percy Coffee House in Rathbone Place, Oxford Street (formerly frequented by James Boswell).[4]

As the 19th century progressed, auction business inevitably gravitated towards the new purpose-built auction rooms. Moreover, coffee houses mostly fell into the ownership of vintners and coffee drinking became a minor attraction. Many coffee houses changed into taverns.

Garraway's finally closed in 1866 with last drinks served on Saturday 11 August. Glyn Mills & Co. of Lombard Street required the site for expansion. Appropriately perhaps it was Farebrother, Lye and Wheeler who sold the furniture and fittings two days after closure.[5] The building

1   Ibid., p. 74.
2   *The Times*, 20 March 1873.
3   D. Kynaston, op. cit., p. 122.
4   B. Lillywhite, op. cit., p. 446.
5   *The Times*, 9 September 1866; D. Kynaston, op. cit., p. 245. For changes in style of coffee houses circa 1810, see M. D. George, *London Life in the 18th Century* (London, 1930), pp. 306–7.

was demolished in 1873: the site is now occupied by Midland Bank at 84 Lombard Street.

Garraway's Coffee-house, Change-alley, Cornhill.—The Furniture and Fixtures of these old-established Sale Rooms and Tavern. FAREBROTHER, LYE, and WHEELER are instructed to SELL by AUCTION, upon the Premises, on Monday next, August 13, at 1 for 2, the whole of the FURNITURE and FIXTURES of the several AUCTION ROOMS, comprising Spanish mahogany and other tables, settees, and forms, oak, mahogany, and grained rostrums and desks, a set of Spanish mahogany dining room chairs, several first-rate dials by Murray, Hawkins, Carpenter, and others, the fittings of the bar, coffee room, and counting-houses, a refrigerator, marble-top lavatory, iron safe, reflectors, three clever pictures, a few fittings of the cellars, gas fittings, and other effects. Catalogues to be obtained on the premises, or of Messrs. Farebrother, Lye, and Wheeler, 8, Lancaster-place, Strand.

1.4 *Progress as an Auctioneer*

By 1803 Charles Farebrother had established himself as a professional auctioneer holding regular sales of increasing prestige. How he was able to reconcile this situation with his nominal apprenticeship to Brasbridge is unclear. Nevertheless from 1803 Farebrother was working from offices and auction rooms at 16 Old Bond Street and had moved his residence from College Street to 7 Beaufort Buildings, Strand.

When Farebrother was carrying out his early auctions, announcements in *The Times* suggest an unusually keen attention to what would now be termed customer relations. On two occasions in 1803 Farebrother, perhaps because he was working without any assistance, placed advertisements designed purely to keep customers informed of the progress of his sales. On February 28th he announced that he would submit for sale in March "a large and highly valuable COLLECTION of ANCIENT STAINED GLASS, which for design and beauty of colouring, will be found to surpass any which has hitherto been offered to the Public". On March 12th it was announced that "MR FAREBROTHER respectfully informs the Public, that the SALE OF PLATE, JEWELLERY, CABINETS etc. which was to have taken place at his Room No.91 New Bond Street, This Day, is unavoidably postponed (on account of his indisposition) for a few days. Timely notice of the sale will be given in future advertisements." The sale was eventually held at New Bond Street on 12 April.

On June 16th 1803 Farebrother held his first sale at Garraway's Coffee House on Exchange Alley, Cornhill. This auction room was to become the principal venue for his sales for more than fifty years. The sale was in two parts. The first part was the sale of "a desirable residence situated at Kennington Green, near the Windmill Tavern ... the purchaser may be accommodated with the genteel household furniture, new within two years, at a valuation." The second part, in complete contrast, was the sale of Price's Wharf on Millbank Street, Westminster, with all the associated warehouses and stock.[1]

As Charles Farebrother's business grew, so the variety of chattels and property offered at auction widened and also the business spread far beyond London. Auctions at Garraway's varied from "An assortment of cottons, muslins, cambrics etc." in January 1805[2] to "The absolute Reversion, certain on the demise of a lady aged 45 years ... of valuable free hold estate" in May 1805.[3] In January 1805 at Garraway's Farebrother carried out the sale of a large estate of 4,360 acres with an annual value of £8,000 and including "that well-known magnificent seat THORN-VILLE ROYAL" near Knaresborough in Yorkshire. Descriptions referred to this as "the most desirable estate in the kingdom ... particularly adapted for a Nobleman or Man of Fashion".[4]

To be selling a property of the importance of Thornville Royal in 1805 was a remarkable achievement for a young man of 22 in what was also the first year in which his name appeared in trade directories. He was described as an auctioneer acting from premises at 16 Old Bond Street.

[1]   *The Times*, 11 June 1803.
[2]   Ibid., 19 January 1805.
[3]   Ibid., 9 May 1805.
[4]   Ibid., 18 January 1805.

SALES BY AUCTION.

MR. FAREBROTHER has the honor to inform
the Nobility and Gentry, that he will submit for SALE in
March (unless previously disposed of by Private Contract), a large
and highly valuable COLLECTION of ANCIENT STAINED
GLASS, which, for design and beauty of colouring, will be found
to surpass any which has hitherto been offered to the Public. Spe-
cimens will be shewn in a few days in Bond-street.—No. 91, · New
Bond-street.

SALES BY AUCTION.

MR. FAREBROTHER respectfully informs the
Public, that the SALE of PLATE, JEWELLERY,
CABINETS, &c. which was to have taken place at his Room.
No. 91, New Bond-street, This Day, is unavoidably postponed
(on account of his indisposition) for a few Days. Timely notice
of the Sale will be given in future Advertisements.
No. 91, New Bond-street, March 11.

By 1809 Charles Farebrother was holding regular sales
at Garraway's and, in keeping with his constant endeavour
to inform the public of his intentions, he issued a statement
committing himself to holding monthly sales at Garraway's.
The lots under offer were to be diverse ranging across
"estates, houses, reversions, life interests, ground rents,
shares in canal property, water works, or any public
institutions". In his statement, Farebrother emphasised the
growing popularity of selling by the auction method. Thus:

It being my intention to establish a Monthly Sale at
Garraway's Coffee House, of the above Description of
Properties, the Object of which is to afford an
Opportunity to the Public, of offering their Property for
Sale by Auction, in lieu of Selling by Private Contract,
which latter Practice has very frequently been adopted to
the great loss of the Seller, in consequence of the Expence
[sic] of Auctions (which Expence will be considerably
lessened where property is bought in) by the above
Establishment, as the whole will be printed in one
Particular, which will not only serve the end of
informing the particular Persons enquiring for one Sale,
but, by laying the whole before the Public, lead to the
almost certainty of the Proprietor selling his property,

17

REVERSIONS.

Particulars and Conditions of Sale
OF THE

ABSOLUTE REVERSION
TO A VALUABLE

Freehold Estate in the County of Leicester,
AMOUNTING TO

Two Hundred & Ninety-one Pounds Thirteen Shillings & Four Pence
PER ANNUM,

Certain on the Demise of a LADY aged Forty-five Years.

ALSO,

THE REVERSION
(Subject to the same Life)

of and to a Valuable FREEHOLD & COPYHOLD Estate,
Of the Annual Value of One Hundred and Forty Pounds,

Situate in the County of Essex.

THE REVERSIONARY LIFE INTEREST
of a Gentleman, aged Twenty Eight Years,
expectant on the Demise of his Mother, aged Forty-Five Years,
In and to Valuable ESTATES in RUTLANDSHIRE, of the present Annual Value of

Two Hundred and Seventy-Two Pounds;

AND

THE PRINCIPAL SUM OF FIVE HUNDRED POUNDS
Certain on the Demise of a LADY aged Sixty Years, provided
a LADY aged Twenty-Eight Years survives her.

The Whole of which will be Sold by Auction,

BY MR. FAREBROTHER,
At Garraway's Coffee House, Exchange Alley,
CORNHILL, LONDON,

On THURSDAY, 9th of May, 1805, at Twelve o'Clock,
IN FOUR LOTS.

The Estates may be Viewed, by Leave of the Tenants—Particulars had, Ten Days prior to the Sale, at the Principal Inns at *Leicester* and *Chinkford*; at the CROWN Inns, *Oakham* and *Stamford*; at GARRAWAY's; of G. J. ROBINSON, Esq. Solicitor, No. 7, Lincoln's *Inn New Square*; and at Mr. FAREBROTHER's Offices, No. 7, *Beaufort Buildings, Strand, London.*

Farebrother in 1805 sells estates in Rutland
by auction at Garraway's

18

THE

Particulars and Conditions of Sale

OF TWO SUBSTANTIAL

BRICK-BUILT RESIDENCES

No. 48 & 49, in Margaret Street, Cavendish Square,

LET TO MESSRS. SUTTON AND WILSON.

TWO PLEASANT

DESIRABLE RESIDENCES,

WITH CAPITAL GARDENS,

Situate Nos. 5, and 6, CRAVEN PLACE, BAYSWATER,

Now in the Occupation of Messrs. JOHNSTON and DARBEY,

FOURTEEEN HOUSES,

IN ARTILLERY PLACE, AND BRUNSWICK ROW,

Near Palmer's Village, Westminster,

PART LET ON LEASE, AND THE REMAINDER TO TENANTS AT WILL.

ALSO,

AN IMPROVED RENT,

OF

TEN POUNDS PER ANNUM for SEVENTEEN YEARS,

ISSUING OUT OF A

Neat Residence, Garden, &c.

No. 5, SOUTHAMPTON ROW, LISSON GREEN.

Which will be Sold by Auction,

BY

Mr. FAREBROTHER,

At Garraway's Coffee House, 'Change Alley,

CORNHILL,

On THURSDAY, the 4th Day of MAY, 1820,

AT TWELVE O'CLOCK, IN FIVE LOTS, WITHOUT RESERVE.

The different Lots may be Viewed by permission of the Tenants, and Particulars had Fourteen Days prior to the Sale, at Garraway's; and of Mr. FAREBROTHER, Beaufort House, Beaufort Buildings, Strand.

Farebrother in 1820 sells estates in London
by auction at Garraway's

and offer a never-failing source for the Speculator to invest his money.

The very important Sales which have been intrusted [sic] to my Care, will I hope, plead a sufficient Excuse for my thus soliciting the Patronage of the Public, in a Concern which will require unabating Zeal and Attention.

I have the Honour to remain, the Public's most faithful humble servant

> CHARLES FAREBROTHER,
> Surveyor, Auctioneer & Appraiser
> 7 Beaufort Buildings, Strand
> March 17, 1809.

At the same time as when he issued the above statement, Farebrother also set out his charges. For each lot, the charges varied from half a guinea to five guineas depending on value with the highest charge introduced when the value exceeded £400. He asked for fifteen days notice to include items in his monthly sale and listed the services offered as: "Estates surveyed, mapped and valued; Timber measured; Live and Dead Farming Stock; Plate, Jewels, Furniture, Linen, Books etc. valued and sold by Private Contract, or by Public Auction."

This announcement accompanied the statement regarding monthly sales at Garraway's, which began on 9 May 1809. Farebrother was using his wide range of skills and experience to offer what was in effect a total property service.

An Elegant SILVER GILT CUP, and THREE Fashionable SILVER DISHES. —By Mr. FAREBROTHER, At his Great Room, No. 91, New Bond-street, on Saturday next, Feb. 5, at one o'clock, the former Purchaser not having completed his Purchase agreeable to the Condition of Sale,

AN Elegant Chased and Gilt fashionable SIDE-BOARD, CUP, and THREE SILVER DISHES. Also some Plated Articles.—To be viewed, and Catalogues had at the Bank Coffee-house; Mr. Lindsil's, Bookseller, Wigmore-street, and in Bond-street.

CHARLES FAREBROTHER

1.5 *The Newstead Sales*

In 1815 Charles Farebrother announced an auction of national importance. This sale, in two parts held at Garraway's on 28 July and 23 October 1815, was for Lord Byron and offered on the two dates respectively Newstead Abbey Estate and its contents. The estate, situated between Nottingham and Mansfield, consisted of the Abbey, the ruins of an older abbey, a castle, farms, mills, quarries, lime kilns etc., a total of 3,200 acres. The contents, listed in the catalogue of the second sale, included "the very elegant furniture (new within a few years)" together with a cellar of wines and the farm stock. The contents were generally impersonal except for some prints of Oxford and Cambridge colleges and one of John 'Gentleman' Jackson, the prize fighter and champion of England: Byron referred to him as "my old friend and corporal pastor and master, John Jackson Esq., Professor of Pugilism."[1]

The July 1815 sale was in fact the second occasion on which Charles Farebrother had offered Newstead Abbey for sale by auction. The first occasion was on 14 August 1812. On that day the bids were insufficient and the Abbey was withdrawn from sale. After this unsuccessful auction, the Abbey was sold privately to a Mr Claughton for £140,000 but he defaulted on the purchase and was obliged to pay Byron a forfeit of £25,000. This fine ruined Claughton but gave Byron some temporary respite from his increasing number of creditors. Moreover, for the time being at least, he retained Newstead.[2]

Although mounting debts forced the sale upon him, Byron was most reluctant to part with Newstead. In March 1809 he wrote to his mother:

> *Newstead* and I *stand* or fall together, I have now lived on the spot, I have fixed my heart upon it,

---

[1]   A. Maurois, *Byron* (London, 1930), pp. 76–7.
[2]   Ibid., pp. 164, 202.

21

NEWSTEAD ABBEY ESTATE,
Nottinghamshire.

THE
PARTICULARS
OF
A CAPITAL, EXTENSIVE, AND VERY VALUABLE
FREEHOLD
TYTHE-FREE ESTATE,
CONTAINING ABOUT
Three Thousand Two Hundred Acres,
CONSISTING OF THE DESIRABLE
MANOR OR LORDSHIP OF NEWSTEAD,
IN THE COUNTY OF NOTTINGHAM,

WITH THE CAPITAL MANSION OF NEWSTEAD ABBEY,
Gardens, Pleasure Grounds, Basins, Fish Ponds, and extensive Offices,
Surrounded by a lofty STONE WALL, and Part of the fine REMAINS of that ANCIENT ABBEY, and

A BEAUTIFUL CASTLE,
STANDING ON AN EMINENCE, AT THE HEAD OF THE GREAT LAKE OF THIRTY ACRES,
With several other extensive Lakes, Woods, and thriving Plantations,
IN THE OCCUPATION OF THE PROPRIETOR.

AND SUNDRY ELIGIBLE FARMS,
MILLS, PUBLIC HOUSES, VALUABLE QUARRIES of excellent FREE STONE, in great Request for BUILDINGS, FLAGS and JAMBS,
AND EXTENSIVE LIME KILNS.

NEWSTEAD
Is a fine compact Property, consisting principally of good WHEAT and TURNIP LAND, and particularly well adapted to the NORFOLK SYSTEM of HUSBANDRY, which may be introduced to great Advantage. It is situated between

NOTTINGHAM AND MANSFIELD,
Within Ten Miles of the former, and Four of the latter, and about One Hundred and Thirty from LONDON, on the great NORTH ROAD, which goes through the Estate. An excellent MANOR of GAME of all Sorts, with which it abounds; and the LAKES, which are extensive, numerous, and grand, are well stocked with FISH, and in the Season much frequented by WILD FOWL, and there are many PACKS of FOX HOUNDS and HARRIERS in the immediate Neighbourhood.

The Whole of the LORDSHIP of NEWSTEAD is extra-parochial, and all the Estate TYTHE-FREE, except about One Hundred and Twenty-seven Acres, which are in the adjoining Parish of LINDBY.—No Church Cess for NEWSTEAD, and the Poor and other Rates very trifling.
There are many grand Scites for erecting a MANSION, and for which there is a great Abundance of Materials in the present Buildings, and the Whole forms a Possession and Domain rarely to be purchased.

There are several very powerful Streams of Water, with sufficient Heads and Falls for Mills and Manufactories of any Magnitude, and considerable Extent of the Land lies remarkably well for Irrigation.

The above MANOR and ESTATES will be SOLD BY AUCTION,

By Mr. FAREBROTHER,

At Garraway's Coffee House, 'Change Alley, Cornhill, London,
On FRIDAY, the 28th Day of JULY, 1815,
AT TWELVE O'CLOCK, IN TWO LOTS.

For a View of the Estate apply to Mr. OWEN MEALEY at the *Hut Public House,* Newstead, near the Turnpike Gate, on the Great North Road, where printed Particulars, with Plans annexed, may be had; also at the Office of JOHN HANSON, Esq. No. 65, Chancery Lane, London; at the Place of Sale; at the *White Lion,* Nottingham; *Swan,* Mansfield; *Bear,* Loughborough; the *Three Crowns,* Leicester; the *Bell,* Derby; the *Black Swan,* York; the *Angel,* Doncaster; the *Bridgewater Arms,* Manchester; the *Hen and Chickens,* Birmingham; the *Bull and Mouth,* Leeds; and of Mr. FAREBROTHER, Beaufort House, Beaufort Buildings, Strand, London.

Sales particulars for Newstead Abbey, 28 July 1815.

22

and no pressure present or future shall induce me to barter the last vestige of our inheritance; I have that pride within me, which will enable me to support difficulties, I can endure privations, but could I obtain in exchange for Newstead Abbey the first fortune in the country, I would reject the proposition – set your mind at ease on that score.[1]

Later that year, 1809, Byron wrote to William Harness (a school friend from Harrow):

Hanson (his friend and lawyer) has at last written and wants *me* to sell Newstead. *I will not*, and though I have in more than one letter to you requested you to corroborate and assist this *negative*, I beg in this and all subsequent communications to entreat you to tell him and all whom it may concern, that I will *not* sell my patrimony.[2]

In January 1811 Byron wrote to Hanson:

I have written my negative to your proposal on the subject of Newstead, by my servant Fletcher, which I presume is delivered by this time, and I write now for the purpose of repeating it – I will *not* sell Newstead, come what may![3]

The depth of Byron's love of Newstead can be appreciated from the opening paragraph of his will drawn up in 1811.

This is the last will and testament of me the Rt. Honourable George Gordon Lord Byron, Baron Byron of Rochdale in the county of Lancaster – I desire that my body may be buried in the vault of the garden at Newstead without any cere-

---

[1] L. A. Marchand (ed.), *Byron's Letters and Journals* (London, 1975), vol.1, pp. 195-6.
[2] Ibid., vol. 2, p. 32.
[3] Ibid., p. 35.

ELEGANT FURNITURE,

PIER AND CHIMNEY GLASSES,

Fine Coloured Prints of the Colleges at Oxford and Cambridge;

CELLAR OF CHOICE WINES,

Brewing Utensils, large Leaden Figures, Three Pleasure Boats;

LIVE & DEAD FARMING STOCK, & EFFECTS,

At Newstead Abbey,

BETWEEN

NOTTINGHAM AND MANSFIELD, IN NOTTINGHAMSHIRE.

A

CATALOGUE

OF THE VERY

ELEGANT FURNITURE,

(NEW WITHIN A FEW YEARS)

CONSISTING OF

Superb State, Four-post, and Tent Bedsteads, with rich Hangings,
Excellent Goose Feather Beds, Hair and Wool Mattresses, fine Witney Blankets and
Marseilles Quilts, Dining, Drawing Room, and Bed Room Curtains;
Capital MAHOGANY GOODS, in Sets of Tables, Sideboards, Bookcases, Mahogany and
Japanned Chairs, Brussels and Kidderminster Carpets, Pier and Chimney Glasses and
Mirrors, a Profusion of Domestic Furniture of every Description;

A small CELLAR of particularly fine-flavoured OLD WINES,
Brewing Copper, Brewing Utensils, large Leaden Figures,

AND VARIOUS EFFECTS——ALSO THE

LIVE AND DEAD FARMING STOCK,

CONSISTING OF

A fine Flock of 500 *SHEEP of the improved Forest, & South-down Breed,*

TEN CART GELDINGS AND MARES,

A Yearling Colt, a Mule, TWENTY HEIFERS with Calves, and in Calf;
Waggons, Carts, Ploughs, 100 Hurdles, Cart and Plough Harness, &c.

About Two HUNDRED and SIXTY QUARTERS of Oats in the Straw;
SEVENTY QUARTERS OF BARLEY IN DITTO,

A STACK of RYE, about Twenty-four Loads, Forty Tons of HAY,

AND VARIOUS FARMING IMPLEMENTS.

Also, the GROWING CROP of TURNIPS on THIRTY ACRES.

Which will be Sold by Auction,

By MR. FAREBROTHER,

ON THE PREMISES,

On MONDAY, 23d of OCTOBER, 1815,

AND FOLLOWING DAYS,

AT ELEVEN O'CLOCK PRECISELY EACH DAY,

BY DIRECTION OF

The Right Honble LORD BYRON.

The Furniture and Effects in the Mansion, may be Viewed after the 13th Instant, and
Catalogues had at the Mansion of Newstead, at 1s. each.
The Farming Stock may be Viewed by applying to Mr. PALING, at Newstead, the Day
preceding the Sale—Catalogues of the Whole had at the White Lion, Nottingham; Swan,
Mansfield; and of Mr. FAREBROTHER, Beaufort House, Beaufort Buildings, Strand,
London.

Sale of furniture and effects, Newstead Abbey, 23 October 1815.

mony or burial service whatever, and that no inscription, save my name and age, be written on the tomb or tablet; and it is my will that my faithful dog may not be removed from the said vault.[1]

In August 1811, faced with the first possible sale by Farebrother, Byron wrote: "I had built myself a bath and a *vault* – and now I sha'n't even be buried in it. It is odd that we can't even be certain of a *grave*, at least a particular one."[2]

In November 1813, just before Claughton defaulted, Byron wrote: "I wonder when that Newstead business will be finished. It cost me more than words to part with it – and to *have* parted with it! What matters it what I do? or what becomes of me?"[3]

When Charles Farebrother conducted the second auction of Newstead in July 1815, Byron was 26 years old and the new Lady Byron was several months pregnant. They had rented a large town house at 13 Piccadilly Terrace with a staff of servants and two carriages. However, Byron's debts were unsustainable. The rent of No.13 was £700 per annum which took all of Lady Byron's income. The Newstead rent roll did not even pay the interest on his debts.

Unfortunately the second sale of Newstead was once again unsuccessful; the bids were insufficient and the property was withdrawn from sale. Eventually, in November 1817, Newstead was sold privately to an old Harrow friend of Byron for 90,000 guineas. After necessary payments for mortgages, annuities and marriage settlements, Byron was left with £22,300 against debts of £28,162. There was to be no respite from debt collectors.

In 1819 Byron was still attempting to raise money and heard rumours of interest in his other estates. He wrote:

[1]   Ibid., p. 72.
[2]   Ibid., vol. 3, p. 96.
[3]   Ibid., p. 209

"Pray what could make Farebrother say that seventeen thousand pounds had been bidden for the undisputed part of Rochdale manor? – it may be so – but I never heard of it before – not even from Spooney – if anybody bids – take it – & send it to me by post – but don't pay away to those low people of tradesmen."[1] Again he wrote: "Cannot Farebrother find this quiet purchaser for Rochdale?"[2]

Byron's income was never sufficient to meet his debts. In December 1821 he wrote from Pisa: "I really can't pay Farebrother or any one else more than the *interest* of their debt at present."[3]

1.6 *Development of the Business*

As Charles Farebrother's business developed it passed through various changes of partnership and style. In 1827, the business became Farebrother, Wilson and Lye. In 1836 it became Farebrother and Lye, and in 1845 the title changed again to Farebrother, Clark and Lye.

The premises from which the business operated also changed during Farebrother's lifetime as follows:

1805	16 Old Bond Street
1806–1814	7 Beaufort Buildings
1815–1824	9 Beaufort Buildings
1825–1826	6 Wellington Street
1827–1835	2 Lancaster Place
1836–1861	9 Lancaster Place

Thereafter, from 1861 the business address was 6 Lancaster Place. In 1882, the business then known as Farebrother, Ellis, Clark & Co. moved to 29 Fleet Street, an address which it was to retain for over 100 years.

---

[1]   Ibid., vol. 6, p. 114.
[2]   Ibid., vol. 6, p. 222.
[3]   Ibid., vol. 9, p. 82.

1.7 *Lord Mayor in Difficult Times*

In the early 19th century, Aldermen of the City of London were elected by the Common Hall of the livery companies and then progressed to the office of Sheriff. This was an essential stage in the ultimate civic advancement to Lord Mayor because only those who had served as Sheriff could be proposed for the office of Lord Mayor.

In 1826 Farebrother was elected to be an Alderman of Lime Street ward and held this office until his death in 1858 when he was the second oldest Alderman in the London Corporation. He became a Sheriff of London and Middlesex in 1826/7. In 1833 he attained the highest municipal office becoming Lord Mayor of London.

The year 1833 in which Charles Farebrother became Lord Mayor was in the middle of a particularly difficult and dangerous period for the government of the City. In June 1832 the Great Reform Act had been passed by Parliament after a struggle which had lasted for two years, and the national feeling in which political tension and exhilaration combined to form a volatile mixture still persisted. The 1832 Act, which came to be regarded as a landmark in British political history, was the first stage in progress towards the modern version of fully representative democracy. Its provisions swept away the pocket boroughs which had been the private fiefdoms of the aristocracy and gentry. Parliamentary seats were re-distributed to the new and growing urban centres of population. New seats were created, including Lambeth where Farebrother lived at Stockwell Common. The franchise was extended within new limits of property ownership or leasehold value: the net effect was to increase the electorate of England and Wales by almost 50%, from 435,000 to 652,000.[1]

---

[1] M. Brock, *The Great Reform Act* (London, 1973); E. J. Evans, *The Great Reform Act of 1832* (2nd ed., London, 1994).

These reforms had not been achieved without serious political tension which spilled over into commotion and riot, some of which involved London, always considered more vulnerable as the seat of government and authority. In April 1831 the House of Commons controlled by the Whigs under Lord Grey with a majority of more than 130, was in favour of reform but the House of Lords was opposed to reform and blocked the bill. Riots broke out in many towns including Bristol, Derby and Nottingham.[1] Much hostility was also directed at the Church because bishops sitting in the House of Lords were known to have voted against reform. In Huddersfield, a bishop was burned in effigy.[2]

The crisis point was reached during the so-called "Days of May" in 1832 when Lord Grey had resigned as Prime Minister following the House of Lords veto. The King, William IV, was opposed to reform and sent for the Duke of Wellington to form a government and to garrison London against civil insurrection. The Duke sent out military forces to defend public buildings and to deliver the King "out of the hands of the radicals". In the event the prospect of another Wellington government was averted.[3]

A very effective weapon used by Reformist groups in the campaign against Wellington was that of creating a run on the banks by withdrawing money. Posters were placed in London proclaiming "To stop the Duke, call for Gold". The intention was to raise general panic, then there would be a run on the Bank of England which would soon be compelled to cease trading and a revolution would follow, or so it was thought. This technique appears to have been very effective in the short term. It was claimed that the Bank of England had to pay out £1,500,000 in a few days

---

[1]   M. Brock, op. cit., pp. 248–50.

[2]   E. A. Smith, *Reform or Revolution, A Diary of Reform in England 1830–32* (Stroud, 1992), p. 108.

[3]   M. Brock, op. cit., pp. 292–301, and E. A. Smith, op. cit., pp. 102–5.

which was about a quarter of the total reserves. After Lord Grey was re-instated as Prime Minister, demand for gold ceased and the financial crisis ended.[1]

When the Reform Act became law in June of 1832 King William IV gave the Royal Assent with great misgivings. He refused to attend the House of Lords to give his assent in person. He directed that there should be no illuminations or fireworks to celebrate the event.[2] Nevertheless there had been a growing inevitability about the passing of a reform act. Many MPs believed that if such an act had not been passed in 1832, violent revolution would have swept away established institutions as had happened in France forty years earlier. A momentum for reform had built up and the next object of attention was local government.

The Municipal Corporations Act of 1835 revolutionised local government in general, sweeping away the old unelected commissions which managed towns, and giving to urban centres the ability to elect their own governing councils. Many towns were investigated by Royal Commission and London was the single subject of the second report of the Commission in 1837. The City of London, over which Charles Farebrother had recently presided, was the object of much criticism.

The City Corporation, which was the oldest and most important of local governing bodies, was seen as "primarily concerned with maintaining its ancient privileges and exclusive rights against the potential encroachments of the rapidly growing town outside its narrow boundaries". A contemporary observer wrote that:

> A common councilman, whether Whig, Radical, or Tory (the exceptions are remarkably few) has not the least notion that he exists to forward any common object in which the inhabitants of the

---

[1] G. Wallas, *The Life of Francis Place 1771–1854* (London, 1908), pp. 310–1.

[2] E. J. Evans, op. cit., p. 1.

whole metropolis are interested, but will honestly state that he considers it his duty to maintain the exclusive rights and privileges of the City of London regardless of any other consideration.[1]

The editor of the *Westminster Review* wrote that "the machinery of local government in the metropolis was about the worst that could be devised".[2]

Although in 1836 the government announced that a bill to reform the government of the City of London would be introduced, the project was dropped. No significant measure was brought forward until 1855.

The atmosphere generated in the City by all of these reforms, both actual and proposed, was very divisive. Reform as an ideal divided everyone even across parties. At Charles Farebrother's civic dinner as outgoing Lord Mayor, the Lord Chancellor stated that "it was his misfortune to differ from some present on public questions, who held views opposite to those which he entertained, and who held them honestly and conscientiously".[3]

Enthusiasm for reform heightened public criticism of the City Corporation although since the early decades of the 18th century, the Corporation was accustomed to being attacked on grounds of "jobbery, corruption and extravagance".[4] Shortly after Farebrother was elected Lord Mayor, the radical Francis Place (later co-author of *The People's Charter*) wrote to the Municipal Corporation Commission complaining about "our corrupt, rotting, robbing, infamous Corporation of London ... and the Court of Aldermen, old men – no, old women, gossiping, guzzling, drinking, cheating, old chandlers'-shop women,

[1] W. A. Robson, *The Government and the Misgovernment of London* (London, 1939), p. 22.
[2] Ibid.
[3] *The Times*, 11 November 1834.
[4] W. A. Robson, op. cit., p. 32.

elected for life". After the passing of the Reform Act in 1832, Place refused to attend the celebratory City banquet on the grounds that "the whole of the City Government was a burlesque on the human understanding more contemptible than the most paltry farce played in a booth at Bartholomew's Fair and more mischievous than any man living is prepared to believe".[1]

Whatever may be the justification of complaints about corruption within the City Corporation, there is clear evidence that to become Lord Mayor in Farebrother's time was expensive and required a substantial financial position. The annual allowance paid to the Lord Mayor was nearly £8,000 which appears to be very generous but he was expected to spend much more than this; in particular, he was expected to make many donations to charity. The Commission of Inquiry on Municipal Corporations 1835-8 reported as follows:

> The annual salary of the Lord Mayor appears at first sight to be enormous, but it is unequal to the demand which custom has inposed upon him. It seems that he is expected to maintain the state of his office by an expenditure much exceeding his salary; the effect of which is to deter persons of moderate incomes from undertaking the office, and to attach to it a character by no means conducive to its real responsibility.[2]

The report of the Commission went on to point out that Sheriffs were also expected to spend much more than their salary of £400-£500 per annum.

---

[1] G. Wallas, op. cit., p. 47. See also M. Thale (ed.)., *The Autobiography of Francis Place 1771-1854* (Cambridge, 1972) and *The Times*, 23 December 1835.

[2] British Parliamentary Papers, Commissioners of Inquiry on Municipal Corporations, Irish University Press, vol. 6 1835-8, pp. 149-51.

It has been suggested elsewhere that even to be an Alderman of the City of London at that time implied ownership of an estate worth £40,000.[1]

Charles Farebrother was installed as Lord Mayor of London on Saturday, 9 November 1833. The procession consisting of the Lord Mayor, Aldermen and other civic officials left Guildhall at 11.30 a.m. and passed through King Street, Cheapside, Poultry, Cornhill, Leadenhall Street, Jewry Street, and Cooper's Row reaching the Tower at 12.30 p.m. They embarked in the civic barge which was rowed to Westminster where "his Lordship was enthusiastically greeted by the assembled crowd, while the military band ... played the national anthem."[2]

In the evening the traditional banquet was held at Guildhall and was attended by "most of the Foreign Ambassadors, the Lord Chancellor, the Duke of Richmond, Viscount Melbourne, Lord Auckland, the Earl of Surrey, Lord Palmerston, Lord Russell, Lord Althorp, the Lord Chief Justice and most of the Judges" together with innumerable others of note. The Hall was "brilliantly lighted" with gas at a cost of £180.

The Lord Mayor and Sheriffs had decided that there should be no ball that year but the rest of the entertainment was lavish. Approximately 1,000 guests sat down to a dinner which began with 150 gallons of turtle soup and continued with similar generosity throughout the courses. The drinks provided consisted of 25 dozen bottles of sherry, 15 dozen of hock, 50 dozen of champagne, 10 dozen each of Madeira and Port and 15 dozen of claret. Three gallons of brandy

---

[1] W. A. Robson, op. cit., p. 31.

[2] *The Times*, 11 November 1833. By the 1840s, the condition of the Thames was so polluted and noxious that procession by river was abandoned and the annual spectacle took to the roads. *The Times* has suggested recently (29.7.1998 – Editorial, 'Burnish the Barge') that the Thames is now so much cleaner that procession by river could and should be resumed.

was served. It is hardly surprising that of the 95 waiters present, five, identified only by their numbers, were "ejected from the Hall intoxicated".

The total cost of the dinner was £2,315 of which £200 was paid from Corporation General Purpose funds. Charles Farebrother was obliged to pay £1,000 and his two Sheriffs paid £450 each.[1]

In his retirement speech as outgoing Lord Mayor in November 1834 Farebrother affirmed that "while he had the honour to fill the high office of Chief Magistrate of the City of London, he had done all in his power to protect the privileges of that great body over which he was called upon to preside, and he had at the same time, whenever the occasion presented itself, done all that lay in his power to uphold the institutions of the country."[2]

In 1835, Farebrother contested Lambeth unsuccessfully for the Conservatives. It is difficult to discern his precise political attitude within Conservatism, but it may be assumed that he was favourably disposed towards reform. This assumption is based on his friendship with the reform-minded Whig MP for Lambeth between 1832 and 1852, Charles Tennyson-d'Eyncourt who, in 1834, wrote a letter recommending Farebrother for re-election as an Alderman.[3] He remained an Alderman for Lime Street ward until his death.

Charles Farebrother died on 20 March 1858 in the 77th year of his age, at his country mansion, Mount House, Stockwell Common, near Clapham. He was described in

[1] Minute Book of Lord Mayor's Entertainment 1833 – MS32 held by Corporation of London Records Office, at Guildhall.
[2] Robson, op. cit.
[3] The letter from Charles Tennyson d'Eyncourt is held in Lambeth Archives Department at the Minet Library. He was one of the two Liberals who won the new seats for Lambeth at the 1835 election in which Farebrother stood as a Conservative and lost.

tributes as "a thorough Conservative municipalist", and his long service and integrity were praised. It was said that "in the dispensation of patronage he had a special eye to the wants of his own constituency but though 'charity' in this respect 'began at home' it was not confined there."[1] References were made to "the loss of a friend and a brother". The Court of Aldermen carried unanimously the following resolution:

> The Court cannot allow the melancholy occasion of the decease of their much respected brother Charles Farebrother, late Alderman of the ward of Lime Street, to pass without placing upon record the expression of their feelings of high estimation of his personal character and his conduct as a magistrate and member of this court for the lengthened period of 32 years.[2]

---

[1] *City Press*, 27 March 1858.

[2] *The Times*, 31 March 1858. It should be noted that the fact that Charles Farebrother, having been Lord Mayor of London, was not knighted is not at all unusual. Between 1800 and 1869, only 25 of 69 Lord Mayors were knighted. In Charles Farebrother's time, say 1820–40, only 5 out of 20 Lord Mayors were knighted.

CHAPTER 2
NEW PROFESSIONS
AND NEW OPPORTUNITIES

2.1. Surveying and Related Professions
The development of the profession of surveying is in most respects directly connected with that of several related activities, e.g. land agency, quantity surveying, valuation, auctioneering, etc. Indeed many companies today still offer a planned combination of these activities. Farebrother remain prominent in this respect.

Land surveying may be traced back to the 16th century when open fields were increasingly subject to enclosure either by compulsion from local squires or by agreement between freeholders.[1] The majority of those who practised land surveying in the 16th to 18th centuries were in effect skilled artisans who used simple methods of measurement and were locally-based in their own regions. Some few of these surveyors who also possessed artistic ability produced the early maps. These map-makers were a highly-skilled minority, however, and their work was obviously not co-ordinated in a national context.[2]

This situation changed with the advent of the Ordnance Survey which began at the end of the 18th century. The first map produced was that of Kent in 1801 followed by Essex

---

[1] W. G. Hoskins, *The Making of the English Landscape* (Harmondsworth, 1985).

[2] The classic account of all these developments is: F. M. L. Thompson, *Chartered Surveyors, the Growth of a Profession* (London, 1968).

Advertisement under the new name of 'Farebrother, Clark & Lye', from the first issue of *The Estates Gazette*, May 1, 1858.

in 1805. By 1844 all of England south of a line from Preston to Hull was mapped. The Isle of Man was the last area to be completed in 1873. The driving force and controlling influence of the Ordnance Survey was provided by military engineers.[1]

Closely associated with surveying was measuring, that is the estimation and costing of necessary materials for building, which was the forerunner of quantity surveying. Measurers flourished in the wave of reconstruction which followed the Great Fire of London in 1666. By the end of

---

[1]   J. B. Harley and C. W. Phillips, *The Historian's Guide to Ordnance Survey Maps* (London, 1964).

the 18th century, a system of negotiation had arisen whereby the price of a building was decided upon after completion and was commonly the final result of argument between two sets of measurers – those employed by the builder on the one hand, and those employed by the commissioners of the building on the other.

With the coming of competitive tendering for buildings in the early 19th century, quantity surveying (for that is what the technique amounted to) became much more sophisticated and professionally organised. The new methods were applied to such major constructions as the new Houses of Parliament designed in 1835/6 and completed in 1865. The quantities for this project were calculated by Henry Arthur Hunt who was later among the original twenty founder members of the Institution of Chartered Surveyors in 1868.[1] Frederick James Clark, senior partner in the practice of Farebrother, Clark and Lye, was a prominent member of this founding group.

When the Institution was founded in 1868 it was established to include such activities as "the improvement of landed estates" and "the management of landed estates". Thus the land agents came under the organisation of surveyors and in many cases (including that of John Clutton, first President of the Institution) the professions of surveyor and land agent were combined.

The position of land agent had arisen largely because economic pressure on landowners had increased greatly in the first half of the 19th century. During the depression which followed the Napoleonic Wars prices obtainable for produce and stock fell and competition rose both nationally and from abroad. Therefore land owners found themselves with much greater incentive to manage their estates more

---

[1]   F. M. L. Thompson, op. cit. See also F. M. L. Thompson, 'The Origins and History of the Royal Institution of Chartered Surveyors', *Estates Gazette*, 8.6 (1968).

efficiently and productively and the professional land agent was introduced to perform this function. Because of their association with the major landowners whom they served, important land agents received considerable deference and respect. They came to be regarded as the elite of the surveying/land management professions. By 1877 it was claimed that the Institution of Chartered Surveyors was "understood to represent the management of something like three-fifths of the landed property of England".[1]

The original twenty founder members of the Institution of Chartered Surveyors in 1868 covered a very wide range of working. There were building and quantity surveyors, valuers, rating consultants and arbitrators, land agents and auctioneers all united under the same general organisation. They represented a new, albeit diverse, profession with its own rising standards.[2] The profession developed rapidly during the mid-19th century particularly in the property market and especially that of London where increasing

---

[1]   F. M. L. Thompson, *Chartered Surveyors*, p. 167. See also F. M. L. Thompson, *English Landed Society in the Nineteenth Century* (London, 1963), pp. 158–61, 258–63.

[2]   By the mid-19th century, people were becoming accustomed to the sight of surveyors in action, often in preparation for the building of the railway or for some other major environmental change to what had previously been a pastoral landscape. Because surveyors were seen as agents of external change, they were not always welcome. George Eliot in *Middlemarch*, published in 1872 but set in 1832, describes how local landowners opposed to the railway inflame country people so that they attack the surveyors, break their instruments and drive them and their working team away with pitchforks. It cannot have been uncommon for surveyors to attract unpopularity in this way. In about 1860 James Green, one of the foremost surveyors and valuers of his day, was given the doubtful distinction of being burned in effigy in Hastings whilst negotiating the sale of West Hill to the Corporation. See *Estates Gazette* Centenary Supplement, 3.5 (1958), p. 79.

prosperity encouraged activity at all levels. Many of the leading surveyors were also auctioneers and the two professions became intermingled. Charles Farebrother and his company were leading exponents of this dual activity.

The great Victorian boom which brought rising prosperity in the mid-century (certainly from 1850 onwards through the third quarter) was accompanied by a great upsurge in commercial activity, especially in property. Leading auctioneers at that time, including Farebrother, Clark and Lye, had annual turnover of about £1 million.[1] There was, however, an accompanying development which was generating immense amounts of work for surveyors, valuers and others in related activities. This was the coming of the railway.

2.2. The Development of the Railways

From the 1830s to the end of the 19th century, the railways were constructed throughout Britain. Competition between a multiplicity of private railway companies ensured a rapid rate of expansion. The majority of the railways were laid down between 1840 and 1860, although construction continued for another fifty years. By 1914 the British railway network had a length of 20,000 miles. The building of the railway was an urgent and sometimes ruthless enterprise and the acquisition of land for this purpose was a major area of contention. The surveyors and valuers were at the centre of this storm.[2]

A new professionalism had entered into the business of land acquisition for industrial development. The contrast with the period when canals were built (ca.1760–1840) was marked. Whereas most of the negotiation for purchasing

---

[1]   F. M. L. Thompson, 'The origins of ... the RICS', loc. cit., p. 17.

[2]   See F. M. L. Thompson, *Chartered Surveyors, the Growth of a Profession* (London, 1968) and J. Simmons, *The Victorian Railway* (New York, 1991).

land in the cause of canal building was conducted by laymen, the corresponding negotiations for railways were carried out by qualified professional men: surveyors, valuers, expert witnesses, arbitrators, etc. Surveyors such as Charles Farebrother and his successors in the business, particularly Frederick Clark and John Whittaker Ellis, became part of the limited group of experts in whose hands the railway companies placed their business.

The power of compulsory purchase of land for railway construction had been strengthened by the Land Clauses Act of 1844. Nevertheless, in order to acquire land and build and operate a railway, each company had to obtain its own individual Act of Parliament. In addition to the basic question of permission to proceed, each railway company had to strive for acceptable costs of compensation for affected landowners and it was in this area that surveyors were continually involved, as expert witnesses in the committee rooms of the Houses of Parliament. These witnesses frequently met in the nearby Westminster Palace Hotel, and it was therefore convenient and appropriate that this hotel should be the venue at which twenty surveyors, including Frederick Clark, should meet to establish the Institution of Chartered Surveyors in 1868.

Although the conflict between railway construction and land ownership was general throughout Britain, the problem in relation to London was particularly acute. All of the railway companies wanted their terminal stations to be in the centre of the city so that innumerable historic buildings and areas of recreation and amenity became vulnerable. In order to protect London, a parliamentary decision was made in 1846 to prohibit railways totally within a large area extending from Park Lane to Bishopsgate and from Euston to the Borough. Only underground railways were to be permitted within this central area.[1]

---

[1]   J. Simmons, op. cit., pp. 164-7.

Ludgate Hill, early twentieth century.

The 1846 ruling survived only until 1858 when a new line was agreed to cross the river at Pimlico: it is now the line into Victoria Station. In 1859 a much more intrusive scheme was put forward in which the London, Chatham and Dover Railway Company proposed to cross the river at Blackfriars and then drive northwards through the city, crossing Ludgate Hill by bridge. After this line was opened in 1866 there was great public reaction against it. One contemporary comment was "That viaduct has utterly spoiled one of the finest street views in the metropolis, and is one of the most unsightly objects ever constructed, in any such situation, anywhere in the world". After further intrusion, when the lines to Charing Cross and to Cannon Street also opened in 1866, public reaction built up again. Although destructive proposals continued to be made, there were no further overground lines built into the centre of London. Even so, by 1900, 5.4% of central London was owned by railway companies.[1]

It is important to appreciate, however, that the barrier to railways operating in the heart of the city was not only aesthetic and environmental but was also economic in terms of the rising cost of the land required. Those who owned land which might be attractive for railway expansion were usually well aware of its potential value.

In December 1881 Whittaker Ellis was engaged in correspondence with the Society of Apothecaries regarding the possibility of letting the southern wing of their hall with frontage on Water Lane and Playhouse Yard, between Ludgate Hill and Queen Victoria Street. Ellis advised that there was unlikely to be much public development in that area in the short term. Moreover, he commented that the London, Dover and Chatham Railway Company had been compelled to abandon plans to expand Ludgate Hill Station because of the cost, and had instead developed at Blackfriars near the river.

Ellis's advice to the Society of Apothecaries is a small but cogent example of the way in which increasing urbanisation and its economic consequences would be dominant influences on the property business in Victorian London.

---

[1] J. R. Kellett, *The Impact of Railways on Victorian Cities* (London, 1969), p. 135.

CHAPTER 3
MID-VICTORIAN DEVELOPMENT

3.1. Sir John Musgrove

When Farebrother, Clark and Co. amalgamated with Gadsden Ellis in 1875, a connection was established with a company which was originally known as Musgrove and Gadsden. It is notable that John Musgrove, a previous senior partner of that company, shared with Charles Farebrother and with John Whittaker Ellis, his former partner in Musgrove Gadsden, the distinction of becoming Lord Mayor of London.

John Musgrove was born at Hackney on 21 January 1793. He was apprenticed for seven years from 1807 to his father, a builder, and was made free of the City of London by servitude in the Clothworkers' Company. Musgrove began his business life as an auctioneer and house agent working from 5 Austin Friars between Old Broad Street and Moorgate Street. Eventually through his participation in Musgrove Gadsden he was able to retire with an "ample fortune in the full vigour of life" in 1858.[1]

Musgrove was not only successful in his chosen profession, he also rose rapidly through the various stages of public life. From 1835 to 1842 he was a Common Councilman for Broad Street ward and an Alderman of that ward from 1842 to 1872. (When he retired in 1872 he was succeeded as Alderman for Broad Street ward by Whittaker Ellis.) In 1844 Musgrove was Master of the Clothworkers'

---

[1] *The Illustrated London News*, 9 November 1850.

Sir John Musgrove, from *The Illustrated London News*
for November 9, 1850

Company and was Master again in 1862/3. In 1843/4 he was
elected as a Sheriff for London and Middlesex. He received
the honour of a knighthood on the occasion of Queen
Victoria opening the Royal Exchange on 28 October 1844.

In 1850/1 John Musgrove was Lord Mayor of London.
Illustrated London News welcomed the appointment and
commended his London origins, his industry as an
auctioneer, his integrity and conduct during ten years of

presiding over public boards.[1] The year 1851 was a particularly prestigious but also a demanding year in which to be Lord Mayor because it was the year of the Great Exhibition.

Held in Hyde Park, in the newly-constructed Crystal Palace, the Great Exhibition was the culminating achievement of Prince Albert and was the result of his wide interests in science and in manufacturing. It was, in effect, a shop window for manufactured goods from all over the world, at a time when British industry was still internationally dominant. The Crystal Palace occupied 26 acres and had a construction of glass supported by steel which was built over and around the trees of Hyde Park. The effect of this structure and exhibition on visitors must have been overwhelming. Excursion trains came from all over the country and, in all, 6 million visitors were recorded at a time when the population of England and Wales was only 18 million. Most of the exhibits were British and they were displayed in a mile of galleries. Not only was the Exhibition a great personal success for Prince Albert, it was also highly profitable and generated £250,000, which was contributed towards the cost of the new museums being built at South Kensington.[2]

At Sir John Musgrove's installation as Lord Mayor the Recorder of London stated that:

> It was an auspicious circumstance, that a gentleman so admirably qualified to maintain the office was appointed to preside over the city in the year 1851. It was fortunate for the public, as well as for the men in high and responsible stations in the country, that upon an occasion which was to bring together such vast assemblages from

[1] Ibid.

[2] R. Porter, *London – a Social History* (Harmondsworth, 1996), pp. 290–1 and T. Richards, *The Commodity Culture of Victorian England. Advertising and Spectacle 1851–1914* (London, 1991), pp. 17–72.

other countries, as well as from all parts of England, Ireland and Scotland, the chair of the City of London would be filled by one who understood so well the duties of the station, and was in every respect so well qualified to promote the noble scheme of Prince Albert by the exertions of his talents and capabilities.[1]

On 9th July 1851, a ball was held at Guildhall in the City to celebrate the Great Exhibition with Queen Victoria and Prince Albert as guests of honour. Shortly after this event, on August 2nd 1851, Sir John Musgrove was created a baronet.

Sir John Musgrove died at his home, Rusthall House, Speldhurst, Kent on 5 October 1881.[2]

3.2. Frederick James Clark
Frederick James Clark was originally articled to Henry Cafe, auctioneer of 48 Great Marlborough Street, off Regent Street. After completing his apprenticeship he built up a considerable reputation as a valuer, referee and expert witness, especially in cases regarding compensation for the construction of railways. In 1844 Clark entered into partnership with Charles Farebrother in the business of Farebrother, Clark and Lye operating from 5 Lancaster Place, Strand. He remained a senior partner in the business until his death in 1875.[3]

During the 1850s and 1860s the business of Farebrother, Clark and Lye was one of three companies which dominated the London auction market. An advertisement from the first issue of *Estates Gazette* published 1 May 1858 (reproduced below, on page 36) is typical of this period.

---

[1]   See *The Illustrated London News*, 9 November 1850.
[2]   *The Times*, 7 October 1881. Corporation of London Records Office at Guildhall (Biographical Notes File).
[3]   F. M. L. Thompson, *Chartered Surveyors, the Growth of a Profession* (London, 1968), pp. 130, 145, 359.

Clark was also notably active in the establishment of an organisational structure for the relatively new profession of surveying. He was one of the twenty surveyors who met at the Westminster Palace Hotel on 23 March 1868 under the Chairmanship of John Clutton and founded the Institution of Surveyors. On the 9 November 1868 the Institution held their first annual meeting in the new premises at 12 George Street which remains their address today. The professional standing and public service of the Institution were recognised by the granting of the prefix 'Royal' in 1946.[1]

Although auctioneers had to wait until 1886 to see the establishment of their own institution, many of them, including F. J. Clark, were also surveyors and had been members of the Institution of Surveyors. Clark was particularly prominent in all of these organisations: in 1858/9 he supported the formation of an auctioneers benevolent fund.

In his later years, from 1871 onwards, Clark was engaged in an interesting case concerning the Chelsea Physic Garden, sometimes also called the Botanic Garden. The garden had been given to the Society of Apothecaries by Sir Hans Sloane and it was intended to contain as far as possible "all the herbs of *Materia Medica* which can grow in the open air, for the instruction of medical students".[2]

Clark was engaged on behalf of the Society of Apothecaries who were claiming compensation from the Metropolitan Board of Works for damage to the garden caused by the flow of the river. The garden was open to the riverbank because the Victoria Embankment, completed in 1854, extended only from Millbank to Chelsea Hospital, slightly short of the garden. Between 1871 and 1874 the

---

[1] F. M. L. Thompson, 'The Origins and History of the Royal Institution of Chartered Surveyors', *Estates Gazette*, 8 June 1968.

[2] E. T. Cook, *Highways and Byways in London* (London, 1911), pp. 234–5.

embankment was extended westward from Chelsea Hospital to Battersea Bridge, but doubts about the safety of the garden remained. The Metropolitan Board of Works considered seeking parliamentary powers to purchase that part of the garden which was adjacent to the Chelsea Embankment.

Eventually the dispute was settled when the Board agreed to build a retaining wall for the garden at a cost of £2,730. Surviving correspondence and accounts for this case show that Clark spent considerable time and effort upon his role as expert witness. Even so, the fee received in 1878, three years after his death, was a modest £10. The Society of Apothecaries declined to accept Clark's original claim for £28 7s. on the grounds that he had not materially influenced the decision to build the wall which resolved the problem.

3.3. Fee Farm Rentals

As Charles Farebrother's business grew, it diversified well beyond the promotion of auction sales. One specific area in which Farebrother obtained considerable business was that of Fee Farm Rentals. These rents were small annual sums payable by the owners of the rentals or occupiers of particular properties and lands scattered throughout England and parts of Wales. The rents had originally been payable to the Crown but they were sold into private ownership by King Charles II in the 17th century. They generally fell due on Lady Day and at Michaelmas. The rents were collected by Farebrother and paid to the owners, for which service Farebrother received a commission.

The calculations of liability to rental were made by Farebrother acting as agents and were quite complex, involving rental, land tax and acquittance. Although the individual sums were small, the total value could be considerable when, as usually happened, rents were consolidated into grouped holdings. For example, in February 1926 Farebrother sold a collection of 73 fee farm rents extending across Buckinghamshire, Leicestershire, Warwickshire, Worcestershire and the City of London. Although some individual rentals were as low as 6*d*. per annum, the total annual value was £120 16*s*. 10*d*.

The liability to pay fee farm rental has produced much legal argument over the past three hundred years. Surviving records in the Farebrother Archive at Guildhall Library show details of disputes in Hereford in 1727–34. During the 20th century there have been frequent debates on the conditions attached to specific fee farm rentals and particular problems have sometimes arisen when new owners have become liable to these rentals when they were not previously aware of the requirement. Neither were they aware in many cases of even the existence of the fee farm rental system.

In these cases, Farebrother had a standard letter which was sent out, certainly from the post-World War II period onwards. The letter contained the explanation:

> These rents were originally Crown rents and were sold in collection to various purchasers by King Charles II in 1672 and conveyed with all the rights and powers of the Crown as to collection and recovery. This rent has been collected since that time by our clients and their predecessors in title.[1]

Today the fee farm rental business is much diminished, but has not entirely disappeared.

3.4 *London – Urbanisation, Expansion and Property Values*

During the 19th century, Charles Farebrother's London changed in all kinds of ways. In the first place, London was expanding as the country became increasingly urban. In 1801 33.8% of the population of England and Wales lived in urban surroundings.[2] By 1851 the figure had risen to 54.0%

---

[1]   I am indebted to Mr George Davies for sight of this letter.

[2]   R. J. Morris and R. Rodger, *The Victorian City. A Reader in*

and by 1911 78.9% of the population were living in towns and cities. Meanwhile, the population of London as a whole had increased steadily. Between 1801 and 1891 the population of London rose from 958,863 to 3,816,483, an average increase of 19% every ten years. Moreover, the overall proportion of the population living in London increased from 9.7% in 1801 to 14.5% at the end of the century.[1]

At the same period, the centre of London including the square mile defined as the City, was undergoing major demographic change. What had formerly been residential areas were cleared for the construction of commercial property – railways, docks, warehouses, factories and offices. Between 1801 and 1901 the population of the City of London actually fell quite substantially from 128,833 in 1801 to only 26,897 in 1901. Although the residential population of the City fell sharply, the increase in available work meant that the daytime population of the City continued to increase. Daytime census figures show an increase from 170,133 in 1866 to 301,384 in 1891. The net result of these changes was to increase overcrowding in the City and to generate large increases in land values. For example, between 1861 and 1881, whilst the population of the City was falling from 113,387 to 51,439, the rateable value of the City area was increasing sharply from £1,332,092 in 1861 to £3,479,428 in 1881 and rising further to £4,858,312 by 1901.[2]

In 1898 it was reported that the value of a range of City streets was as follows (presented in walking sequence):[3]

British Urban History 1820-1914 (London, 1993), p. 3.

[1] K. Young and P. L. Garside, *Metropolitan London, Politics and Urban Change 1837-1981* (New York, 1982), p. 15.

[2] G. S. Jones, *Outcast London. A Study in the Relationship between Classes in Victorian Society* (Harmondsworth, 1984), p. 161.

[3] G. L. Gomme, *London in the Reign of Victoria 1837-1897* (London, 1898).

Street	Number of houses	Value per annum (£)
Lombard Street	41	116,946
Cheapside	130	93,373
St Paul's Churchyard	61	47,981
Ludgate Hill	72	48,047
Fleet Street	143	60,883
Strand	406	169,224
Pall Mall	132	99,750
Piccadilly	241	165,924
Bond Street	234	124,751
Oxford Street	600	201,276
Regent Street	321	154,865

These figures show that by 1898 many individual streets in London had a greater value than entire towns elsewhere in England, e.g. Canterbury £111,000; Northampton £205,000; Yarmouth £177,000; Gloucester £157,000; Winchester £92,000; Rochester £104,000; Margate £128,000; Ramsgate £134,000; and Bedford £124,000. Clearly the commercial activities of surveyors, valuers, land agents and auctioneers were of high and rising importance in the City.

The urbanisation which had been the principal demographic trend of Victorian Britain continued into the Edwardian era and the cities spread outwards. The word "suburbia" was coined in the 1890s to describe the semi-rural developments growing up around London. At the end of the nineteenth century the area within six miles of the centre of London had lost population to the so-called "outer ring" which comprised most of Middlesex and parts of Essex, Surrey, Kent and Hertfordshire. Between 1881 and 1911 the population of the outer ring grew from 936,000 to 2,730,000. The railway network expanded to support suburbanisation around major cities, increasing from 13,562 miles in 1870 to 20,038 miles UK total in 1914.[1]

---

[1]   J. Stevenson, *British Society 1914–45* (Harmondsworth, 1984).

Engraved portrait of John Whittaker Ellis, as Lord Mayor of
London, 1881–2, with facsimile signature.

CHAPTER 4
SIR JOHN WHITTAKER ELLIS

John Whittaker Ellis was born on 25 January 1829 at Petersham, Surrey, the fifth son and one of thirteen children of Joseph Ellis, proprietor of the Star and Garter Hotel, Richmond. Before moving to Petersham, the family had lived at Marylebone where Joseph Ellis kept a well-known coffee house, the Yorkshire Stingo, which was later frequented by Charles Dickens. Joseph Ellis had previously worked at the London Coffee House on Ludgate Hill and had visited Richmond, possibly in connection with his original trade as a hairdresser and wig maker.[1]

In Richmond, Joseph Ellis expanded his business interests. He enlarged the Star and Garter Hotel and terraced the garden. He bought his competitor, the Castle Hotel, and added a banqueting suite and ballroom. At that time it was fashionable to drive out of town to Richmond for dinner so that business was good. In about 1822 Joseph Ellis founded Ellis & Sons, wine merchants, in Hill Street. In 1840 he planted a vine there which can still be seen, well kept and flourishing, opposite the Old Town Hall. By the

---

[1] These details and many others in this chapter are drawn from the excellent summary of information about Ellis which is available from Richmond Local Studies Collection. There is also a summary available from the Corporation of London Records Office at Guildhall (Biographical Notes File). The Yorkshire Stingo, which closed in 1848, was noted for the concerts held every evening; omnibuses ran from the Bank at a fare of one shilling. See E. B. Chancellor, *The London of Charles Dickens* (London, 1924), pp. 68 and 74.

middle of the 19th century the hotels and the wine business had been sold out of the family. The Castle Hotel and Assembly Rooms were, however, re-purchased by John Whittaker Ellis in 1888.

Whittaker Ellis was educated locally in Richmond at the Reverend William Allen's School. In 1844, at the age of fifteen, he was apprenticed to Henry Francis Gadsden, a senior partner in Musgrove and Gadsden, auctioneers and estate agents of Old Broad Street in the City. Whittaker Ellis duly served his apprenticeship, and on 5 April 1854 he became free of the Merchant Taylors' Company and was admitted as a liveryman on 27 April. In 1854 he became a partner in Musgrove and Gadsden. At the early age of twenty-five he was successful and well established. In 1858 he married Mary Ann, youngest daughter of John Staples of Belmont, near Salisbury.

Whilst working at Musgrove, Gadsden, which from 1858 became Gadsden, Ellis of 18 Old Broad Street, Ellis built up a considerable reputation as an expert witness in compensation cases, e.g. the site required for the Royal Courts of Justice, the closing of Sun Street by the Great Eastern Railway. In 1875 he acquired the business of the late Frederick John Clark at 5/6 Lancaster Place, Strand and the business continued as Farebrother, Ellis, Clark & Company. The new merged company, with Ellis as senior partner, maintained the tradition of great expertise in compensation. Ellis himself was a leading exponent of the views of claimants and was very successful in obtaining high levels of compensation.[1]

When the Metropolitan bridges were freed from tolls, Ellis approached the question both logically and systematically by carrying out calculations of expected

---

[1]   Most of the information regarding compensation practice is from the reminiscences of Sir Whittaker Ellis published in *Estates Gazette*, 5 and 12 October 1912.

income based on a forward projection of population and traffic. By this method he obtained very high levels of compensation for the toll owners of the Albert and Battersea bridges, much more than was given for Vauxhall and Waterloo bridges which had been decided by arbitration.

In a case in which Ellis acted for wharf owners affected by the widening of Battersea Bridge, he claimed £30,000 but had to settle for half of that amount when the valuer of the Metropolitan Board of Works wrote as follows:

Dear Ellis,
    In matters of commerce, the fault of the Dutch, is giving too little and asking too much. (Canning)
    I offer you £15,000 without prejudice.

The construction of the Manchester Ship Canal gave Ellis an outstanding opportunity when he acted on behalf of the principal landowner affected, both in parliamentary committee and at arbitration. The compensation awarded was £37,620.

The building of reservoirs to hold water for the rapidly growing towns and cities of Victorian England gave Ellis much profitable occupation. In the case of Eccup Reservoir, Ellis appeared as expert witness for Leeds Corporation and Lord Harewood's claim for £80,000 was reduced to an award of £25,000. On the opposite side of the compensation debate, Ellis appeared on behalf of Lord Lanesborough to determine the price of land required to construct Swithland Reservoir near Leicester: an award of £27,700 was achieved.

At this time Ellis was involved in a wide diversity of proceedings. For example, he acted for the freeholders of Smithfield Market regarding their hours of working and rights to impose tolls. He was expert in the rating of public buildings, and in 1895 was a central figure in the action whereby the Imperial Institute in South Kensington were given a 24% reduction in rateable value from £15,473 to

£11,771. Ellis also gave his expert opinion on the rating of all types of building including convents, licensed houses, lunatic asylums and prisons.

An experience of Ellis whilst surveying trade premises in London throws an interesting light on the Victorian art market. He was being asked to support a substantial claim for loss of earnings by a somewhat pretentious dealer in paintings whose premises were subject to compulsory purchase. When Ellis asked to see the stock, he was enjoined to secrecy and shown a heap of spurious 'old masters' undergoing various stages of artificial ageing by smoking and curing. These were destined for gradual introduction into the reputable art market and would, Ellis was assured, fetch high prices without any difficulty.

The above cases, although important individually, are relative side-issues to the main business in which Ellis achieved overwhelming reputation and success – the affairs of railways and particularly railway compensation. At various times he carried out actions against every important railway company in and out of London and was frequently concerned in giving evidence as an expert witness in related parliamentary proceedings.

In one of his most notable cases Ellis represented the Duke of Portman, whose estates were affected by the Great Central Railway (previously known as the Manchester, Sheffield and Lincolnshire Railway) passing through North London to the new Marylebone terminal, opened in 1899. The terminal was built on the site of Blandford and Harewood Squares. With the associated goods and coal depots, the project necessitated the purchase of 51 acres of land south of St John's Wood Road.[1] The claim in this case exceeded £2.5 million.

---

[1] A. A. Jackson, *London's Termini* (Newton Abbot, 1985), p. 333.

Ellis acted for the Duke of Norfolk against Midland Railway in respect of estates at Sheffield and was also involved in claiming against North British Railways for damaging the amenities of Princes' Gardens in Edinburgh.

By 1881 Ellis's prowess as an expert witness and, indeed, negotiator in the business of railway compensation had achieved a level at which he was regularly retained as principal witness by both public bodies and railway companies. This increased status may well have been encouraged by Ellis's talent for restrained self-promotion as displayed to perfection in the following letter sent to Robert Ritchie.

My dear Ritchie,

I hope you will not forget that by my being engaged for the Railway Company in the cases heard during the beginning of last month, it has got abroad that I am entirely retained by the Railway Company and consequently I am cut out from the extraneous business which would undoubtedly have fallen to me. I find also upon your reference to the list of cases mentioned by you when you first spoke to me on the subject, that Teape's and others were mentioned as those in which the Company would retain me. It also seems that they were settled after all in court. I can quite understand that assuming the Trial had gone on and I had not given evidence, there might have been a question as to what my fee should be, but that could always be arranged.

I think however you might put me permanently on your staff and then you could employ me when opportunity offered without going into the Box and I shall have no objection to some arrangement as to that.

It is quite probable that I might be of considerable service to you in settling cases as I think I am not wrong if I say that I have considerable influence with many of the surveyors whom you must meet.

I am sure you quite understand the object of my letter is that I should like to aid you in any way I can, and also that I do not like to be out of these matters more than I can help.

> Yours very truly,
> J. Whittaker Ellis.[1]

Ellis was principal witness for numerous cases concerning the City, Metropolitan and District Railways. He became surveyor for the London and South Western Railway and also for the London, Brighton and South Coast Railway for whom he arranged the purchase of property in connection with the enlargement of Victoria Station. In this latter case, Ellis's evidence convinced the jury to reduce the London Authority claim for £30,000 to an award of only £7,500.

Ellis was retained as an expert witness both by the Office of Works and by the War Office. He became an official valuer to the Board of Trade. He dealt directly with Parliament in the original negotiations for construction of the Bakerloo underground. Ellis was entrusted with the settlement of claims arising from the Bakerloo work and also from work on the Waterloo and City tube lines.

In later years Ellis attributed much of his success in obtaining high levels of railway compensation to the fact that Crown Authorities were always over-represented by eminent legal experts who lacked the technical expertise required in cross-examination to damage the evidence of a skilled valuer acting as expert witness. Opposing counsels, on the other hand, suggested that Ellis frequently took refuge in a flood of eloquence which was irritating and thought to be intended to confuse and divert. The appeal was heard "Pray, Sir Whittaker, spare us a speech and answer the question".

In addition to his remarkable professional achievements, Whittaker Ellis was very prominent in public life. He was Master of the Merchant Taylors' Company in 1884/5. In

---

[1] Guildhall Library MS 22,365.

1864 he became a Common Councillor of the City of London and in 1872 he was unanimously elected to succeed Sir John Musgrove (his former professional colleague) as Alderman for the Broad Street ward, an office which he held until 1909 when he had reached the age of 80. In 1874/5 he was elected as a Sheriff of London and Middlesex and in 1881/2 was Lord Mayor of London.

Ellis later said that his proudest moment as Lord Mayor was when Epping Forest was presented to the nation in May 1882. On horseback, he escorted the Queen's carriage through the forest and she remarkably conceded to him the right to declare the forest open with the pronouncement: "It is my wish that the Lord Mayor should open the Forest to my people for all time." A fortnight after this event the Queen conferred upon Whittaker Ellis the honour of a baronetcy. Contemporary newspaper reports stressed that during the first six months of his Lord Mayoralty, Ellis had engaged in an exceptionally large number of public and philanthropic projects and that the honour was richly deserved.[1]

Ellis established a close relationship with the Royal Family and with senior political and professional figures of the time. At his riverside home, Buccleuch House, Richmond, he and Lady Ellis entertained lavishly. Guests included the Prince of Wales (later King Edward VII), the Duke of Cambridge, the Duke and Duchess of Teck, the Duke of Albany, the Queen of Sweden, W. E. Gladstone, Joseph Chamberlain, Lord Salisbury and A. J. Balfour.[2]

Buccleuch House had originally been owned by the Duke of Buccleuch who died in 1886. After the Duke died, his son put the estate up for sale. There was dismay in Richmond because of clear indications that speculators would buy the estate and build villas; "What is vulgarly

---

[1] *Richmond and Twickenham Times*, 27 May 1882.
[2] *Richmond Biographies*, held at Richmond Local Studies Collection.

Hand-coloured illuminated address commemorating the presentation of Epping Forest to the nation during the mayoralty of Sir John Whittaker Ellis in May 1882.

termed development" as one objector wrote to *The Times*.[1] The much-admired view of Richmond was under threat: who could "save Richmond Hill from its threatened vandalistic builders?"[2] The *Daily News* asked the question

---

[1]   *The Times*, 8 July 1901.

"What man owns the glory that Turner has painted?"[2]

When the local vestry found the asking price of the estate prohibitive, Ellis came forward as "Richmond's defender". He bought the estate, retaining the house, the library at the foot of the famous terrace gardens, and some land along the riverside. He then offered the vestry very favourable terms to buy the remainder of the estate. Thus the terrace gardens were saved and were opened to the public in 1887.[3] The local press commended Ellis for "his valiant attempt to keep this delightful piece of Surrey inviolate ... he will deserve the thanks of all nature-loving people ... (he) may be regarded as Richmond's Godfather."[4]

Buccleuch House had been built in the early Georgian period. When Ellis lived there the house stood on a seven acre site and was justifiably described as "one of the most delightful residences on the banks of the River Thames".[5] The walls had been built to an unusually substantial thickness in order to maintain an even temperature throughout the year. The spaces between the floor joists were filled with sea shells to give sound-proofing. Ellis had pleasant gardens laid out on the opposite bank of the river; his guests were rowed across. Buccleuch House was eventually bought by Richmond Borough in 1937 and demolished. The site is now part of the public gardens below the Old Town Hall.

From the 1880s onwards, Ellis increased his involvement in the political and social affairs of Richmond both nationally and locally. In 1884 he became the Conservative MP for mid-Surrey and won the seat again in

[1]   From Richmond Local Studies Collection.

[2]   *Daily News*, 13 July 1901.

[3]   J. Cloake, *Richmond Past*, p. 123 includes a photograph of the rain-soaked opening ceremony of the Terrace Gardens.

[4]   From Richmond Local Studies Collection.

[5]   Farebrother, Ellis, Egerton, Breach & Co., sale particulars, 23 October 1902.

"*BUCCLEUCH HOUSE*,"
RICHMOND,

With its Grounds sloping to the Banks of the River, on both sides of the Thames, commanding within its purview Petersham Meadows and Woods, Richmond Park, and the beautiful Gardens and Terrace on Richmond Hill. One of the most delightful Residences on the banks of the River Thames.

Particulars and Conditions of Sale

OF A VERY VALUABLE AND

BEAUTIFUL RESIDENCE,

KNOWN AS

"Buccleuch House,"

erected in the best period of the Georgian Age of Architecture, in a most substantial manner ; it is approached by a handsome Stone Porch, and contains Outer and Inner Halls.

SUITES OF CHARMING RECEPTION ROOMS,

All facing the Lawns with River Views, Fourteen Bed Rooms, Two Bath Rooms, Dressing Rooms, &c., having ample ACCOMMODATION FOR A FAMILY OF POSITION.

The PLEASURE GROUNDS & GARDENS,

SITUATED ON BOTH SIDES OF THE THAMES,

AND

FORMING ONE OF THE CHIEF FEATURES OF THE RIVER SCENERY,

have been laid out with great taste at a very large outlay, having EXTENSIVE LAWNS, adorned with grand timber Trees, also TWO HANDSOME CONSERVATORIES, GARDENER'S RESIDENCE, all requisite GLASS-HOUSES, ORCHARD, FRUIT AND FLOWER GARDENS.

EXCELLENT STABLING.

Dwelling Houses, Laundry Premises, &c. The Whole occupying an Area of about

SEVEN ACRES.

The Property has been maintained for many years past in complete order and condition, and possesses amenities which it is impossible to surpass within the same distance of London.

POSSESSION WILL BE GIVEN UPON THE COMPLETION OF THE PURCHASE.

TO BE SOLD BY AUCTION,

BY MESSRS.

FAREBROTHER, ELLIS, EGERTON, BREACH
AND CO.

At the Mart, Tokenhouse Yard, near the Bank of England, E.C.

On THURSDAY, the 23rd day of OCTOBER, 1902,

AT TWO O'CLOCK PRECISELY (unless in the meantime an acceptable offer is made).

Particulars with Conditions of Sale may be obtained of Messrs. HOLLAMS, SON, COWARD & HAWKSLEY, Solicitors, Mincing Lane, E.C. ; at the Auction Mart, E.C. ; and of MESSRS. FAREBROTHER, ELLIS & CO., 29, Fleet Street, Temple Bar, E.C.

Title-page from 1902 sales catalogue for Buccleuch House

62

1888 when it was re-organised as the Kingston Division of Surrey. Ellis remained a member of Parliament for eight years, retiring in 1892 despite being petitioned to stay on by more than 5,000 constituents. Politically he was 'staunchly Conservative' with a specific interest in the so-called "Irish Question" in which he was a powerful opponent of Home Rule. During his year as Lord Mayor he was urged by the citizens of London to organise some concerted opposition to Charles Stuart Parnell who was considered to be waging war against landlords in Ireland. With the consent of Gladstone, who was Prime Minister at the time and would later regret his support, Ellis formed a society called the Irish Defence Association which was pledged to protect the rights of those who owned property in Ireland. He was so active in this cause across the whole of the United Kingdom that the Home Secretary, Sir William Harcourt, complained: "Why, the Lord Mayor is governing Ireland."[1]

Ellis was a patriotic imperialist who summarised his own views as follows:

> All classes of society are influenced materially by the overwhelming power of those who direct the public affairs of the Empire. When the aims of statesmen at the helm are great and far-seeing, they should be guided by Disraeli's observation: they should possess courage to make the Empire still greater. If they abandon this for lesser considerations, it will have a powerful influence on all classes, and cannot fail to influence our municipal and every other phase of life.[2]

When Ellis retired from public life in 1902 he commented on the conflicting pressures of his working life and showed that he was still the active head of Farebrother,

[1] *The Veteran City Alderman Talks of His 50 Years of Public Life, Memories of Politics*. Richmond Local Studies Collection.

[2] For details of opposition to Ellis, see G. F. Bartle, 'Late Victorian Politics in Richmond', *Richmond History*, vol. 13 (1992), and vol. 14 (1993).

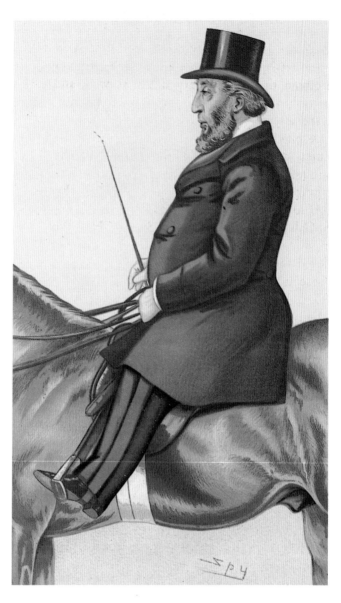

Sir John Whittaker Ellis as lord mayor of London,
1881–2; Spy cartoon from *Vanity Fair*

Ellis. At the age of 73 he wrote "I decided to retire from the political arena. I found that I could not conduct my business and attend to parliamentary duties as well, and as I was reasonably sure of success in the former, and not so sure of it in the latter, I relinquished my work at the House."[1]

Despite this comment, Ellis did in fact retire from the business of Farebrother, Ellis in 1902. The business continued under the direction of the partners whom Ellis had introduced in 1897: these were Mr H. D. Egerton, Mr B. l'Anson Breach, Mr Ralph Staples Ellis (his nephew), Mr V. S. Galsworthy and Mr Alfred Skingle. His office had also been a respected training ground for many who later achieved their own distinction elsewhere. These included Mr Joseph Stower, Mr W. Hurst Flint of Humbert, Flint, Mr G. E. Knight of Dowsett, Knight and Taylor, and Mr P. A. Mence of Wigram, Mence.

When Richmond was granted borough status in 1890 Ellis was obviously a strong candidate for the position of Mayor and was supported by the local newspaper, *Richmond and Twickenham Times*. At first Ellis declined nomination pleading the surely credible excuse of pressure of work since at that time he was both a member of Parliament and described as sole partner of Farebrother, Ellis. Nevertheless he changed his mind and was elected Mayor but not without opposition. Local Liberals claimed that his attendance at Westminster had been unsatisfactory, that he had shown little interest in local affairs and that nothing would change. He was accused of having been "practically useless in parliament" and it was claimed that "his bitter attacks on the working classes had produced a feeling of the greatest antagonism to him in the breasts of the workmen of this district". There were fears expressed that "he will fling money left and right whenever it will

---

[1] *The Veteran City Alderman Talks of His 50 Years of Public Life, Memories of Politics.* Richmond Local Studies Collection.

answer his purpose".[1]

After Ellis was elected Mayor he presented the Borough with the land on which the new Town Hall was to be built. This was the site of the Castle Hotel and Assembly Rooms which his family had once owned and which he had re-purchased in 1888. The vestry of Richmond had previously tried to buy these premises but the price was prohibitive. Ellis had then intervened to buy the whole of the property on condition that an appropriate municipal building was constructed on the site and that a road was made to the river so that the public could have access to the waterside. The town hall building was opened in 1893 by the Duke of York. The road down to the river was named Whittaker Avenue. Public subscription was raised to pay for a marble bust of Ellis which was unveiled in 1895 by the Duchess of Teck and still stands at the head of the stairs in Richmond Old Town Hall.[2]

After Ellis's year as Mayor had ended in 1891 he took much less direct interest in the local politics of Richmond. In 1894 he offended many local Conservatives by summarily demanding greatly increased rent of £1,200 from their clubs which he had previously financed. He gave them no alternative but to pay or leave the premises. The result was the closure of Unionist clubs in Richmond, Kingston and Mortlake.[3]

In 1901 Lady Ellis died aged 77. Their long marriage lasting nearly 42 years had been childless. The King and Queen sent messages of sympathy; the Prince and Princess of Wales sent flowers to which the Princess added the hand-written message, "A last token of sincere regard from the Prince and Princess of Wales, December 1901." Five

---

[1]   See Note 2, p. 63, above.
[2]   J. Dunbar, *A Prospect of Richmond* (London, 1966). See also *Death of Sir Whittaker Ellis – his public work for Richmond*, held at Richmond Local Studies Collection.
[3]   See Note 2, p. 63, above.

hundred messages of condolence were received at Buccleuch House. Lady Ellis had been held in great esteem, especially in Richmond. The *Herald* commented that

> of her Ladyship's efforts in the sacred cause of charity, it is impossible to speak too highly. She was ever ready with her services and her purse to assist deserving institutions and hardly a month passed but what some gathering for the purpose of charity was held at Buccleuch House, under her auspices.[1]

After the death of Lady Ellis, Sir Whittaker left Richmond and moved to a new residence, Wormleybury at Broxbourne in Hertfordshire.

In 1904 Whittaker Ellis, now aged 74, re-married. His bride was Marion Bailey, daughter of the vicar of Holy Trinity, Cowes, and rural dean of the Isle of Wight. The wedding and honeymoon were spectacular, even by the lavish standards of wealthy Edwardian England. Ellis gave his new bride two diamond stars, a diamond ring, a diamond and sapphire ring, a pearl and diamond pendant and a jewelled necklace. The wedding took place at St Peter's, Eaton Square and was conducted by Canon Clement Smith, Chaplain to the King. The bride and bridegroom then set out on a remarkable honeymoon. They travelled by train to Southampton where they embarked on Sir Whittaker's steam yacht *Latona*. They then proceeded via Holland and the Kiel Canal to St Petersburg, thence by train to Moscow, returning via Stockholm three months later.[2]

Sir Whittaker Ellis was clearly a wealthy man. Company records indicate that in 1898 his annual withdrawal from Farebrother, Ellis was at least £5,000. His private papers suggest that his household expenditure in 1911 exceeded £12,000 a year.

1   *The Herald*, 21 and 28 December 1901.
2   *Richmond and Twickenham Times*, 6 June 1903.

In 1909 he celebrated his eightieth birthday and finally retired from public life. He died in 1912 aged 83. The King and Queen sent messages of sympathy to Lady Ellis. Obituary notices recorded his many civic and public offices.[1] He had received the Order of Mercy from Queen Victoria on the recommendation of the Prince of Wales (later King Edward VII). The King of Holland had given him the Order of the Golden Lion of Nassau when he visited The Hague in 1882. As Sheriff of London and Middlesex in 1874/5 he accompanied the Lord Mayor on the first municipal state visit to Paris. His charitable work was much praised, particularly the raising of £109,000 for the relief of persecuted Jews in Russia. He also raised £17,000 for Irish ladies in distress. For ten years, Ellis was Governor of the Honourable Irish Society, the body of trustees appointed to manage the Corporation of London's estates in Ulster. In his long and distinguished career Ellis achieved high office in many societies, hospitals, banks and assurance companies. He was a director of the Alliance Bank in 1880 and chairman in 1883–86. He was chairman of the Emmanuel Hospital, and was also a JP in both Surrey and in Londonderry.[2]

Sir John Whittaker Ellis was greatly respected both within his own profession and throughout the City. *The Times* stated that the news of his death would cause "sincere regret in the City, for it severs a connexion [sic] with civic affairs of over 40 years".[3]

[1]   The obituary is in *The Times*, 21 September 1912, and the funeral details in *The Times*, 27 September 1912.

[2]   There are summaries of Sir Whittaker Ellis's many offices and honours in the papers referred to in Note 21 and also in *Who Was who 1897–1916*, p. 227. In order to avoid spoiling the moment, I have omitted to mention in the main text that the splendidly-named Golden Lion of Nassau was awarded in the second class.

[3]   *The Times*, 21 September 1912.

CHAPTER 5
THE GALSWORTHY CONNECTION

In 1897 Farebrother, Ellis incorporated the company of Messrs Egerton, Breach and Galsworthy of Searle Street, Lincoln's Inn. The foundation of this latter company may be traced back through various changes of partnership and style to the establishment by Frank Gissing Debenham of Debenham, Tewson and Chinnocks at 80 Cheapside in April 1853. The company became major land agents and surveyors. For example in 1874, operating as Chinnock, Galsworthy & Chinnock from 11 Waterloo Place, Pall Mall, they sold Her Majesty's Theatre and Opera House, the whole of the Opera Arcade and the United Hotel and Clergy Club. This unusually large block of property yielded a leasehold income of £5,406 14s. per annum. The catalogue stated that "the attention of Capitalists and others is particularly invited to this Sale, so vast a Property has rarely been offered to the Public for investment". The theatre and opera house was described as "a noble pile of buildings lately rebuilt from the foundations, by the eminent architect, CHARLES LEE Esq., the original form, so much admired, being to a great extent retained and supplemented by all the advantages modern Art and Ingenuity could devise."

After 1897 the new merged company was originally operated under the combined but unwieldy name of Farebrother, Ellis, Egerton, Breach and Galsworthy but in 1898 they reverted to the much more convenient title of 'Farebrother, Ellis'.

Frederick Thomas Galsworthy was one of the partners in the new company and an uncle of John Galsworthy, the

69

Title-page from the sale catalogue for Her Majesty's Theatre and Opera House by Chinnock, Galsworthy and Chinnock in May , 1874.

70

writer. Frederick was an auctioneer and estate agent who had built up his practice in the precursor company of Chinnock, Galsworthy and Chinnock. He was a substantial property owner and lived in a large house at 8 Queens Gate, Kensington. He became the inspiration for the character of Uncle Swithin "Four-in-Hand" Forsyte in *The Man of Property*.

Although John Galsworthy drew extensively on his own family to derive his fictional characters, he was himself opposed to the respectable Toryism which was the hallmark of the fictional Forsytes. He described himself as a 'liberal humanist' and took great pleasure in the Liberal revival of 1906. He consistently campaigned for reformist causes such as improvements in prison conditions, reform of the divorce laws and abolition of censorship. He denounced the Boer War, advocated reform of the House of Lords, and even refused a knighthood.[1]

John Galsworthy's father was a wealthy London solicitor and company director who suffered from serious misgivings about the large fortune which he had amassed. He was the model for Old Jolyon in the Forsyte saga although in that case the fictional fortune was derived from the tea trade. Old Jolyon is described thus:

> He was too old to be a liberal, had long ceased to believe in the political doctrines of his Club, had even been known to allude to them as 'wretched stuff' and it afforded him pleasure to continue a member in the teeth of principles so opposed to his own. He had always had a contempt for the place, having joined it many years ago when they refused to have him at the 'Hotch Potch' owing to his being 'in trade'. As if he were not as good as any of them! He naturally despised the club that *did* take him. The members were a poor lot, many of them in the City – stockbrokers, auctioneers, what not! ... secretly he

[1] G. Harvey, 'Introduction' to *The Forsyte Saga*, World's Classics (Oxford, 1995), p. x.

thought them a common lot.[1]

These somewhat uncertain attitudes have some similarities with John Galsworthy's own views which he related to his rural ancestry in a letter written in 1907 to his friend the literary editor, Edward Garnett:

> What queer mixtures we all are; and yet it's remarkable how, up to this century, class and locality kept themselves to themselves. Look at my origin for instance; as far as I can make out, my Dad's forbears were absolutely of the small farmer class for hundreds of years, and all from the same little corner of South Devon. And my mother's absolutely of the provincial Squire class ...
>
> The Galsworthys rising into the middle class for two generations with all its tenacity and ability (of a sort) now seem in the third generation all abroad, as if melting away again into a more creative sphere or nothing at all, muddling out as architects, writers, painters, engineers, do nothing at all, a non-practising barrister, a musicianly solicitor, one doctor, and a curious dandified land agent, alone represent the truly middle-class element and very poorly at that.[2]

The 'curious' dandified land agent' was Frederick Galsworthy, who was depicted as the reactionary and socially pretentious Uncle Swithin. Swithin is a man of great wealth. "Since his retirement from house agency, a profession deplorable in his estimation, especially as to its auctioneering department, he had abandoned himself to naturally aristocratic tastes."[3]

Swithin's own taste is qualified by the description "great if somewhat luxurious".[4] It tends towards the ostentatious and reflects his boastful attitude regarding the display of

---

[1]   J. Galsworthy, *The Forsyte Saga* (Oxford, 1995), p. 36.

[2]   E. Garnett (ed.), *Letters from John Galsworthy 1900–1932* (London, 1934), pp. 133–5.

[3]   See J. Galsworthy, *The Forsyte Saga* (Oxford, 1995), p. 46.

[4]   Ibid.

possessions. When the intrinsic value of one of his Italian statuary groups is questioned in *The Man of Property*, he turns sharply on his brother, Old Jolyon, with the rejoinder: "I should like to see anything you've got in your house half as good."[1]

Others can see that Swithin's taste is not only undiscriminating and designed for display, but it is also old-fashioned and passé. "Vieux Jeu" as Soames thought it, "hopelessly of the last generation."[2] Swithin has "a love of Ormolu", that type of gilded bronze which by the time *The Man of Property* was published in 1906, was rejected as quite out-moded, a forgotten fad of high Victorianism. The direct connection between Swithin and Frederick Galsworthy is demonstrated clearly by the sale catalogue of the contents of the latter's house in Queen's Gate after his death in 1917. Ormolu is present in profusion.

LOT

173 A PAIR OF 18IN. SEVRES CHINA VASES, with paintings of pastoral subjects after Watteau, on a turquoise coloured ground, with gem enrichments and chased ormolu mounts, fitted with electric lamps and shades

174 *A 14in. Blue and White Japanese Porcelain Vase*, with ormolu mounts, electric lamp and fittings

175 Another similar vase en suite fitted with duplex lamp and receiver

176 A PAIR OF 10IN. CHASED ORMOLU 2-HANDLED CHINA VASES, exotic birds and flowers on a blue ground, with electric lamp and shades

177 A PAIR OF 18IN. CHASED ORMOLU RUSTIC CANDELABRA, with male and female supports, having four branches, three fitted for electric light

178 *A Pair of 7in. Chased Ormolu Candlesticks*, with vine branches and young Bacchanalian figures, on scroll bases

---

Lots of ormolu in the sales of the contents of 8, Queen's Gate.

---

[1] Ibid., p. 58.
[2] Ibid., p. 58.

Swithin in fact personified the uncertainty of those who had entered the ranks of the upper middle class by wealth, but whose trades and even professions tended to undermine their confidence in occupying a relatively high social position.

> Born too soon, Swithin had missed his vocation. Coming upon London twenty years later, he could not have failed to become a stockbroker, but at the time when he was obliged to select, this great profession had not as yet become the chief glory of the upper-middle class. He had literally been forced into auctioneering.[1]

Many wealthy Victorians attempted to buttress their social stability by providing themselves with more creditable antecedents. They took additional names which often simulated Norman French and acquired through the Heralds' Office coats of arms, crests and family mottoes. John Galsworthy describes Swithin obtaining arms in this way and using them on his coach and note paper: "It strengthened his conviction that he was a gentlemen."[2]

Frederick Galsworthy lived to the age of 90. It is very probable that his attitudes were largely similar to those of the fictional Swithin, although John Galsworthy may have been less than generous in his writing. After all, Frederick had a profound influence on one stage of the life of his nephew.

John Galsworthy was in love with Ada, the wife of his cousin Arthur John, the son of Frederick. The marriage between Arthur and Ada had degenerated and Ada (who is often considered to be the model for Irene in the Forsyte saga) was drawn to John Galsworthy. Although Arthur was agreeable to divorce Ada, who had become unfaithful, it has been claimed that his father Frederick forbade the divorce because of the prevailing attitude in Edwardian society. A

---

[1]   Ibid., p. 122.
[2]   Ibid., p. 163.

divorce would have been disastrous because the associated public scandal would have severely damaged the family's social position. It is further claimed that the reason why Frederick was able to prevent Arthur proceeding to divorce was that Arthur was dependent upon his father for his allowance of £700 per annum.[1] After the death of Frederick in 1917, Arthur divorced Ada who married John.

Title-page to the sales catalogue for 8, Queen's Gate.

---

1   D. Barker, *The Man of Principle. A View of John Galsworthy* (London, 1963). See also A. Fréchet, *John Galsworthy: A Reassessment* (London, 1982).

29 Fleet Street from which the company traded 1882–1987

CHAPTER 6
EXPANSION AND SPECIALISATION, 1900-1939

A random selection of sales carried out by Farebrother, Ellis between 1900 and 1920 not only confirms the increasing value of property in London, but also illustrates the wide variety of business which the practice dealt with in all regions of England. Lots offered at auction included commercial, domestic and industrial properties together with building sites: locations ranged over London, Windsor, Bristol, Manchester, Bolton, Leicester, etc. The unusually wide range of activity reflected the growing diversity of society itself. For example, in 1899 the firm was acting for the Vicar of Belgrave parish (Leicester) in collecting rents for allotments[1] and then in 1902 they were selling the magnificent Buccleuch House, Richmond, for Whittaker Ellis.

At the turn of the century there began what was to be a continuing association with the London theatre. In May 1902 Farebrother, Ellis sold the Ealing Theatre which also included a masonic temple and a ballroom; the main theatre had a seating capacity of 1,354. In April 1907 the practice sold the London Coliseum, described at the time as "the most palatial and up to date house of entertainment in the metropolis" with "the largest proscenium in the Kingdom". The seating capacity was 2,200. The building had been

---

[1] The allotment rents, which were payable six months in advance, were charged at a rate of 4s. 6d. for 300 sq. ft. and pro rata.

NOTICE.

BELGRAVE
GLEBE ALLOTMENT
GARDENS.

NOTICE IS HEREBY GIVEN, that we shall attend in the Superintendent's Hut in the Allotment Gardens, on Saturday, the *30* day of *Sept.* 1899, between the hours of *2* and *3·30* p.m., to receive the two Quarters' Rent due in advance to the *25* day of *December* 1899.

All Tenants who fail to pay their rents on the day hereby appointed are liable without notice, to be deprived of their Gardens, and to legal proceedings for recovery of the amount due.

FAREBROTHER, ELLIS & CO.,
Agents for the Vicar of Belgrave.

29, Fleet Street,
London, E.C.

Allotment-rent collection in Leicester.

designed by Frank Matcham in 1904 and had two remarkable new features – the 15 feet diameter illuminated globe at the top of the building, and the famous revolving stage. This stage was described as "75 feet in diameter, made up of 3 concentric tables each 25 feet across which are fitted to run together or independently by electric power". Much later, in 1931, Farebrother, Ellis sold the Royal Court Theatre in Sloane Square which had a seating capacity of

78

Farebrother Ellis & Co., agents for the London Coliseum.

614. The sale particulars emphasised that the lease of July 1888 from the Cadogan Estate contained a covenant stipulating that "the theatre shall only be used for the representation of such Dramatic or Musical Entertainments as are usually performed in Theatres in London under licence of the Lord Chamberlain". This covenant would become very relevant in 1956 when the Royal Court gave the first showing of John Osborne's *Look Back in Anger* and

The colour painting of the London Coliseum,
used for the cover of the sales catalogue.

Farebrother Ellis & Co., agents for the Royal Court Theatre.

went on to stage other plays by the new writers classified by the press as the 'Angry Young Men' who wrote 'kitchen sink' drama.

In April 1913 Farebrother, Ellis sold the premises which they currently occupy, No.1 Pemberton Row. At the time it was described as suitable for "printer, publisher, lithographer or allied trades".

During the First World War, the new danger of aerial bombardment caused concern among the people of London, and this is reflected in the particulars of a house sold in July 1918. The property, which was in Dorking, is described as "outside the air raid danger zone", and this could well have been a significant selling point. The recent air raid of May 1918 on London had been the heaviest of the war. On one of the four nights of bombardment, 40 German bombers dropped 20 tons of high explosive on British targets, of which 11 tons fell on London. More than 1,000 houses and

81

FLEET STREET

CLOSE TO

West Harding Street and Fetter Lane.

Particulars, Plan and Conditions of Sale

OF THE COMPACT

FREEHOLD BUILDING SITE

OCCUPIED BY No.

1, Pemberton Row, Gough Square,

Extending to and having the advantage of an additional Entrance from

JOHNSON'S COURT AT THE REAR,

Adapted for the Erection of Premises suitable for

PRINTER, PUBLISHER, LITHOGRAPHER or ALLIED TRADES

The Property has a

Frontage of 18 feet by a Depth of 92 feet.

And occupies an Area of

1,700   square   feet.

POSSESSION ON COMPLETION OF THE PURCHASE.

Which will be Sold by Auction by Messrs.

FAREBROTHER, ELLIS & Co.

AT THE MART, TOKENHOUSE YARD, E.C.,

On THURSDAY, APRIL the 3rd, 1913

At TWO o'clock precisely.

Particulars with Plan and Conditions of Sale may be had of Messrs. H. J. & T. CHILD, Solicitors, 2, Paul's Bakehouse Court, Godliman Street, St. Pauls, E.C.; at the Mart; and of Messrs. FAREBROTHER, ELLIS & Co., Auctioneers and Surveyors,

29, Fleet Street, Temple Bar, E.C.

NOTE.—For Order of Sale see "The Times" of the day preceding the Auction.

The 1913 sale of 1, Pemberton Row, the premises which
Farebrother currently occupy.

'Outside the Air Raid Danger Zone' in 1918.

business premises were either destroyed or damaged and British casualties totalled 226 including 49 dead, all Londoners. At the time of the sale it was not yet apparent that Germany had decided to abandon the bombing campaign known as operation "Turk's Cross". There were no further raids.[1]

---

[1] R. H. Fredette, *The First Battle of Britain 1917–1918 and the Birth of the Royal Air Force* (London 1966), pp. 207–215. See also J. H. Morrow Jnr., *German Air Power in World War I* (Lincoln & London, 1982).

83

The 1926 sales of Somerton Court. Landscape-shaped sales
catalogues were fashionable between the two world wars.

After the First World War business began to return to
normality, but not without disruption and difficulties to be
overcome. One such difficulty was the General Strike of
1926: sale particulars for Somerton Court in Somerset due
to be sold on 20 May 1926 carry an additional label which
states that "in consequence of the General Strike, this sale
has been postponed to Wednesday 9th June 1926 at 3
o'clock precisely".

The Great Depression had a severe effect on the
property market and activity was restrained for a time. The
peak of the Depression was in 1931 which was an exceptionally difficult year for Farebrother, Ellis, with profits down
by about 80%. A temporary reduction in staff wages was
necessary.[1] Even so, a job in the City was always prized.

---

[1]   Farebrother, Ellis also reduced the travel requirement for
valuation from 1st to 3rd class rail fare in 1931.

Mr George Davies, formerly Chief Cashier of Fare-brother, joined the company in the early 1930s as an office boy at a wage of £1 per week. After a few weeks of menial work and errands, he was told to accompany the rent collector to Tottenham Court Road and to learn that side of the business. After they had visited several addresses and extracted rent from unwilling and impoverished tenants, he was told by the collector that he had seen enough and was now qualified to do the job himself. He was instructed as follows: "Now lad, you do No. 26 but listen carefully to what I say. Knock on the door and you'll hear a shuffling movement inside. Open the door but only about three inches and hold it. There'll be an almighty thud, then it's safe to open the door and collect the rent."

George followed the recommended procedure, felt and heard the thud on the door, waited a moment, and opened it. Inside was a man of terrifying appearance preparing to throw a second hatchet into the back of the door. As they fled, the rent collector explained to George that the man was a Polish circus knife-thrower who really meant no harm and that the second hatchet would have come close but not actually hit him. The collector also admitted, to no surprise, that rent had not been collected from No. 26 for several years.

During the 1920s and 1930s the practice was principally concerned with three aspects of changing society: (1) the sale of great estates and country houses, sometimes into changed functions; (2) property sales related to new styles of living, and (3) sales connected with the continually developing structure of London.

The prime example of selling a great estate into changed circumstances was the sale of Stowe in 1922. Stowe House was the seat of the Grenvilles, Dukes of Buckingham and Chandos from 1710 to 1921. The family had risen from Buckinghamshire gentry and had acquired Stowe through marriage with the Temples. By the early nineteenth century they owned more than 70,000 acres across England and Ireland, two fine London houses and a collection of four country houses in addition to Stowe. After 1820 the family incurred increasing debts and in 1849 the second Duke was declared bankrupt. By 1845, when the Duke was entertaining Queen Victoria at Stowe on a lavish scale, his debts had exceeded £1 million.[1]

The contents of Stowe were originally sold in 1848 by Christie & Manson of King Street, St James' Square. The total proceeds of £75,562 gave little relief against the debt and the prices obtained were regarded at the time as very disappointing. Many of the items purchased were restored to Stowe.

Eventually the house, by then unoccupied, was put up for sale by auction in July 1921 by Jackson, Stops. The house with the surrounding 1,435 acres, gardens, temples and statuary together with the village of Dadford, was bought by Mr Harry Shaw of Benham Court, Newbury, for £50,000. Mr Shaw's declared intention was to save the house from destruction but his subsequent efforts to find a suitable use for Stowe were unsuccessful. Therefore the house and contents were auctioned again in October 1922 as a joint operation by Jackson, Stops and Farebrother, Ellis. The event was described as "a sale no connoisseur should miss".

The catalogue for this sale was a substantial 120-page, well-illustrated publication: the production cost was 18 shillings per copy and the original price was a generous 5 shillings, later increased to 10 shillings. The catalogue described the house as "One of the Most Palatial Residences in the Kingdom, the Noble and Stately Palace of Stowe". It

---

[1]   J. Beckett, *The Rise and Fall of the Grenvilles, Dukes of Buckingham and Chandos*, 1710–1921 (Manchester, 1994), pp. 241–50, 281–8.

PARTICULARS OF

Stowe House

NEAR BUCKINGHAM

and the Remaining Portions of the Estate

to be sold by Auction by direction of H. SHAW, Esq.

The Sale will take place in the Marble Saloon, Stowe House

on

WEDNESDAY, OCTOBER 11th, 1922

AT 2.30 O'CLOCK

and will be followed on the TWO SUCCEEDING DAYS

AT 11 O'CLOCK EACH DAY

By the Sale of the Temples, Monumental Columns, Edifices, Unique Statuary, Mantelpieces, Heirloom Tapestries, Remaining Furniture, Panellings and Fittings

Solicitors :

Messrs. BOYDELL & COOKE
1 South Square, Gray's Inn, W.C.

Messrs. WITHERS, BENSONS, CURRIE WILLIAMS & CO.
Howard House, 4 Arundel Street, Strand, W.C.

Messrs. SMALL & BARKER, Town Hall, Buckingham

Auctioneers :

Messrs. JACKSON STOPS
Mowbray House, Norfolk Street, Strand, W.C. Tel. 3224
Northampton. Tel. 610
Town Hall, Towcester. Tel. 16

Messrs. FAREBROTHER, ELLIS & CO.
29 Fleet Street, London, E.C.4. Tel.: Holborn 6344-5
26 Dover Street, Piccadilly, W.1. Tel.: Regent 6368-9

STOWE HOUSE

BUCKINGHAM.

Renowned for its

MAGNIFICENCE AND INTENSE HISTORICAL INTEREST

Wonderful Grounds and Parks,

Temples, Lakes, Arches & Lodges.

HOME FARM	-	323 Acres.
PAVILION FARM	-	132 Acres.
CULLEY'S PARK	-	63 Acres.

Accommodation Land & Cottages.

About 957 Acres

MESSRS.

JACKSON STOPS

IN CONJUNCTION WITH MESSRS.

FAREBROTHER, ELLIS & CO.

Will Sell the above by Auction, IN THE MARBLE SALOON, STOWE HOUSE,

On Wednesday, October the 11th, 1922

At TWO o'clock precisely.

Followed on THE TWO SUCCEEDING DA'S by the SALE of the REMAINING CONTENTS of the MANSION.

Solicitors: Messrs. BOYDELL & COOKE, 2, South Square, Gray's Inn, London, W.C.;
Messrs. WITHERS, BENSONS, CURRIE WILLIAMS & Co., 4, Arundel St., W.C.;
Messrs. SMALL & BARKER, Town Hall, Buckingham.

Auctioneers: Messrs. JACKSON STOPS, Northampton and Towcester;
Messrs. FAREBROTHER, ELLIS & Co., 29, Fleet St., & 26, Dover St., Piccadilly.

Illustrated Catalogues, 10s. each.

SMITH & BATAY, Ltd., Printers, 60, Kennington Park Road, S.E.11. 'Phone: Hop 1388.

THE Remaining Treasures
OF
STOWE HOUSE
Buckingham

COMPRISING

Wonderful Mantelpieces and Exquisite Carvings,

HEIRLOOM TAPESTRIES,

CHAPEL CEDARWOOD PANELLING

Lead Figures, Statuary, Pictures and Works of Art,

UNIQUE FITTINGS OF THE PALACE.

Will be Sold by Auction, *IN THE MARBLE SALOON,*

On **THURSDAY, OCT. 12th, 1922**
and following Day

At *ELEVEN* o'clock precisely each Day, by Messrs.

JACKSON STOPS
IN CONJUNCTION WITH MESSRS.

FAREBROTHER, ELLIS & Co.

Illustrated Catalogues at 10s. Each.

Auctioneers: Messrs. JACKSON STOPS, Northampton & Towcester;
Messrs. FAREBROTHER, ELLIS & Co.,
29, Fleet Street, E.C., & 26, Dover St., Piccadilly, W.

SMITH & BAYLEY, Ltd., Printers, 382, Kennington Park Road, S.E.11.   Phone, Hop. 2286

89

was explained that: "strenuous but unavailing efforts have been made to save this wonderful place from sharing the fate of so many stately homes throughout the country, by using it for some national purpose, such as a great public school, and the present vendor has been reluctant to decide that dismemberment and the sale of the unique and priceless fittings is the only course open to him."

In the event the buildings, gardens and park were acquired on behalf of an educational trust which represented the board of the proposed new school. The house was re-opened as a public school on 11 May 1923.

With regard to the houses and estate, Mr Shaw generally recovered his original expenditure. The house sold for £30,000 as part of the total estate proceeds of £54,000 compared to £50,000 paid in the previous year. In relation to the sale of contents, the vendor was less fortunate. A life-size equestrian statue of King George I, bought for 700 guineas in 1921, realised only 400 guineas. The stone *alto relievo* of 1485 showing the Battle of Bosworth Field sold for 420 guineas compared with 1,000 guineas in 1921.

The prices obtained for the paintings were remarkably low. A landscape attributed to Poussin sold for £17. In a few cases, where items had been returned to Stowe, comparison can be made with the results of the 1848 sale.[1] Thus, the large painting by Corregio of "Venus and Mercury teaching Cupid", which had sold for £157 10s. in 1848 went for £20. Sir Joshua Reynolds' painting of the Marquess of Granby, which had sold for £210 in 1848, sold for £100. A painting of "Diana de Poitiers at her Toilet" had been attributed to Leonardo da Vinci in 1848 when it sold for £111 6s. In 1922 it was attributed to Clouet and went for £100.

The sale of Stowe was one of many country estate sales conducted by Farebrother, Ellis in the 1920s and 1930s. During these two decades Farebrother, Ellis, together with

---

[1]   *The Times*, 23 June 1921.

The sales catalogue for Bransgore House estate in 1932, showing
title-page and one of the aerial photographs as a frontispiece.

Knight, Frank and Rutley were leading figures in this type
of business with regular advertisements in *Country Life*.
This branch of the practice was carried out from the West
End office at 26 Dover Street; the City Office at 29 Fleet
Street was more concerned with commercial property.

During the 1920s and 1930s photography became an
increasingly important aid to the sale of property, and the
technique was used by Farebrother, Ellis very effectively.
The photographs of Stowe for the 1922 sale were particularly well produced. When aerial photography was introduced, it enabled the whole area of an estate to be displayed
to maximum advantage. An early example is the sale of
Bransgore House, Hampshire, in 1932 when a fine set of
photographs by Aerofilms Ltd. of Hendon cost Farebrother, Ellis £25 out of a total advertising budget of £85.

Across the first three decades of the twentieth century
there were major changes in the design of houses and in the
environmental requirements for their surroundings. In 1922

91

The unusual frontispiece used for the sales catalogue for the King's Hall Palace of Dancing, 1926. It combines photography and drawing and illustrates the English taking their pleasure seriously.

Farebrother, Ellis advertised a house in Croydon built in 1902 with Arts and Crafts features as "a delightful house for the artistic family".

In the early 1930s Farebrother, Ellis acted as agents for the sale of the houses on Marlow Manor Park, "a beautifully planned private park on the banks of the River Thames" with more than 700 feet of private river frontage. At the access from the park, the river was to be widened and deepened. There were to be 26 houses on plots of about half an acre each; some of the houses were planned to have rustic design features such as Norfolk reed thatched roofing. The brochure stated that in the lodge-keeper's cottage "an attendant will be constantly on duty to afford every assistance to residents".

This luxurious development at Marlow represented a partial reversion to the aristocratic way of life where privacy was sought either in a closed estate or in a gated and enclosed London square. It was emphasised that "the privacy of the environment will be jealously maintained".

Commuters were assured that the drive to Hyde Park Corner using the new Great Western Road over Kew Bridge would take about an hour. As an alternative, fast trains were advertised which would cover the 30 miles into London in less than 30 minutes.

Throughout the 1920s and 1930s the activities of Farebrother, Ellis, although centred on the sale of major town and country properties, showed great diversity ranging from the sale of a Palace of Dancing (The King's Hall, Elephant and Castle) in 1926, to the valuation of a large estate in Mexico in 1924.

The Mexico project was carried out by the senior partner, Mr B. l'Anson Breach who, with his assistants, spent three months, October to December 1923, inspecting the 800 square mile estate which included two cotton factories, two sugar mills and an alcohol distilling plant which utilised the by-products of the sugar mills, a tobacco plantation, widespread forestry and livestock activity including 19,000 head of cattle. The estate was truly as Mr l'Anson Breach described it: "a Little Empire". The estate, out of which large fortunes had been made in the past, was identified as having great potential but national instability and the danger of unreasonable taxation were identified as serious threats. The valuation finally quoted was the dollar equivalent of £1,276,000.

In the early years of the twentieth century, many historic sites in London were re-developed. In July 1903 Farebrother, Ellis sold Clifford's Inn in Fleet Street and thereafter held an auction of the seventeenth-century woodwork and carving removed from the building. The sale catalogue showed chimney pieces and panelling attributed to Grinling Gibbons and described as "of the date and style of Sir Christopher Wren".

Redevelopment adjacent to the Strand was particularly extensive. The process had begun in March 1915 when Farebrother, Ellis sold the Tivoli site "in the heart of

Farebrother, Ellis produced three sales catalogues for the Adelphi Terrace sales, one for the land and two for the architectural salvage. The above photograph was issued in the last catalogue and preserves the appearance of the terrace just before demolition.

Theatre Land" on the south side of the Strand. On the building site created by this sale had previously stood The Old Tivoli Theatre. Following this sale, the Strand was widened. After the end of the First World War, development resumed and in October 1931 Farebrother, Ellis began the sale of the adjoining Adelphi estate. The whole area was to be redeveloped to include the construction of new headquarters for Shell-Mex, opened in 1933.

This project necessitated the destruction of one of London's architectural masterpieces – Adelphi Terrace and the surrounding streets. The main residential blocks of the Adelphi had been designed by Robert and James Adam and constructed from 1768 onwards. Originally the Adam brothers, Robert, James and William, had obtained in 1768 a ninety-nine year lease from the Duke of St. Albans for

94

𝕺𝖍𝖊 𝕬𝖉𝖊𝖑𝖕𝖍𝖎

Catalogue of the remaining

Marble and Wood Chimneypieces, Columns,
Shutters, Dado Rails, Skirting Boards, Doors,
Oak Flooring, Balconettes, Outside Pilasters
and Door Ways, Iron Railing, etc.

at

1-10, ADELPHI TERRACE, 1-10, JOHN STREET
5 & 6, ROBERT ST. and 19 & 20, ADAM ST.
STRAND

built by

Robert and James Adam

For Sale by Auction by Messrs.

FAREBROTHER, ELLIS & CO.

At 6 and 7, ADELPHI TERRACE, STRAND, W.C.

On Thursday, 7th May, 1936

At ONE o'clock

On View, May 5th and 6th, between the hours of 10 a.m. and 5 p.m.

Solicitors: Messrs. FLADGATE & CO., 70, Pall Mall, S.W.1.
Auctioneers:
Messrs. FAREBROTHER, ELLIS & CO.,
26, DOVER STREET, W.1, and
29, Fleet Street, E.C.4.

Title-page of the last of the Adelphi Terrace sales catalogues.

what was then the site of Durham House. In 1771 the
brothers obtained an Act of Parliament permitting
reclamation of a shallow area of the Thames on which they
built an arched wharf supporting blocks of houses south of
Adelphi Terrace. At the time, this was the finest riverside
building in London: Robert and James Adam and also
David Garrick took up residence in the new development.
Unfortunately, the Adelphi was not a commercial success.
The river was becoming increasingly commercialised,
crowded and polluted; living near to it was ceasing to be

fashionable.[1]

It has been claimed that exterior remodelling of the Adelphi area in 1872 had resulted in Victorian over-elaboration, destroying the original Adam design.[2] The Farebrother, Ellis sale catalogues of 1936 give clear photographic evidence of the lost elegance, a little of which survives today in John Adam Street. In two sales, held in April and May 1936 after demolition, Farebrother, Ellis sold the architectural salvage: the chimney pieces, balconies, wainscoting, doors, grates, etc. Every kind of structure was sold ranging from the white marble chimney pieces from the houses of the Adam brothers and David Garrick, to the patterned pilasters and cornices from the exterior of the buildings.

In March 1930 Farebrother, Ellis sold the freehold site vacated by the House of Harrison, printers, in St. Martin's Lane, Charing Cross: the expected price was equivalent to £10 14s. per square foot. In the sale catalogue the vendor commented on the "remarkable" increase in rates which had taken place since the company first moved into St. Martin's Lane in about 1840 when the rate was 4d. in the pound. By 1930 the rate applied in the City of Westminster had risen to 8s. 10d. in the pound and clearly Harrison considered that it was uneconomical to carry out necessary expansion on a West End site. It was suggested that the site might be more suitable for "some other purpose – perhaps for the erection of a great place of entertainment".

In 1930 Farebrother, Ellis sold the contents of Grand Buildings in Trafalgar Square where the Grand Hotel, sold in 1928, had been situated. Again a different usage of the property was suggested. The catalogue claimed that Trafalgar Square, described by Sir Robert Peel as "the finest

---

[1]   R. Porter, *London. A Social History* (Harmondsworth, 1996), p. 114.

[2]   J. Summerson, *Georgian London* (London, 1962), p. 138.

For the 1930 sale of St Martin's Lane, Charing Cross, Farebrother used this attractive colour painting for their brochure, appropriately enough for the premises of the long-established printers Harrison & Sons.

site in London" was becoming an attractive area for commercial activity: thus, "there was a time when what was called the 'Business Quarter' was narrowed down to one locality within the confines of the City of London – of recent years the trend has been towards the West."

Before this trend had shown much evidence of coming into effect, property development in the mid 1930s was overtaken by national concern over fears of impending war.

CHAPTER 7
POST-WAR CHANGES: FOCUSING THE PRACTICE

From 1938 onwards, fears of war began to weaken the property market, and when war was declared in September 1939 there was a sharp decline in property values, especially in London.[1] During the ensuing conflict 3.25 million properties in the United Kingdom were either damaged or destroyed, of which the largest single group, 43%, was in London with a further 11% elsewhere in the south east. The majority of the affected properties – 93% – were houses.[2] In the City of London, bombing destroyed 225 acres, about one-third of the total area.[3]

After the war the City authorities attempted to control re-development by operating compulsory purchase, by which means they became one of the largest urban landlords in the country. There were many controls applied to property, and development required an appropriate licence, but in 1954 the system of building licences was ended and the property boom was under way.

---

[1] O. Marriott, *The Property Boom* (London, 1967), pp. 43–56.

[2] B. P. Whitehouse, *Partners in Property: a History and Analysis of the Provision of Institutional Finance for Property Development* (London, 1964).

[3] The Farebrother archives contain a partially burnt cheque drawn on Coutts & Co. for £1 2s. 9d. in favour of Messrs. Fuller Watts, from whose safe the cheque was recovered after the premises were destroyed by enemy action on the night of 10/11 May 1941.

98

Business as usual in Chancery Lane, 1941.

In areas such as Fetter Lane between Holborn Circus and Fleet Street, the old street patterns were largely re-created and it was to this area that Farebrother, Ellis would eventually move in 1987, transferring from Fleet Street to Bream's Buildings and in 1993 to Pemberton Row.

For Farebrother, Ellis, the ending of World War II brought a return to the pre-war pattern of business in the short term, but also marked the beginning of a fundamental change in the work of the practice. The very diverse range of activities which characterised the operation in the 1930s became increasingly unrealistic in the competitive post-war world. To continue selling all forms of chattels and property was no longer feasible. Some concentration of the business was inevitable.

The practice had suffered a considerable loss from the death of four senior staff during the war, and this reduced the strength of the company in dealing with house sales.[1] Nevertheless, major country house sales continued up to the 1960s, and usually included contents. During the 1960s, however, there began a gradual evolution towards focusing the business on mainly commercial property within the City and Holborn, the area which was to become known as Midtown.

In the immediate aftermath of the war, returning staff found some small relaxation in the strict rules of behaviour and dress which had been enforced in the 1930s. The requirement to wear a black coat, striped trousers and white shirt was very gradually weakened. The West End Office in Dover Street and the City Office in Fleet Street employed about 100 staff in total and social relations between staff became freer. One consequence of this, not long after the war ended, was a challenge by the West End Office for Fleet Street to play them in a football match. Many of the participants had to play in their old army boots and the match was long remembered not only for its violence but the convincing score of 13–0 in favour of West End. Not surprisingly, the fixture was never renewed.

A little later, the Dover Street office was closed, and thereafter the business was all conducted from 29 Fleet Street which had been the home of the practice since 1882 and remained so for more than 100 years until the move to 7/9 Bream's Buildings in 1987. Until the mid-1960s the

---

[1] The staff who died in World War II were: Alan Wheen Ellis, Gilbert Valentine Farrell OBE, Andrew Paterson and Sidney John Scott Wilde.

working conditions in 29 Fleet Street were somewhat Dickensian with clerks sitting on high stools and working behind grilles on rent days.

Fleet Street had seen the introduction of many changes in working practice, including the introduction of the telephone. When this novelty was first installed, a clerk was instructed to sit all day by the instrument and await incoming calls. For four days, nothing happened and then the phone rang. The senior partner was out at lunch and the nervous clerk was obliged to take a message. He later reported to the senior partner that "his Lordship had rung" but was unable to answer the question "Which bloody Lord?".

Among the major country house sales carried out at this time was that of Benham Park, Newbury, which had been the home of the late Sir Richard V. Sutton, Bart. who had bought several important items from the Stowe sale in 1922. At the Benham Park sale, held in May 1951, Mr George Davies was acting as auctioneer's clerk and noticed that the auctioneer was ignoring bids from a well-dressed gentleman at the back of the room. When he mentioned this, the auctioneer asked him to go up to the gentleman and say "Good morning, Captain X, Mr Rodgers presents his compliments and says he saw you at the Curzon Street sale last week". This was done and when Mr Davies returned to his post, he noticed that Captain X had gone. The auctioneer explained that this was his intention: he was not sure what game the bogus Captain X was operating, but he wanted him out.

This period of the 1950s was a time in which the sales of substantial country houses were often very personal activities in which the vendors had traditional and long-established linkages with Farebrother, Ellis. The principal contact for many of these sales was Philip Buckland.

Philip Harry Beale Buckland was born in 1906 into an old Kent family with a long tradition of agriculture and country sport. His grandfather ran a pack of hounds in Ashford Valley in 1850 and his father continued the tradition. Buckland retained a lifelong enthusiasm for horses and hunting, and was joint master of the Ashford Valley Foxhounds from 1961 to 1978. He was also a keen point-to-point rider and an amateur National Hunt jockey in both England and Ireland. He was on the panel of the British Show Jumping Association and was a major figure in agriculture in Kent.

During the Second World War, Philip Buckland was second in command of the British force which invaded Iceland in 1940. This action was notable for being a peaceful invasion carried out with the full support of the Icelanders. The operation was launched as a pre-emptive measure because the Germans had occupied Denmark in 1940 and there was much concern that Iceland also could be occupied and U-boats would threaten shipping on the great circle route between Halifax, Nova Scotia and Scotland.[1] Iceland provided a valuable base for allied escort ships and aircraft. Buckland thereafter saw service in the Faroe Islands and across the continent of Europe, finishing in Berlin.

Philip Buckland had joined the regular army in August 1939 after the mobilisation of his Territorial Army unit, but he had already qualified as a chartered surveyor having been apprenticed to Bannister & Co. of Haywards Heath. After the war, when he was a partner at Farebrother, Ellis he worked in a very personal manner through direct contact with a range of well-established customers. Once a week, however, it was accepted that he would be away hunting. He was a much-loved personality. When he died in 1985, his record of service to equestrian sport and agriculture was highly commended.[2]

---

[1] W. S. Churchill, *The Second World War*, vol. III (London, 1950), p. 120.

[2] *Horse and Hound*, 9 August 1985.

Buckland's colleague as senior partner was Leslie Philip Woolf, a very different man in many ways. Woolf spent his entire working life with Farebrother, Ellis, a period of 54 years followed by 10 years as a consultant. He came from a family of solicitors, B. A. Woolf, in the City of London. However, he did not follow the family business but became apprenticed in 1926 to S. H. Wilde, a partner in Farebrother, Ellis, for the sum of £300. Three years later, at the beginning of the Great Depression, Woolf was earning £150 per annum plus a commission for any new business which he might introduce. In 1936 he became a partner, although this was after some disagreement between the existing partners who were reluctant to train a new partner during those difficult times. In 1955 Woolf became the senior partner and remained so until his retirement in 1980 at the age of 70.[1] He became a consultant and finally retired from any involvement in 1990 on medical advice. Three years earlier the practice had moved from 29 Fleet Street to Bream's Buildings. Therefore Woolf spent more than 60 years working in the same building.

Woolf was an old-fashioned figure. Like Buckland, he maintained a long tradition of personal service to particular clients. He had an amazing memory for detail and indeed was somewhat obsessive about it; he was particularly upset when the practice was referred to as anything other than Farebrother, Ellis & Co. (never "Company"). He insisted that only he should be empowered to sign letters on behalf of the company and he did this in small writing always using a particular square-nibbed pen.

Woolf was highly respected for his professional ability and was very successful as an expert witness. He was not,

---

[1]   The partnership deed dated 8 May 1962 confirms that after the retirement of Ernest Munro Runtz, Woolf and Buckland agreed to continue the business of Farebrother, Ellis & Co. with the capital account of £12,000 credited in the ratio of 2:1 respectively, i.e. Woolf £8,000, Buckland £4,000.

Lowndes Square Estate in Knightsbridge. Farebrother assembled this estate during the 1950s and 1960s and have managed it ever since on behalf of Sun Life Properties. Farebrother's management even includes the maintenance of the central square gardens.

however, a communicative man; neither was he at all gregarious. Although his method of working personally and exclusively with specific clients brought in much business, Woolf's lack of overall communication and his resistance to change meant that he would be overtaken by time. Despite his success he led a very modest lifestyle and travelled about London on foot or by bus.

Apart from flat racing and his membership of the Worshipful Company of Paviours, of which he was a Past

Master, Woolf had few outside interests except the Reform Club. He was a long-time member and took lunch there every day, often alone. He became chairman of the Club and was also a trustee, an honorary but also very honourable position. When the club was temporarily without a secretary, Woolf took on this duty in addition to his role as chairman. When he died in 1995 at the age of 85, the Reform Club was a major beneficiary of his estate.

When Philip Buckland and Leslie Woolf were the principal partners, they both possessed in their different ways a great talent for personal business service provided for traditional long-standing clients; but communication within the practice was lacking. The problem was exacerbated by the labyrinthine structure of 29 Fleet Street which was in effect a building on ten separate floors. In 1980 the incoming senior partner, Michael Bridges Webb, recognised this deficiency and corrected it. Communication was established at all levels and this gave a major improvement in the flexibility of the practice. Nevertheless, the personal aspect was retained with individual partners dealing with specific clients as far as possible, and this is still a feature today. In some cases the personal relationship with clients has been developed over more than a hundred years of mutual business. Examples of such traditional clients include the Apothecaries Company and the Maryon Wilson estate in Hampstead, administered on behalf of Viscount Gough.

After 1970 the practice gradually acquired a sharper focus and further evolution of this process led to a concentration on dealing with principally commercial property in the City and Holborn area, usually referred to now as "Midtown". This area extends east–west from St. Paul's to Trafalgar Square and north–south from King's Cross to the river. To accompany this new definition of the market, the name of the practice was changed in 1980 from Farebrother, Ellis & Co. to the simplified shorter title – Farebrother.

CHAPTER 8
FROM 1980 TO 1999: MIDTOWN,
CHARLES FAREBROTHER'S WORLD

Since 1980 Farebrother have continued to reorganise as necessary in order to remain at the forefront of the property business, which has evolved into an increasingly complex activity making greater demands on the professional skills of those involved in all of its aspects. In 1980 the present senior partner of Farebrother, Christopher Woodbridge, addressed the Insurance Institute of London on the subject of 'Management of Real Estate by Trustees' and emphasised how the responsibilities of property trustees had increased both in quantity and in detail. There were increasing volumes of relevant law, in particular the law relating to trusts was becoming "long and involved ... specialised and complicated". Christopher Woodbridge summarised the increasing complexity of the property business in his conclusion as follows:

> There are many problems that can arise with property. Not only are there very many statutes that now affect property, but the case law has increased dramatically in the last few years. Certainly it takes a considerable amount of time to keep abreast of the changes that occur and some of these changes can be absolutely vital because they can directly affect the value of property almost overnight."[1]

---

[1]   C. Woodbridge, 'Management of Real Property by Trustees', a talk given to The Insurance Institute of London, 8 October 1980, R.I.C.S. Library, London.

These changes in the nature of the property business have multiplied and diversified since 1980. Furthermore buildings themselves have become technically more sophisticated especially with regard to computerised environmental control. All of these developments have made, and continue to make, rising demands on the property business. Computerisation is a subject in which Farebrother were at the forefront of progress in pioneering a database for the office market.

In order to address this climate of change, the firm has organised the practice into departments, principally Agency, Management, Professional Services, Investment and Building. There are also specialist services which cross over and interact with the main departments: these services comprise Development, Asset Management and Residential Consultancy. It is important to emphasise, however, that all business continues to receive expert attention without losing any of the traditional personal relationship with the client. Although specific members of staff specialise in particular mainstream departments, the total property service is delivered by Farebrother as a personally co-ordinated product which utilises all the expertise of the practice.

An example of the way in which this approach has operated is represented by the acquisition, refurbishment and continued management of the Lowndes Square Estate in Knightsbridge. Farebrother assembled this estate during the 1950s and 1960s and have managed it ever since on behalf of Sun Life Properties. Farebrother carried out a review of the leasing arrangements which generated funds for re-investment, refurbishment and planned maintenance. The practice continues to supply a management team who deal with routine matters including maintenance of the central square gardens.

Continuing property management is a major feature of the work of the practice. For example, Farebrother have managed all of the regional offices of the Confederation of

British Industry for many years. As an interesting contrast to the work for CBI, Farebrother have acted as surveyors to the print union NGA, subsequently GPMU, a connection which arose through the long association with Fleet Street.

The Holborn Estate, managed since 1991 on behalf of the Bedford Charity, represents a more recently established ongoing project. This estate consists of six acres of land remaining from thirteen acres to the north of High Holborn given by Sir William Harpur, Lord Mayor of London, in 1566 in order to endow Bedford School and for other charitable purposes in Bedford. The estate is situated in Lamb's Conduit Street and Bedford Row and includes many Georgian buildings. The Charity has recently sought to diversify its investment and Farebrother have realised some £15 million from the sale of two sites which the Charity had owned for several centuries. These sites consisted of a shopping centre in Bedford and almost an entire street in Midtown.

Also situated in Holborn is an estate owned by Rugby School. There are approximately 80 buildings and those sections of the estate which are in Lamb's Conduit Street and in Rugby Street were in part built by the seventeenth century speculative housing developer Nicolas Barber. There is an additional area covering Great Ormond Street which was developed in the early 1700s with further construction in the mid-nineteenth century. Farebrother have managed this estate since 1991.

The thirty years elapsing between the acquisition of Lowndes Square and the establishment of estate management in Holborn for the Bedford Charity and for Rugby School bridge the transition period between early post-war resumption of property development and the very different and more constrained situation of the 1990s. During this period there have been various phases in which the economics of the property market have fluctuated markedly and this has conditioned the way in which the market has developed. From the mid-1950s onwards, development flourished until the depression of activity which arose from the oil crises of the 1970s. Thereafter, development was of necessity much more demanding in terms of strategic planning to maximise returns.

An example of the early 1980s approach is provided by development for the Worshipful Society of Apothecaries of London with whom Farebrother have a business history of over one hundred years. The project involved a review of the Society's property in Blackfriars Lane. Between 1980 and 1985 Farebrother conceived, project-managed and let the redevelopment of a major part of the site. The remaining buildings were refurbished. As a result of this work, the long term finances of the Society were secured.

In the late 1980s a new development occurred in that foreign companies began to make major investments in property in the City of London. In early landmark projects, Farebrother acted on behalf of two of the largest corporations in Japan. Firstly, Bow Bells House in Bread Street, off Cheapside, was acquired for Mitsubishi giving 120,000 square feet of office space. Secondly, in 1990, Farebrother advised Mitsui & Co. and Mitsui Fudosan in the acquisition of 20 Old Bailey, a new 200,000 square feet office building. Mitsui relocated their European head-quarters to the top two floors of 20 Old Bailey and Farebrother have managed the property on their behalf ever since. Both of these projects were overseen by Christopher Woodbridge and carried out across the whole of the practice.

Structural and demographic change continued in Midtown throughout the 1980s and beyond. The whole area, which had originally been segmented into traditional business and trade sectors, opened out. Foreign investment was attracted. The freeing of space in Fleet Street following the departure of newspaper production led to business in general moving into Midtown. Because of improved communication techniques there was no longer any

In 1990 Farebrother advised Mitsui & Co. and Mitsui Fudosan in the acquisition of 20 Old Bailey, a new 200,000 square feet office building. Mitsui relocated their European headquarters to the top two floors of 20 Old Bailey and Farebrother have managed the property on their behalf ever since.

necessity for specific categories of profession and business to be located together in close proximity.

The Advent of 'Big Bang' on the Stock Exchange in October 1986 raised the demand for office space in London. However, after the events of 'Black Monday' in October 1987 office rents fell sharply to half or less of the previous values and there was a new tendency for older office property to be converted to residential or mixed residential/commercial usage. Farebrother were the first company to research the relationship between supply and demand and to set up a database in this area.

This situation is illustrated by the most recent phase of the long relationship between Farebrother and Shell UK

Plan for development in Blackfriar's Lane, EC4, for the
Worshipful Society of Apothecaries of London.

Limited. The relationship began before the second world
war when Farebrother managed an extensive range of
premises for Shell. More recently Farebrother have been
closely involved with property owned by Shell and situated
near to the head office, Shell-Mex House, off the Strand.
Wellington House, which lies on the corner of Strand and
Lancaster Place, was refurbished under the direction of
Farebrother who continue to manage the property.
Farebrother are also advising on their building, Cecil
Chambers, which stands between Shell-Mex House and the
Strand.

In 1980, Farebrother were one of the first companies to sponsor polo at Windsor, and this sponsorship continued for ten years. The practice still supports and enjoys a range of sporting activities for staff and clients, including sailing and golf.

The demand for both residential and commercial property in Midtown remains high. Farebrother are centrally positioned within this attractive market and have been recognised as 'The Midtown Niche Player'. Although Midtown is the focus of Farebrother's business, the practice is well equipped to offer a total service on all aspects of property throughout the British Isles.

Farebrother have been involved in many major transactions in Central London in recent years and have been retained by BT plc to dispose of their surplus premises, many of which are in Midtown. BT's disposals are a result of a dramatic restructuring in the global telecommunications market and the practice has also advised WorldCom International, an American competitor, in acquiring

The partners today. From left to right: Iain Malcolm, John Nugent, Myles Bridges, Christopher Woodbridge, Alistair Subba Row, Bruce Clitherow, Huw Colwyn Foulkes and Trevor Graves.

significant amounts of space in Central London as they expand into Europe.

The current strategy of the practice may be summarised as the intention to grow and build from a Midtown strength, acting for large institutions on most aspects of commercial and residential property. Clients are normally, but not exclusively, London-based. The practice is an entirely independent partnership so that there are no external influences which might affect the independence of advice given to clients. The depth of expertise held by Farebrother gives unique strength in providing strategic advice: the practice can justifiably claim to have a total understanding of property.

It is notable that the two recent projects for Shell UK Limited are on the actual sites of Charles Farebrother's original addresses. Wellington House is on the corner of Lancaster Place where Charles Farebrother lived between 1827 and 1861; Cecil Chambers stands on the site of the Cecil Hotel, demolished in 1930, which in turn stood on the site of Beaufort Buildings where Charles Farebrother lived between 1806 and 1824.

Thus the business can be viewed as having come through a full circle in two hundred years because the particular strengths on which Charles Farebrother first established his own successful practice were those which characterise Farebrother today – independent personal service and an informed market commitment to what was in effect Charles Farebrother's world and is now known as Midtown. It may reasonably be concluded that Charles Farebrother would recognise and approve these unique strengths of the business which he began two hundred years ago.

Opposite: Full-circle: the 1799 map of central London by R. Norwood was issued during the year when Charles Farebrother began his working life and shows 7 & 9 Beaufort Buildings, Farebrother's addresses from 1806 to 1824. Beaufort Buildings was later demolished and the site is currently occupied by Cecil Chambers, which is being refurbished and redeveloped as this book goes to press, a project for which Farebrother are acting as advisers.

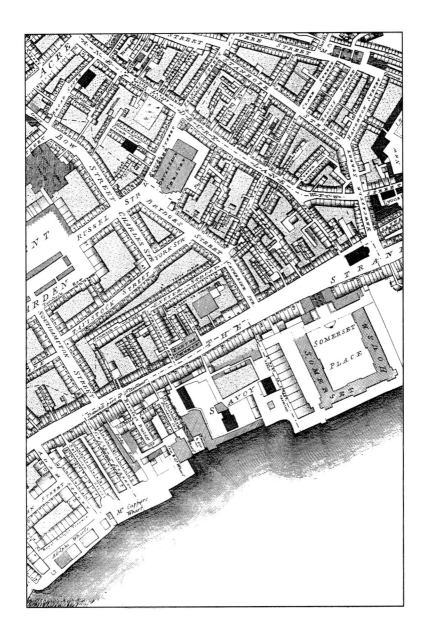

APPENDIX 1
RELATIVE VALUES OF MONEY

In 1962 Mitchell and Deane opened their article on "Wages and the standard of living" as follows: "In travelling backwards from the twentieth century to the nineteenth, the student of wages passes from a highway to a thorny path."[1] This caution is very true and particularly apposite in attempting to make any comparison between current values of money and corresponding values at the beginning of the nineteenth century. There is no doubt that the value of £1 in 1800 was a good deal higher than that of £1 today, but the multiplication factor is really impossible to define with any confidence. Wages are relevant only as far as they relate to living conditions at the time, to the cost of accommodation and to that of food. Moreover, types of housing are greatly different across the past 200 years. In Victorian times, most people lived in rented accommodation.

Some indication of relative value may be obtained by considering some actual figures. For example, in the 1860s, an upper class man living on a substantial private income without the necessity of working would be receiving up to about £5,000 per annum. An upper middle class professional or manufacturer might earn £500 p.a. which would enable him to live in a house at £50 p.a. rental and keep three female servants. A lower middle class man such as a clerk might earn £100 p.a. and live without a resident servant in a house rented for £15 p.a. The average doctor might have £300 p.a. to live on after deducting the expenses of his practice. In 1875, the stationmaster of St. Pancras was paid £265 p.a. In the 1860s, a skilled artisan, e.g. a watch maker or an engine driver, would receive a weekly wage of 35 shillings. The wages of the working class would then be graded downwards depending on skill: for example postmen and miners would be paid about 22 shillings a week, and at the bottom of the scale would come

---

[1] B. R. Mitchell & P. Deane, *Abstract of British Historical Statistics* (Cambridge, 1962), pp. 338–45.

general labourers at 14 shillings per week.[1]

It is virtually impossible to make an accurate comparison between the value of money across the past two centuries. It has been attempted on a basis of calculating the amount of money required in modern times to purchase the goods which could have been bought for £1 in past years. The results appear to give a rather low estimate for the value of Georgian and Victorian currency in modern terms. The calculation is quite rightly unacceptable to an economist, but it is better than nothing and it does provide a very rough guide. With these major reservations, the results are quoted below.

Year	Value of £1 in 1998
1800	28.5
1810	27.1
1820	33.2
1830	39.7
1840	35.4
1850	46.5
1860	41.7
1870	40.7
1880	42.8
1890	50.8
1900	52.5
1910	47.9
1920	18.1
1930	28.5
1940	24.7
1950	19.4
1960	13.1
1970	8.8
1980	2.4

---

[1] G. Best, *Mid-Victorian Britain 1851–75* (London, 1971), pp. 93–168.

APPENDIX 2
SCALE OF FEES 1865

The scale of fees charged by Farebrother, Ellis, Clark & Co. in compensation and railway cases depended on the results of the case and was as follows:

Award or Verdict in £, with fee in Guineas

100	5	3800	32	8400	55
200	7	4000	33	8600	56
300	9	4200	34	8800	57
400	11	4400	35	9000	58
500	13	4600	36	9200	59
600	14	4800	37	9400	60
700	15	5000	38	9600	61
800	16	5200	39	9800	62
900	17	5400	40	10000	63
1000	18	5600	41	11000	68
1200	19	5800	42	12000	73
1400	20	6000	43	13000	78
1600	21	6200	44	14000	83
1800	22	6400	45	15000	88
2000	23	6600	46	16000	93
2200	24	6800	47	17000	98
2400	25	7000	48	18000	103
2600	26	7200	49	19000	108
2800	27	7400	50	20000	113
3000	28	7600	51		
3200	29	7800	52	Above 20000: by
3400	30	8000	53	special arrange-
3600	31	8200	54	ment

In addition to the above, 5 guineas per day for attending before an Arbitrator or Jury. Plans and travelling expenses extra.

Farebrother, Ellis, Clark & Co.
5 & 6 Lancaster Place, Strand, W.C.
and 18 Old Broad Street, E.C.